GUNSMITH ガンスミスキャッツ CATS

Misfire

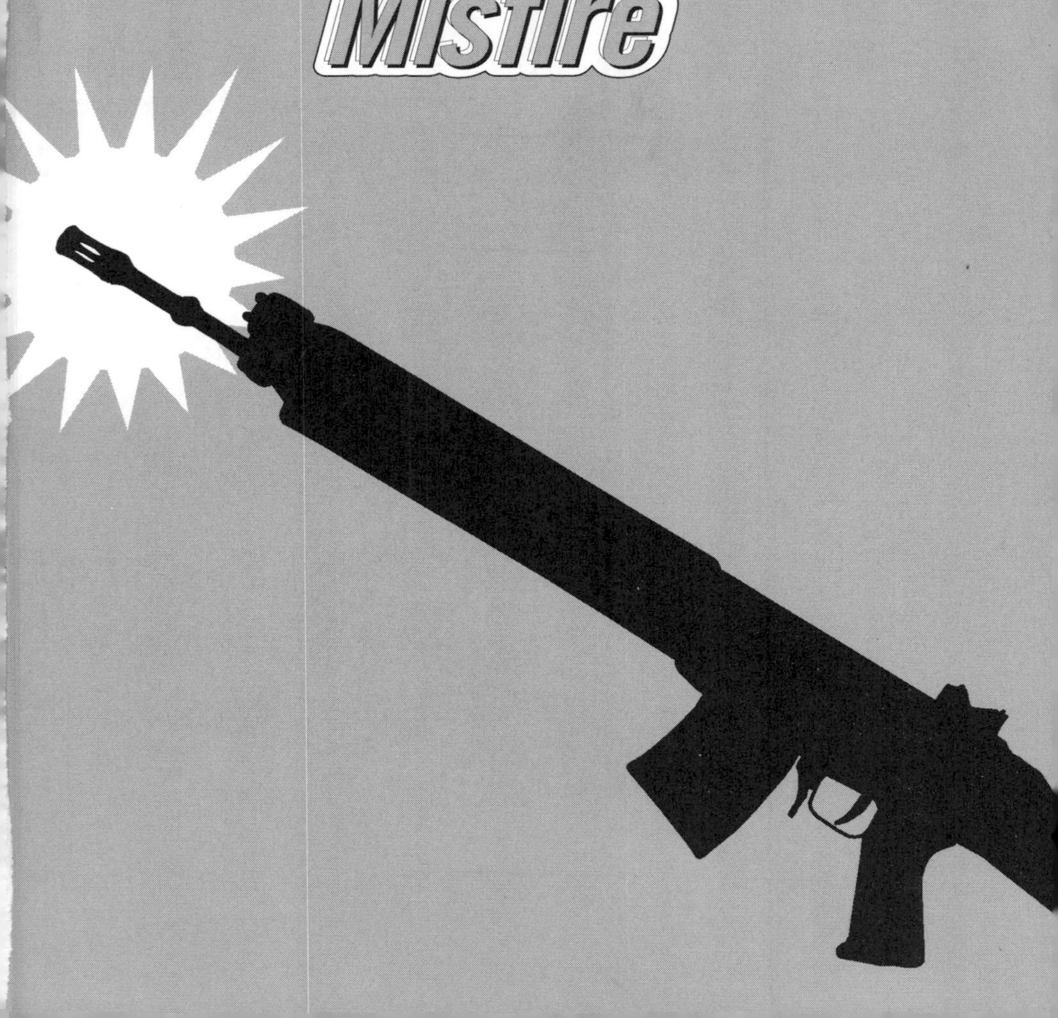

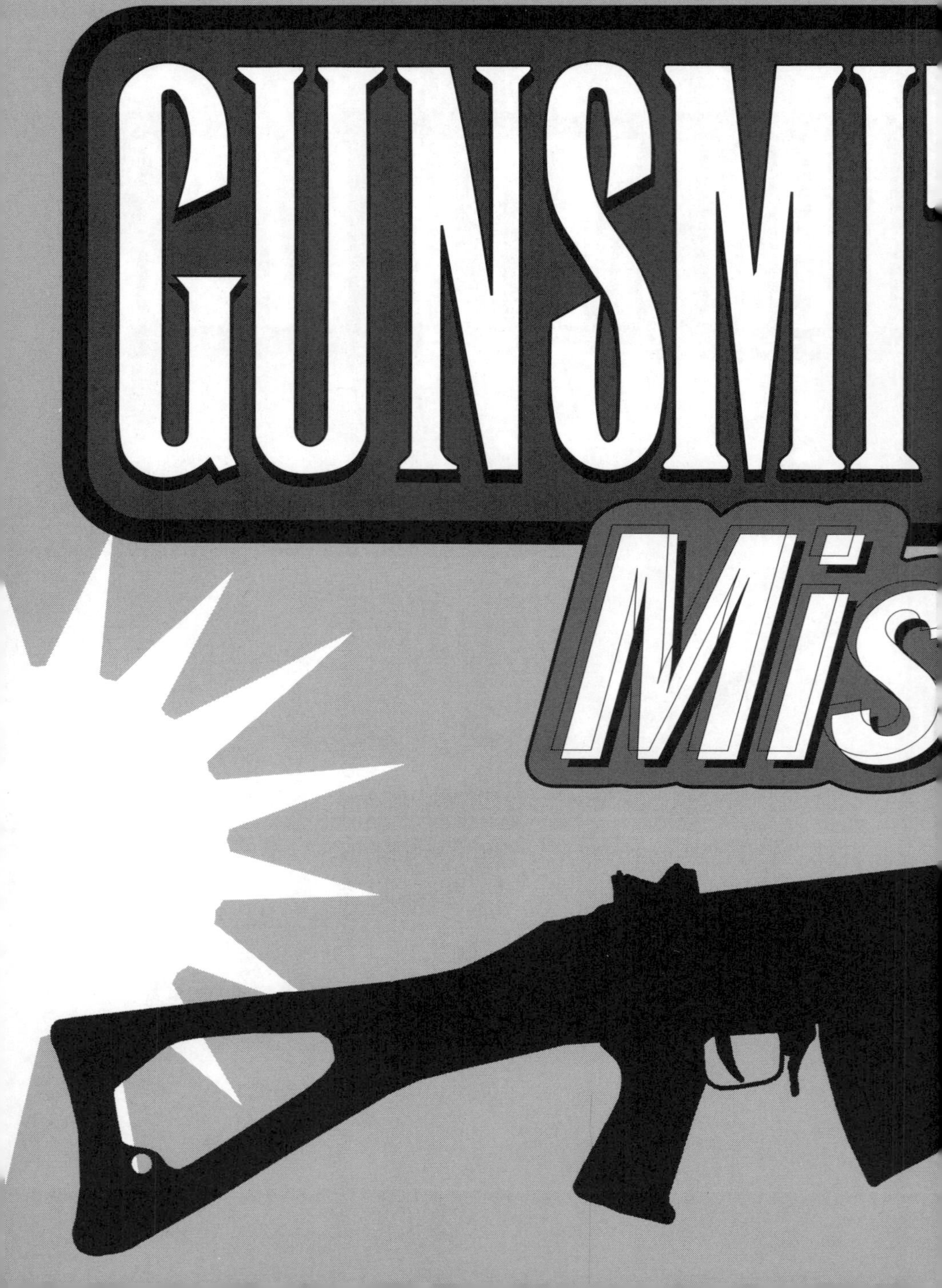
GUNSMI
Mis

TH CATS

ガンスミスキャッツ

fire

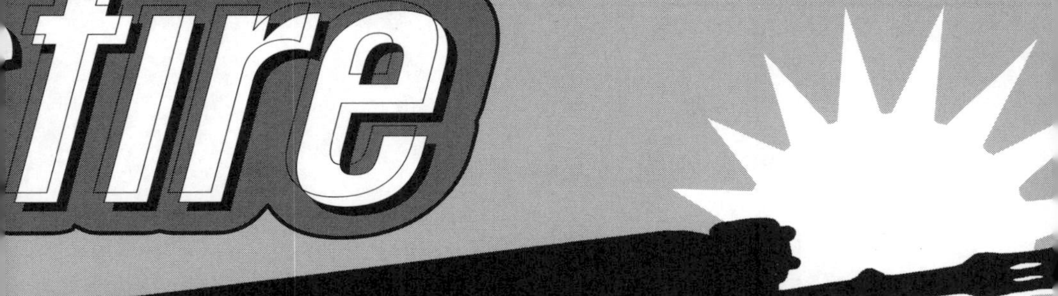

story and art by *KENICHI SONODA*

translation by *DANA LEWIS & TOREN SMITH*

lettering and retouch by *TOMOKO SAITO*

DARK HORSE COMICS®

publisher **MIKE RICHARDSON**
series editor **DAVE CHIPPS**
collection editor **SUZANNE TAYLOR**
collection designer **HARALD GRAHAM**
collection design manager **BRIAN GOGOLIN**

GUNSMITH CATS VOL. 2: MISFIRE

English-language version produced by Studio Proteus for Dark Horse Comics, Inc.

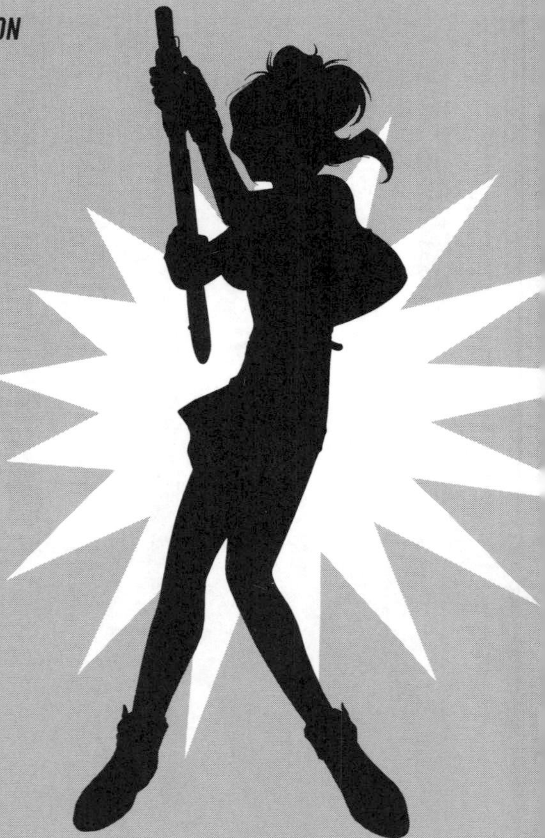

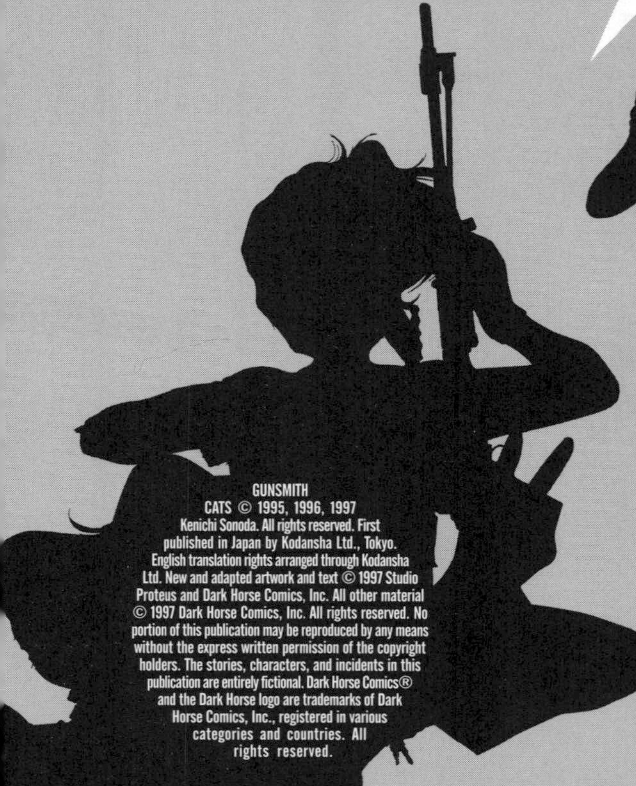

This book collects issues 7-10 of the Dark Horse comic-book series Gunsmith Cats *and issues 1-3 of the Dark Horse comic-book series* Gunsmith Cats: The Return of Gray.

Published by
Dark Horse Comics, Inc.
10956 SE Main Street
Milwaukie, OR 97222

First edition: August 1997
ISBN: 1-56971-253-0

4 6 8 10 9 7 5 3
Printed in Canada

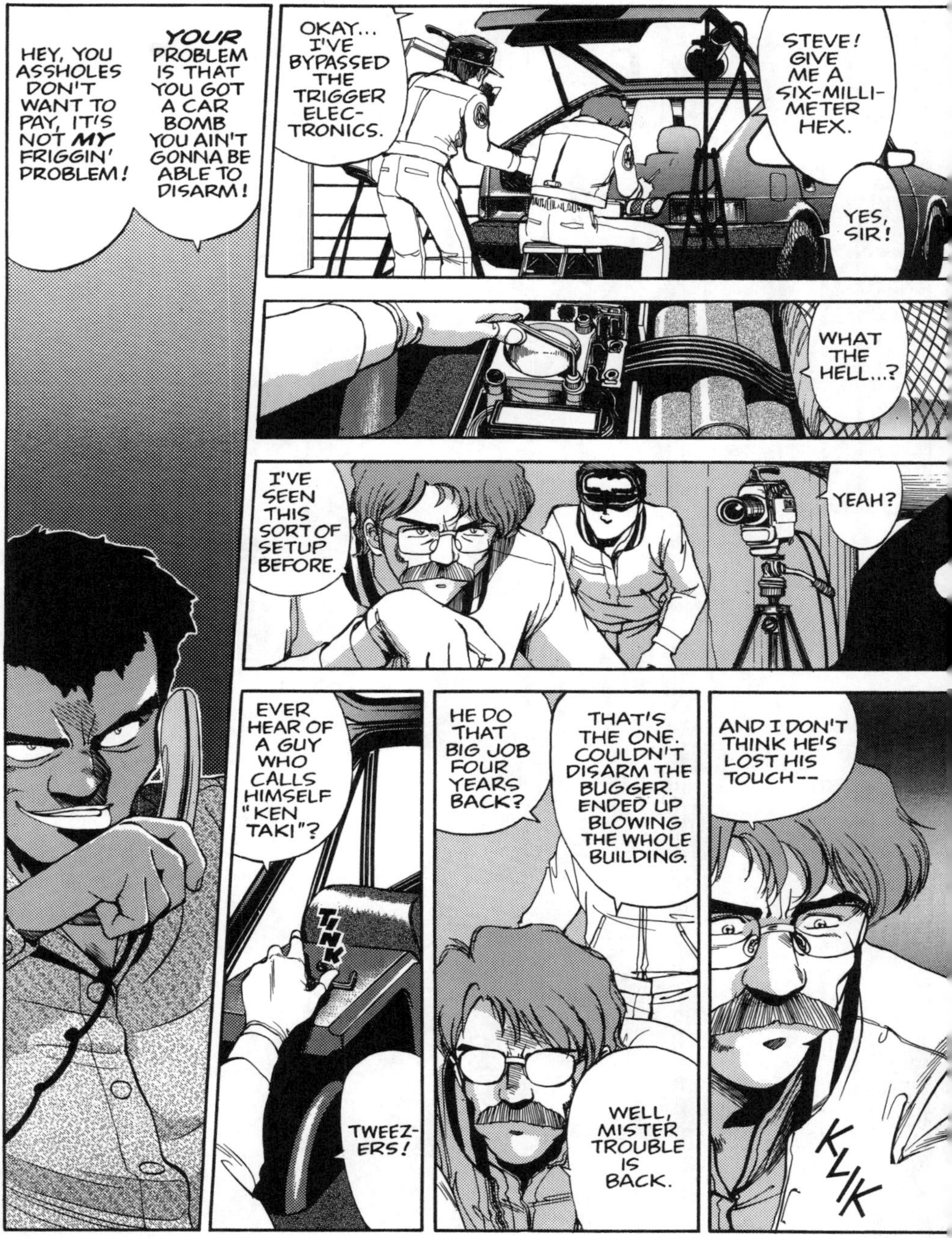

HEY, YOU ASSHOLES DON'T WANT TO PAY, IT'S NOT ***MY*** FRIGGIN' PROBLEM!
YOUR PROBLEM IS THAT YOU GOT A CAR BOMB YOU AIN'T GONNA BE ABLE TO DISARM!
OKAY... I'VE BYPASSED THE TRIGGER ELEC-TRONICS.
STEVE! GIVE ME A SIX-MILLI-METER HEX.
YES, SIR!
WHAT THE HELL...?
I'VE SEEN THIS SORT OF SETUP BEFORE.
YEAH?
EVER HEAR OF A GUY WHO CALLS HIMSELF "KEN TAKI"?
TINK
TWEEZ-ERS!
HE DO THAT BIG JOB FOUR YEARS BACK?
THAT'S THE ONE. COULDN'T DISARM THE BUGGER. ENDED UP BLOWING THE WHOLE BUILDING.
WELL, MISTER TROUBLE IS BACK.
AND I DON'T THINK HE'S LOST HIS TOUCH--
KLIK

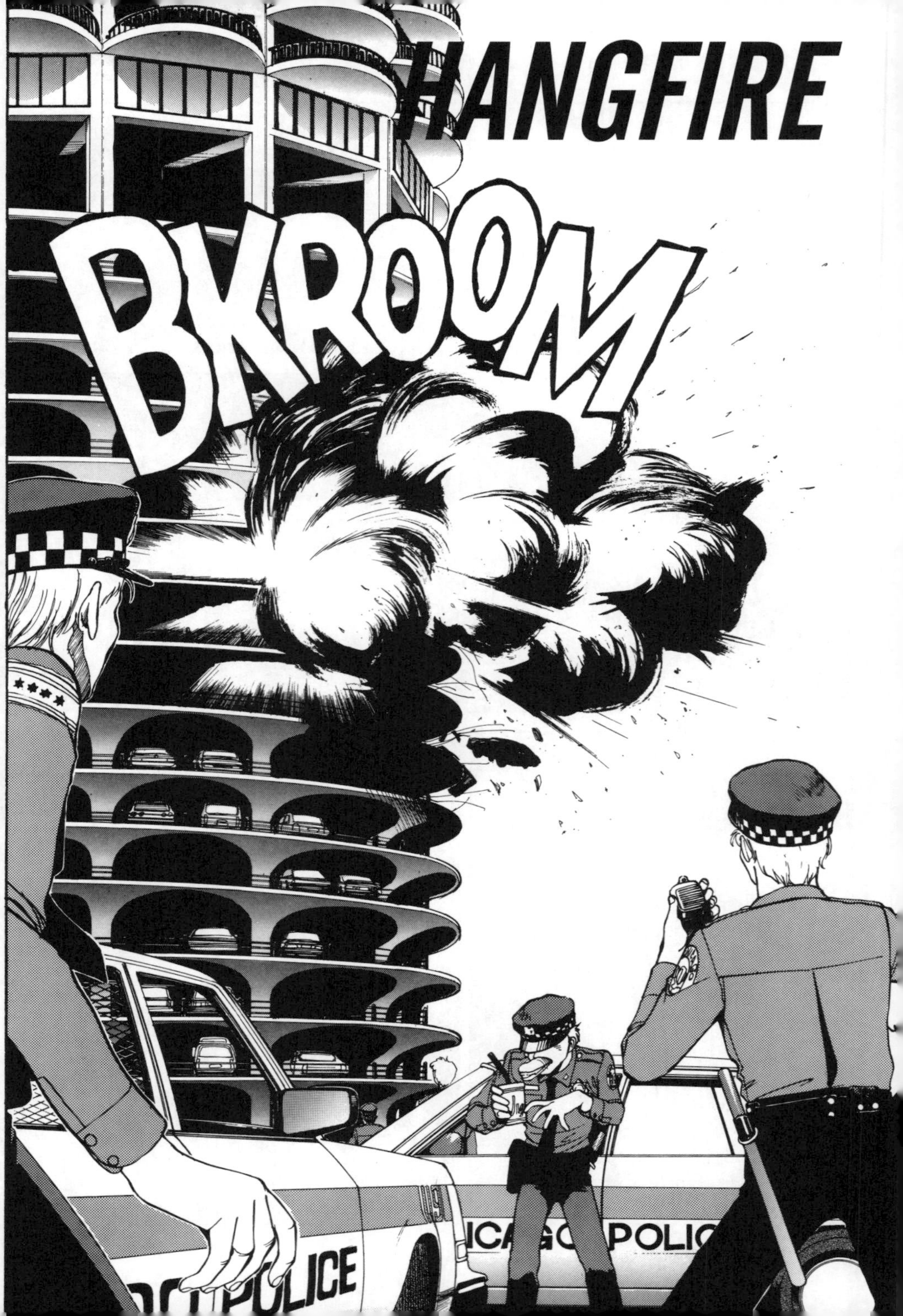
HANGFIRE
BKROOM
POLICE

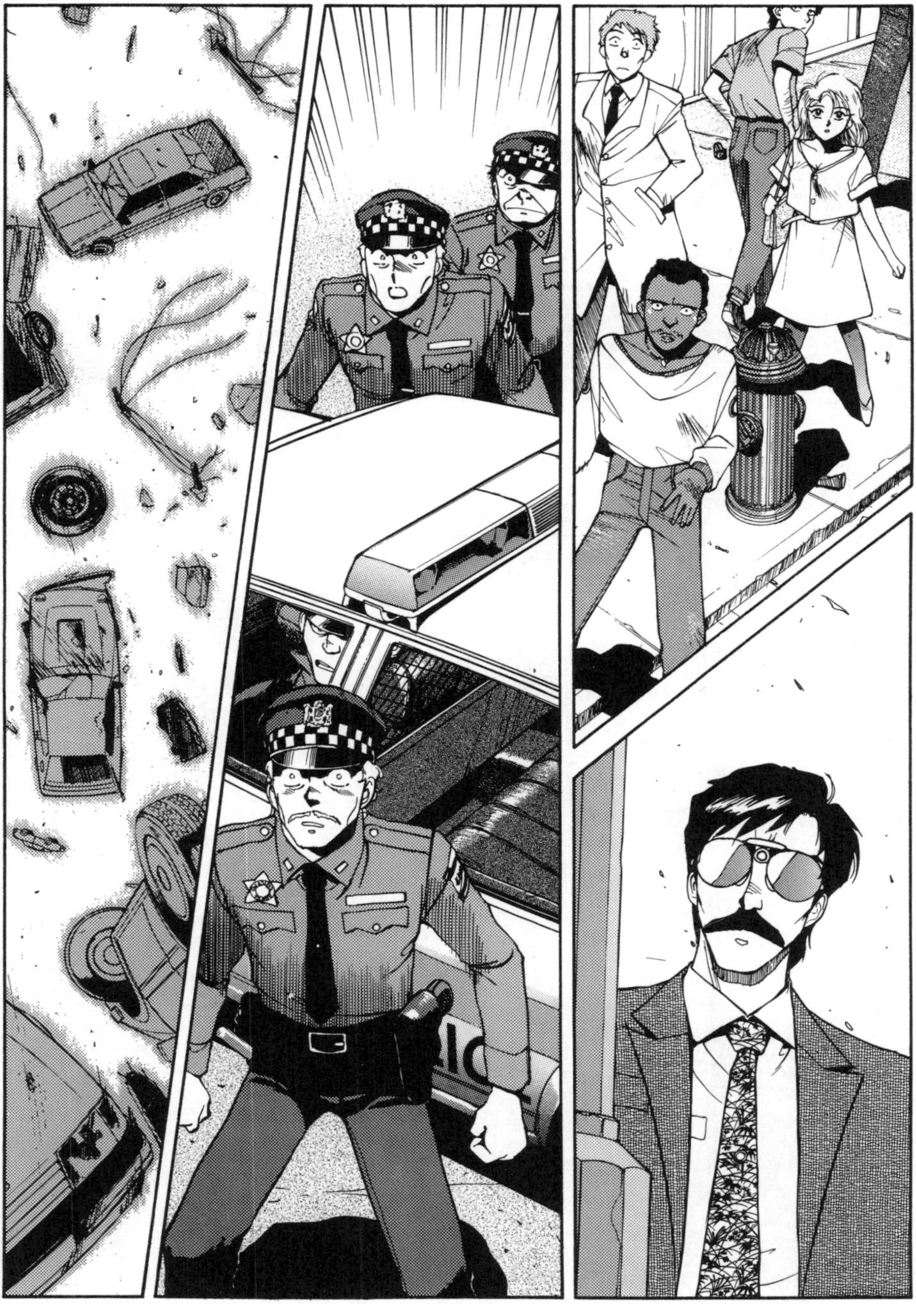

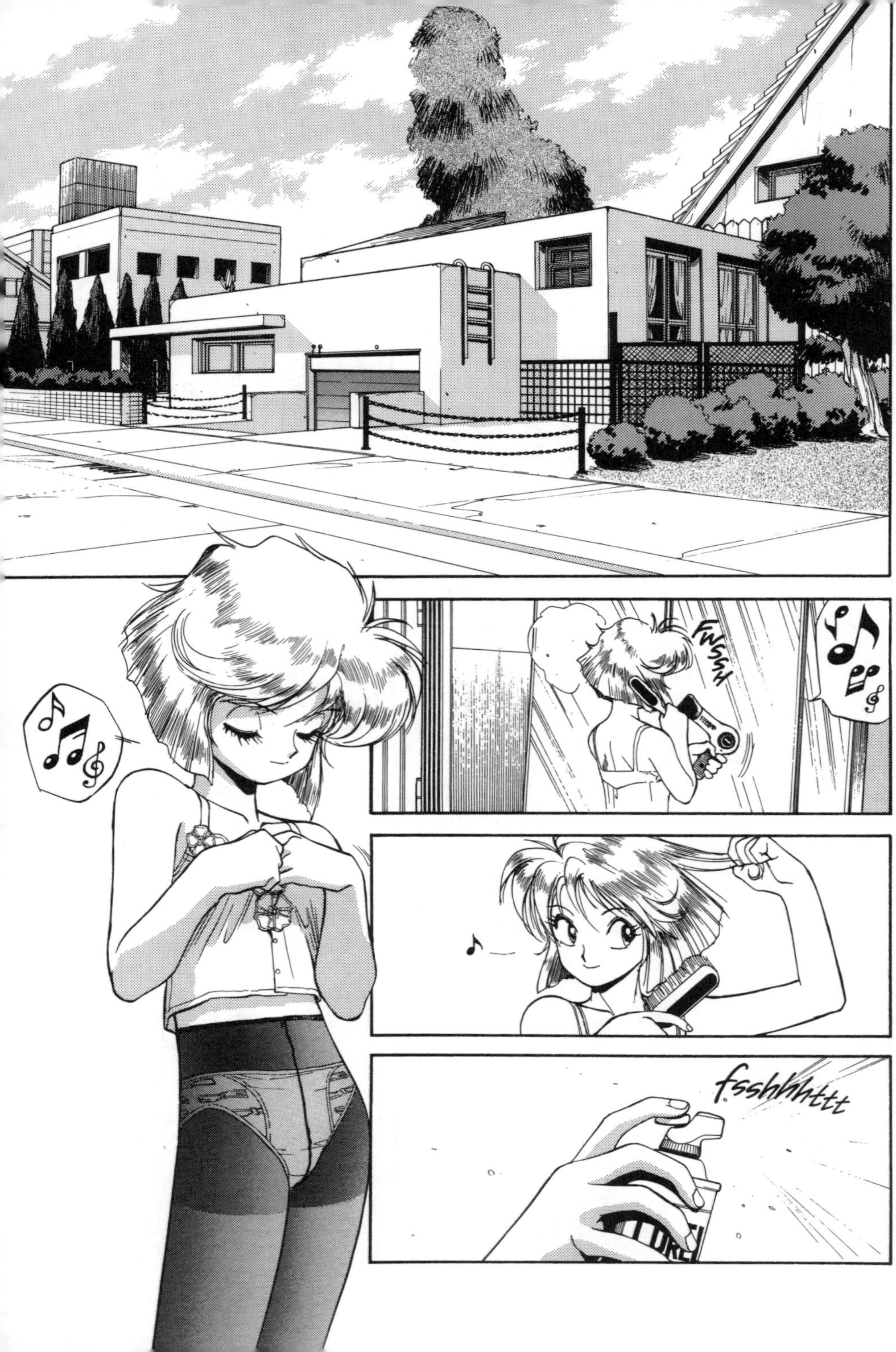
FWSSH
fsshhhttt

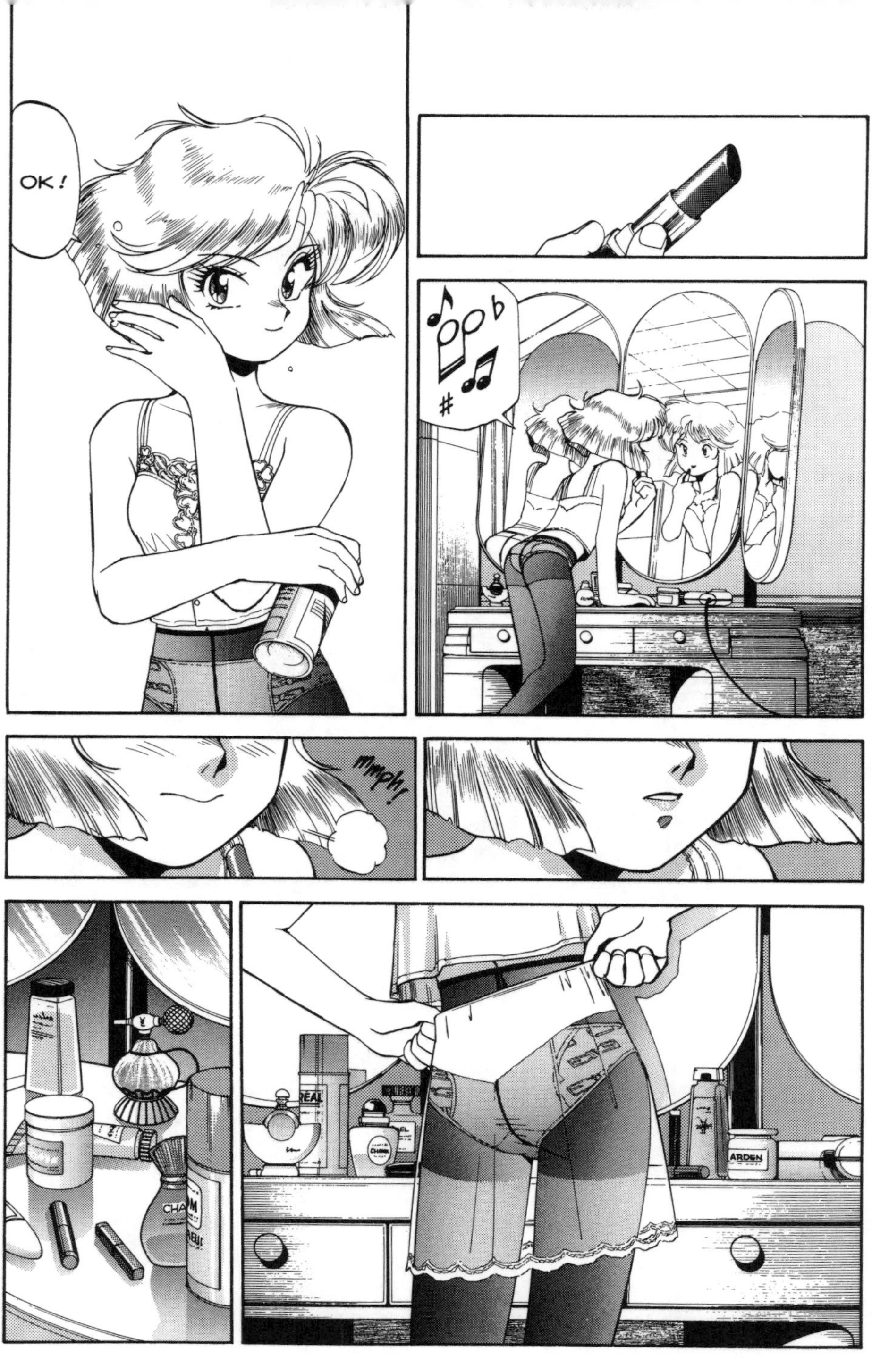
OK!
mmph!

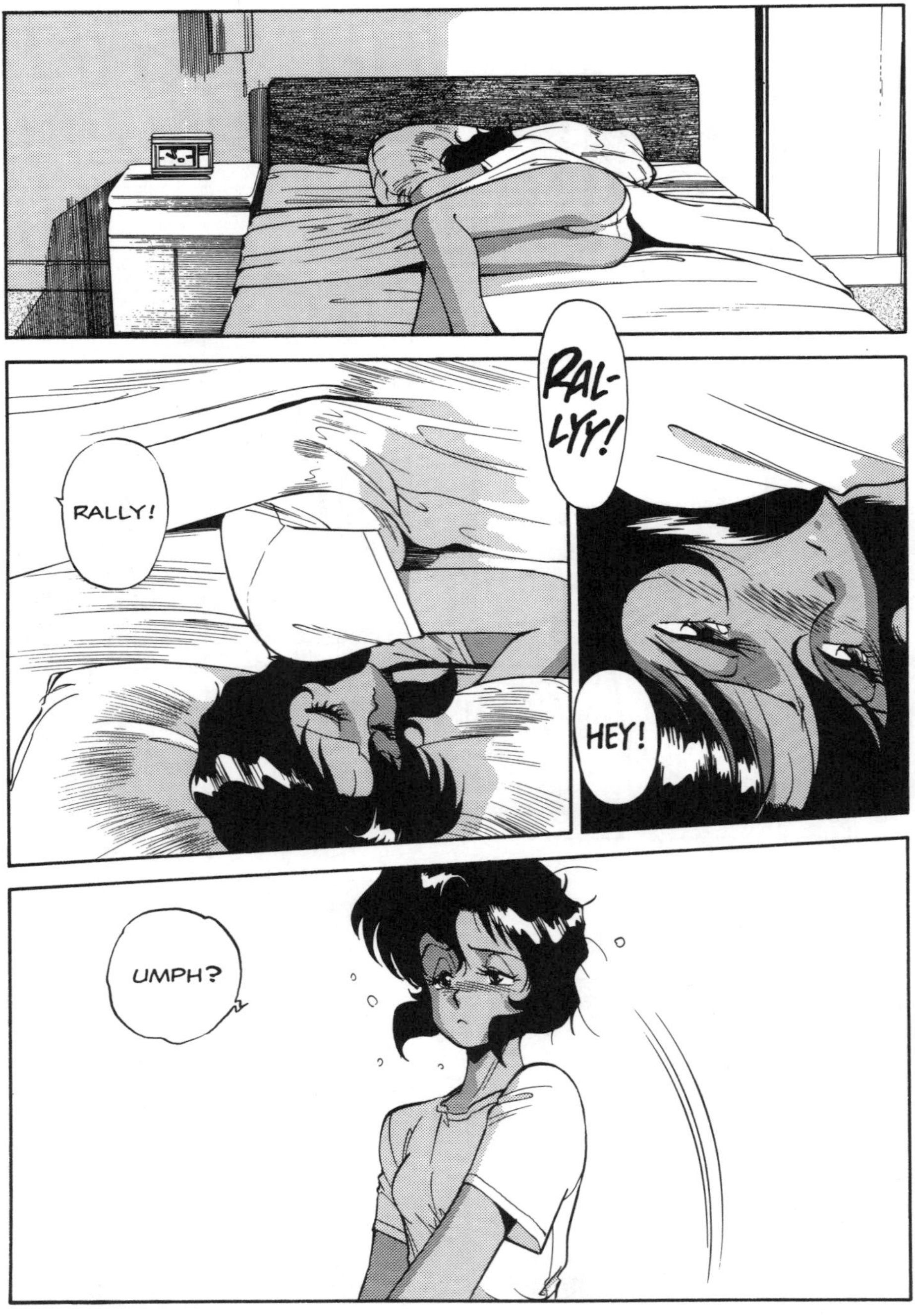
RAL-
LYY!
RALLY!
HEY!
UMPH?

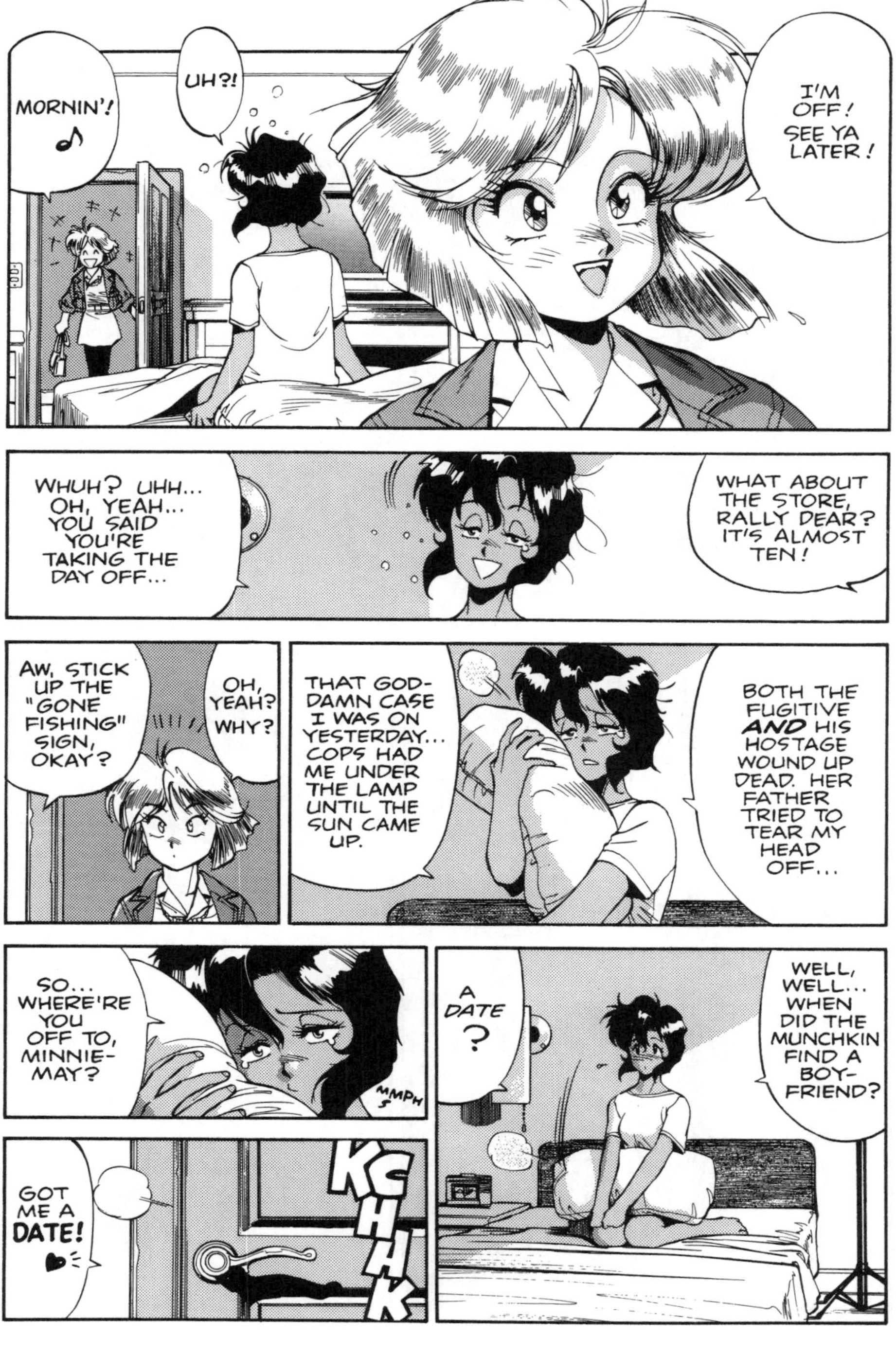
MORNIN'! ♪
UH?!
I'M OFF! SEE YA LATER!
WHUH? UHH... OH, YEAH... YOU SAID YOU'RE TAKING THE DAY OFF...
WHAT ABOUT THE STORE, RALLY DEAR? IT'S ALMOST TEN!
AW, STICK UP THE "GONE FISHING" SIGN, OKAY?
OH, YEAH? WHY?
THAT GOD-DAMN CASE I WAS ON YESTERDAY... COPS HAD ME UNDER THE LAMP UNTIL THE SUN CAME UP.
BOTH THE FUGITIVE AND HIS HOSTAGE WOUND UP DEAD. HER FATHER TRIED TO TEAR MY HEAD OFF...
SO... WHERE'RE YOU OFF TO, MINNIE-MAY?
MMPHS
GOT ME A DATE! ♥
KCHHK
A DATE?
WELL, WELL... WHEN DID THE MUNCHKIN FIND A BOY-FRIEND?

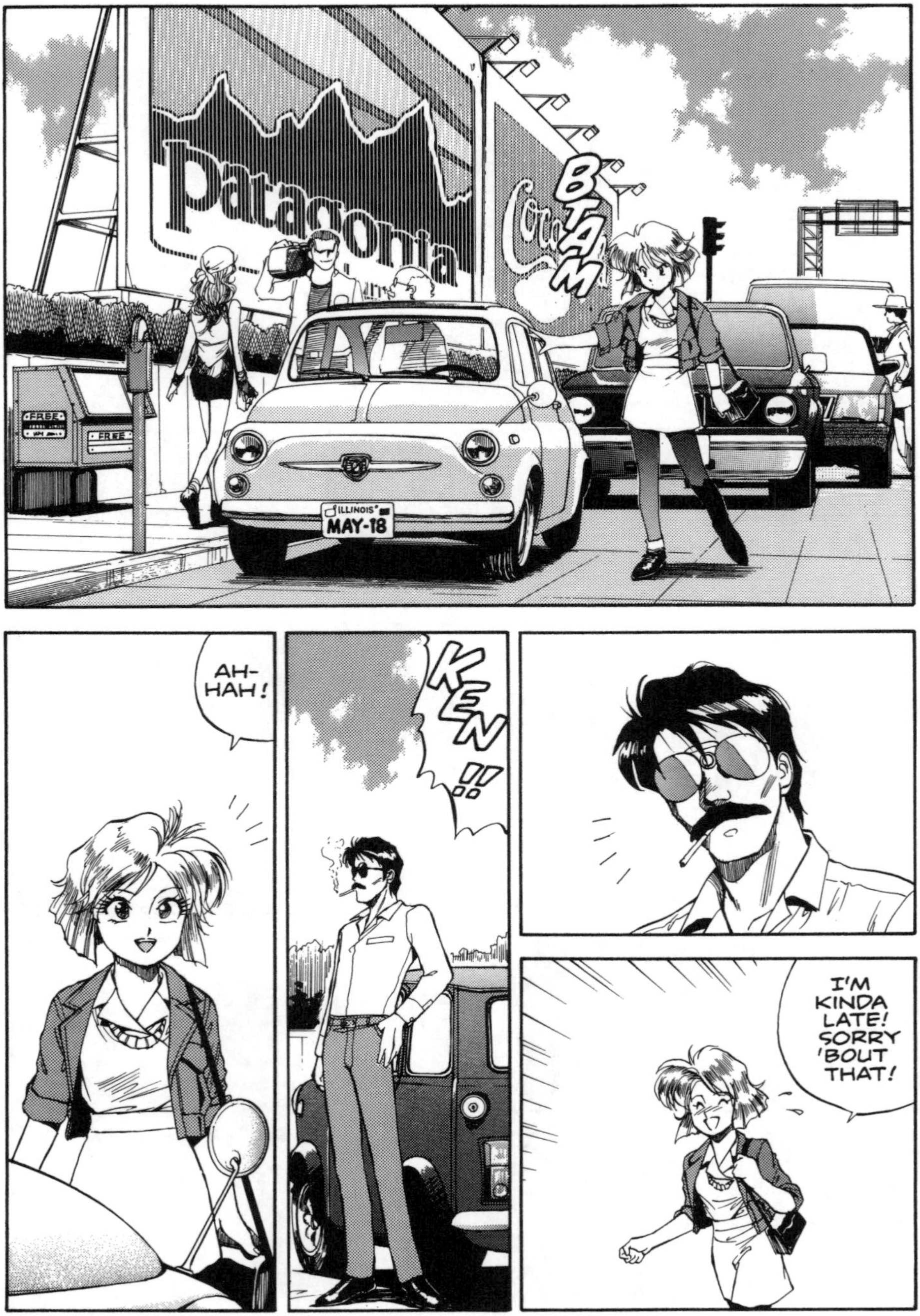
patagonia
FREE
ILLINOIS
MAY-18
BTAM
AH-HAH!
KEN!!
I'M KINDA LATE! SORRY 'BOUT THAT!

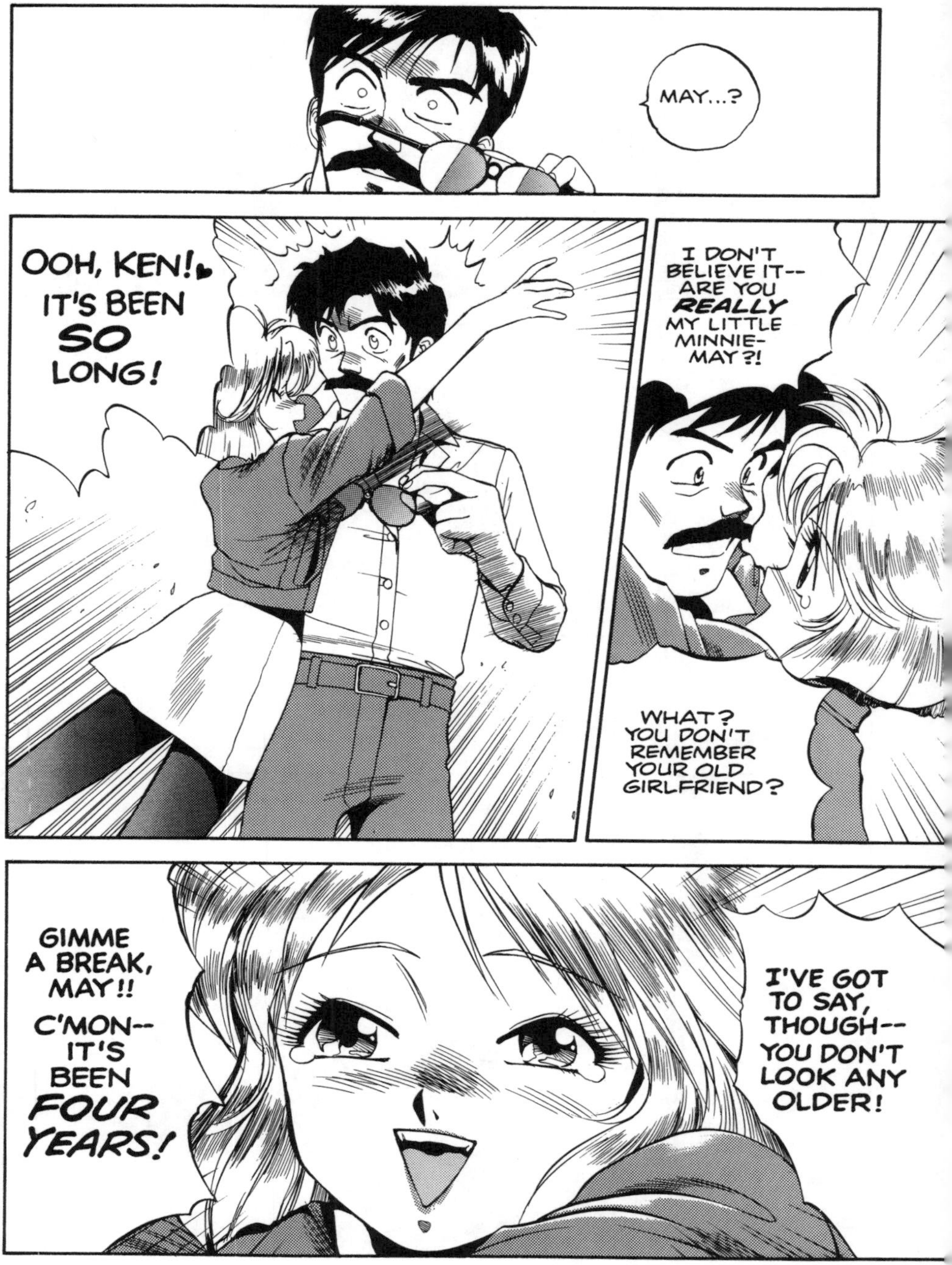
MAY...?
OOH, KEN!♥ IT'S BEEN SO LONG!
I DON'T BELIEVE IT-- ARE YOU REALLY MY LITTLE MINNIE-MAY?!
WHAT? YOU DON'T REMEMBER YOUR OLD GIRLFRIEND?
GIMME A BREAK, MAY!!
C'MON-- IT'S BEEN FOUR YEARS!
I'VE GOT TO SAY, THOUGH-- YOU DON'T LOOK ANY OLDER!

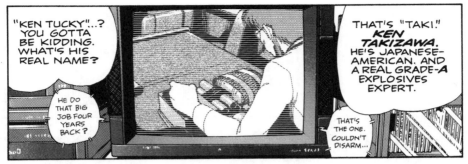

"KEN TUCKY"...? YOU GOTTA BE KIDDING. WHAT'S HIS REAL NAME?

HE DO THAT BIG JOB FOUR YEARS BACK?

THAT'S "TAKI." *KEN TAKIZAWA.* HE'S JAPANESE-AMERICAN. AND A REAL GRADE-*A* EXPLOSIVES EXPERT.

THAT'S THE ONE. COULDN'T DISARM...

NEVER HEARD OF HIM.

YEAH, WELL, IT'S BEEN FOUR YEARS SINCE HIS LAST BIG SHOW.

PLUS, HE'S ALWAYS WORKED THE EAST COAST BEFORE.

THIS IS PROBABLY HIS CHICAGO DEBUT.

HERE!!

KLIK

THE BOMB WENT UP RIGHT AFTER HE CUT THAT CABLE. THE TAPE ENDS HERE, TOO, OF COURSE.

I DUNNO, ROY-- MAYBE THE TIMER WAS STILL COUNT-ING DOWN?

NAW, THIS WAS AFTER HE LOCKED OUT THE COMPUTER. COULDN'T HAVE BEEN THAT.

SO...?

KLIK

DiNG!

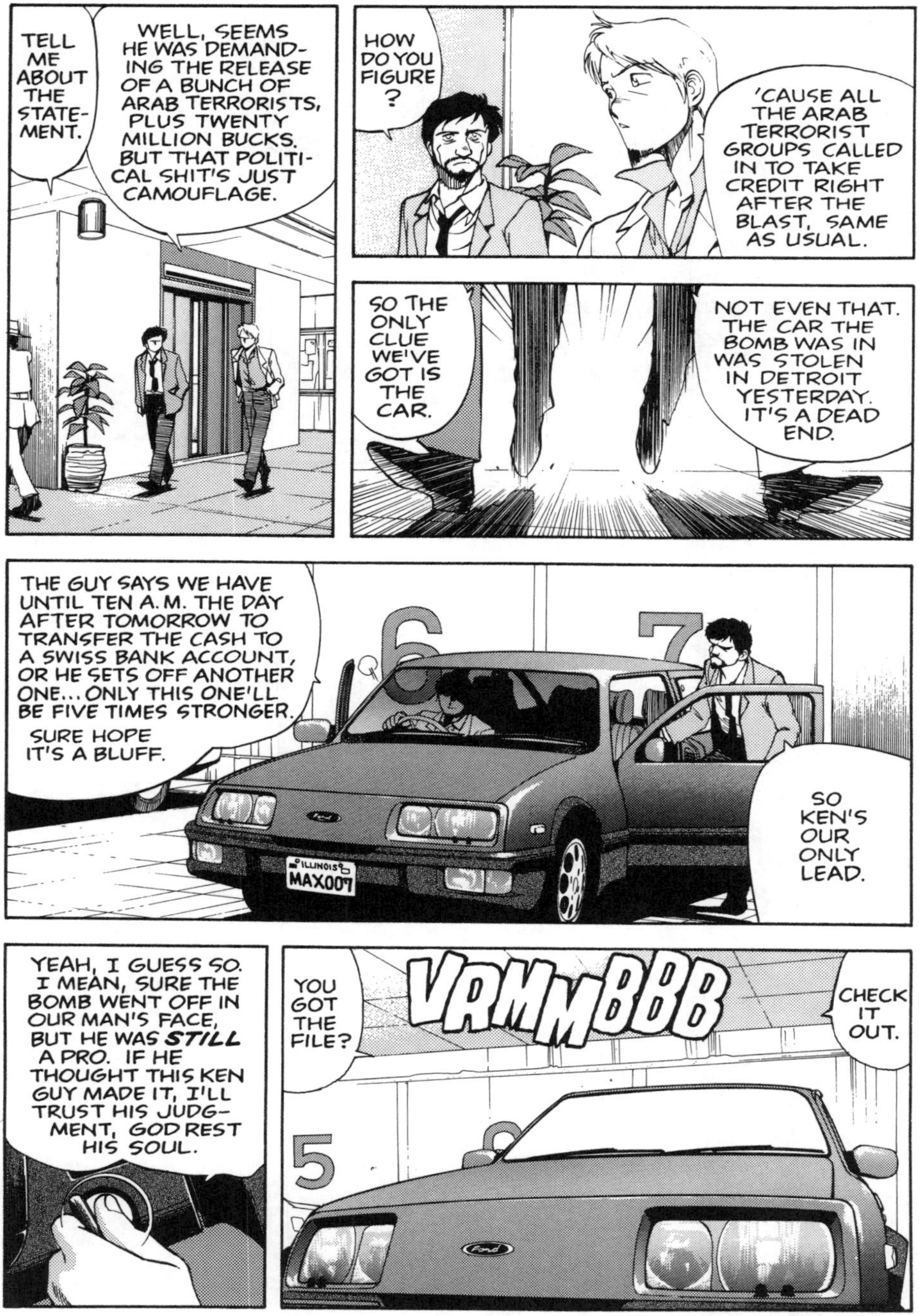
TELL ME ABOUT THE STATEMENT.
WELL, SEEMS HE WAS DEMANDING THE RELEASE OF A BUNCH OF ARAB TERRORISTS, PLUS TWENTY MILLION BUCKS. BUT THAT POLITICAL SHIT'S JUST CAMOUFLAGE.
HOW DO YOU FIGURE?
'CAUSE ALL THE ARAB TERRORIST GROUPS CALLED IN TO TAKE CREDIT RIGHT AFTER THE BLAST, SAME AS USUAL.
SO THE ONLY CLUE WE'VE GOT IS THE CAR.
NOT EVEN THAT. THE CAR THE BOMB WAS IN WAS STOLEN IN DETROIT YESTERDAY. IT'S A DEAD END.
THE GUY SAYS WE HAVE UNTIL TEN A.M. THE DAY AFTER TOMORROW TO TRANSFER THE CASH TO A SWISS BANK ACCOUNT, OR HE SETS OFF ANOTHER ONE... ONLY THIS ONE'LL BE FIVE TIMES STRONGER.
SURE HOPE IT'S A BLUFF.
6
7
ILLINOIS
MAX007
SO KEN'S OUR ONLY LEAD.
YEAH, I GUESS SO. I MEAN, SURE THE BOMB WENT OFF IN OUR MAN'S FACE, BUT HE WAS STILL A PRO. IF HE THOUGHT THIS KEN GUY MADE IT, I'LL TRUST HIS JUDGMENT, GOD REST HIS SOUL.
YOU GOT THE FILE?
VRMMBBB
CHECK IT OUT.
5
Ford

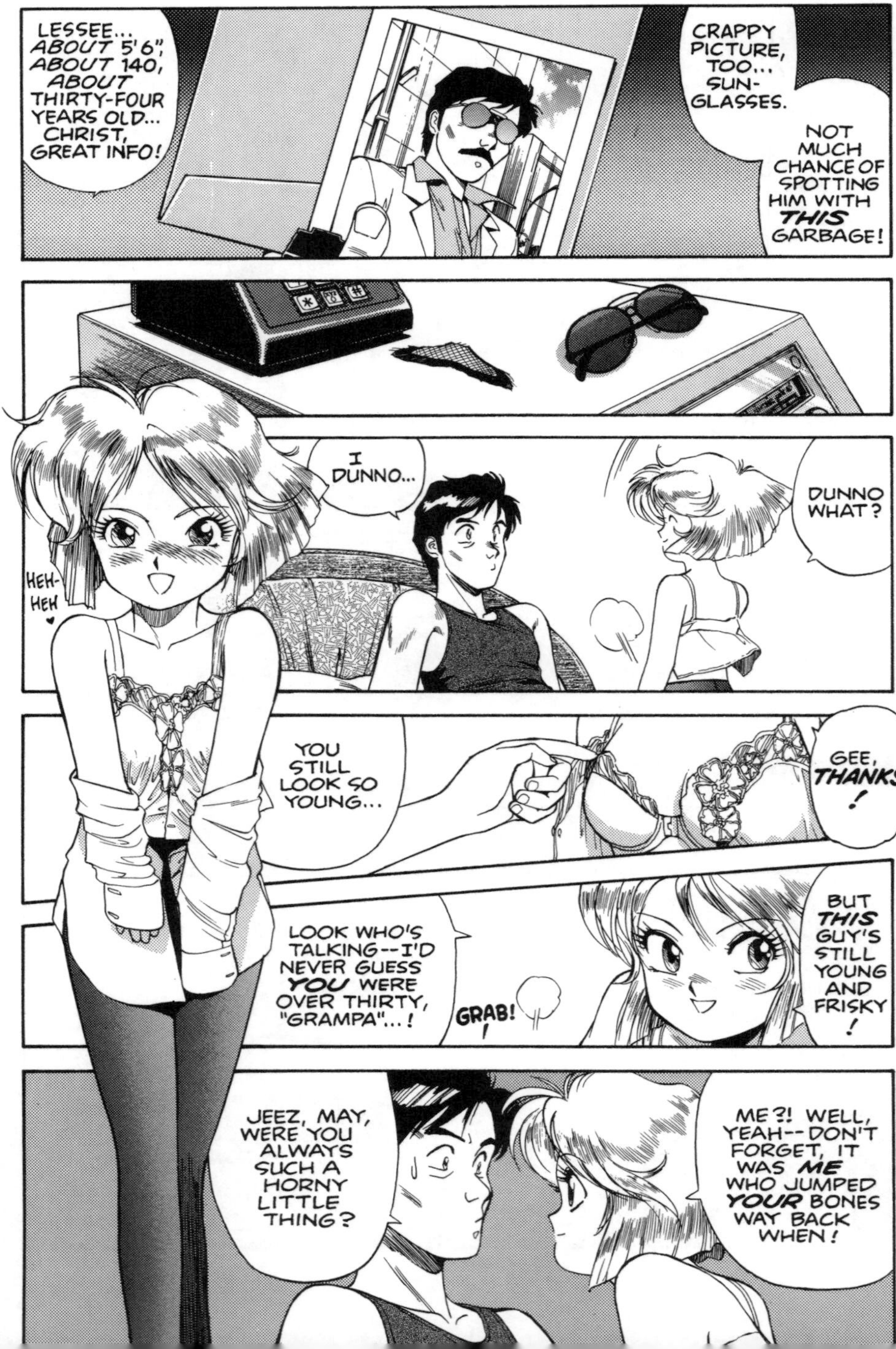
LESSEE... ABOUT 5'6", ABOUT 140, ABOUT THIRTY-FOUR YEARS OLD... CHRIST, GREAT INFO!
CRAPPY PICTURE, TOO... SUN-GLASSES.
NOT MUCH CHANCE OF SPOTTING HIM WITH THIS GARBAGE!
HEH-HEH ♥
I DUNNO...
DUNNO WHAT?
YOU STILL LOOK SO YOUNG...
GEE, THANKS!
LOOK WHO'S TALKING--I'D NEVER GUESS YOU WERE OVER THIRTY, "GRAMPA"...!
GRAB!
BUT THIS GUY'S STILL YOUNG AND FRISKY!
JEEZ, MAY, WERE YOU ALWAYS SUCH A HORNY LITTLE THING?
ME?! WELL, YEAH--DON'T FORGET, IT WAS ME WHO JUMPED YOUR BONES WAY BACK WHEN!

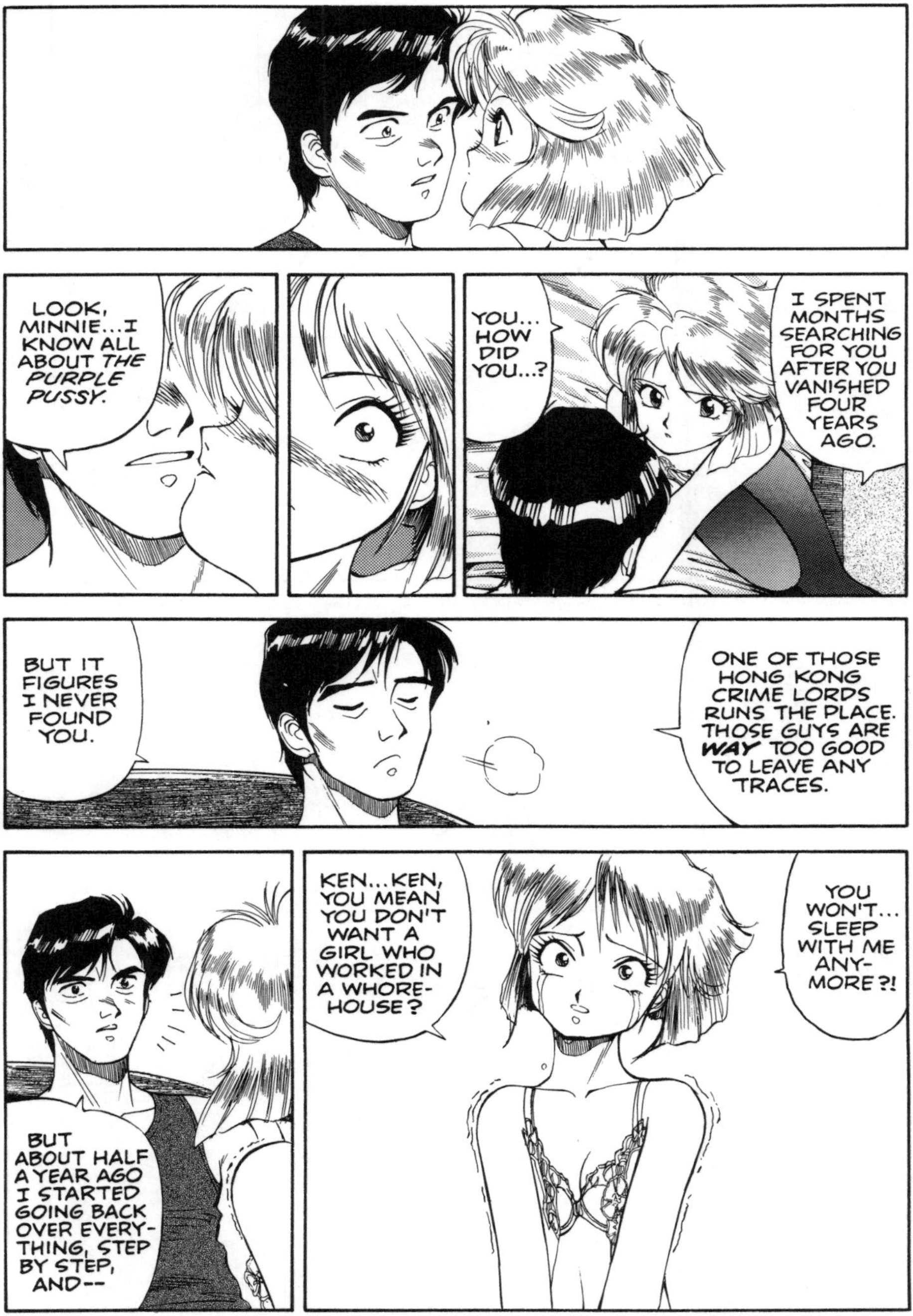
LOOK, MINNIE...I KNOW ALL ABOUT *THE PURPLE PUSSY.*
YOU... HOW DID YOU...?
I SPENT MONTHS SEARCHING FOR YOU AFTER YOU VANISHED FOUR YEARS AGO.
BUT IT FIGURES I NEVER FOUND YOU.
ONE OF THOSE HONG KONG CRIME LORDS RUNS THE PLACE. THOSE GUYS ARE *WAY* TOO GOOD TO LEAVE ANY TRACES.
BUT ABOUT HALF A YEAR AGO I STARTED GOING BACK OVER EVERY-THING, STEP BY STEP, AND--
KEN...KEN, YOU MEAN YOU DON'T WANT A GIRL WHO WORKED IN A WHORE-HOUSE?
YOU WON'T... SLEEP WITH ME ANY-MORE?!

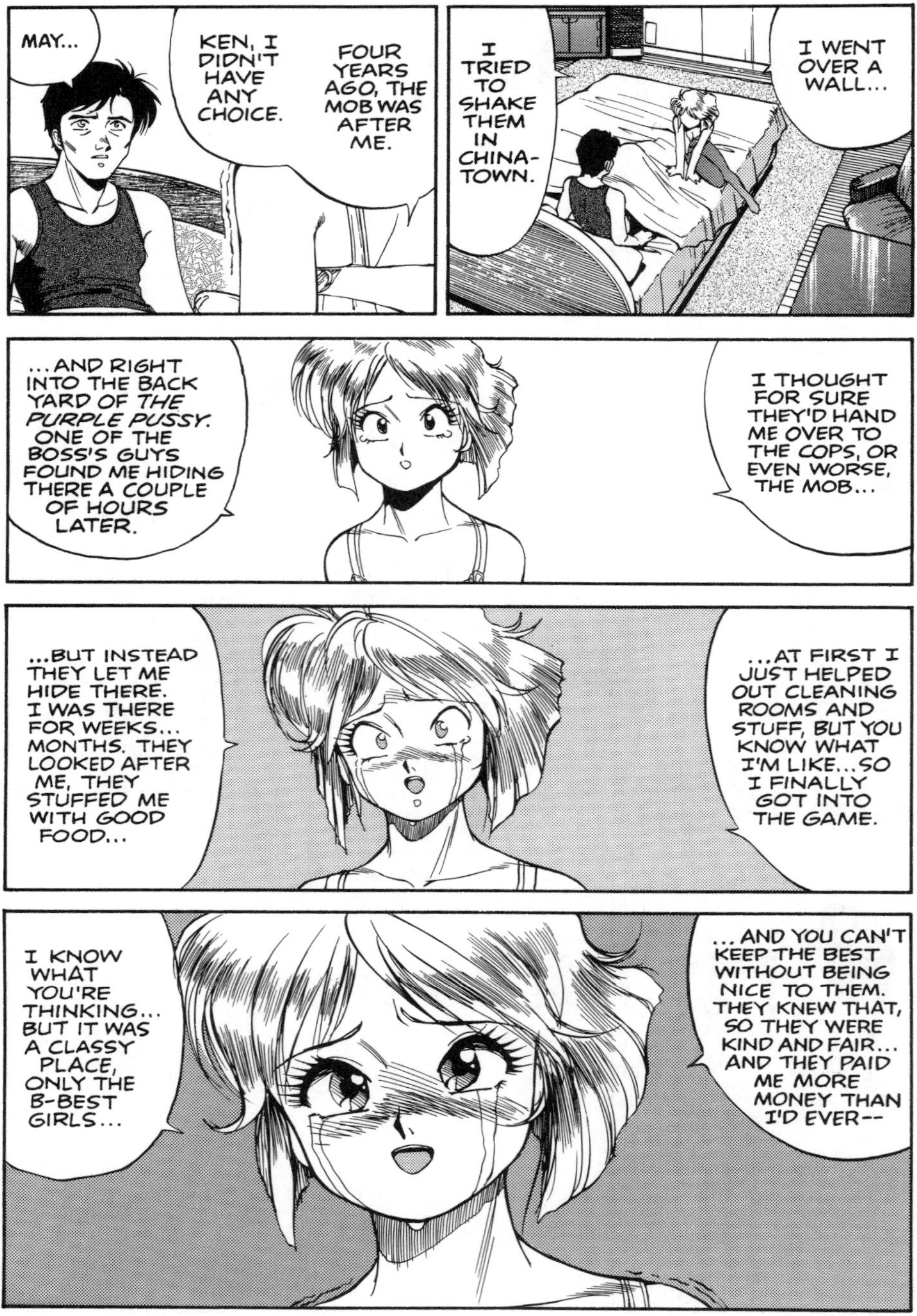
MAY...
KEN, I DIDN'T HAVE ANY CHOICE.
FOUR YEARS AGO, THE MOB WAS AFTER ME.
I TRIED TO SHAKE THEM IN CHINA-TOWN.
I WENT OVER A WALL...
...AND RIGHT INTO THE BACK YARD OF *THE PURPLE PUSSY.* ONE OF THE BOSS'S GUYS FOUND ME HIDING THERE A COUPLE OF HOURS LATER.
I THOUGHT FOR SURE THEY'D HAND ME OVER TO THE COPS, OR EVEN WORSE, THE MOB...
...BUT INSTEAD THEY LET ME HIDE THERE. I WAS THERE FOR WEEKS... MONTHS. THEY LOOKED AFTER ME, THEY STUFFED ME WITH GOOD FOOD...
...AT FIRST I JUST HELPED OUT CLEANING ROOMS AND STUFF, BUT YOU KNOW WHAT I'M LIKE...SO I FINALLY GOT INTO THE GAME.
I KNOW WHAT YOU'RE THINKING... BUT IT WAS A CLASSY PLACE, ONLY THE B-BEST GIRLS...
...AND YOU CAN'T KEEP THE BEST WITHOUT BEING NICE TO THEM. THEY KNEW THAT, SO THEY WERE KIND AND FAIR... AND THEY PAID ME MORE MONEY THAN I'D EVER--

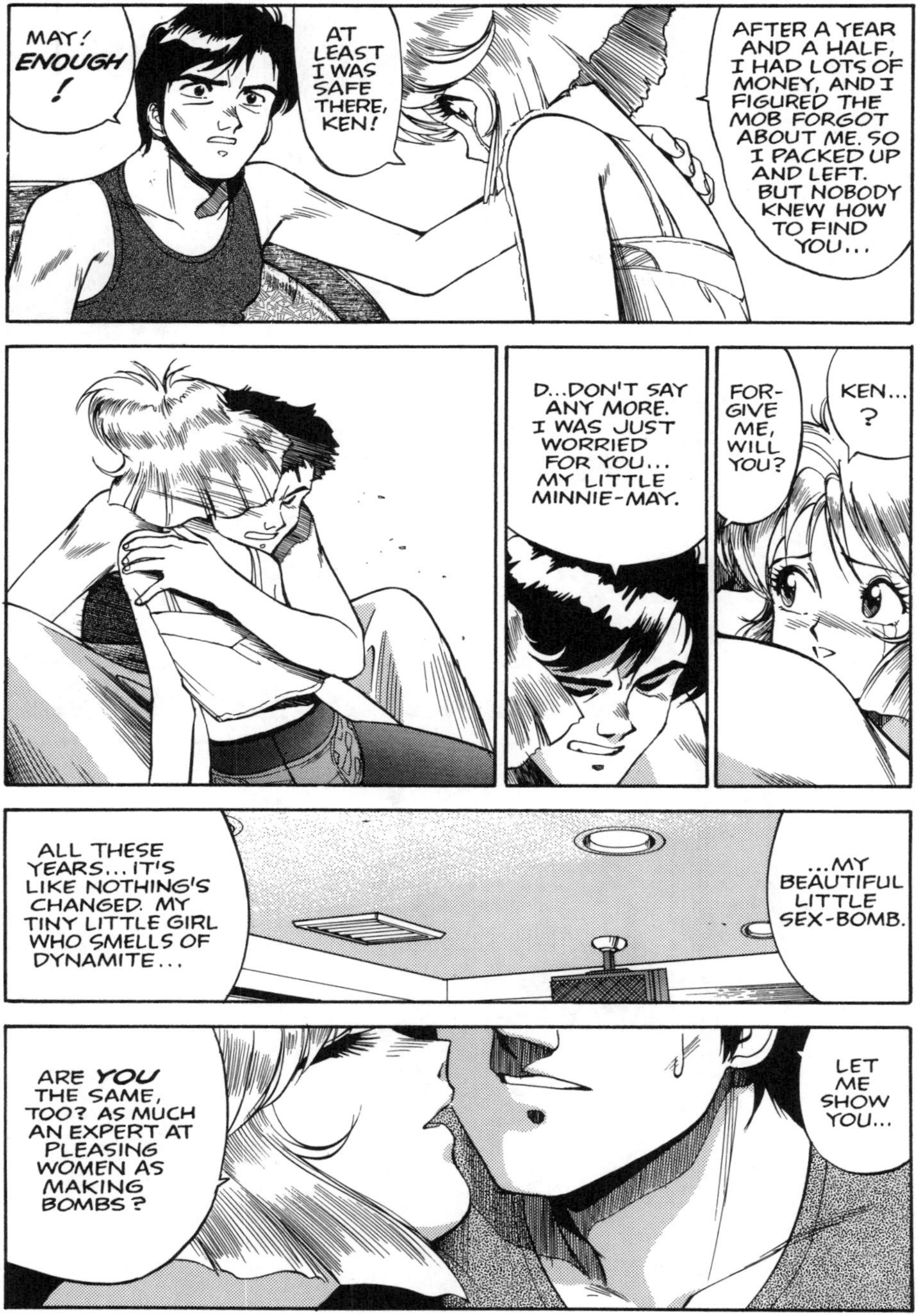
MAY! ENOUGH!
AT LEAST I WAS SAFE THERE, KEN!
AFTER A YEAR AND A HALF, I HAD LOTS OF MONEY, AND I FIGURED THE MOB FORGOT ABOUT ME. SO I PACKED UP AND LEFT. BUT NOBODY KNEW HOW TO FIND YOU...
D...DON'T SAY ANY MORE. I WAS JUST WORRIED FOR YOU... MY LITTLE MINNIE-MAY.
FOR-GIVE ME, WILL YOU?
KEN... ?
ALL THESE YEARS... IT'S LIKE NOTHING'S CHANGED. MY TINY LITTLE GIRL WHO SMELLS OF DYNAMITE...
...MY BEAUTIFUL LITTLE SEX-BOMB.
ARE YOU THE SAME, TOO? AS MUCH AN EXPERT AT PLEASING WOMEN AS MAKING BOMBS?
LET ME SHOW YOU...

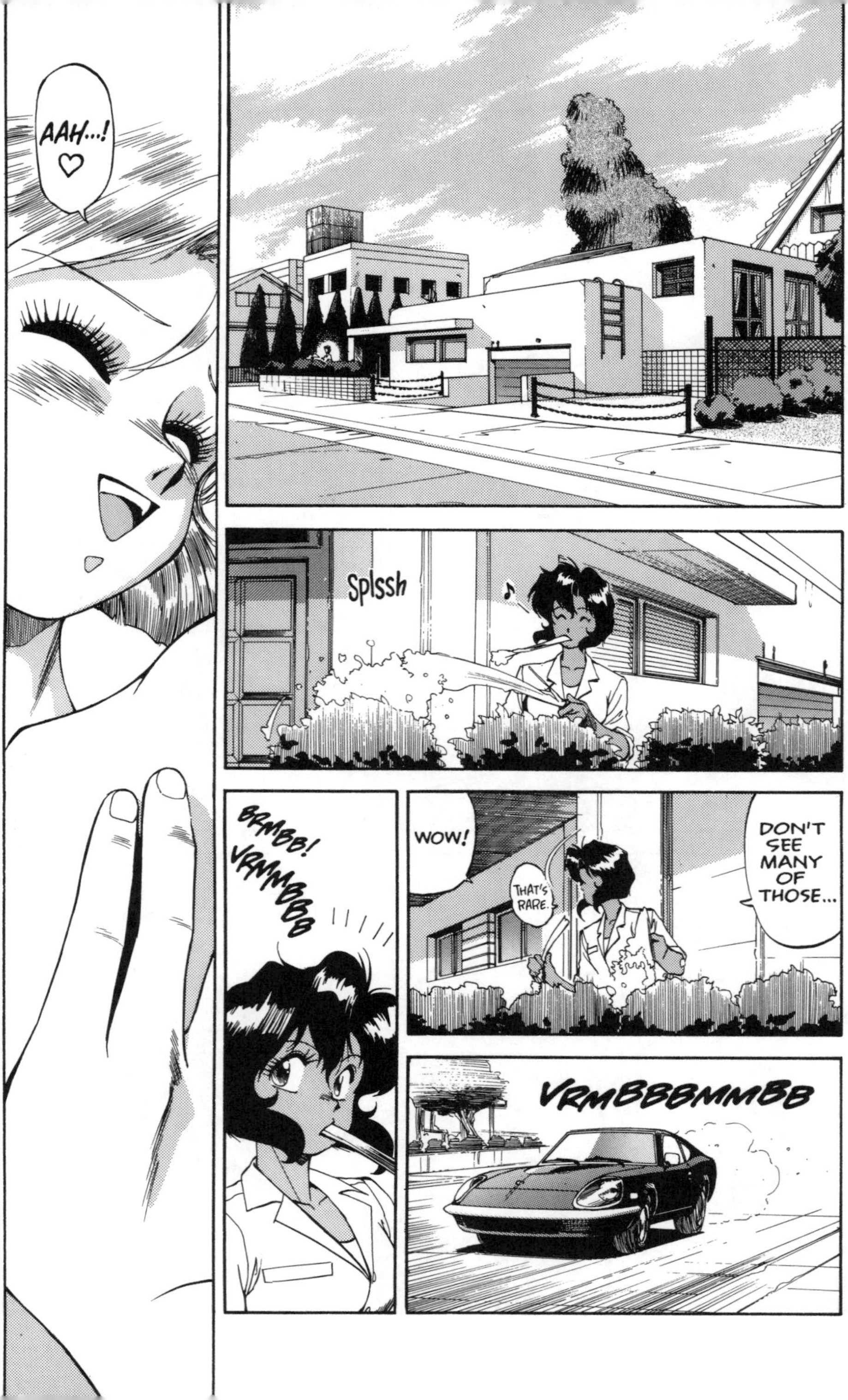
AAH...! ♡
Splssh
BRMBB!
VRMMBBB
WOW!
THAT'S RARE.
DON'T SEE MANY OF THOSE...
VRMBBBBMMBB

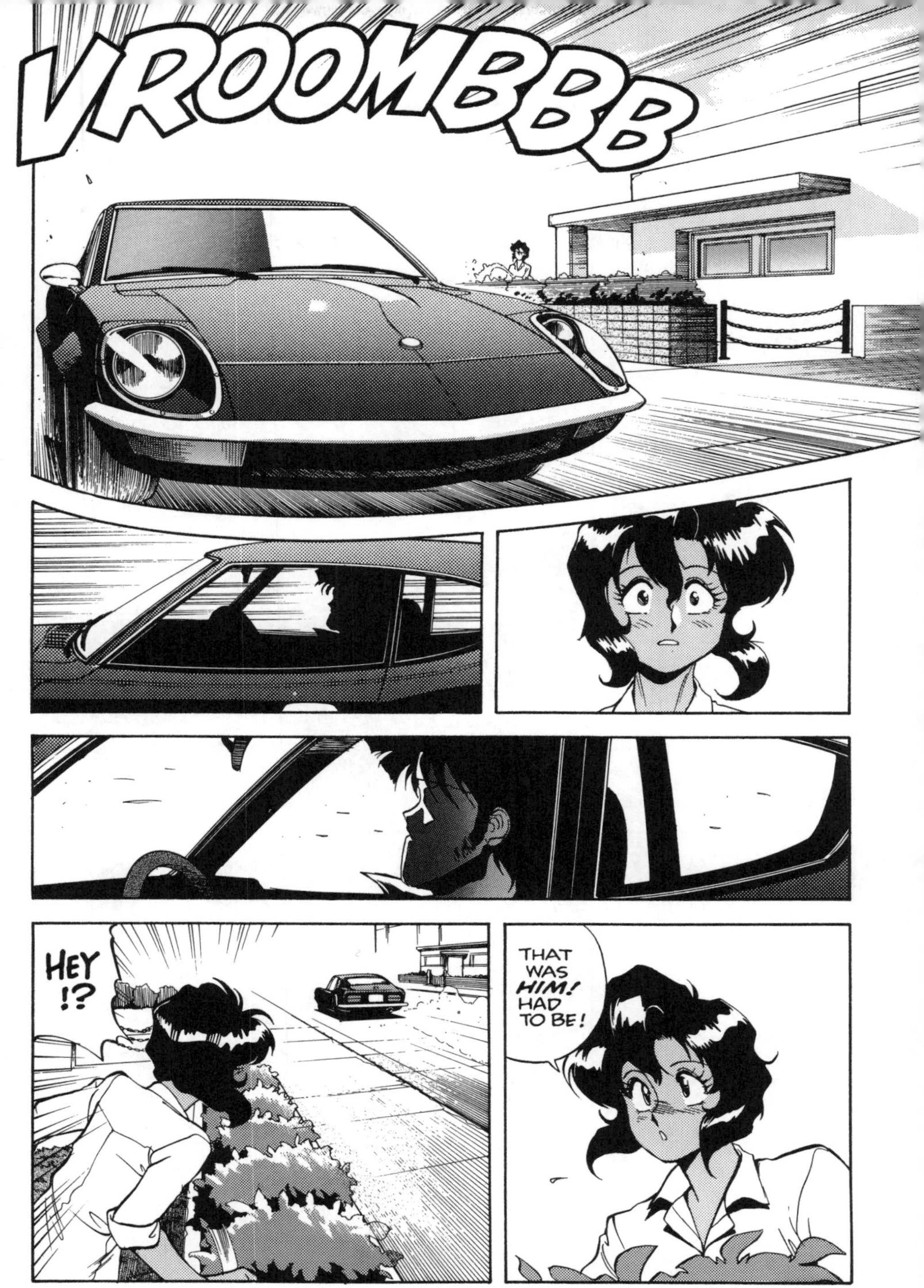
VROOMBBB
HEY !?
THAT WAS HIM! HAD TO BE!

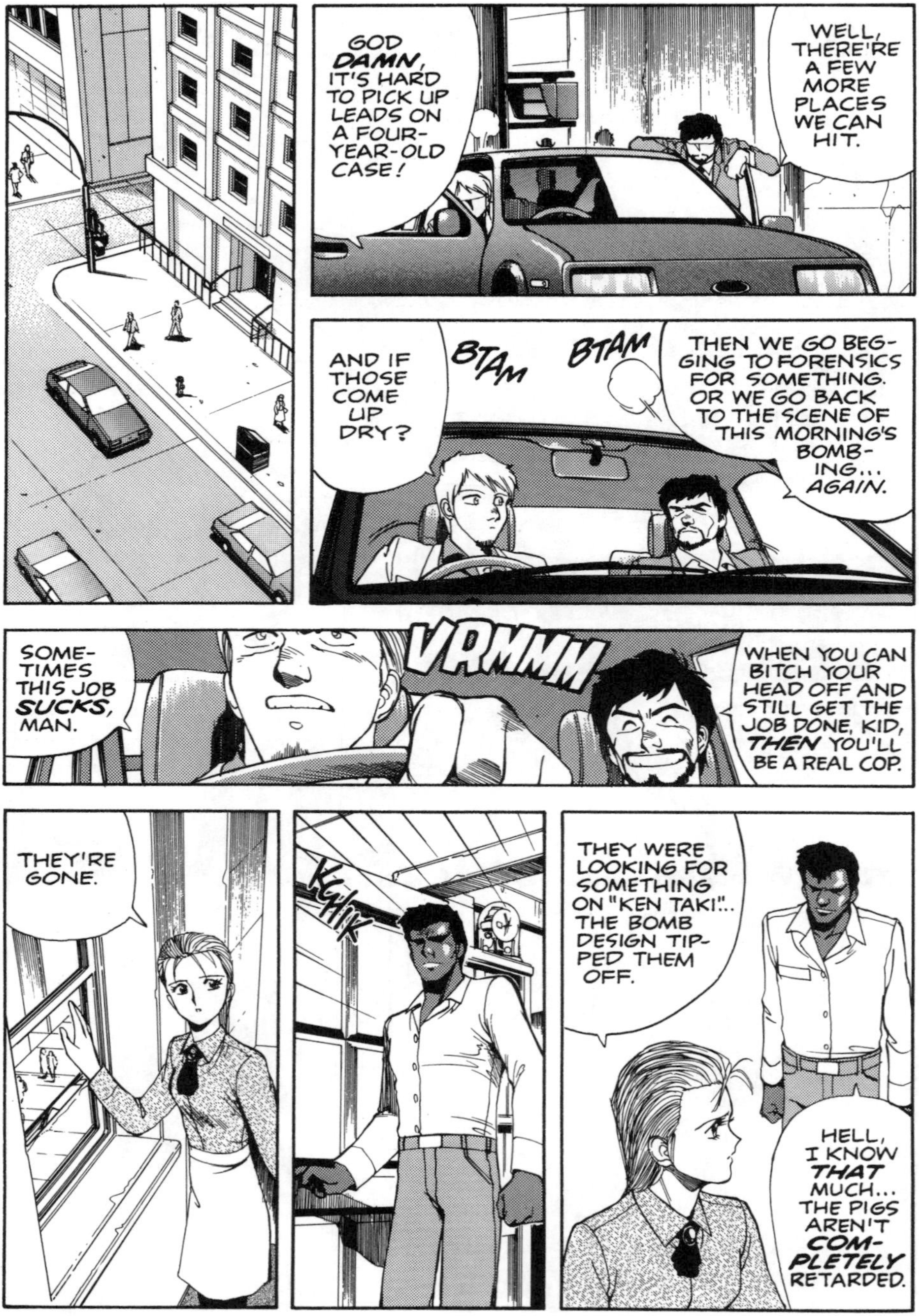
GOD DAMN, IT'S HARD TO PICK UP LEADS ON A FOUR-YEAR-OLD CASE!
WELL, THERE'RE A FEW MORE PLACES WE CAN HIT.
AND IF THOSE COME UP DRY?
BTAM
BTAM
THEN WE GO BEGGING TO FORENSICS FOR SOMETHING. OR WE GO BACK TO THE SCENE OF THIS MORNING'S BOMBING... AGAIN.
SOMETIMES THIS JOB SUCKS, MAN.
VRMMM
WHEN YOU CAN BITCH YOUR HEAD OFF AND STILL GET THE JOB DONE, KID, THEN YOU'LL BE A REAL COP.
THEY'RE GONE.
KCHIK
THEY WERE LOOKING FOR SOMETHING ON "KEN TAKI"... THE BOMB DESIGN TIPPED THEM OFF.
HELL, I KNOW THAT MUCH... THE PIGS AREN'T COMPLETELY RETARDED.

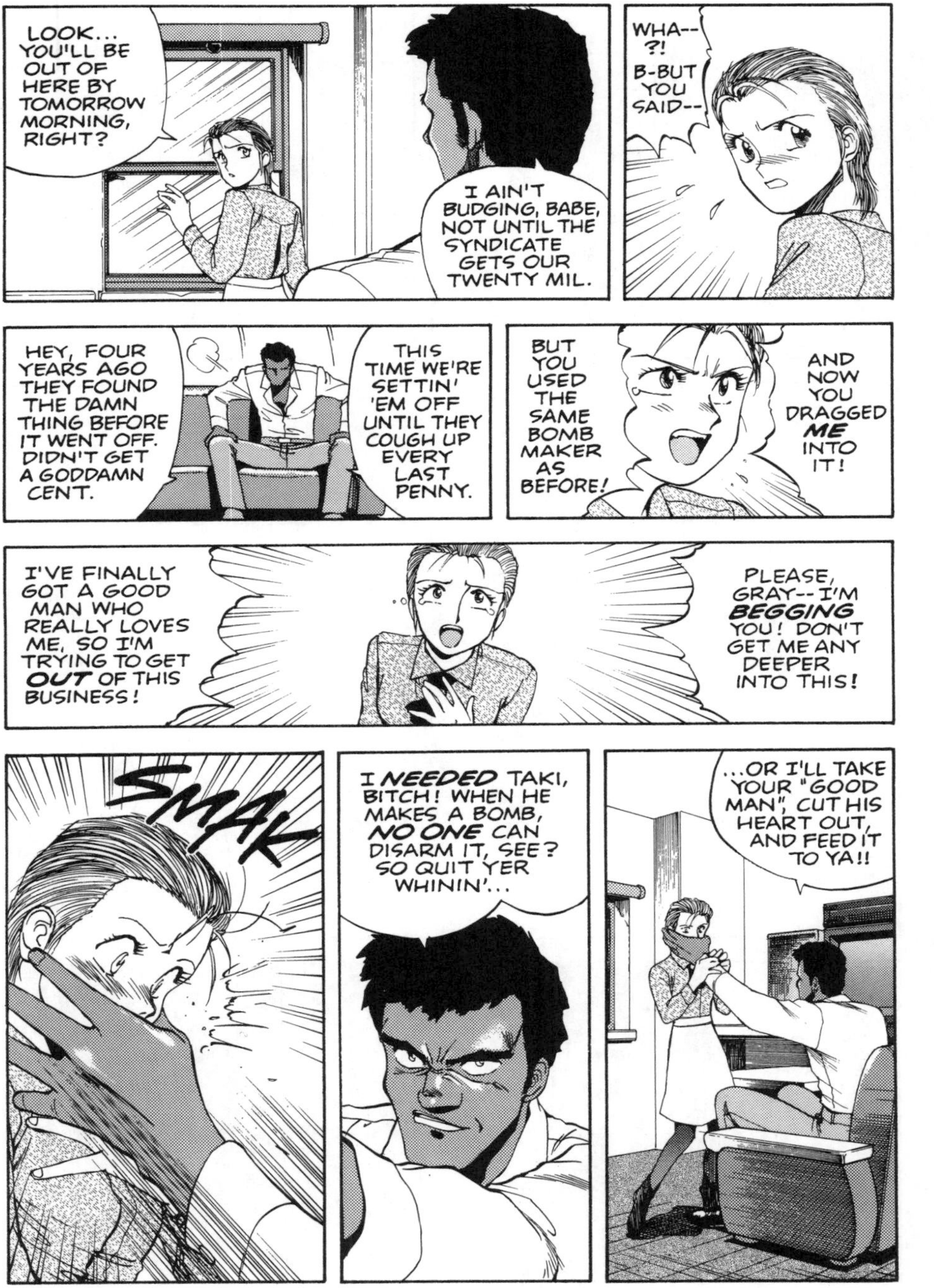
LOOK... YOU'LL BE OUT OF HERE BY TOMORROW MORNING, RIGHT?
I AIN'T BUDGING, BABE, NOT UNTIL THE SYNDICATE GETS OUR TWENTY MIL.
WHA-- ?!
B-BUT YOU SAID--
HEY, FOUR YEARS AGO THEY FOUND THE DAMN THING BEFORE IT WENT OFF. DIDN'T GET A GODDAMN CENT.
THIS TIME WE'RE SETTIN' 'EM OFF UNTIL THEY COUGH UP EVERY LAST PENNY.
BUT YOU USED THE SAME BOMB MAKER AS BEFORE!
AND NOW YOU DRAGGED ME INTO IT!
I'VE FINALLY GOT A GOOD MAN WHO REALLY LOVES ME, SO I'M TRYING TO GET OUT OF THIS BUSINESS!
PLEASE, GRAY-- I'M BEGGING YOU! DON'T GET ME ANY DEEPER INTO THIS!
SMAK
I NEEDED TAKI, BITCH! WHEN HE MAKES A BOMB, NO ONE CAN DISARM IT, SEE? SO QUIT YER WHININ'...
...OR I'LL TAKE YOUR "GOOD MAN", CUT HIS HEART OUT, AND FEED IT TO YA!!

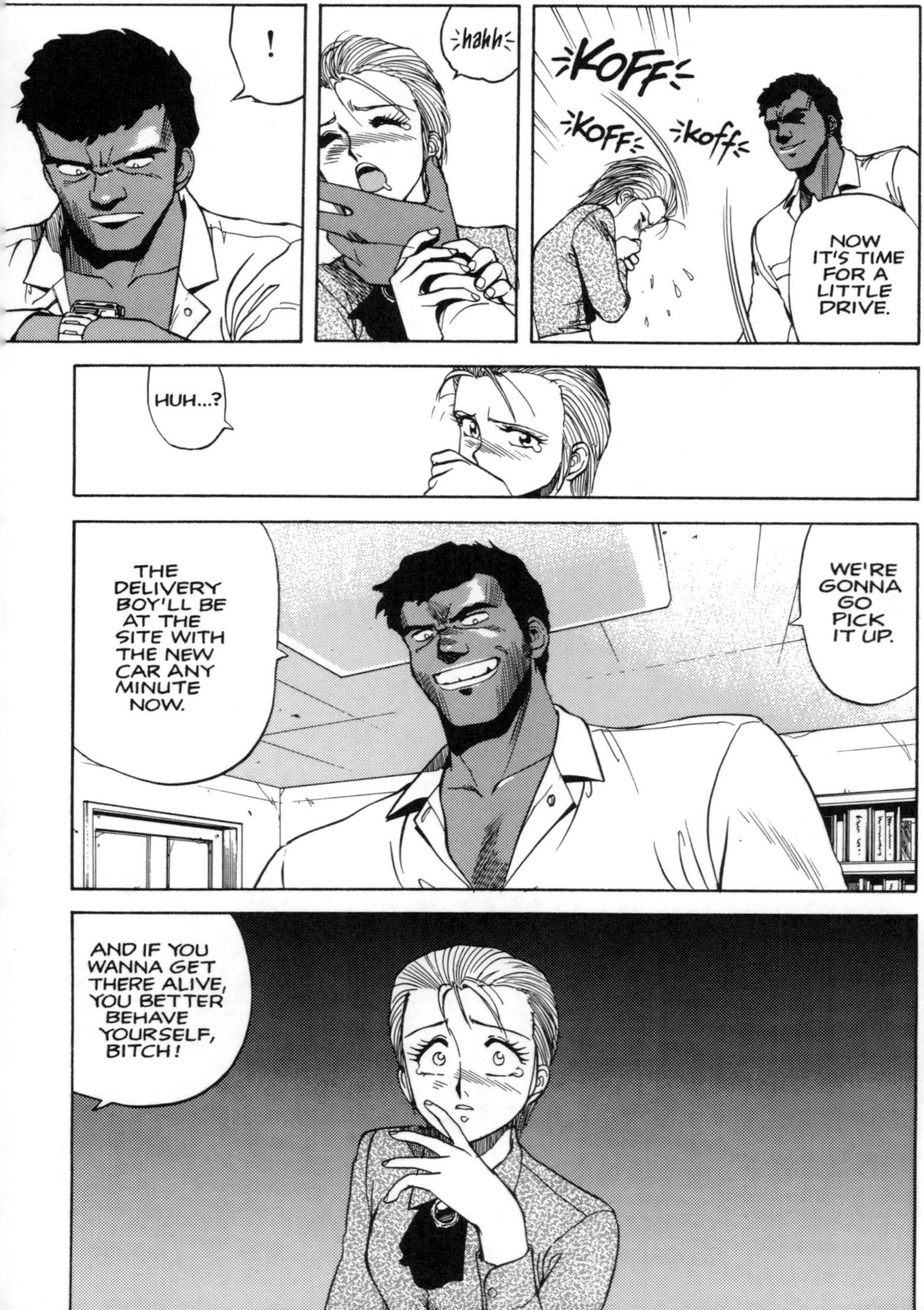
!
hahh
KOFF
KOFF
koff
NOW IT'S TIME FOR A LITTLE DRIVE.
HUH...?
THE DELIVERY BOY'LL BE AT THE SITE WITH THE NEW CAR ANY MINUTE NOW.
WE'RE GONNA GO PICK IT UP.
AND IF YOU WANNA GET THERE ALIVE, YOU BETTER BEHAVE YOURSELF, BITCH!

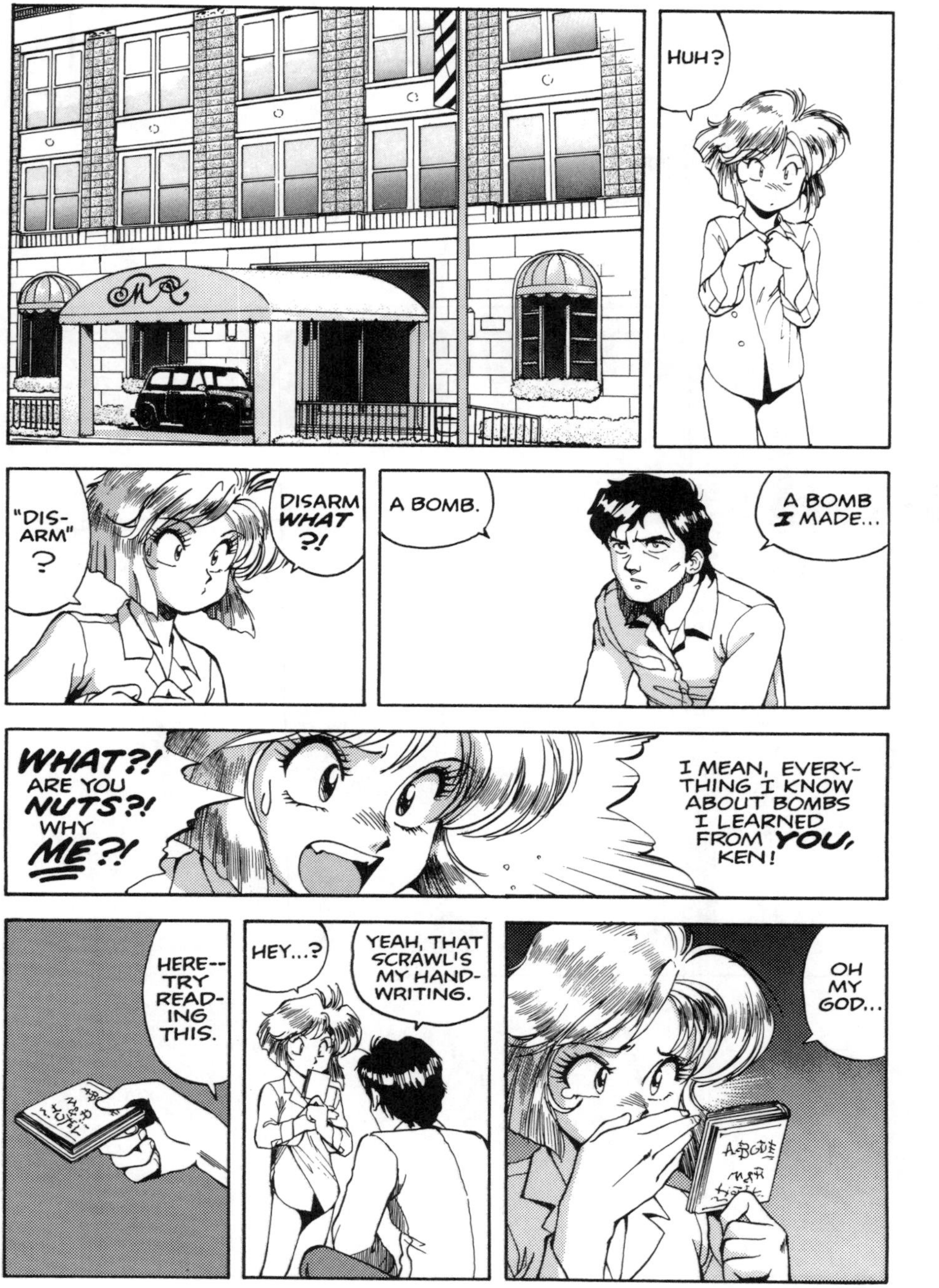
HUH?
"DIS-ARM"?
DISARM WHAT?!
A BOMB.
A BOMB I MADE...
WHAT?! ARE YOU NUTS?! WHY ME?!
I MEAN, EVERY-THING I KNOW ABOUT BOMBS I LEARNED FROM YOU, KEN!
HERE-- TRY READ-ING THIS.
HEY...?
YEAH, THAT SCRAWL'S MY HAND-WRITING.
OH MY GOD...

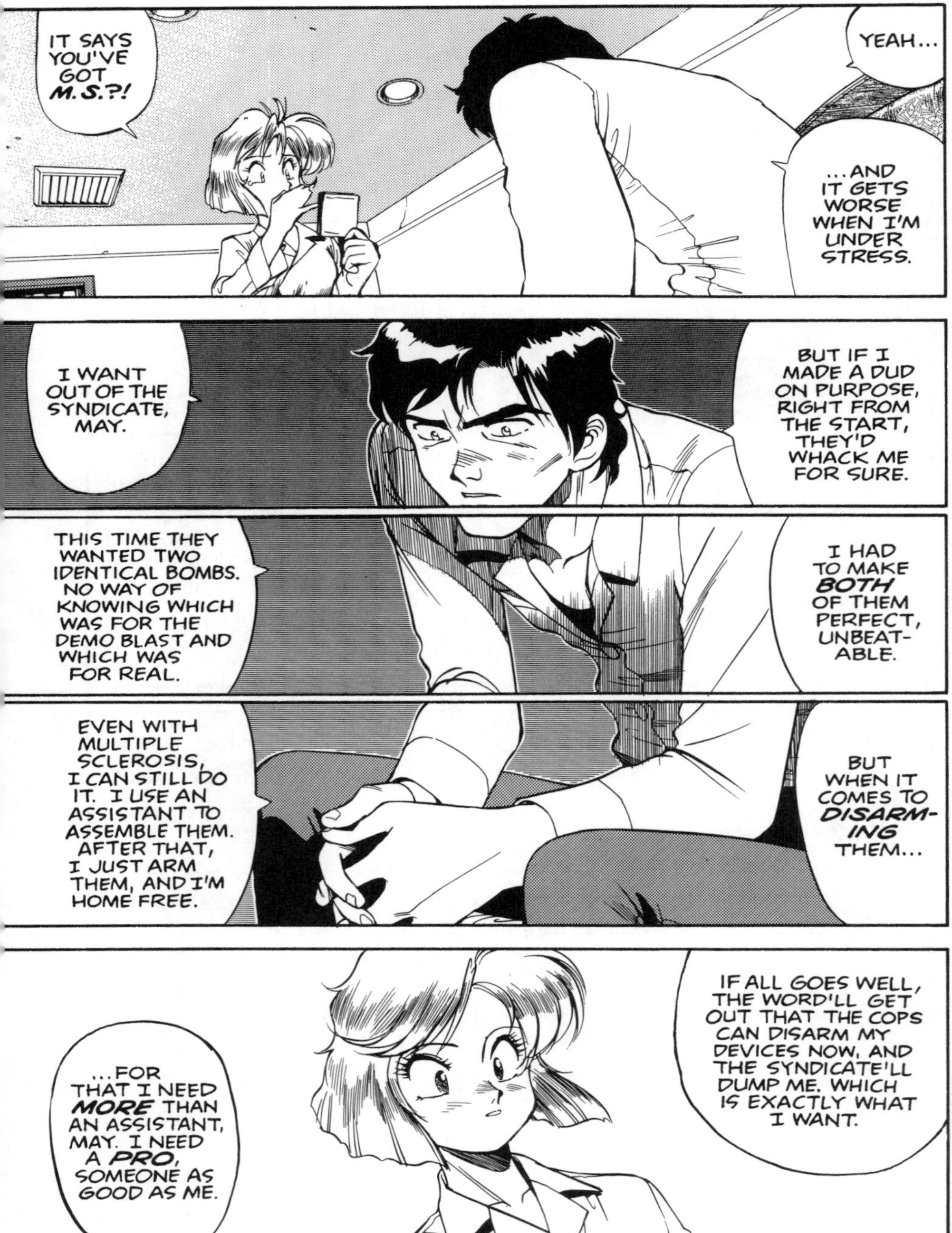
IT SAYS YOU'VE GOT **M.S.?!**
YEAH...
...AND IT GETS WORSE WHEN I'M UNDER STRESS.
I WANT OUT OF THE SYNDICATE, MAY.
BUT IF I MADE A DUD ON PURPOSE, RIGHT FROM THE START, THEY'D WHACK ME FOR SURE.
THIS TIME THEY WANTED TWO IDENTICAL BOMBS. NO WAY OF KNOWING WHICH WAS FOR THE DEMO BLAST AND WHICH WAS FOR REAL.
I HAD TO MAKE **BOTH** OF THEM PERFECT, UNBEAT-ABLE.
EVEN WITH MULTIPLE SCLEROSIS, I CAN STILL DO IT. I USE AN ASSISTANT TO ASSEMBLE THEM. AFTER THAT, I JUST ARM THEM, AND I'M HOME FREE.
BUT WHEN IT COMES TO ***DISARM-ING*** THEM...
...FOR THAT I NEED **MORE** THAN AN ASSISTANT, MAY. I NEED A ***PRO***, SOMEONE AS GOOD AS ME.
IF ALL GOES WELL, THE WORD'LL GET OUT THAT THE COPS CAN DISARM MY DEVICES NOW, AND THE SYNDICATE'LL DUMP ME. WHICH IS EXACTLY WHAT I WANT.

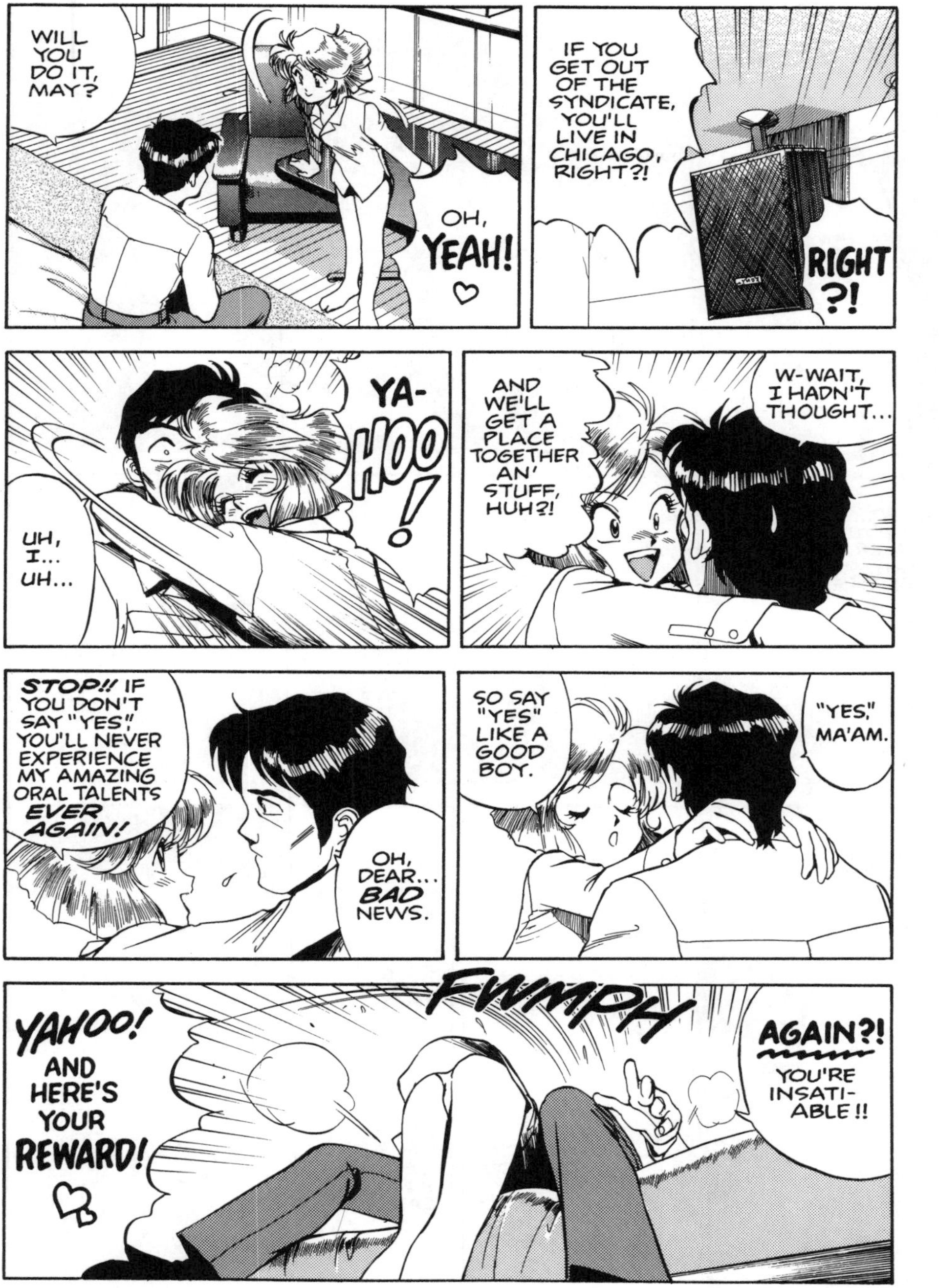
WILL YOU DO IT, MAY?
OH, YEAH!
IF YOU GET OUT OF THE SYNDICATE, YOU'LL LIVE IN CHICAGO, RIGHT?!
RIGHT ?!
YA-HOO!
UH, I... UH...
AND WE'LL GET A PLACE TOGETHER AN' STUFF, HUH?!
W-WAIT, I HADN'T THOUGHT...
STOP!! IF YOU DON'T SAY "YES," YOU'LL NEVER EXPERIENCE MY AMAZING ORAL TALENTS EVER AGAIN!
OH, DEAR... BAD NEWS.
SO SAY "YES" LIKE A GOOD BOY.
"YES," MA'AM.
YAHOO! AND HERE'S YOUR REWARD!
FWMPH
AGAIN?!
YOU'RE INSATI-ABLE!!

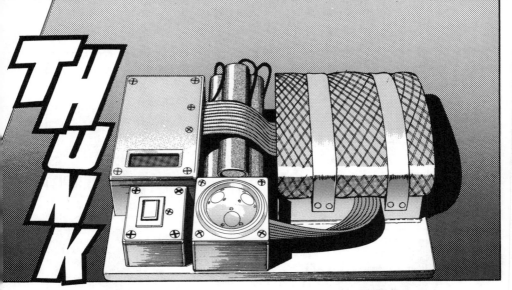

TH UNK

EEP... I... I'VE NEVER SEEN THIS TYPE BEFORE...

IT'S MY NEWEST MODEL.

DON'T WORRY-- THE EXPLOSIVES AREN'T REAL.

THE FIRST BARRIER IS THE COMPUTER SECURITY PROGRAM.

YOU CAN HACK INTO IT WITH THIS LAPTOP.

AFTER THAT, ALL YOU HAVE TO KNOW IS THE CONNECTOR SYSTEM. YOU CAN USE THIS DISK TO SPIKE THE SOFTWARE.

IF YOU DON'T DISABLE THE SECURITY CORRECTLY, THE WHOLE THING INSTANTLY GOES OFF IN YOUR FACE.

SO BE CARE-FUL!

THE REAL ONE'S INSTAL-LED IN A CAR...

...AND INSTEAD OF THE USUAL MERCURY SWITCH, IT USES A GYRO SENSOR.

SO IT KNOWS WHEN IT'S BEING MOVED. ONCE IT'S BEEN SET, IT'LL GO OFF IF YOU SHIFT THE CASE OR CHANGE THE CASE ORIENTATION MORE THAN THREE TIMES.

FIRST YOU'LL WANT TO USE A SET OF CORNER JACKS TO FREEZE THE CAR POSITION...

HEY, WAIT! THE *CAR*!

HOW ARE WE GONNA EVEN KNOW WHERE IT IS?

I DON'T KNOW THE EXACT MODEL, BUT I *DO* KNOW WHERE THEY'RE PARKING IT...

...AND THAT IT'LL HAVE MICHIGAN PLATES. THAT SHOULD NARROW IT DOWN ENOUGH.

OKAY, MAY-- WE'VE ONLY GOT TWENTY-SIX HOURS.

SO WE'RE NOT GOING TO GET MUCH SLEEP TONIGHT...

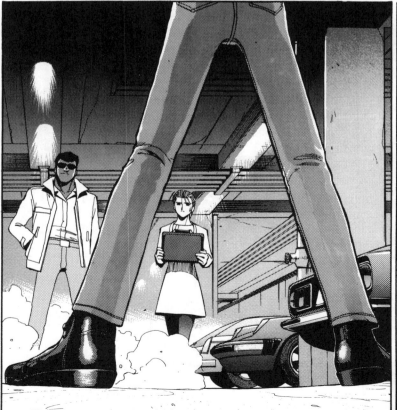

YOU BROUGHT HER OVER NICE AND SMOOTH, RIGHT?

DIDN'T EVEN SPILL MY BEER, MAN.

ALL RIGHT. HERE'S YOUR FORTY GRAND.

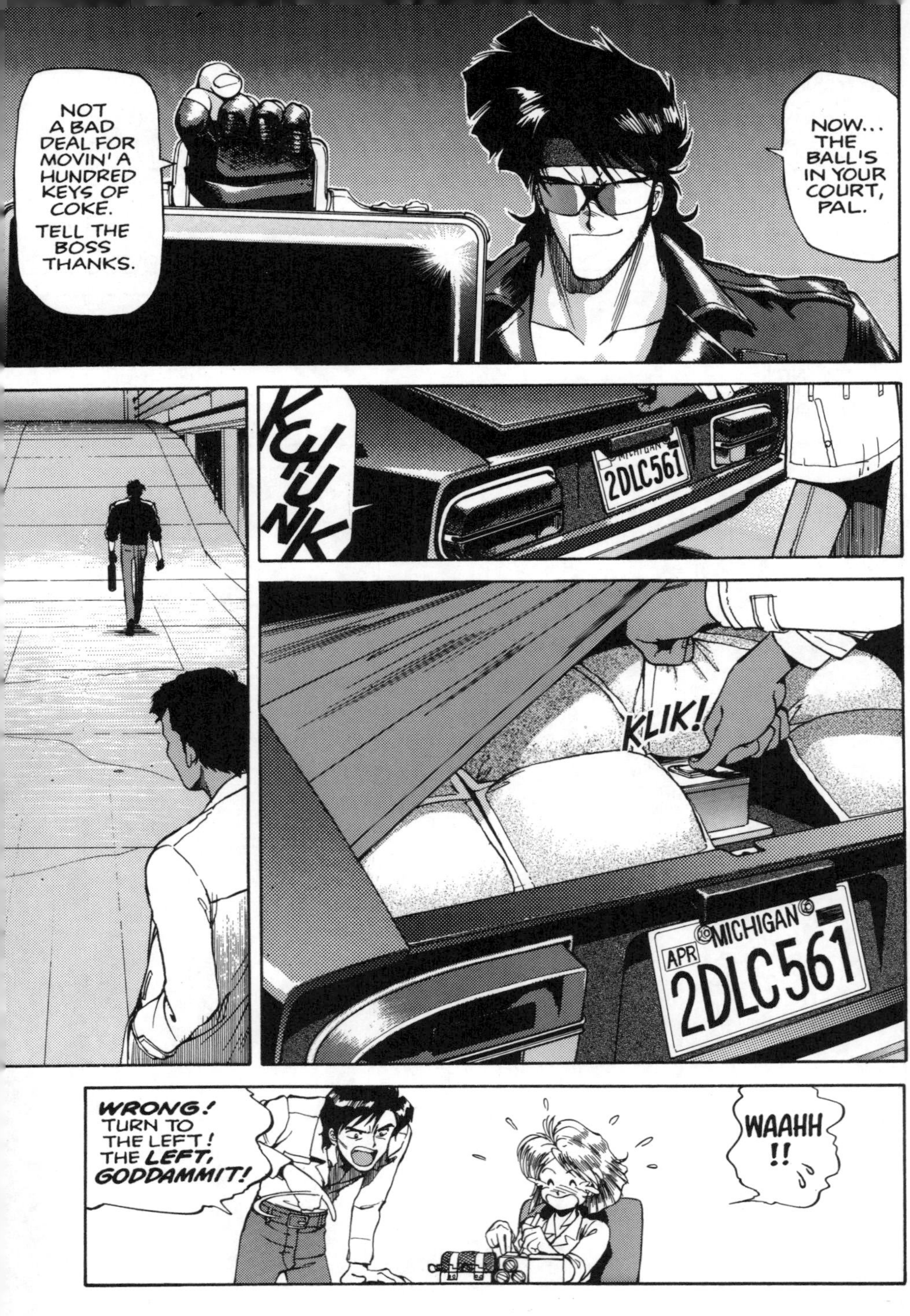
NOT A BAD DEAL FOR MOVIN' A HUNDRED KEYS OF COKE. TELL THE BOSS THANKS.
NOW... THE BALL'S IN YOUR COURT, PAL.
KCHUNK
MICHIGAN
2DLC561
KLIK!
APR MICHIGAN
2DLC561
WRONG! TURN TO THE LEFT! THE LEFT, GODDAMMIT!
WAAHH !!

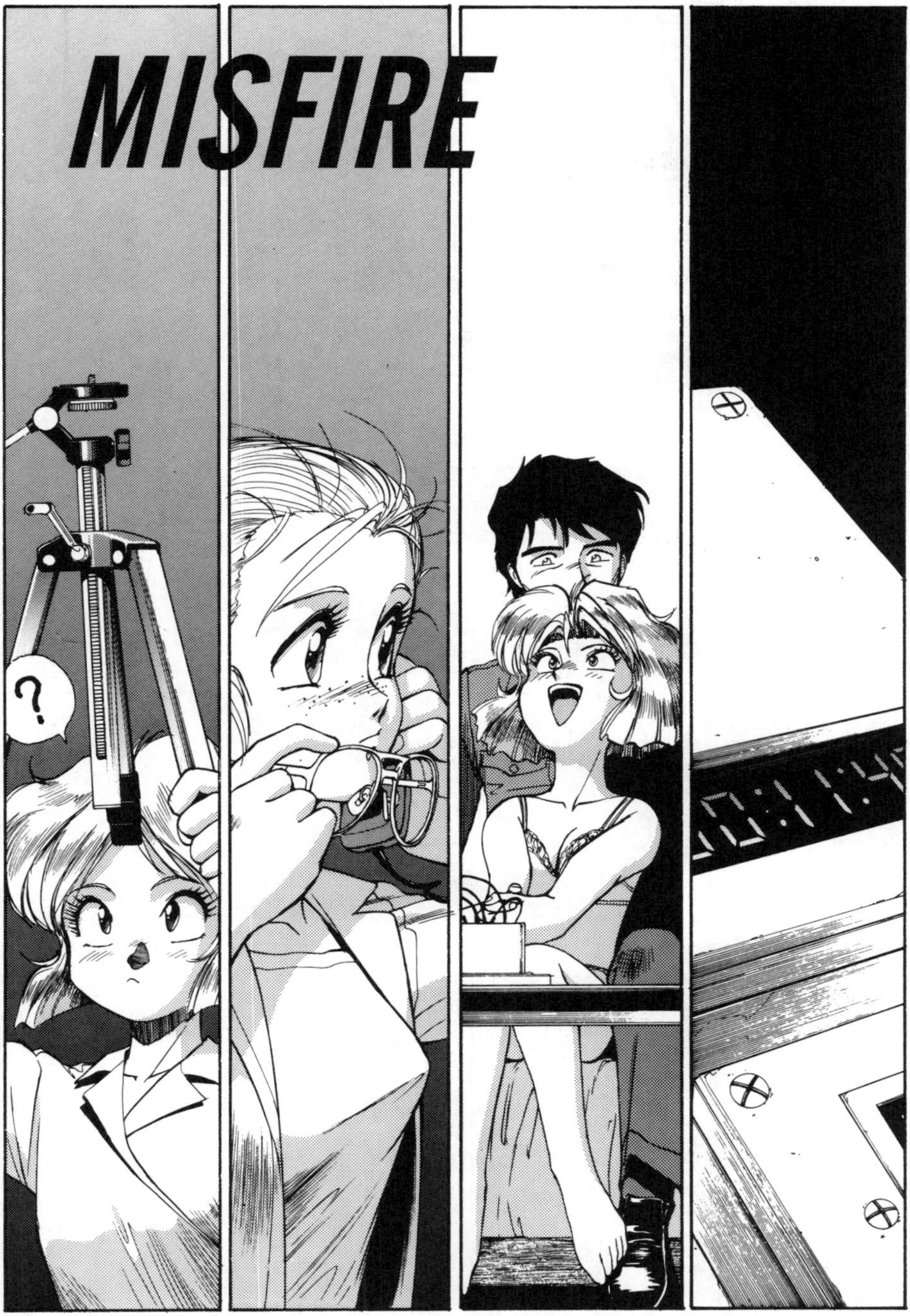
MISFIRE
?

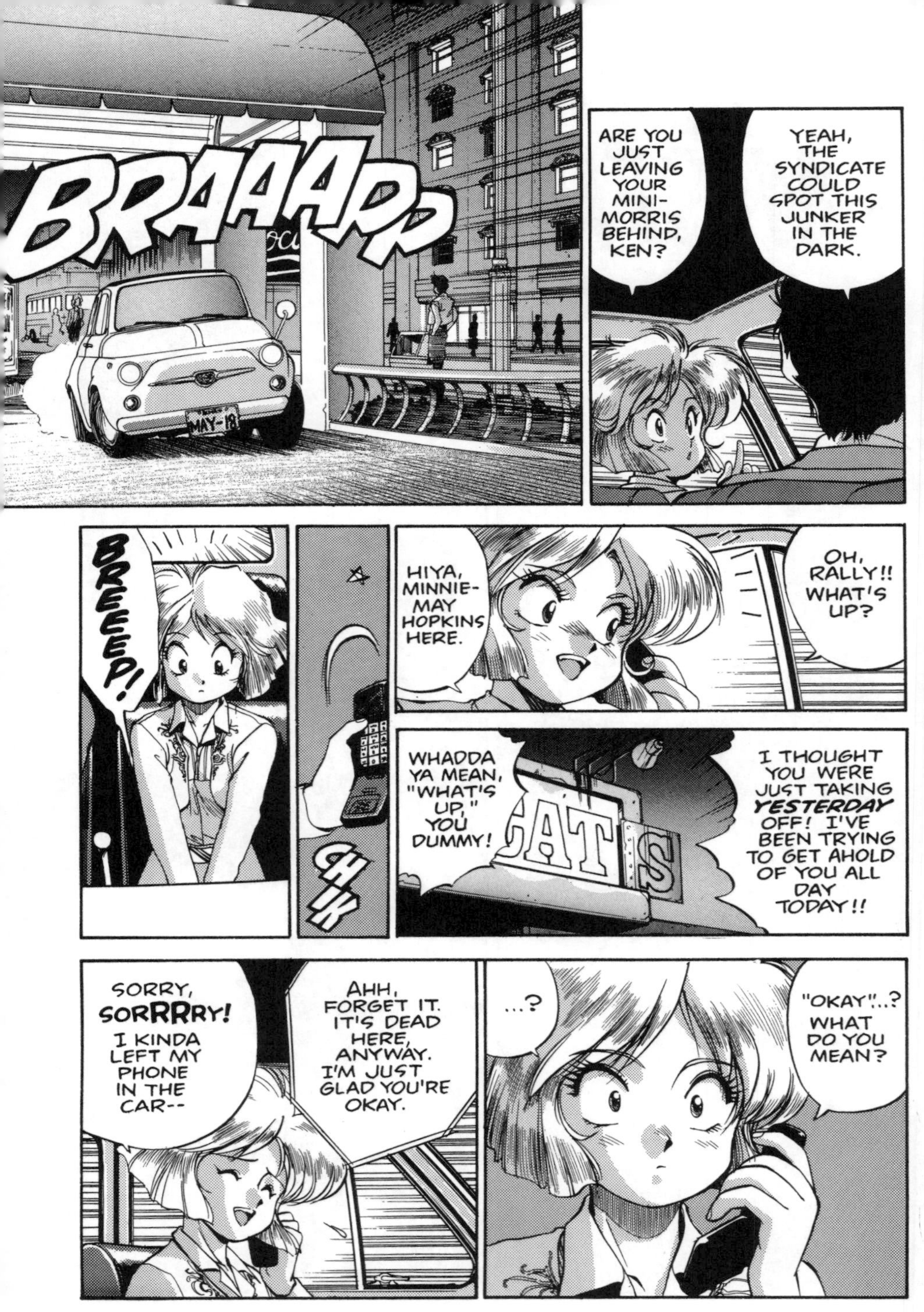
BRAAAARP
ARE YOU JUST LEAVING YOUR MINI-MORRIS BEHIND, KEN?
YEAH, THE SYNDICATE COULD SPOT THIS JUNKER IN THE DARK.
BREEEP!
CHIK
HIYA, MINNIE-MAY HOPKINS HERE.
OH, RALLY!! WHAT'S UP?
WHADDA YA MEAN, "WHAT'S UP," YOU DUMMY!
I THOUGHT YOU WERE JUST TAKING ***YESTERDAY*** OFF! I'VE BEEN TRYING TO GET AHOLD OF YOU ALL DAY TODAY!!
SORRY, **SORRRRY!** I KINDA LEFT MY PHONE IN THE CAR--
AHH, FORGET IT. IT'S DEAD HERE, ANYWAY. I'M JUST GLAD YOU'RE OKAY.
...?
"OKAY"..? WHAT DO YOU MEAN?

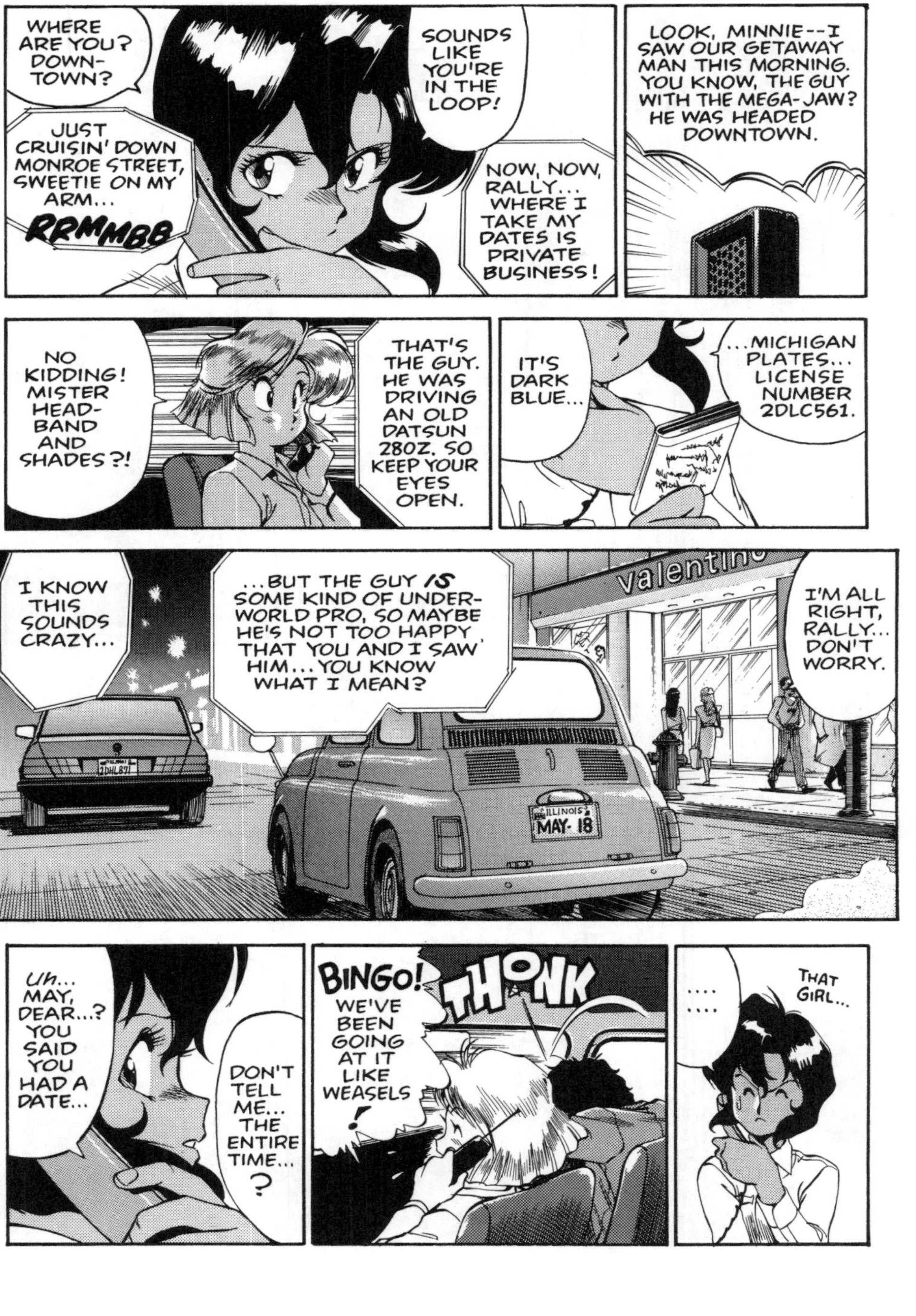
WHERE ARE YOU? DOWN-TOWN?
JUST CRUISIN' DOWN MONROE STREET, SWEETIE ON MY ARM...
RRMMBB
SOUNDS LIKE YOU'RE IN THE LOOP!
NOW, NOW, RALLY... WHERE I TAKE MY DATES IS PRIVATE BUSINESS!
LOOK, MINNIE--I SAW OUR GETAWAY MAN THIS MORNING. YOU KNOW, THE GUY WITH THE MEGA-JAW? HE WAS HEADED DOWNTOWN.
NO KIDDING! MISTER HEAD-BAND AND SHADES?!
THAT'S THE GUY. HE WAS DRIVING AN OLD DATSUN 280Z. SO KEEP YOUR EYES OPEN.
IT'S DARK BLUE...
...MICHIGAN PLATES... LICENSE NUMBER 2DLC561.
I KNOW THIS SOUNDS CRAZY...
...BUT THE GUY IS SOME KIND OF UNDER-WORLD PRO, SO MAYBE HE'S NOT TOO HAPPY THAT YOU AND I SAW HIM... YOU KNOW WHAT I MEAN?
valentino
ILLINOIS MAY-18
I'M ALL RIGHT, RALLY... DON'T WORRY.
Uh... MAY, DEAR...? YOU SAID YOU HAD A DATE...
DON'T TELL ME... THE ENTIRE TIME...?
BINGO!
THONK
WE'VE BEEN GOING AT IT LIKE WEASELS!
....
THAT GIRL...

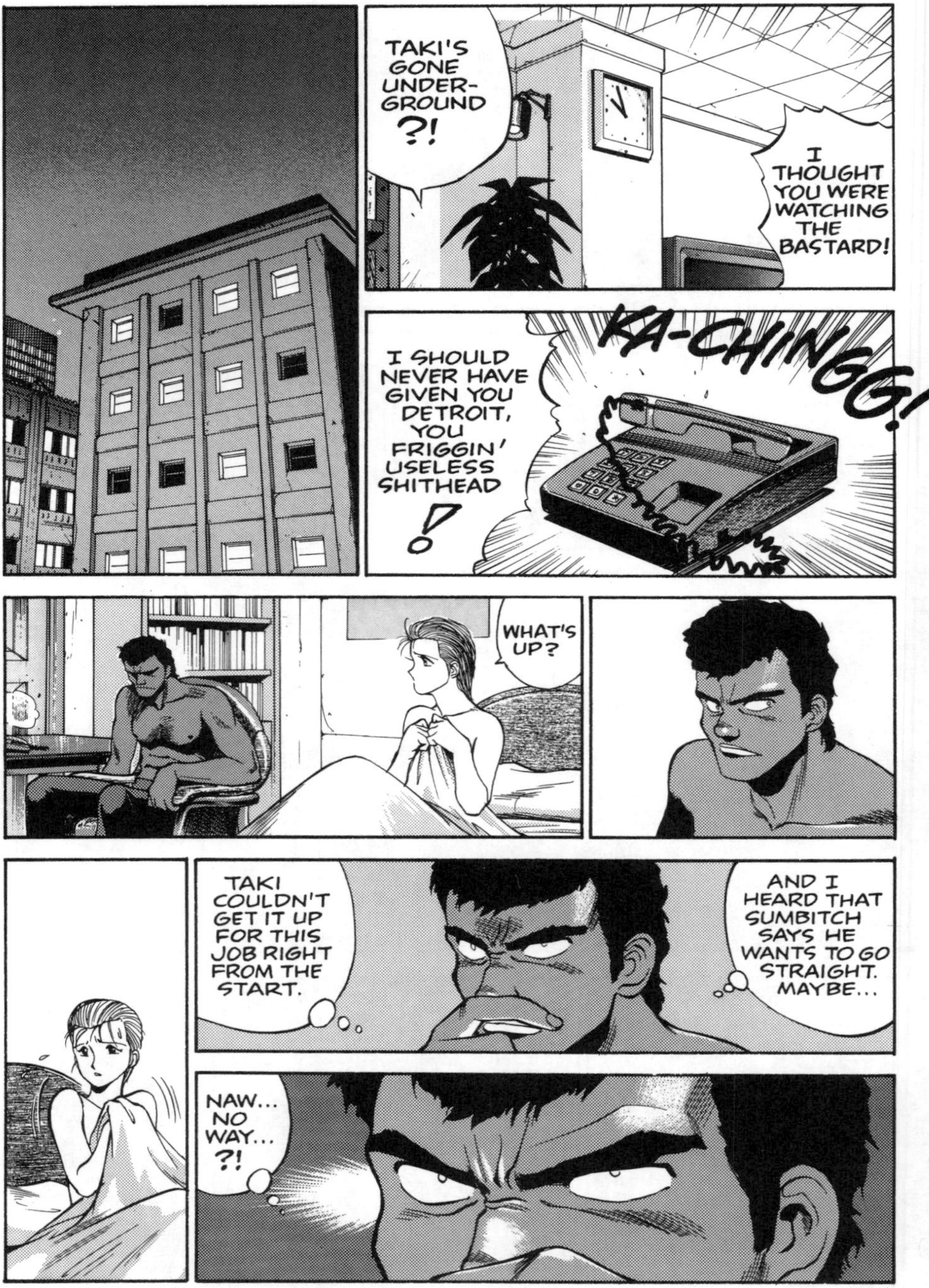
TAKI'S GONE UNDER-GROUND ?!
I THOUGHT YOU WERE WATCHING THE BASTARD!
I SHOULD NEVER HAVE GIVEN YOU DETROIT, YOU FRIGGIN' USELESS SHITHEAD !
KA-CHINGG!
WHAT'S UP?
TAKI COULDN'T GET IT UP FOR THIS JOB RIGHT FROM THE START.
AND I HEARD THAT SUMBITCH SAYS HE WANTS TO GO STRAIGHT. MAYBE...
NAW... NO WAY... ?!

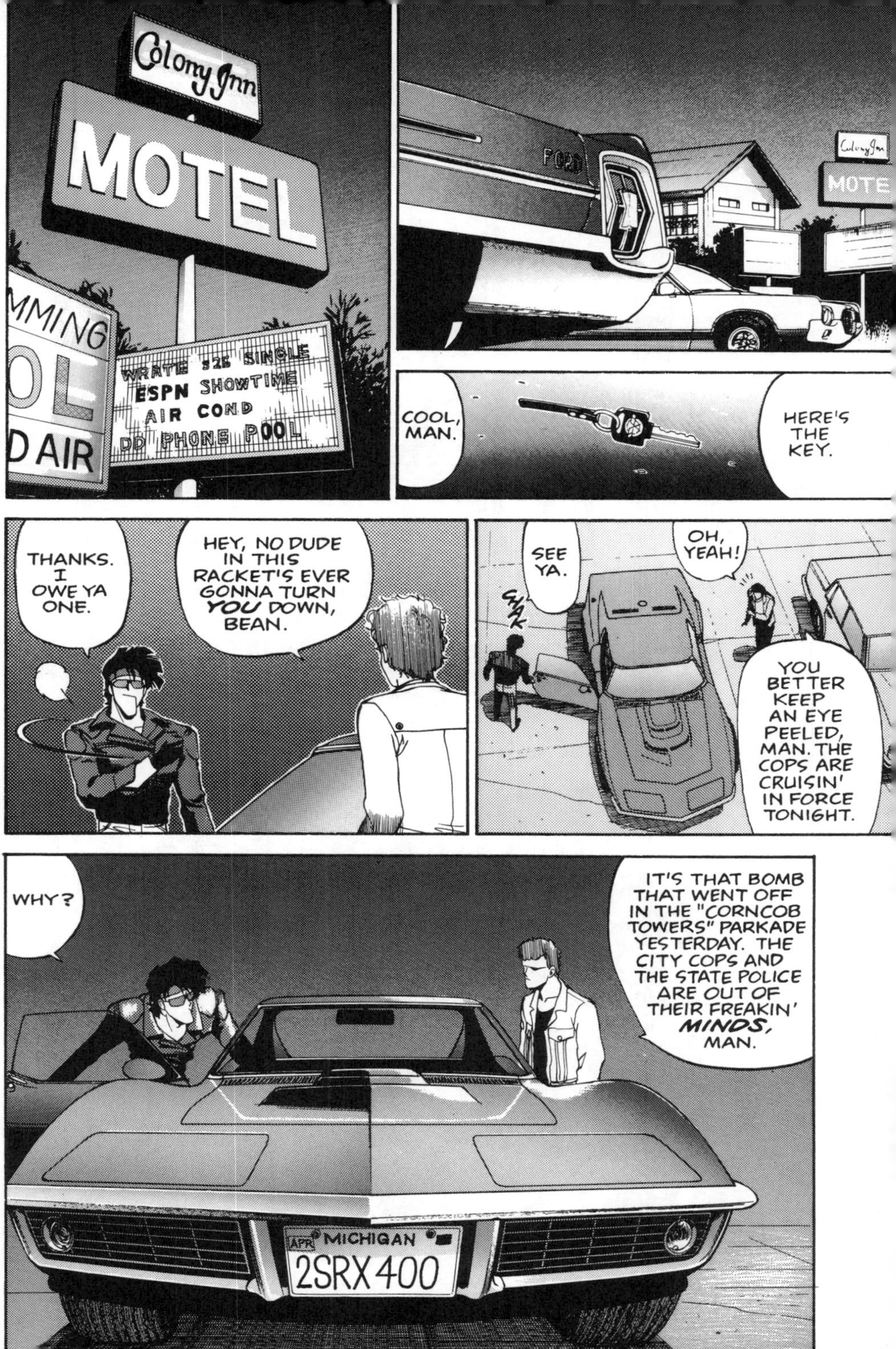

Colony Inn
MOTEL
ESPN SHOWTIME
AIR COND
FORD
Colony Inn
MOTE
HERE'S THE KEY.
COOL, MAN.
THANKS. I OWE YA ONE.
HEY, NO DUDE IN THIS RACKET'S EVER GONNA TURN *YOU* DOWN, BEAN.
SEE YA.
OH, YEAH!
YOU BETTER KEEP AN EYE PEELED, MAN. THE COPS ARE CRUISIN' IN FORCE TONIGHT.
WHY?
IT'S THAT BOMB THAT WENT OFF IN THE "CORNCOB TOWERS" PARKADE YESTERDAY. THE CITY COPS AND THE STATE POLICE ARE OUT OF THEIR FREAKIN' ***MINDS,*** MAN.
APR MICHIGAN
2SRX400

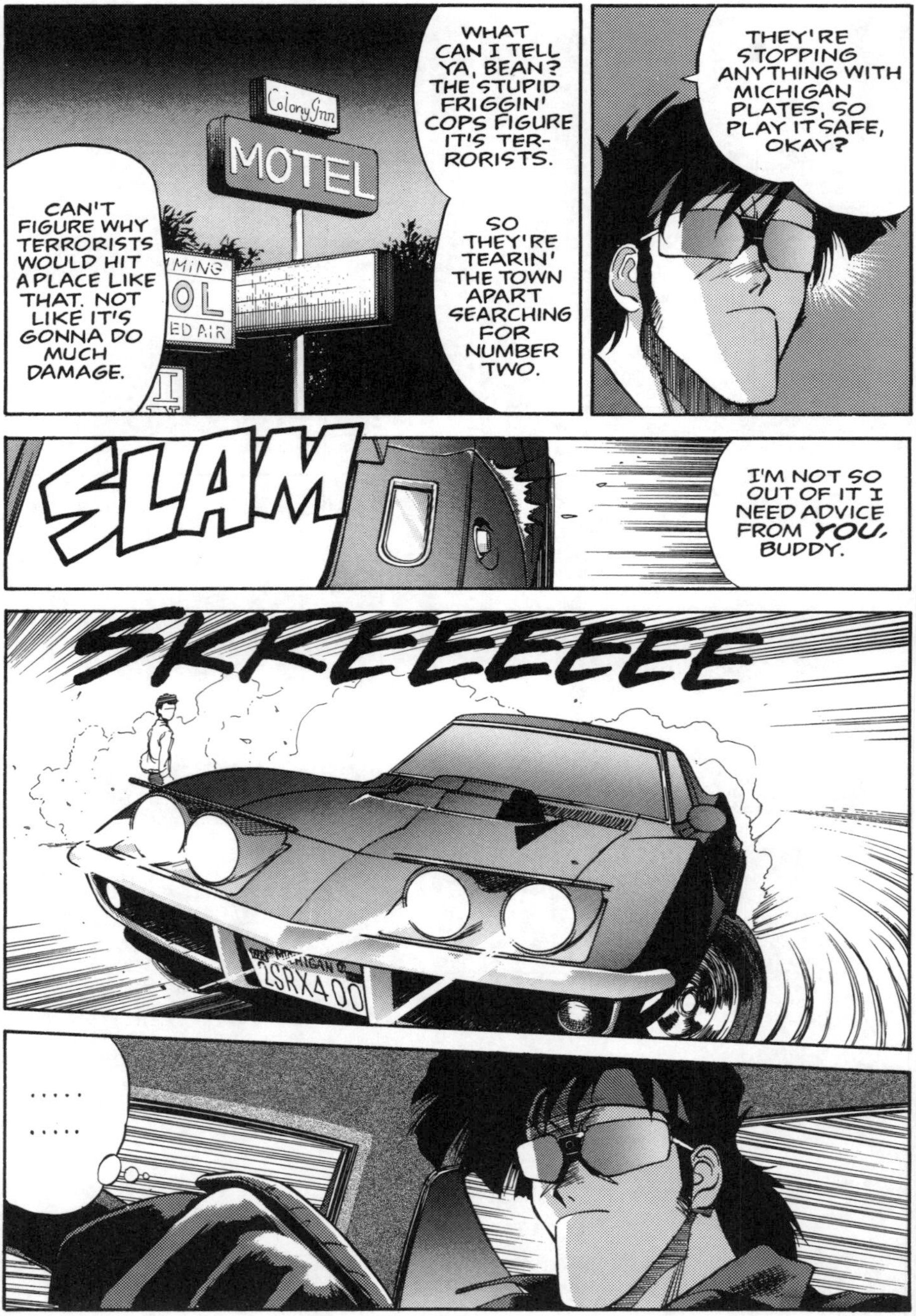
Colony Inn
MOTEL
CAN'T FIGURE WHY TERRORISTS WOULD HIT A PLACE LIKE THAT. NOT LIKE IT'S GONNA DO MUCH DAMAGE.
WHAT CAN I TELL YA, BEAN? THE STUPID FRIGGIN' COPS FIGURE IT'S TERRORISTS.
SO THEY'RE TEARIN' THE TOWN APART SEARCHING FOR NUMBER TWO.
THEY'RE STOPPING ANYTHING WITH MICHIGAN PLATES, SO PLAY IT SAFE, OKAY?
SLAM
I'M NOT SO OUT OF IT I NEED ADVICE FROM YOU, BUDDY.
SKREEEEEEE
2SRX400
.....
.....

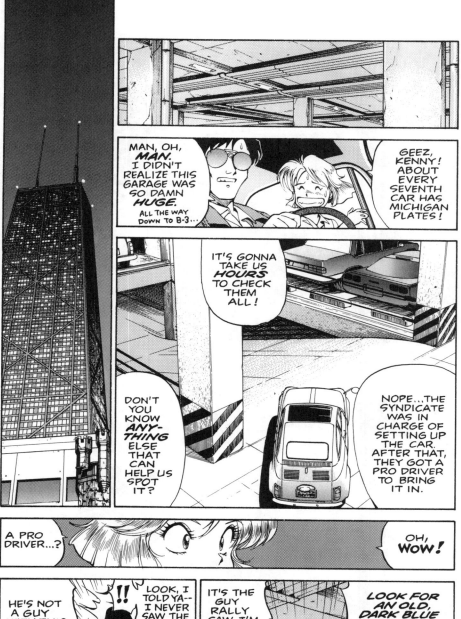

MAN, OH, *MAN.* I DIDN'T REALIZE THIS GARAGE WAS SO DAMN *HUGE.* ALL THE WAY DOWN TO B-3...

GEEZ, KENNY! ABOUT EVERY SEVENTH CAR HAS MICHIGAN PLATES!

IT'S GONNA TAKE US *HOURS* TO CHECK THEM ALL!

DON'T YOU KNOW *ANYTHING* ELSE THAT CAN HELP US SPOT IT?

NOPE...THE SYNDICATE WAS IN CHARGE OF SETTING UP THE CAR. AFTER THAT, THEY GOT A PRO DRIVER TO BRING IT IN.

A PRO DRIVER...?

OH, *WOW!*

HE'S NOT A GUY WITH THIS *BIG OL' JAW,* IS HE?!

LOOK, I TOLD YA-- I NEVER SAW THE DRIVER!

IT'S THE GUY RALLY SAW, I'M *POSITIVE!!*

LOOK FOR AN OLD, DARK BLUE DATSUN 280Z, LICENSE PLATE 2DLC561!

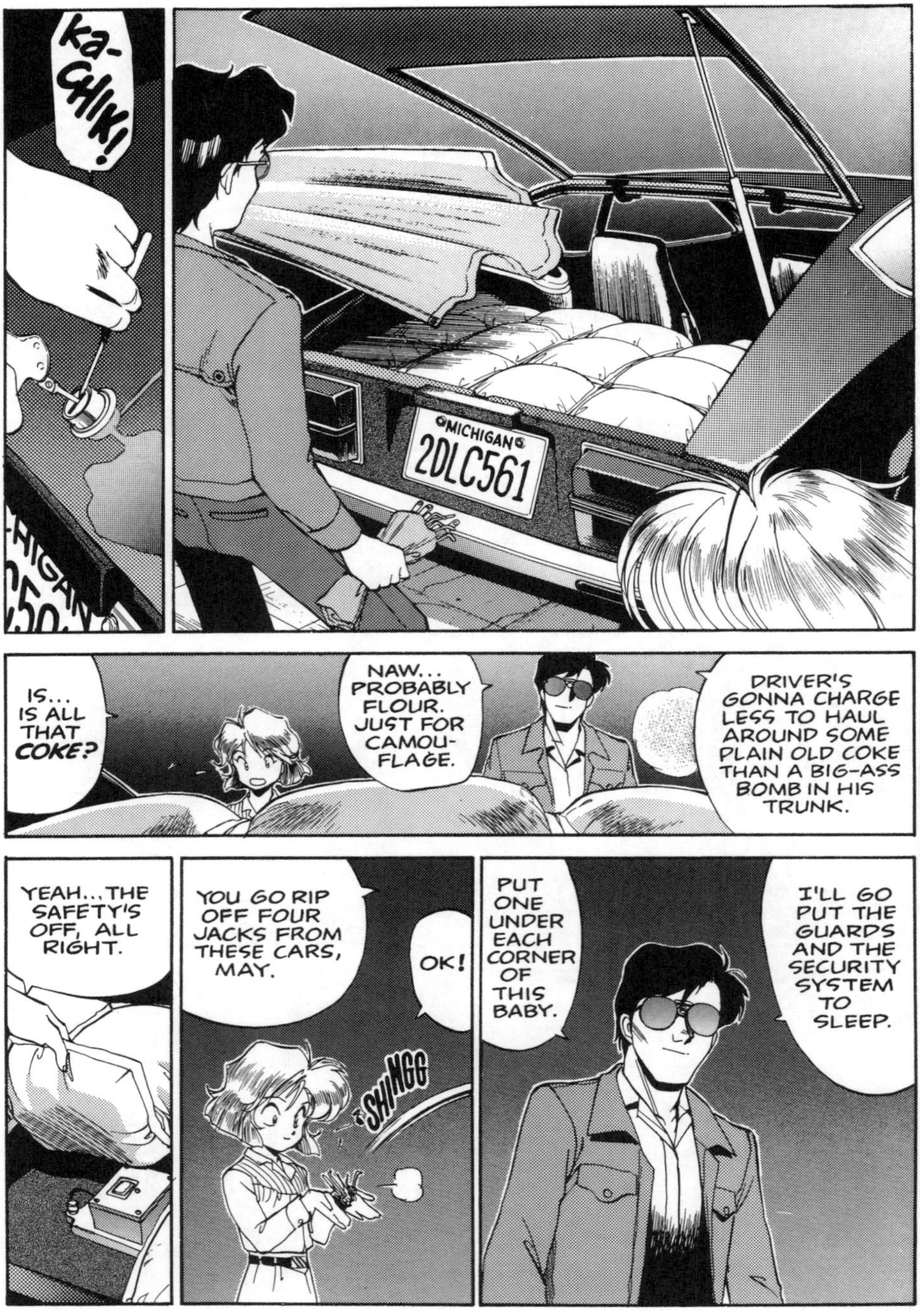
ka-CHIK!
MICHIGAN
2DLC561
IS... IS ALL THAT *COKE?*
NAW... PROBABLY FLOUR. JUST FOR CAMOU-FLAGE.
DRIVER'S GONNA CHARGE LESS TO HAUL AROUND SOME PLAIN OLD COKE THAN A BIG-ASS BOMB IN HIS TRUNK.
YEAH... THE SAFETY'S OFF, ALL RIGHT.
YOU GO RIP OFF FOUR JACKS FROM THESE CARS, MAY.
OK!
SHINGG
PUT ONE UNDER EACH CORNER OF THIS BABY.
I'LL GO PUT THE GUARDS AND THE SECURITY SYSTEM TO SLEEP.

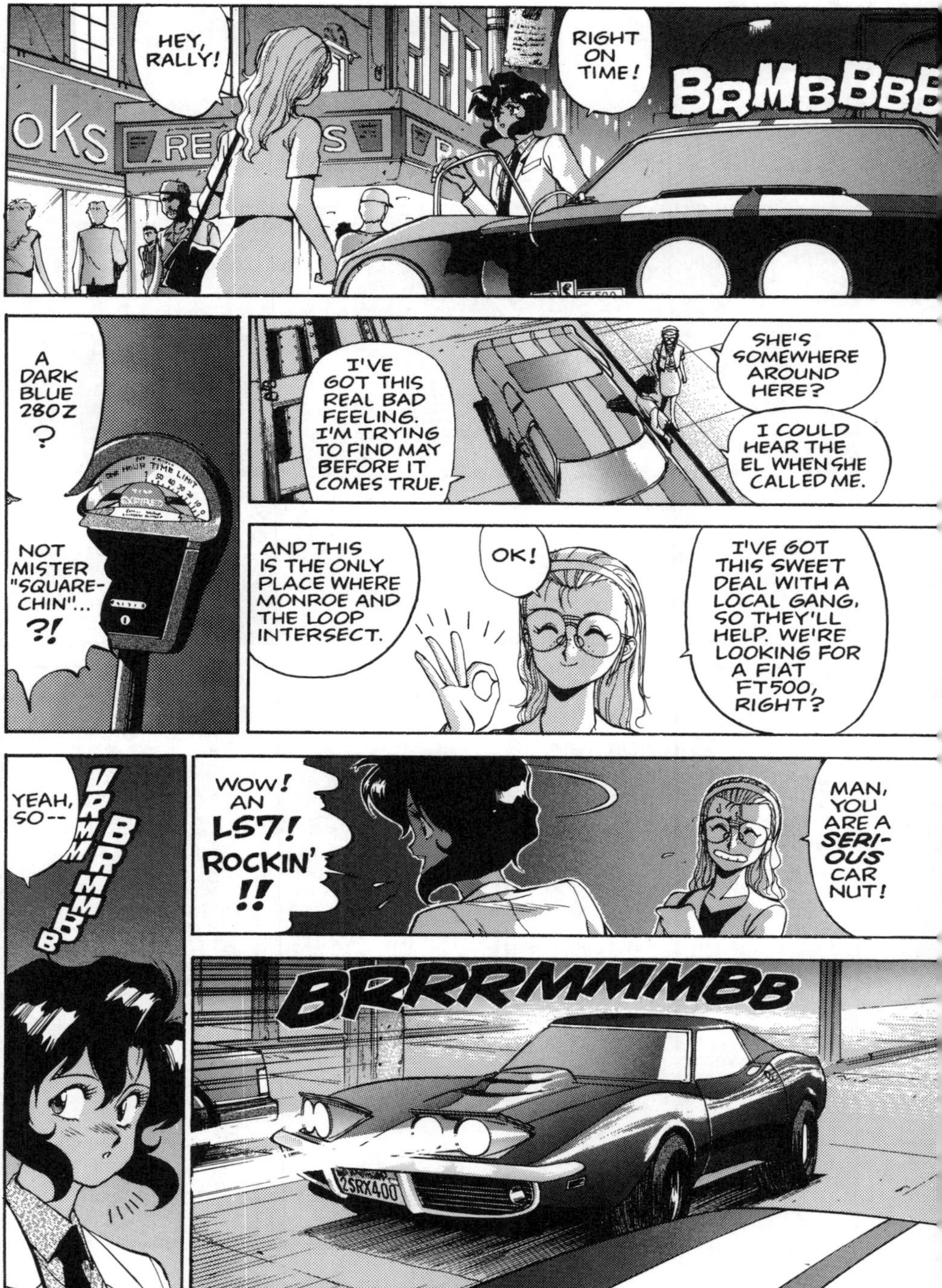
HEY, RALLY!
RIGHT ON TIME!
BRMBBBB
A DARK BLUE 280Z?
NOT MISTER "SQUARE-CHIN"... ?!
I'VE GOT THIS REAL BAD FEELING. I'M TRYING TO FIND MAY BEFORE IT COMES TRUE.
SHE'S SOMEWHERE AROUND HERE?
I COULD HEAR THE EL WHEN SHE CALLED ME.
AND THIS IS THE ONLY PLACE WHERE MONROE AND THE LOOP INTERSECT.
OK!
I'VE GOT THIS SWEET DEAL WITH A LOCAL GANG, SO THEY'LL HELP. WE'RE LOOKING FOR A FIAT FT500, RIGHT?
YEAH, SO--
VRMMM
BRRMMBB
WOW! AN LS7! ROCKIN'!!
MAN, YOU ARE A SERIOUS CAR NUT!
BRRRMMMMBB
2SRX400

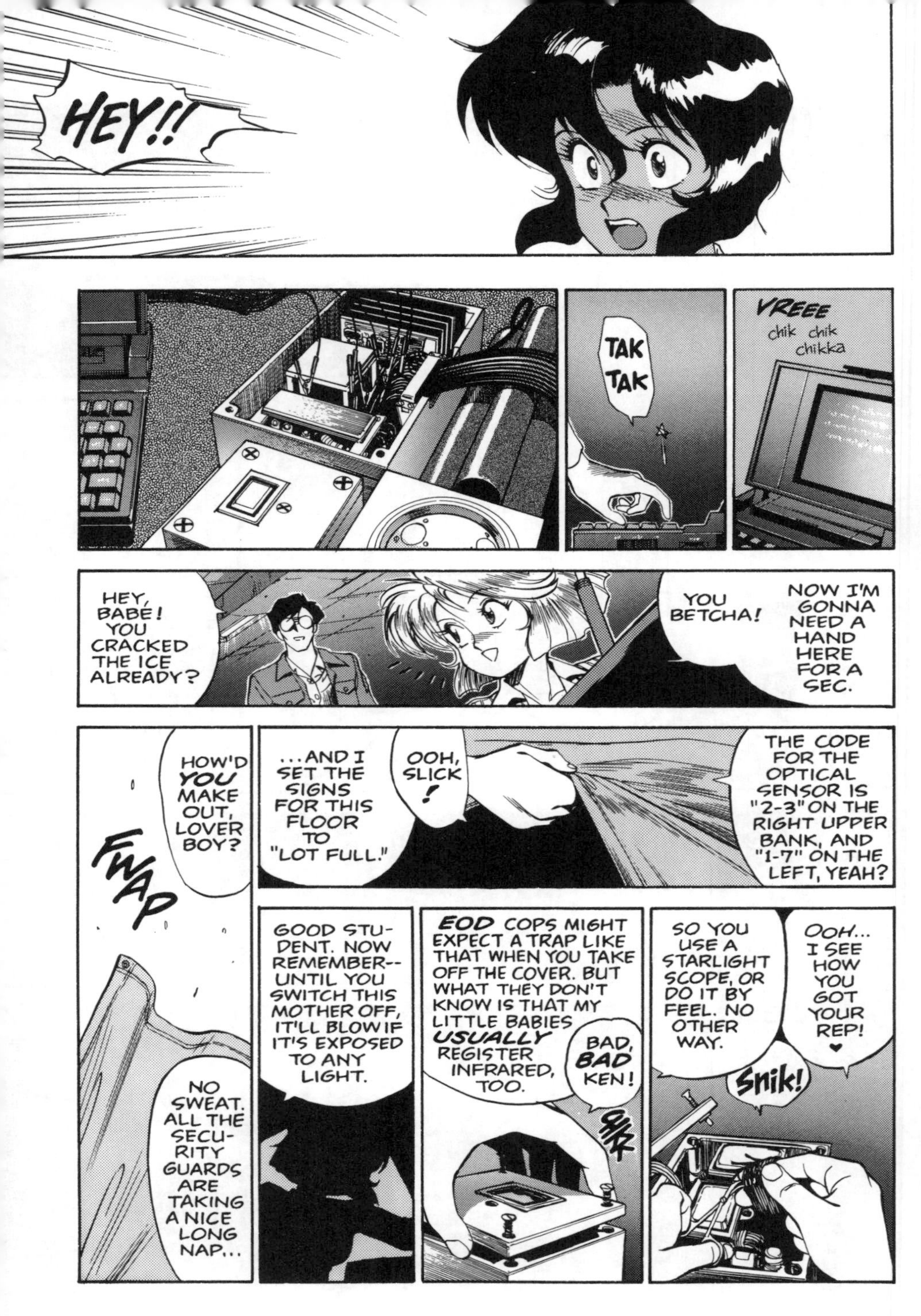
HEY!!
TAK TAK
VREEE
chik chik chikka
HEY, BABÉ! YOU CRACKED THE ICE ALREADY?
YOU BETCHA!
NOW I'M GONNA NEED A HAND HERE FOR A SEC.
HOW'D YOU MAKE OUT, LOVER BOY?
FWAP
NO SWEAT. ALL THE SECU-RITY GUARDS ARE TAKING A NICE LONG NAP...
...AND I SET THE SIGNS FOR THIS FLOOR TO "LOT FULL."
OOH, SLICK!
THE CODE FOR THE OPTICAL SENSOR IS "2-3" ON THE RIGHT UPPER BANK, AND "1-7" ON THE LEFT, YEAH?
GOOD STU-DENT. NOW REMEMBER-- UNTIL YOU SWITCH THIS MOTHER OFF, IT'LL BLOW IF IT'S EXPOSED TO ANY LIGHT.
EOD COPS MIGHT EXPECT A TRAP LIKE THAT WHEN YOU TAKE OFF THE COVER. BUT WHAT THEY DON'T KNOW IS THAT MY LITTLE BABIES USUALLY REGISTER INFRARED, TOO.
BAD, BAD KEN!
SO YOU USE A STARLIGHT SCOPE, OR DO IT BY FEEL. NO OTHER WAY.
OOH... I SEE HOW YOU GOT YOUR REP! ❤
Snik!

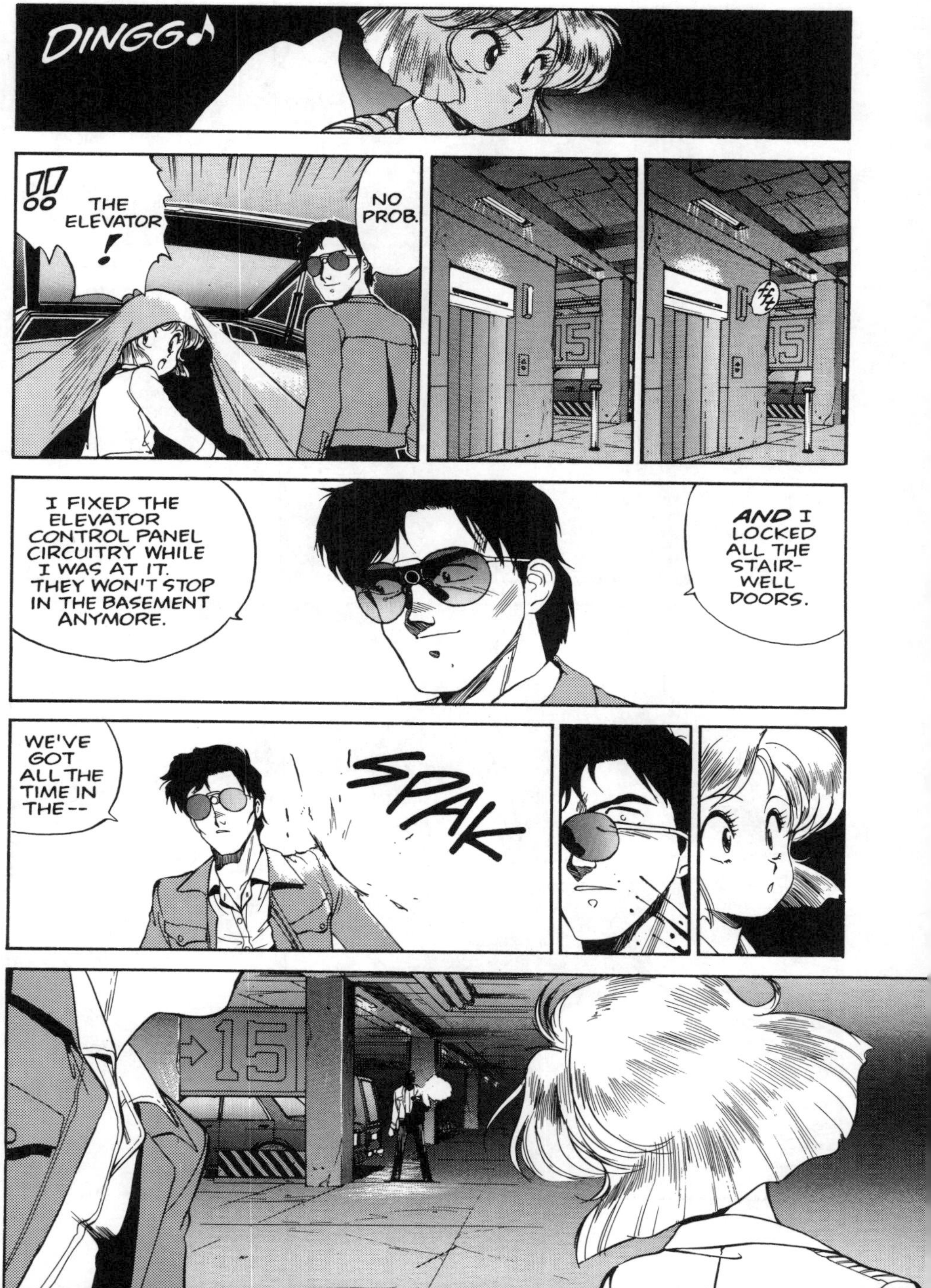
DINGG♪
!!
THE ELEVATOR!
NO PROB.
I FIXED THE ELEVATOR CONTROL PANEL CIRCUITRY WHILE I WAS AT IT. THEY WON'T STOP IN THE BASEMENT ANYMORE.
AND I LOCKED ALL THE STAIR-WELL DOORS.
WE'VE GOT ALL THE TIME IN THE--
SPAK
15

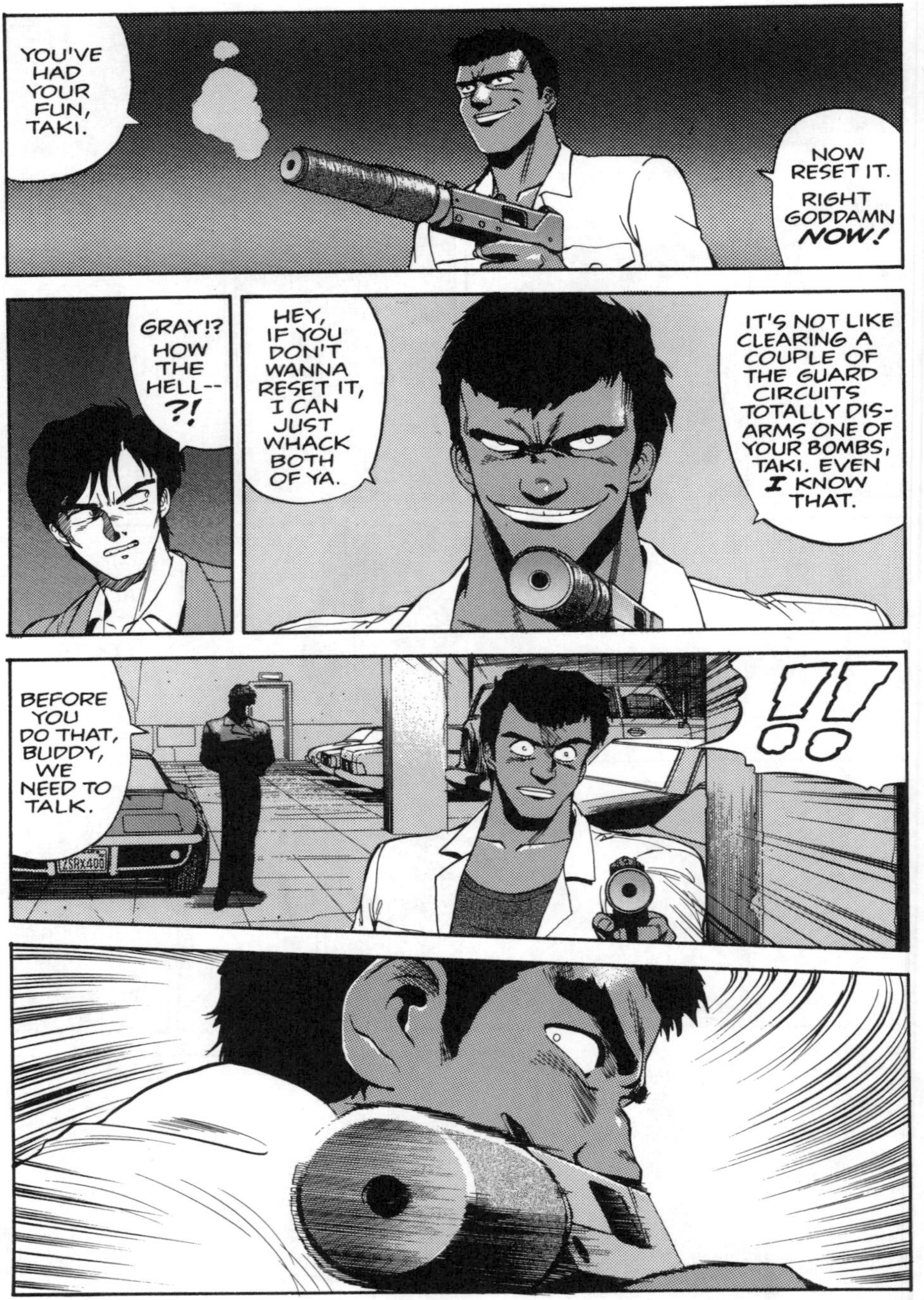
YOU'VE HAD YOUR FUN, TAKI.
NOW RESET IT.
RIGHT GODDAMN ***NOW!***
GRAY!? HOW THE HELL-- ?!
HEY, IF YOU DON'T WANNA RESET IT, I CAN JUST WHACK BOTH OF YA.
IT'S NOT LIKE CLEARING A COUPLE OF THE GUARD CIRCUITS TOTALLY DISARMS ONE OF YOUR BOMBS, TAKI. EVEN ***I*** KNOW THAT.
BEFORE YOU DO THAT, BUDDY, WE NEED TO TALK.
!!

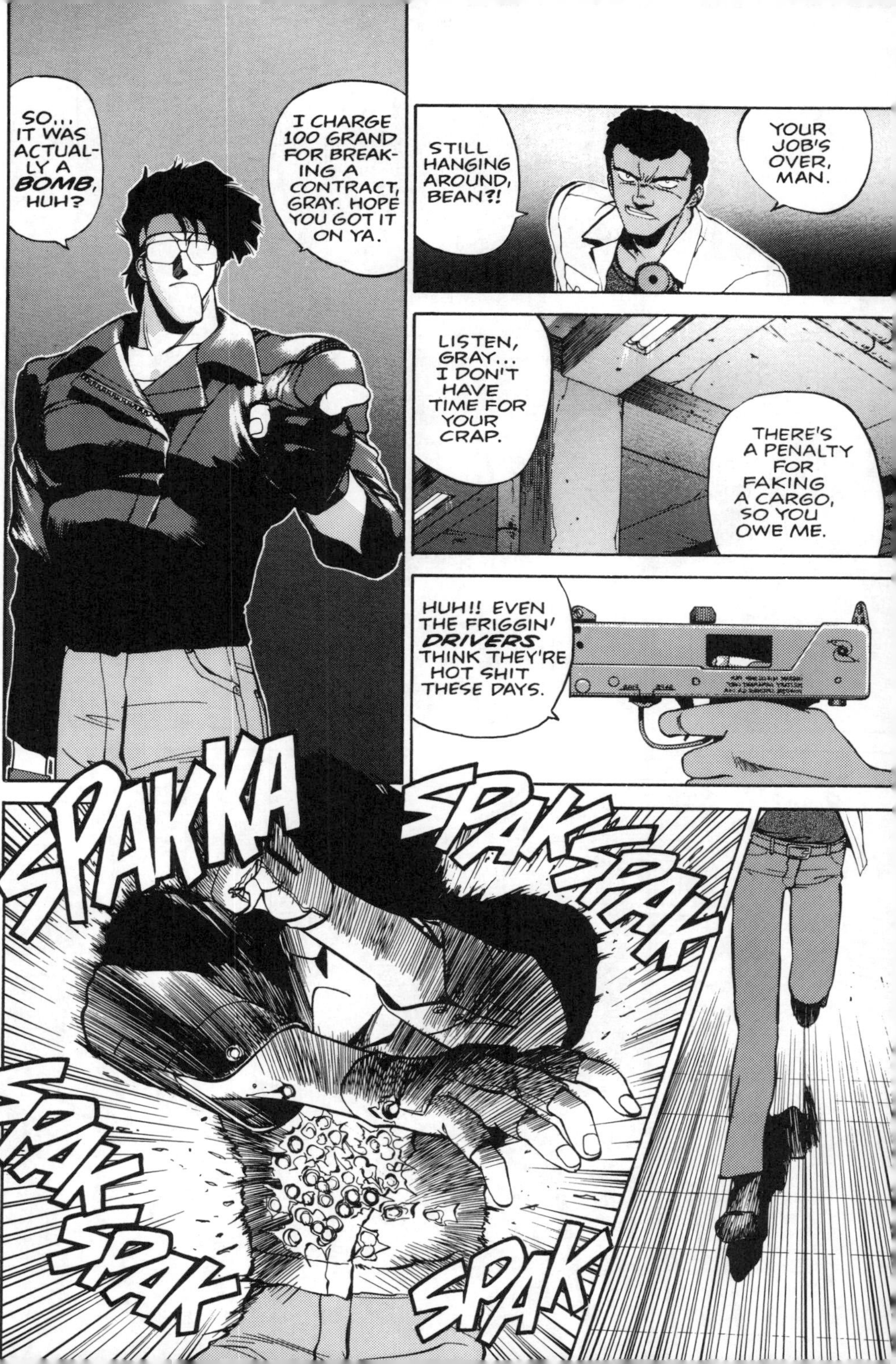
SO... IT WAS ACTUAL-LY A BOMB, HUH?
I CHARGE 100 GRAND FOR BREAK-ING A CONTRACT, GRAY. HOPE YOU GOT IT ON YA.
STILL HANGING AROUND, BEAN?!
YOUR JOB'S OVER, MAN.
LISTEN, GRAY... I DON'T HAVE TIME FOR YOUR CRAP.
THERE'S A PENALTY FOR FAKING A CARGO, SO YOU OWE ME.
HUH!! EVEN THE FRIGGIN' DRIVERS THINK THEY'RE HOT SHIT THESE DAYS.
SPAKKA
SPAKSPAKSPAK
SPAK SPAK SPAK
SPAK

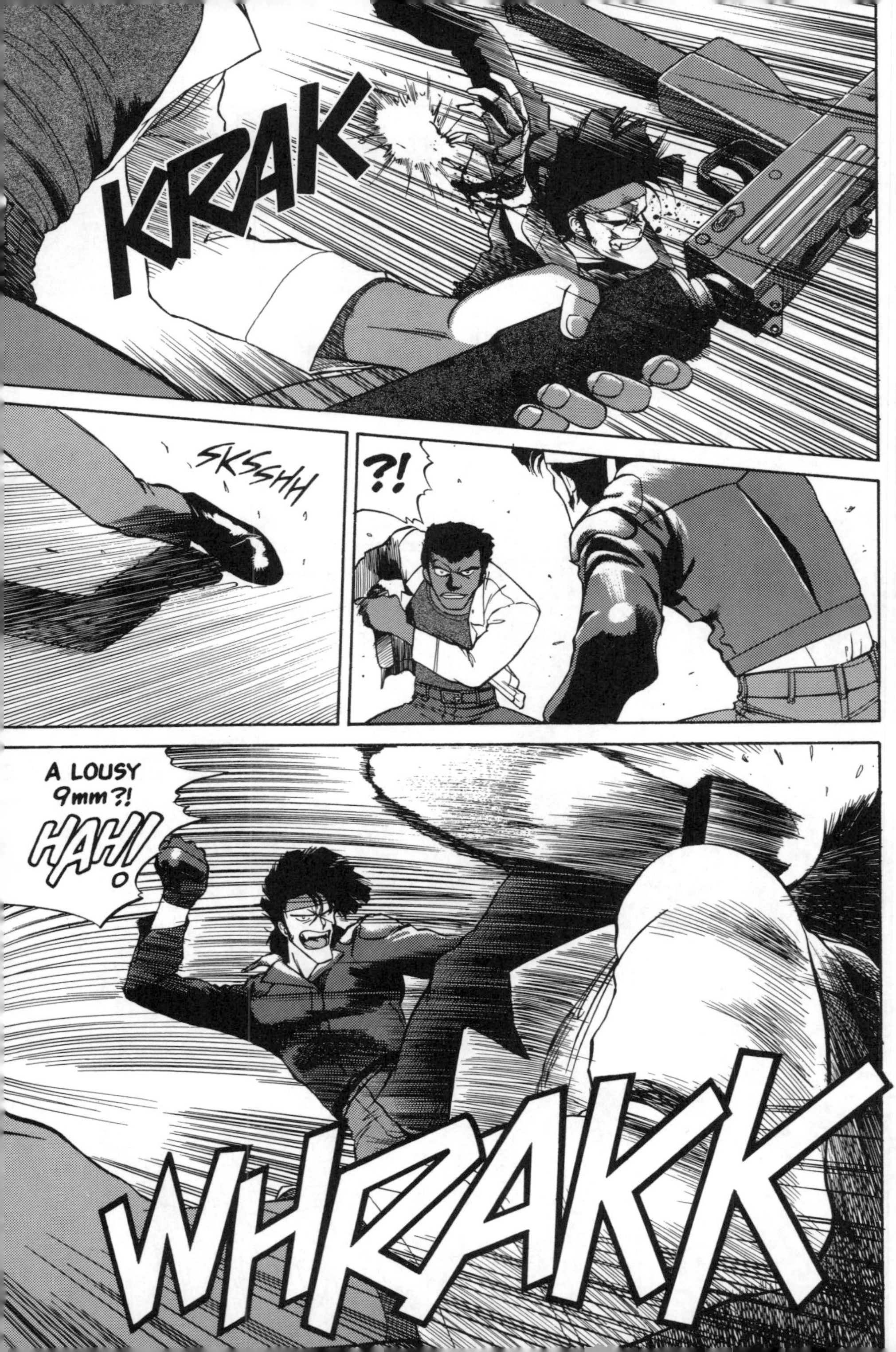
KRAK
SKSSHH
?!
A LOUSY 9mm?!
HAH!
WHRAKK

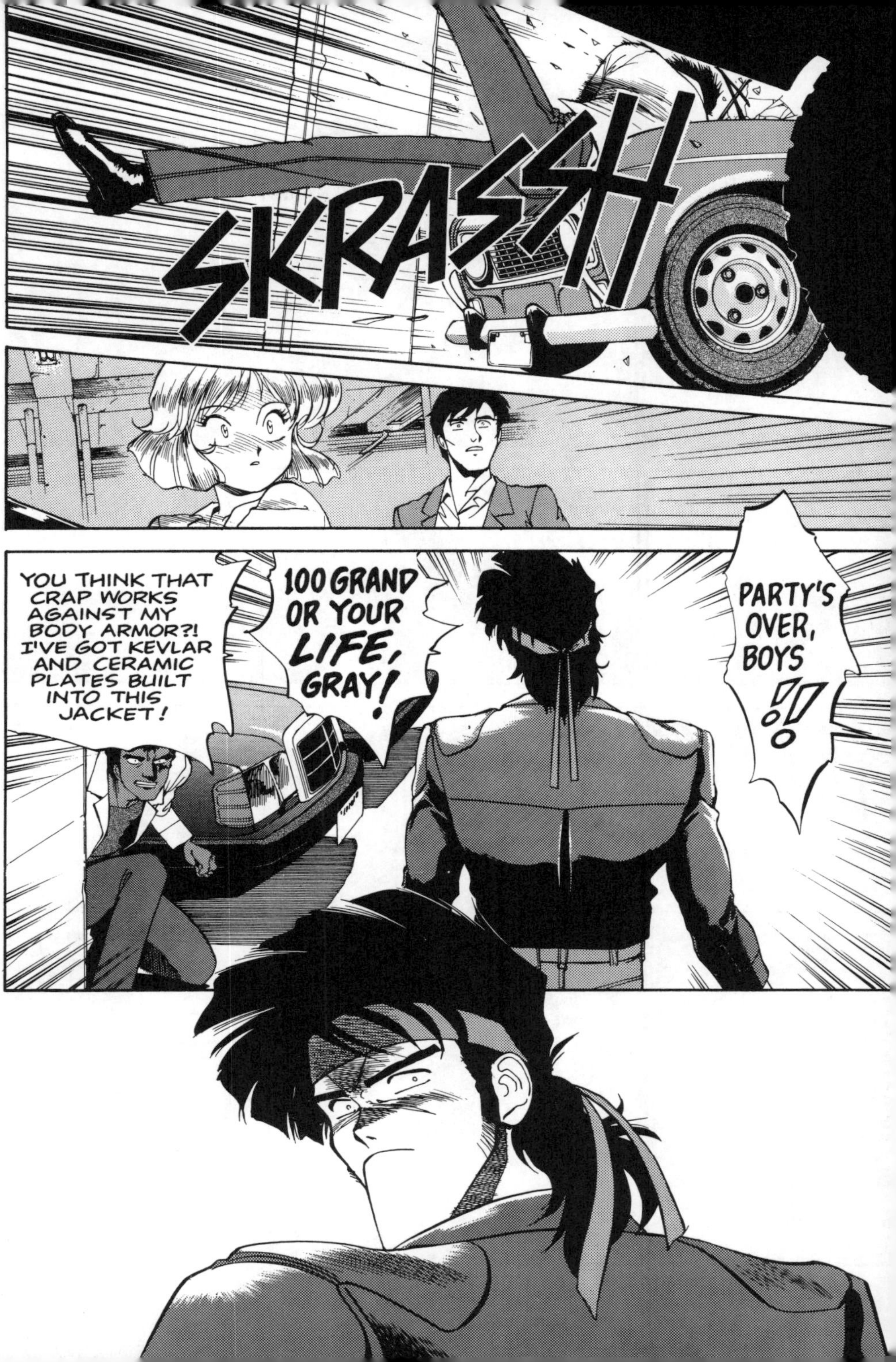
SKRASSH
YOU THINK THAT CRAP WORKS AGAINST MY BODY ARMOR?! I'VE GOT KEVLAR AND CERAMIC PLATES BUILT INTO THIS JACKET!
100 GRAND OR YOUR LIFE, GRAY!
PARTY'S OVER, BOYS ?!

THERE'S A TEN GAUGE CHECKING OUT YOUR CRANIUM...

...MISTER "BIG-JAW"!

NO, WAIT! KEN, *STOP!*

AS LONG AS GRAY KNOWS...

...EITHER I KILL HIM, OR THE SYNDICATE TRACKS ME DOWN.

BKAM BKAM

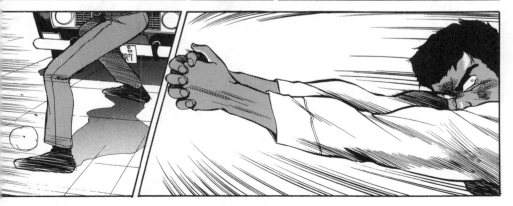

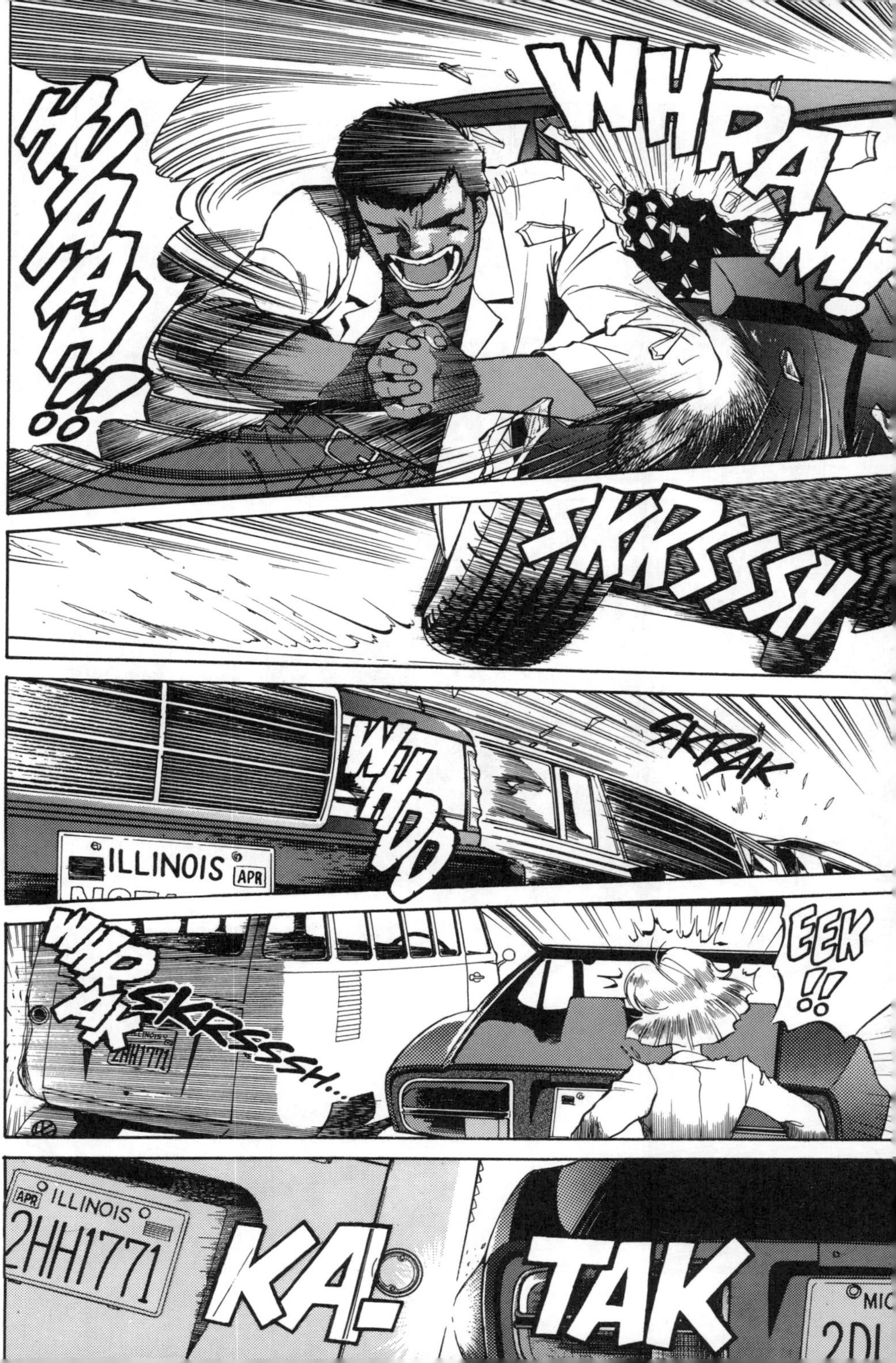
HWAAAAH!!
WHRAM!
SKRSSSH
ILLINOIS
APR
WHOO
SKRAK
WHRAK
SKRSSSH...
EEK!!
APR ILLINOIS
2HH1771
KA-TAK

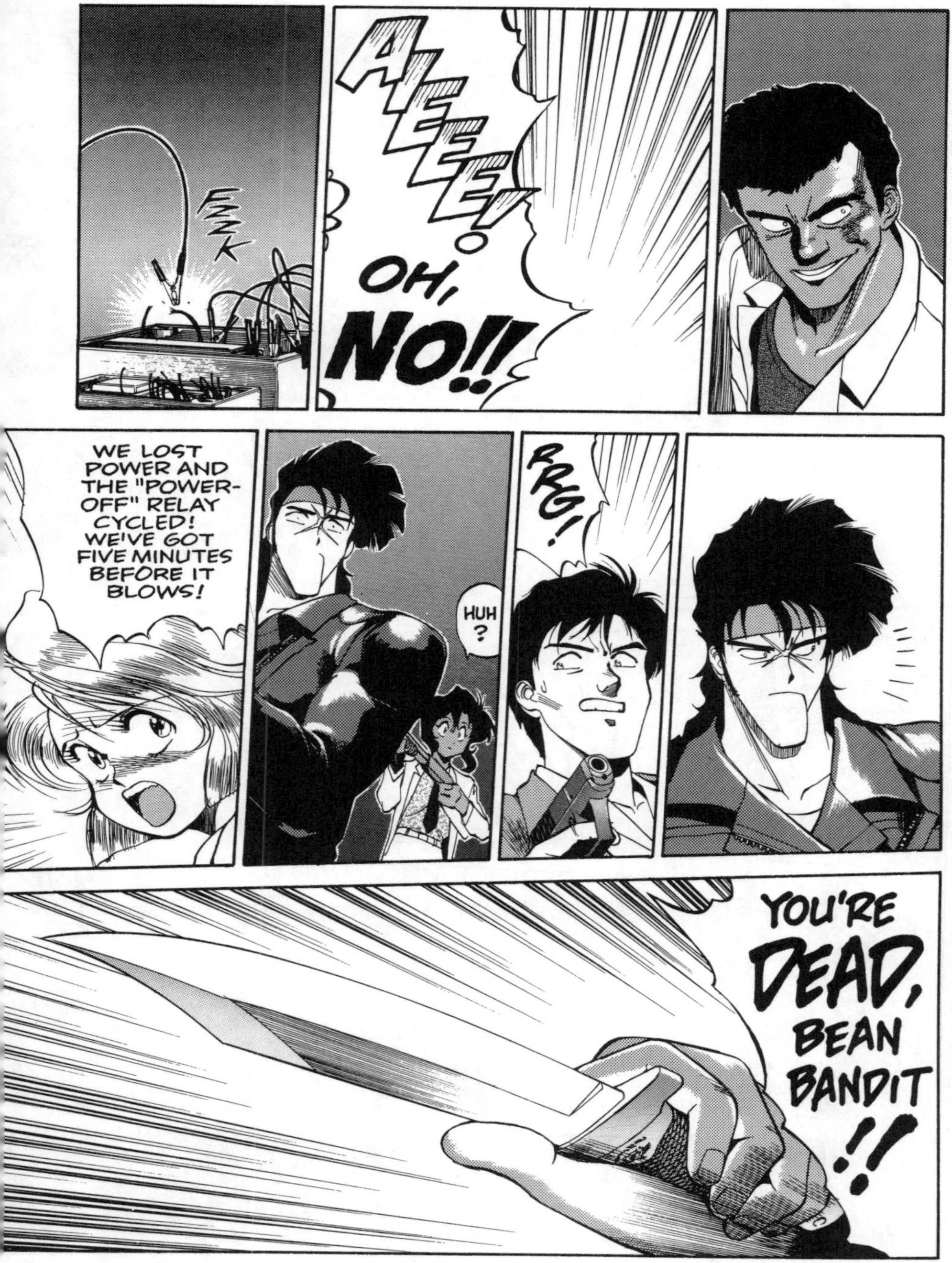
FZZK
AIEEEE!
OH, NO!!
WE LOST POWER AND THE "POWER-OFF" RELAY CYCLED! WE'VE GOT FIVE MINUTES BEFORE IT BLOWS!
HUH?
RRG!
YOU'RE DEAD, BEAN BANDIT!!

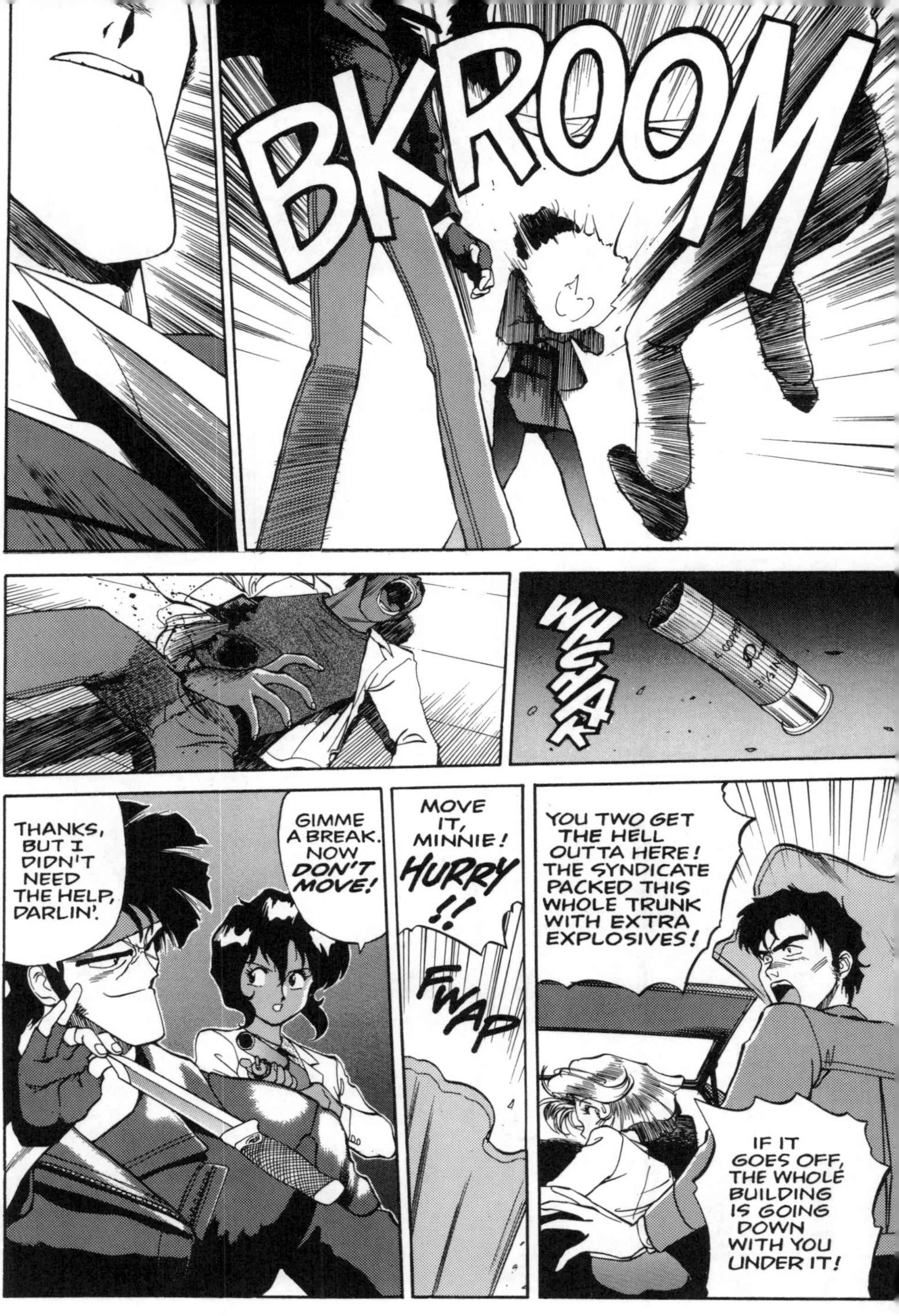
BKROOM
WHGHAK
THANKS, BUT I DIDN'T NEED THE HELP, DARLIN'.
GIMME A BREAK. NOW DON'T MOVE!
MOVE IT, MINNIE!
HURRY !!
FWAP
YOU TWO GET THE HELL OUTTA HERE! THE SYNDICATE PACKED THIS WHOLE TRUNK WITH EXTRA EXPLOSIVES!
IF IT GOES OFF, THE WHOLE BUILDING IS GOING DOWN WITH YOU UNDER IT!

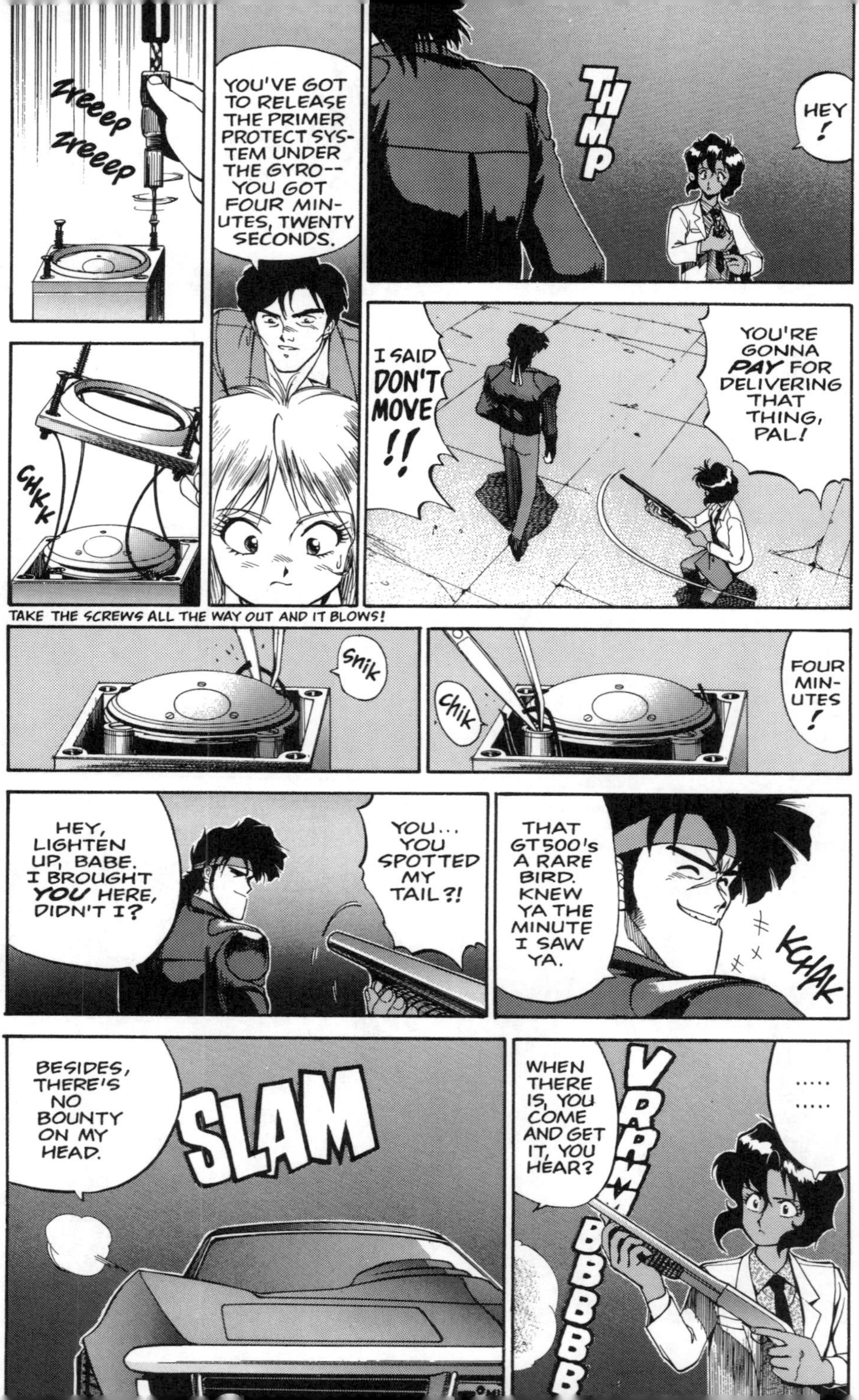
zreeep
zreeep
CHKK
YOU'VE GOT TO RELEASE THE PRIMER PROTECT SYSTEM UNDER THE GYRO-- YOU GOT FOUR MINUTES, TWENTY SECONDS.
THMP
HEY!
I SAID DON'T MOVE!!
YOU'RE GONNA PAY FOR DELIVERING THAT THING, PAL!
TAKE THE SCREWS ALL THE WAY OUT AND IT BLOWS!
snik
chik
FOUR MINUTES!
HEY, LIGHTEN UP, BABE. I BROUGHT YOU HERE, DIDN'T I?
YOU... YOU SPOTTED MY TAIL?!
THAT GT500's A RARE BIRD. KNEW YA THE MINUTE I SAW YA.
KCHAK
BESIDES, THERE'S NO BOUNTY ON MY HEAD.
SLAM
WHEN THERE IS, YOU COME AND GET IT, YOU HEAR?
VRRMMBBBBB
.....
.....

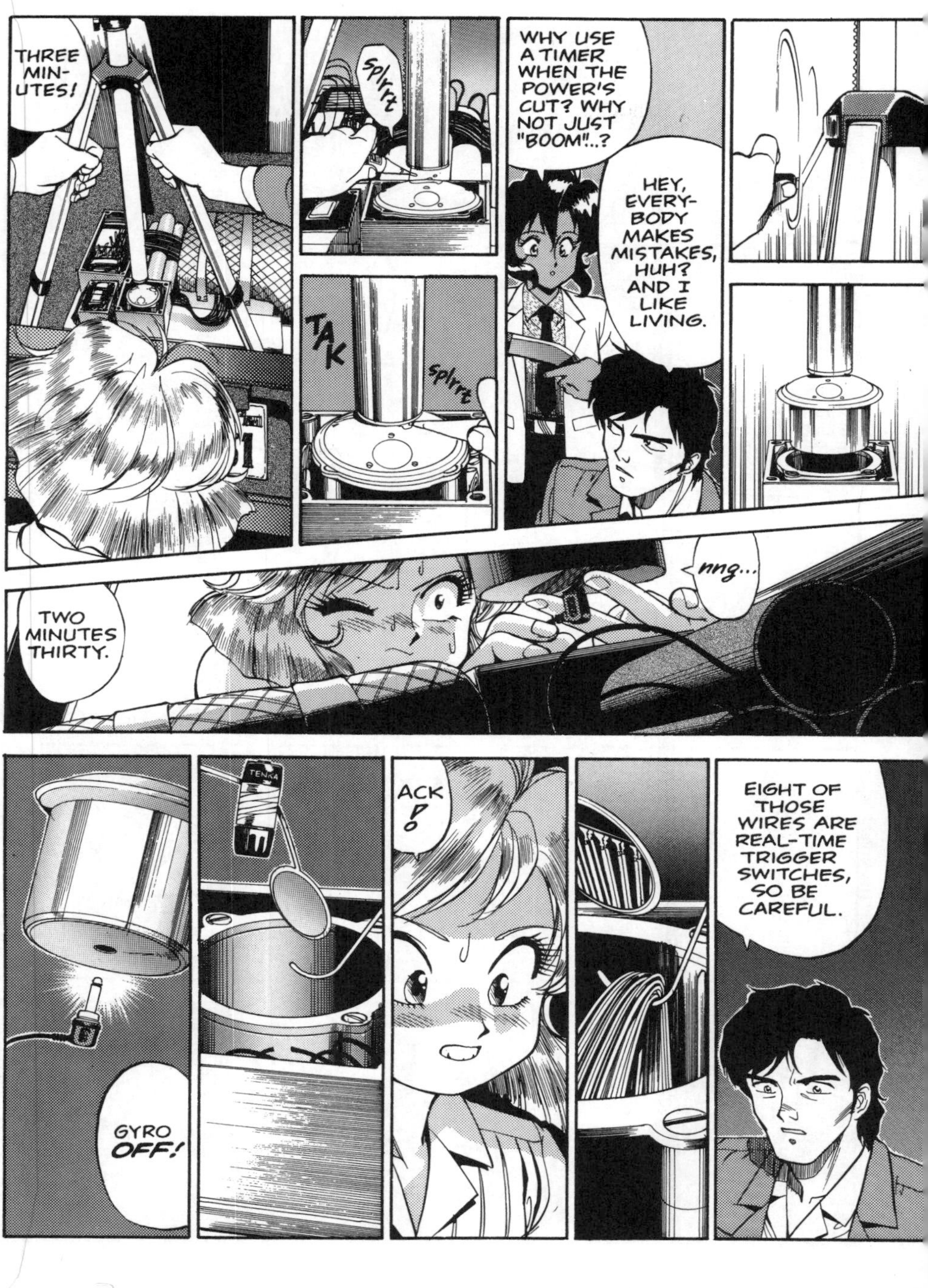
THREE MIN-UTES!
splrrt
TAK
splrrt
WHY USE A TIMER WHEN THE POWER'S CUT? WHY NOT JUST "BOOM"..?
HEY, EVERY-BODY MAKES MISTAKES, HUH? AND I LIKE LIVING.
TWO MINUTES THIRTY.
nng...
GYRO OFF!
ACK!
EIGHT OF THOSE WIRES ARE REAL-TIME TRIGGER SWITCHES, SO BE CAREFUL.

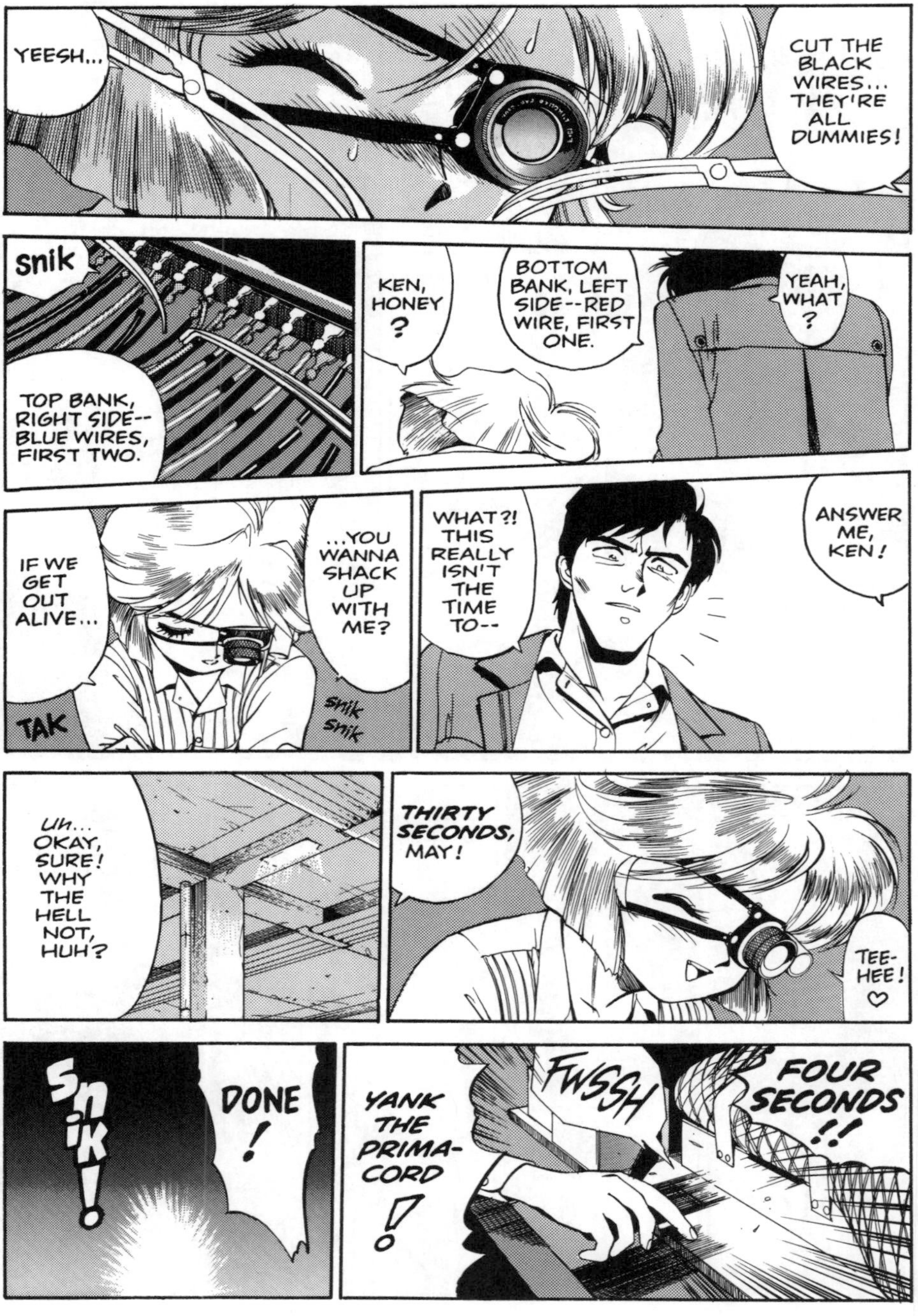
YEESH...
CUT THE BLACK WIRES... THEY'RE ALL DUMMIES!
snik
TOP BANK, RIGHT SIDE-- BLUE WIRES, FIRST TWO.
KEN, HONEY ?
BOTTOM BANK, LEFT SIDE--RED WIRE, FIRST ONE.
YEAH, WHAT ?
IF WE GET OUT ALIVE...
...YOU WANNA SHACK UP WITH ME?
TAK
snik snik
WHAT?! THIS REALLY ISN'T THE TIME TO--
ANSWER ME, KEN!
Uh... OKAY, SURE! WHY THE HELL NOT, HUH?
THIRTY SECONDS, MAY!
TEE-HEE! ♡
Snik!
DONE!
YANK THE PRIMA-CORD!
FWSSH
FOUR SECONDS!!

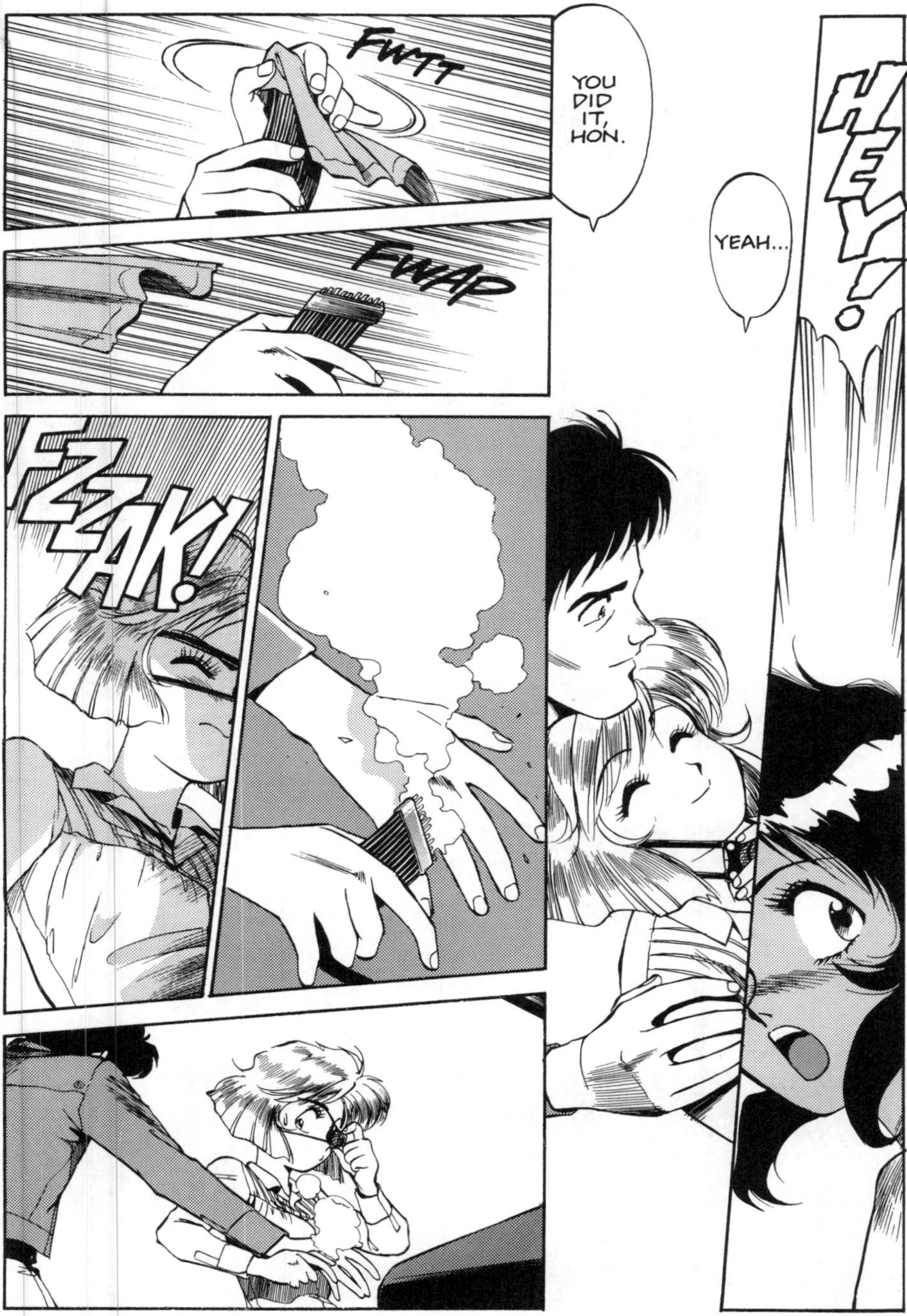
FWTT
FWAP
FZZAK!
YOU DID IT, HON.
YEAH...
HEY!

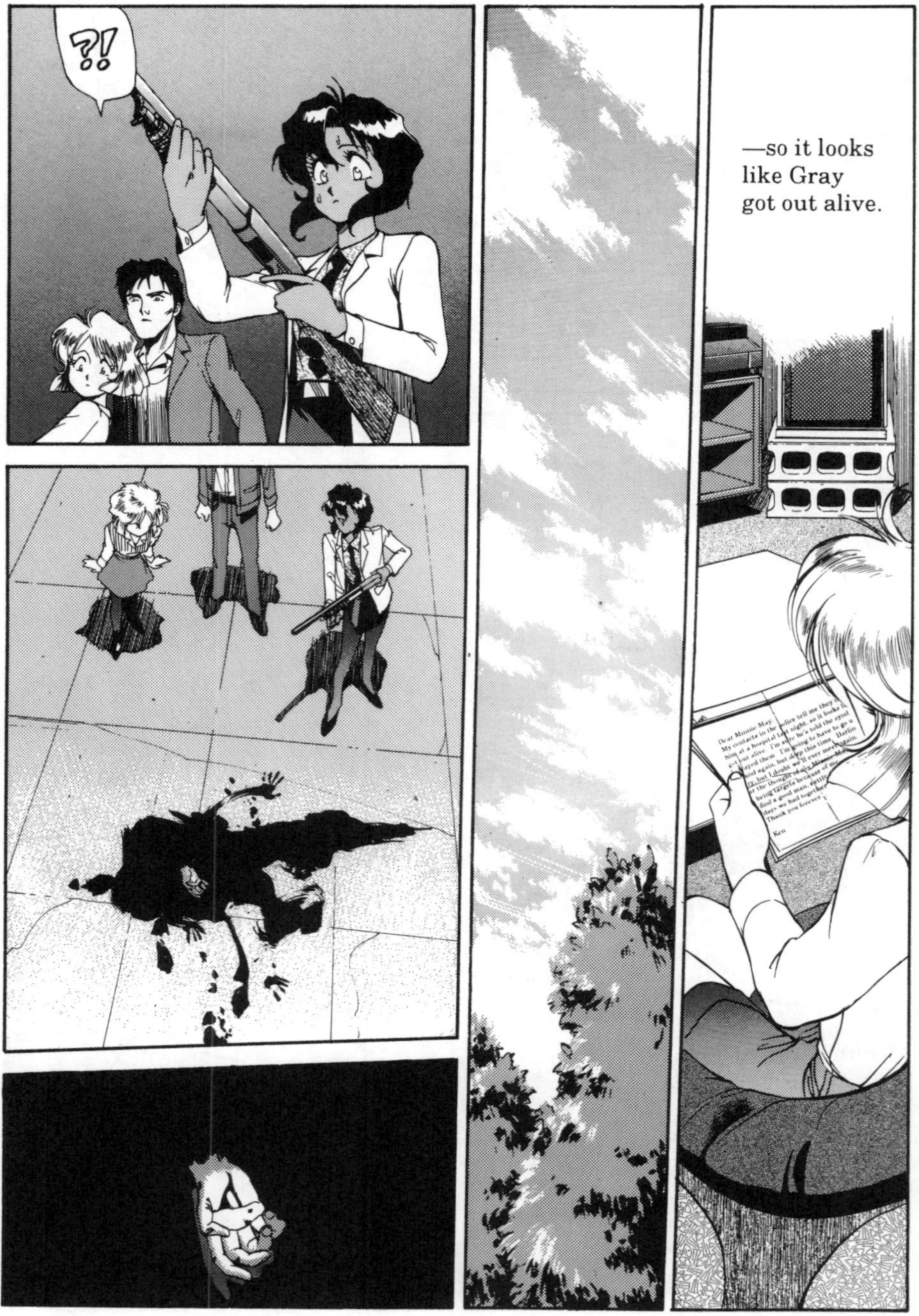
?!
—so it looks like Gray got out alive.

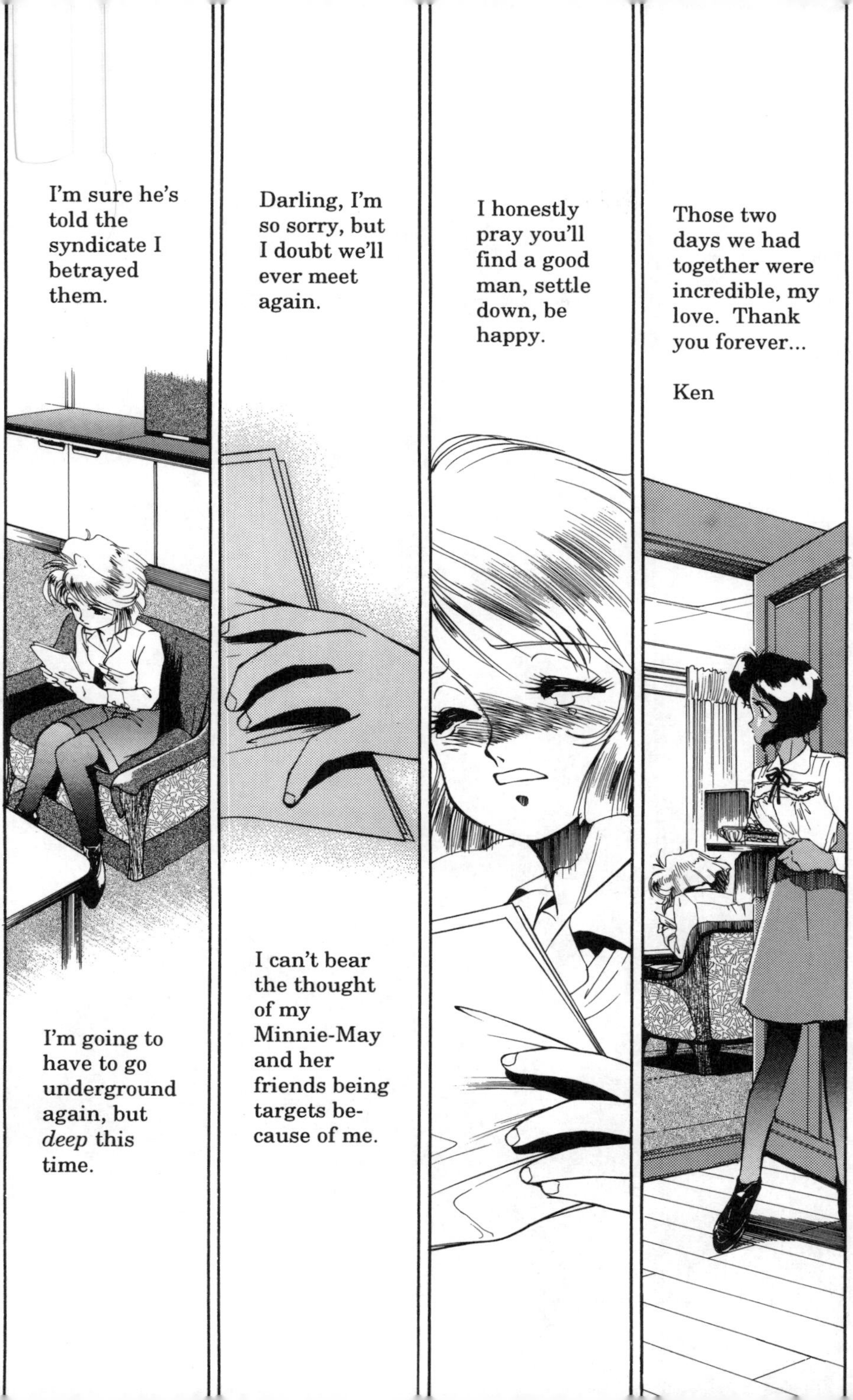
I'm sure he's told the syndicate I betrayed them.
I'm going to have to go underground again, but *deep* this time.
Darling, I'm so sorry, but I doubt we'll ever meet again.
I can't bear the thought of my Minnie-May and her friends being targets be-cause of me.
I honestly pray you'll find a good man, settle down, be happy.
Those two days we had together were incredible, my love. Thank you forever...
Ken

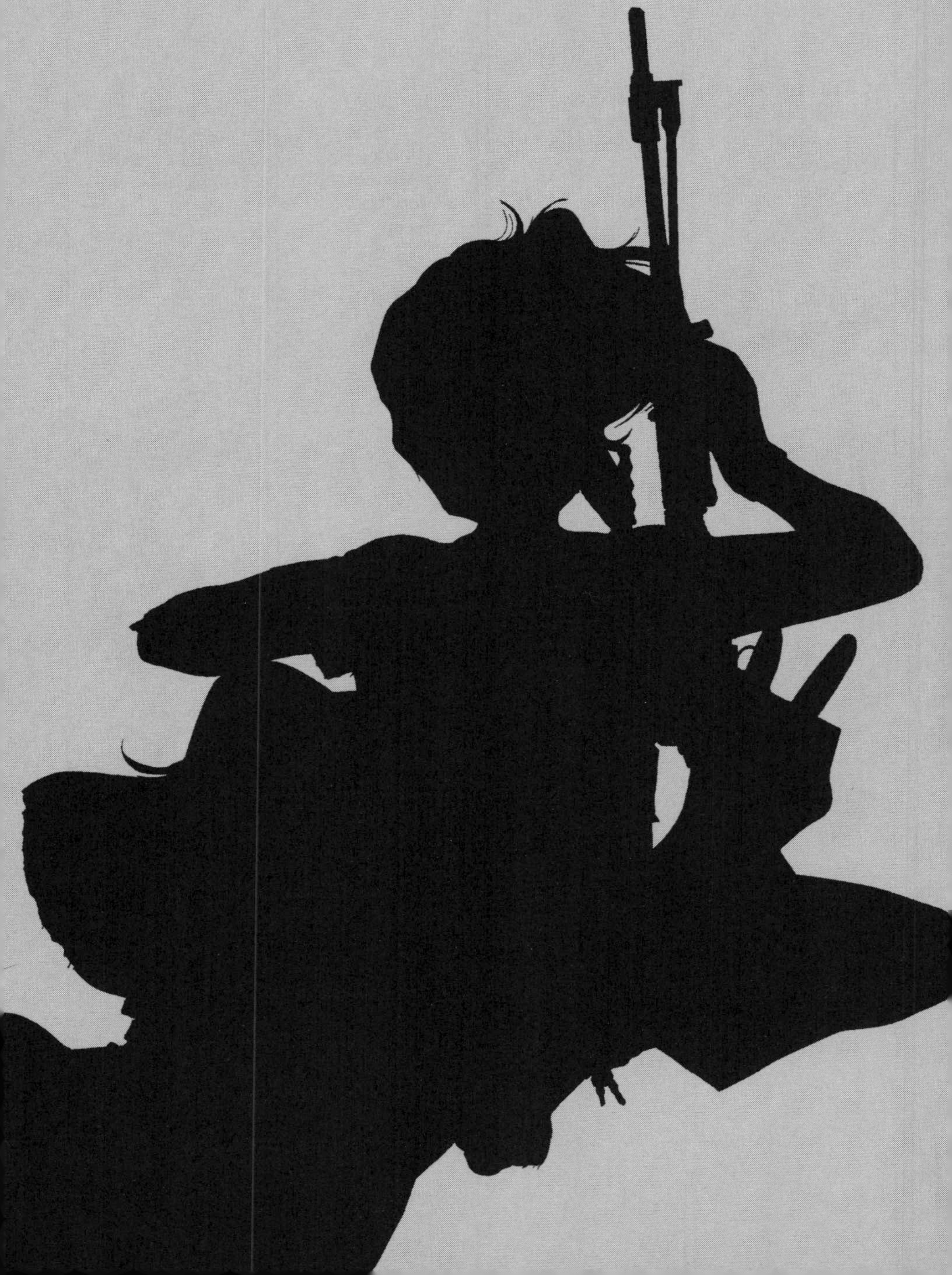

JAMMING

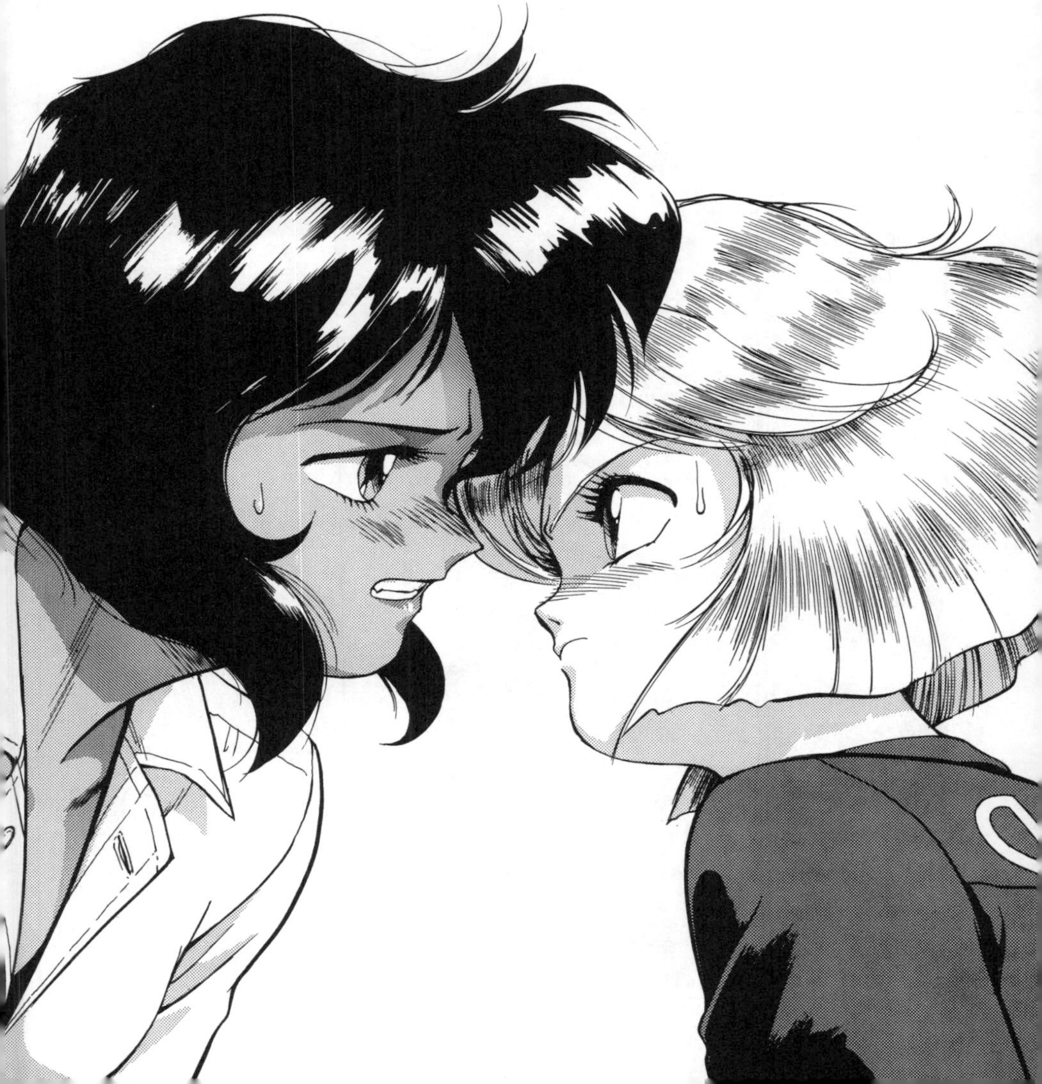

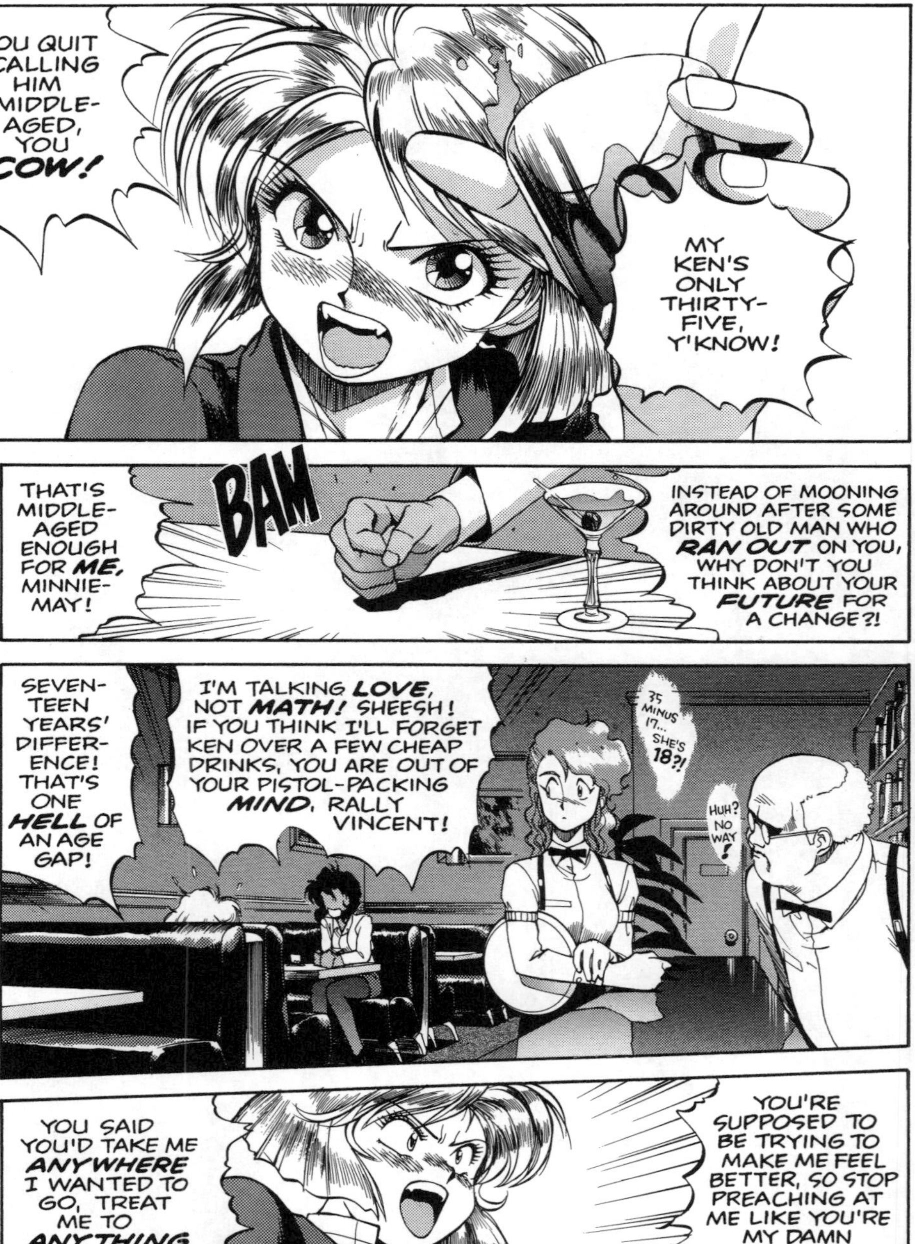
YOU QUIT CALLING HIM MIDDLE-AGED, YOU COW!
MY KEN'S ONLY THIRTY-FIVE, Y'KNOW!
THAT'S MIDDLE-AGED ENOUGH FOR ME, MINNIE-MAY!
BAM
INSTEAD OF MOONING AROUND AFTER SOME DIRTY OLD MAN WHO RAN OUT ON YOU, WHY DON'T YOU THINK ABOUT YOUR FUTURE FOR A CHANGE?!
SEVENTEEN YEARS' DIFFERENCE! THAT'S ONE HELL OF AN AGE GAP!
I'M TALKING LOVE, NOT MATH! SHEESH! IF YOU THINK I'LL FORGET KEN OVER A FEW CHEAP DRINKS, YOU ARE OUT OF YOUR PISTOL-PACKING MIND, RALLY VINCENT!
35 MINUS 17... SHE'S 18?!
HUH? NO WAY!
YOU SAID YOU'D TAKE ME ANYWHERE I WANTED TO GO, TREAT ME TO ANYTHING I WANTED TO EAT!
YOU'RE SUPPOSED TO BE TRYING TO MAKE ME FEEL BETTER, SO STOP PREACHING AT ME LIKE YOU'RE MY DAMN MOTHER OR SOMETHING!

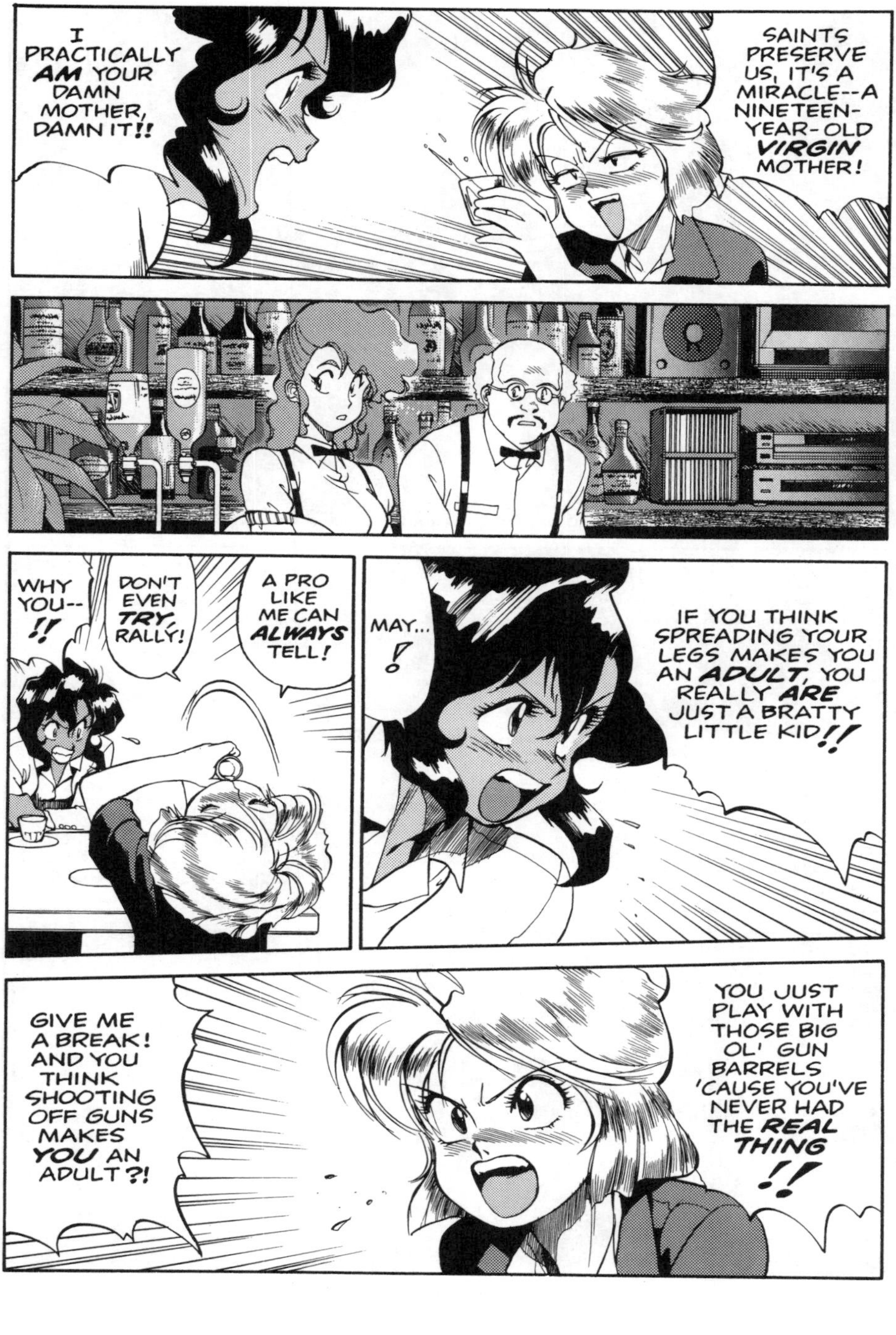
I PRACTICALLY AM YOUR DAMN MOTHER, DAMN IT!!
SAINTS PRESERVE US, IT'S A MIRACLE--A NINETEEN-YEAR-OLD VIRGIN MOTHER!
WHY YOU-- !!
DON'T EVEN TRY, RALLY!
A PRO LIKE ME CAN ALWAYS TELL!
MAY... !
IF YOU THINK SPREADING YOUR LEGS MAKES YOU AN ADULT, YOU REALLY ARE JUST A BRATTY LITTLE KID!!
GIVE ME A BREAK! AND YOU THINK SHOOTING OFF GUNS MAKES YOU AN ADULT?!
YOU JUST PLAY WITH THOSE BIG OL' GUN BARRELS 'CAUSE YOU'VE NEVER HAD THE REAL THING !!

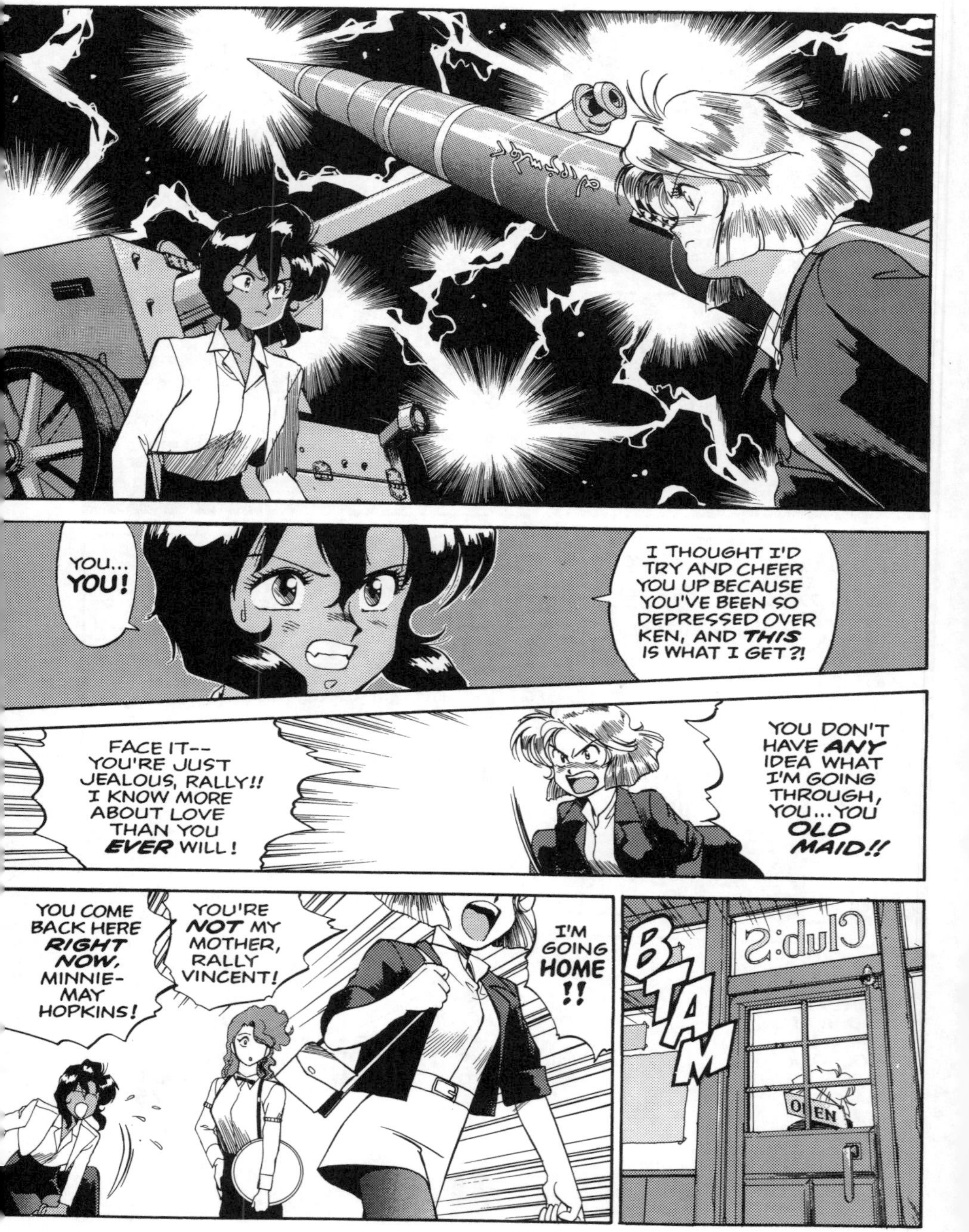
YOU... YOU!
I THOUGHT I'D TRY AND CHEER YOU UP BECAUSE YOU'VE BEEN SO DEPRESSED OVER KEN, AND THIS IS WHAT I GET?!
FACE IT-- YOU'RE JUST JEALOUS, RALLY!! I KNOW MORE ABOUT LOVE THAN YOU EVER WILL!
YOU DON'T HAVE ANY IDEA WHAT I'M GOING THROUGH, YOU... YOU OLD MAID!!
YOU COME BACK HERE RIGHT NOW, MINNIE-MAY HOPKINS!
YOU'RE NOT MY MOTHER, RALLY VINCENT!
I'M GOING HOME!!
BTAM
Club:S
OPEN

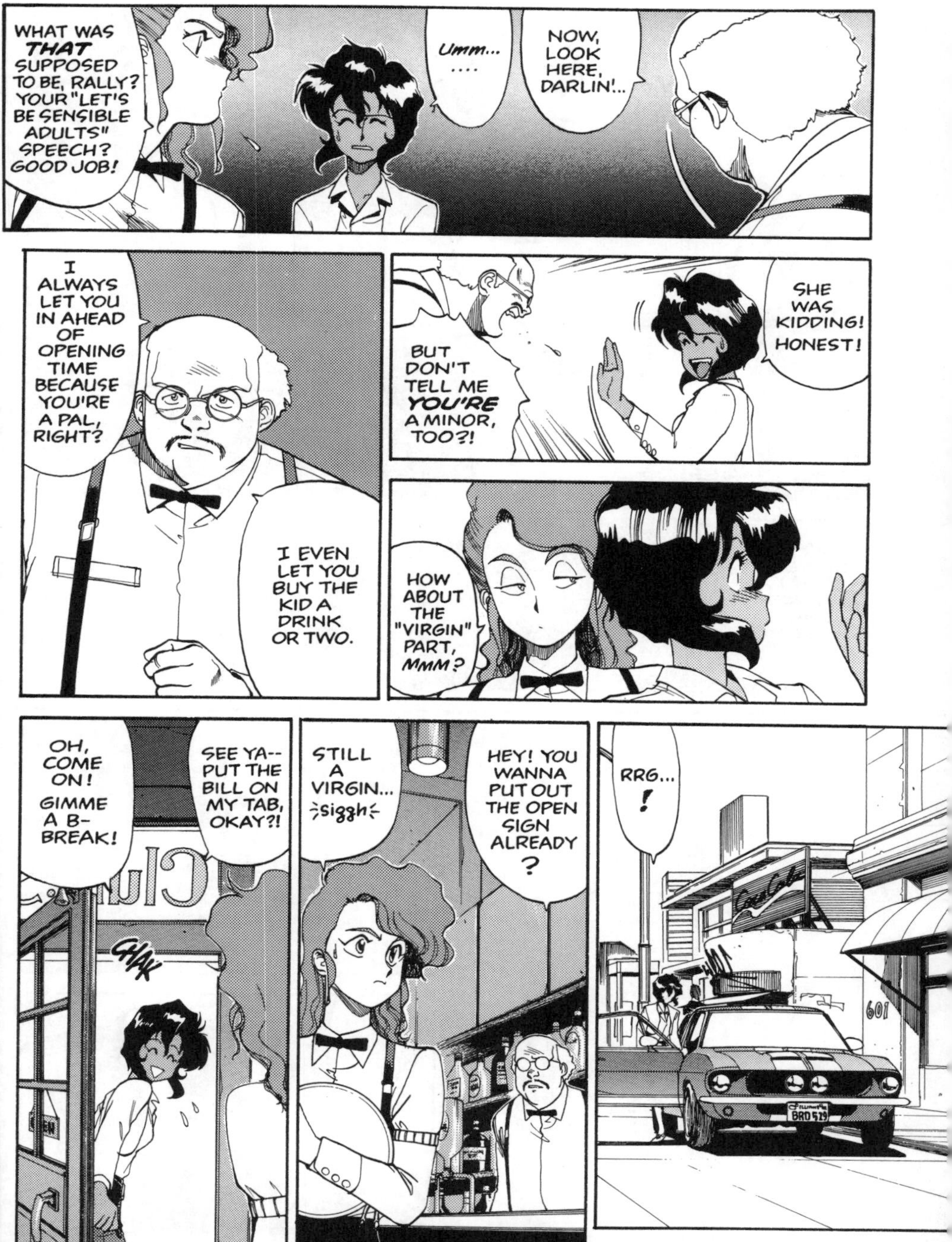
WHAT WAS THAT SUPPOSED TO BE, RALLY? YOUR "LET'S BE SENSIBLE ADULTS" SPEECH? GOOD JOB!
Umm... ....
NOW, LOOK HERE, DARLIN'...
I ALWAYS LET YOU IN AHEAD OF OPENING TIME BECAUSE YOU'RE A PAL, RIGHT?
I EVEN LET YOU BUY THE KID A DRINK OR TWO.
BUT DON'T TELL ME YOU'RE A MINOR, TOO?!
SHE WAS KIDDING! HONEST!
HOW ABOUT THE "VIRGIN" PART, MMM?
OH, COME ON! GIMME A B-BREAK!
SEE YA-- PUT THE BILL ON MY TAB, OKAY?!
CHAK
STILL A VIRGIN... sigggh
HEY! YOU WANNA PUT OUT THE OPEN SIGN ALREADY?
RRG... !

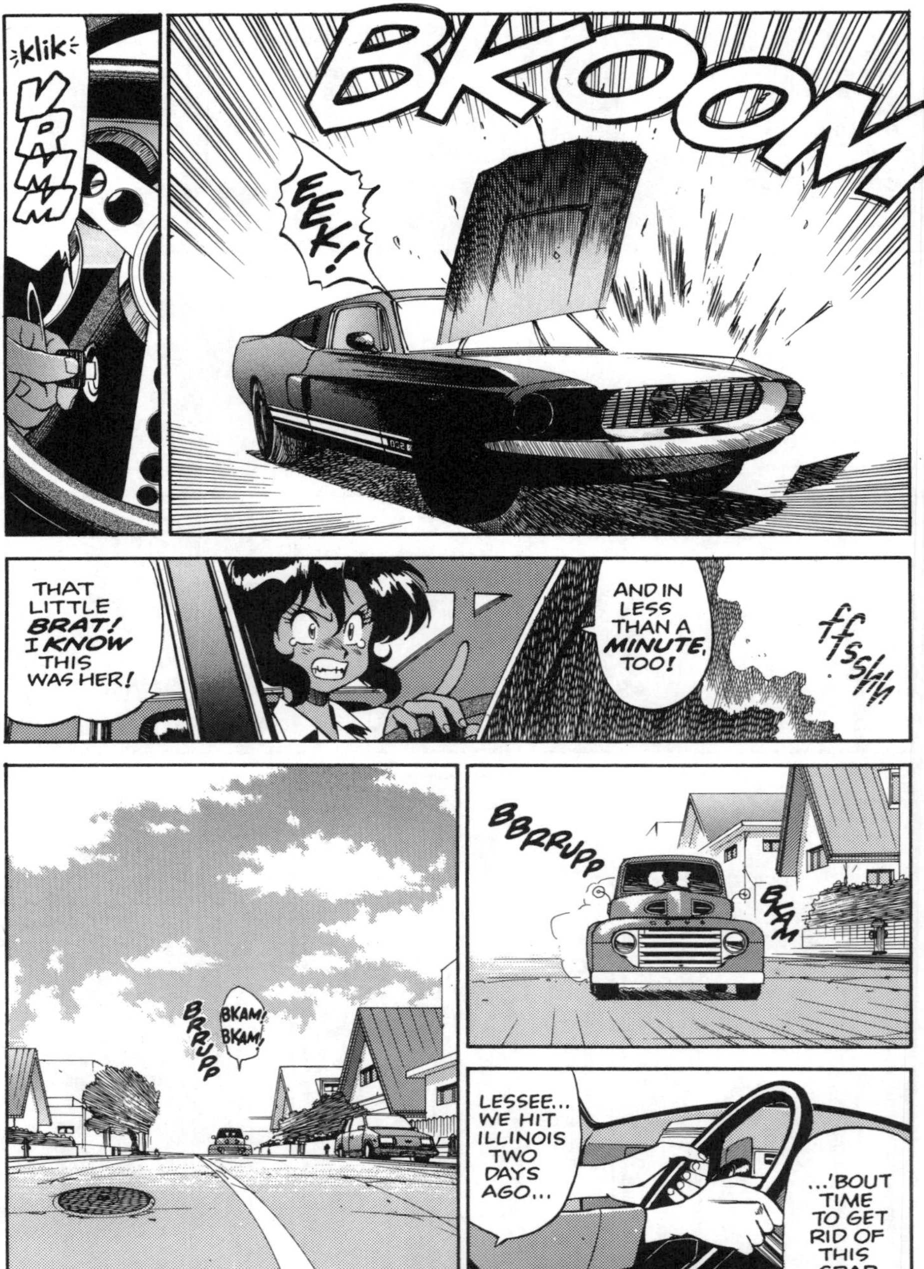
klik
VRMM
BKOOM
EEEK!
THAT LITTLE BRAT! I KNOW THIS WAS HER!
AND IN LESS THAN A MINUTE, TOO!
ffsshh
BRRUPP
BKAM! BKAM!
BBRRUPP
BKAM
LESSEE... WE HIT ILLINOIS TWO DAYS AGO...
...'BOUT TIME TO GET RID OF THIS CRAP TRUCK.

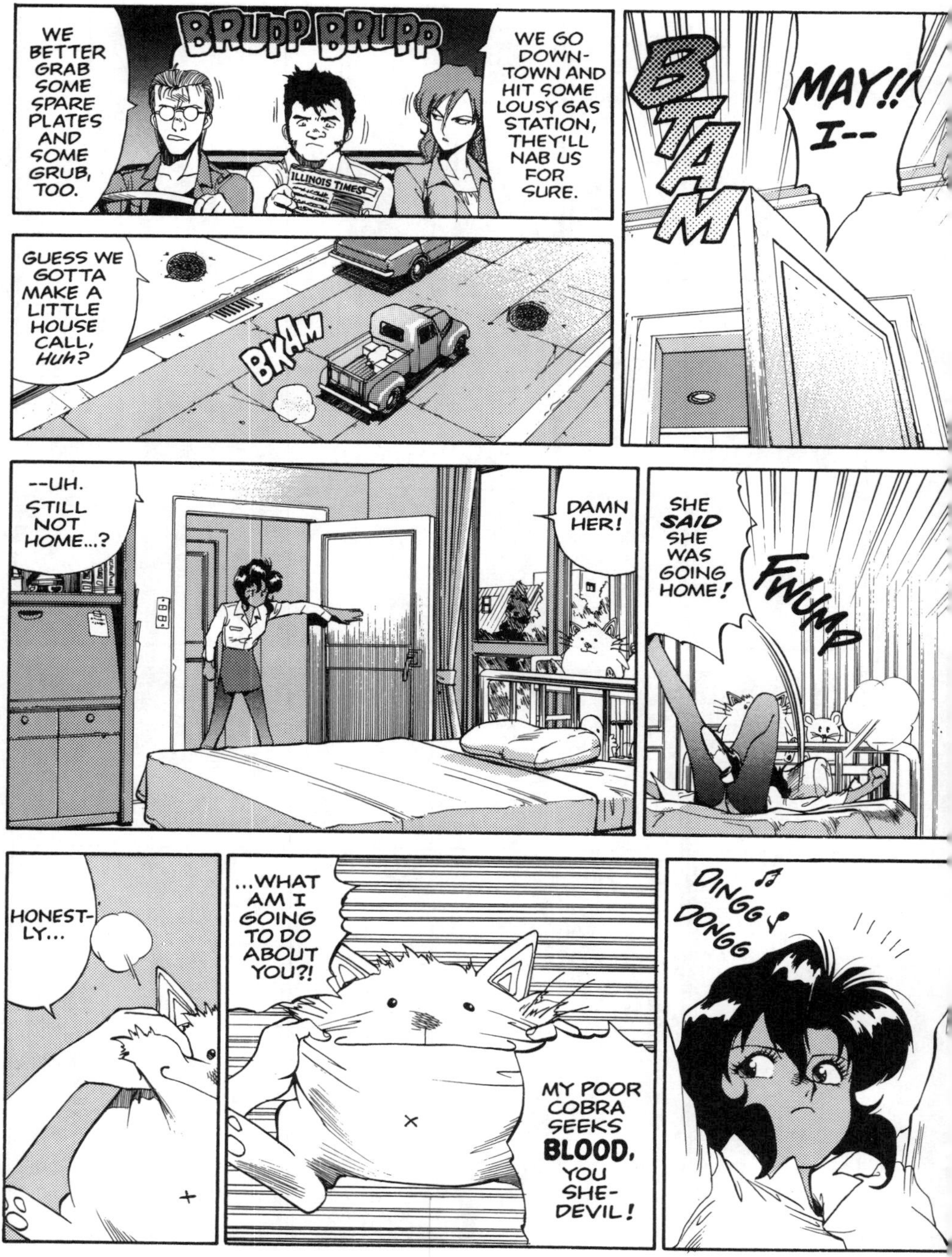
BRUPP BRUPP
WE BETTER GRAB SOME SPARE PLATES AND SOME GRUB, TOO.
ILLINOIS TIMES
WE GO DOWN-TOWN AND HIT SOME LOUSY GAS STATION, THEY'LL NAB US FOR SURE.
GUESS WE GOTTA MAKE A LITTLE HOUSE CALL, *Huh?*
BKAM
BTAM
MAY!! I--
--UH. STILL NOT HOME...?
DAMN HER!
SHE **SAID** SHE WAS GOING HOME!
FWUMP
HONEST-LY...
...WHAT AM I GOING TO DO ABOUT YOU?!
MY POOR COBRA SEEKS **BLOOD**, YOU SHE-DEVIL!
DINGG DONGG

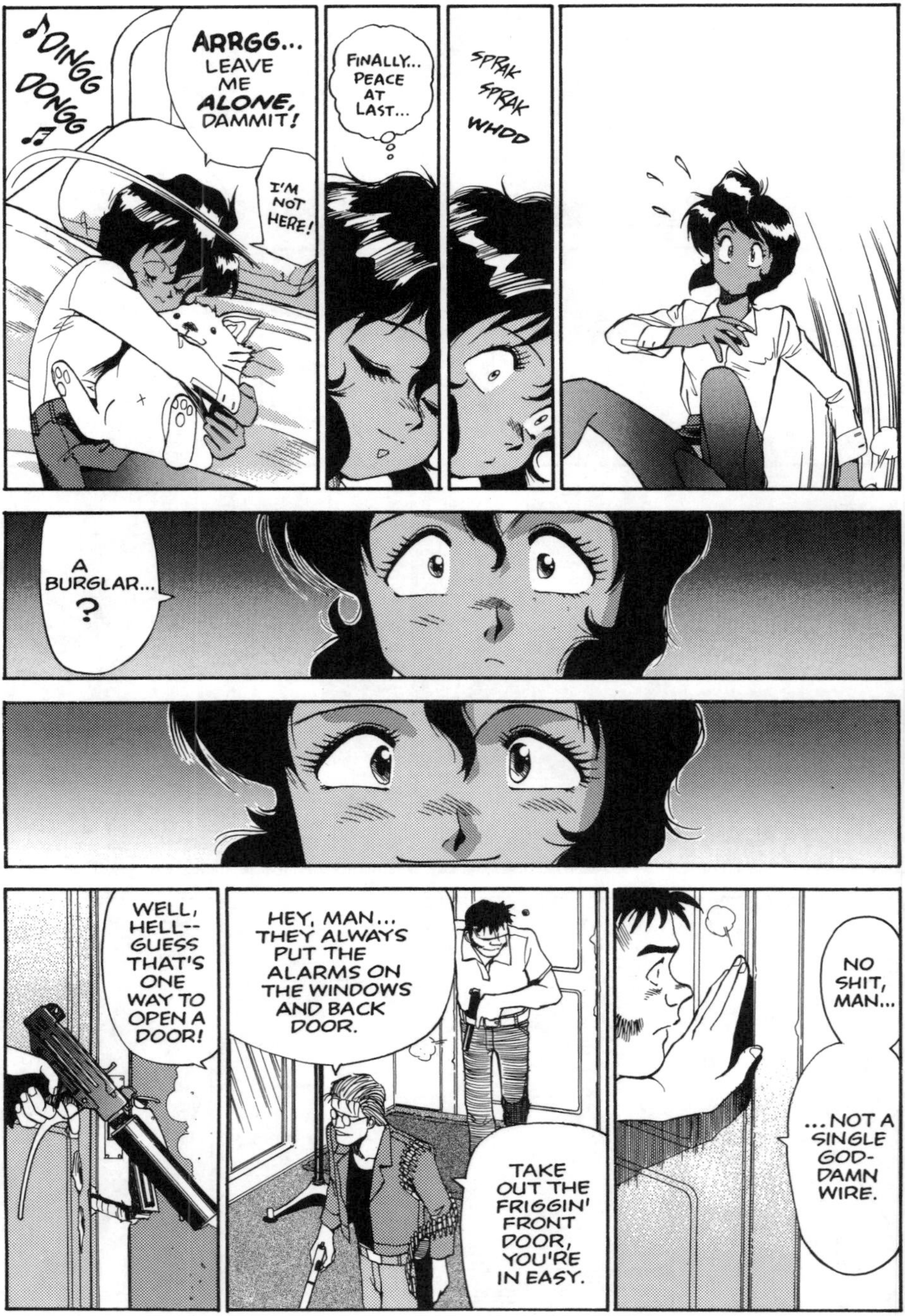
♪DINGG DONGG♪
ARRGG... LEAVE ME ALONE, DAMMIT!
I'M NOT HERE!
FINALLY... PEACE AT LAST...
SPRAK SPRAK WHDD
A BURGLAR... ?
WELL, HELL-- GUESS THAT'S ONE WAY TO OPEN A DOOR!
HEY, MAN... THEY ALWAYS PUT THE ALARMS ON THE WINDOWS AND BACK DOOR.
TAKE OUT THE FRIGGIN' FRONT DOOR, YOU'RE IN EASY.
NO SHIT, MAN...
...NOT A SINGLE GOD-DAMN WIRE.

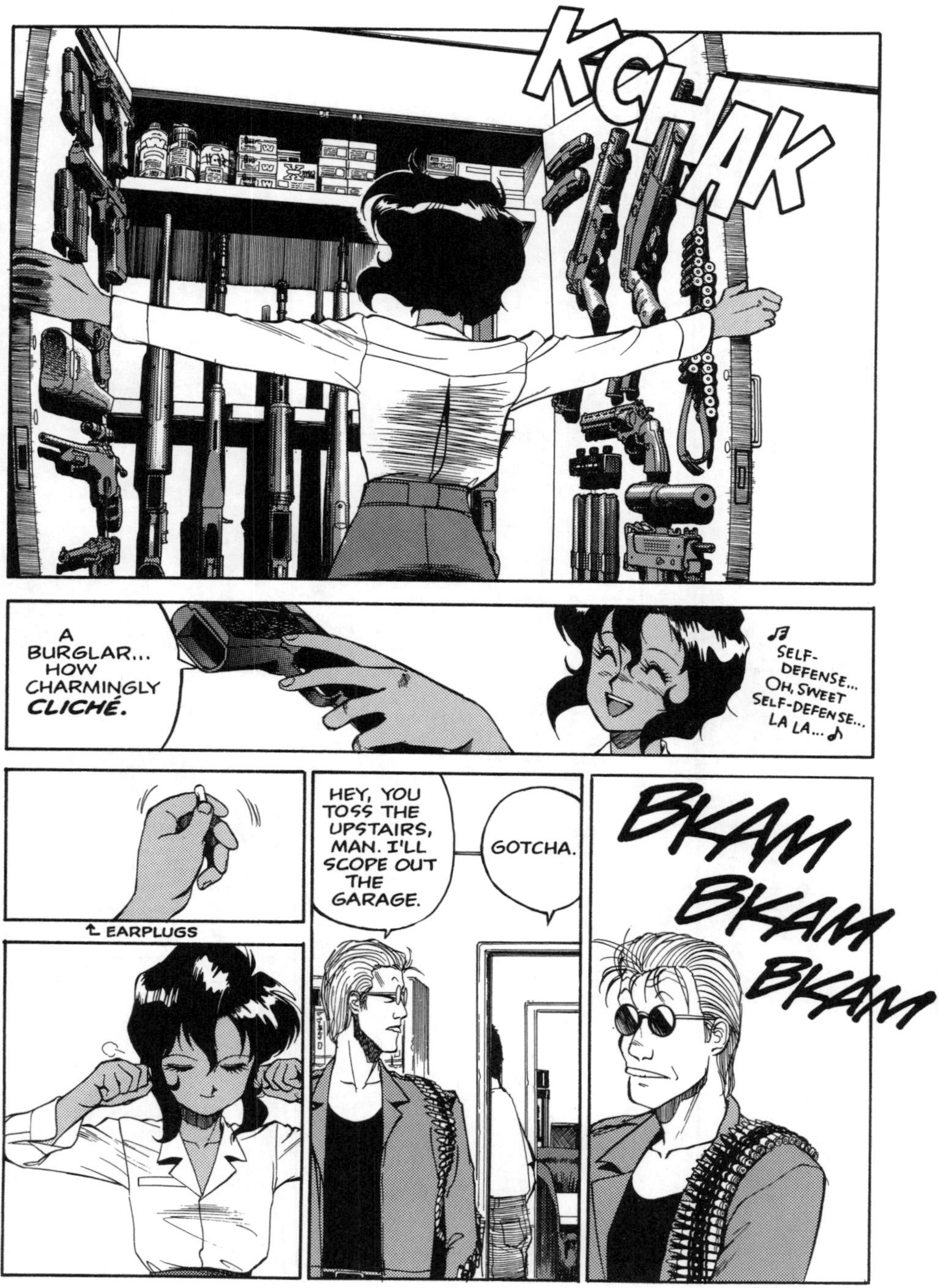
KCHAK
A BURGLAR... HOW CHARMINGLY CLICHÉ.
SELF-DEFENSE... OH, SWEET SELF-DEFENSE... LA LA...
EARPLUGS
HEY, YOU TOSS THE UPSTAIRS, MAN. I'LL SCOPE OUT THE GARAGE.
GOTCHA.
BKAM BKAM BKAM

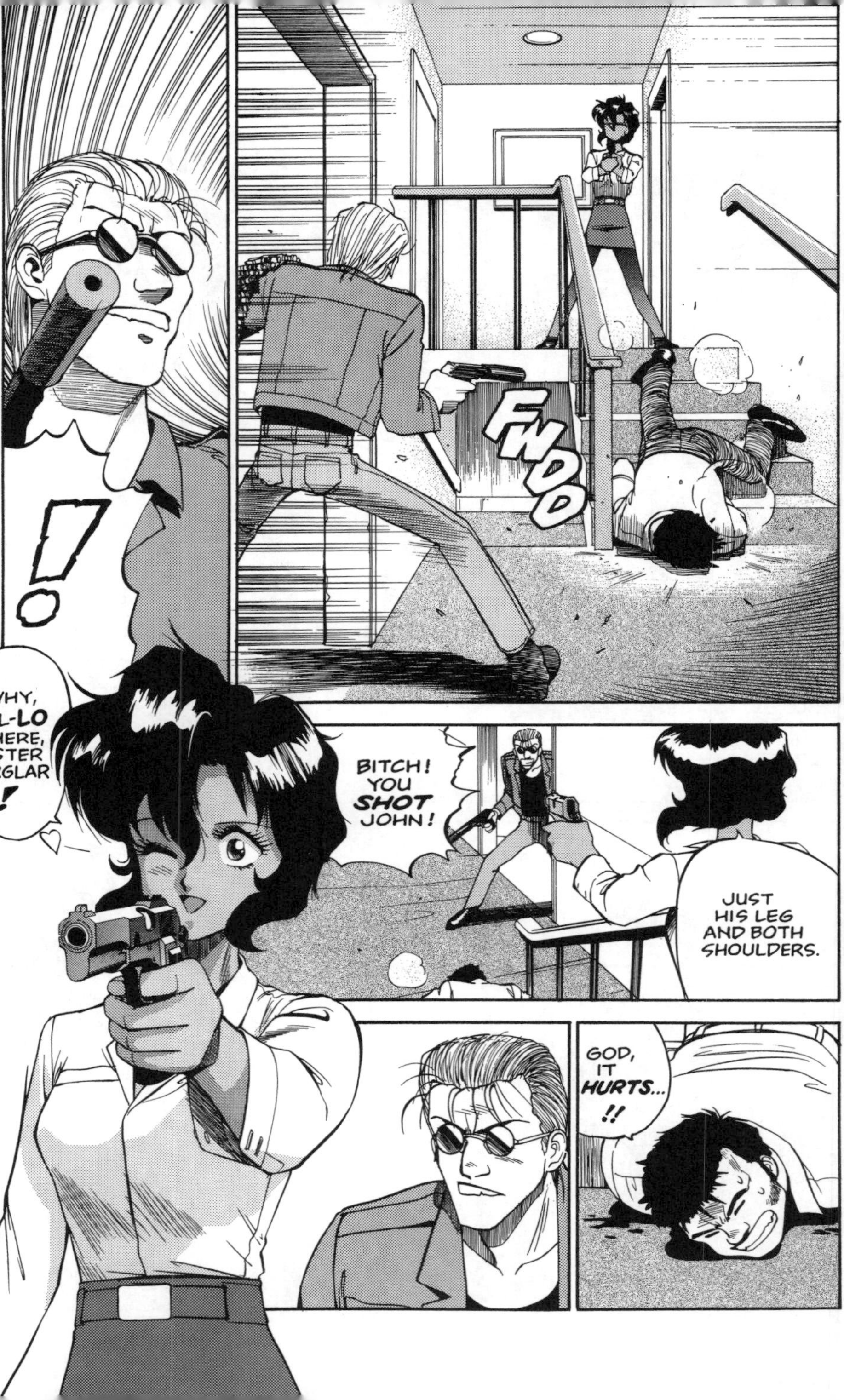
!
FWOO
WHY, HEL-LO THERE, MISTER BURGLAR!
BITCH! YOU SHOT JOHN!
JUST HIS LEG AND BOTH SHOULDERS.
GOD, IT HURTS... !!

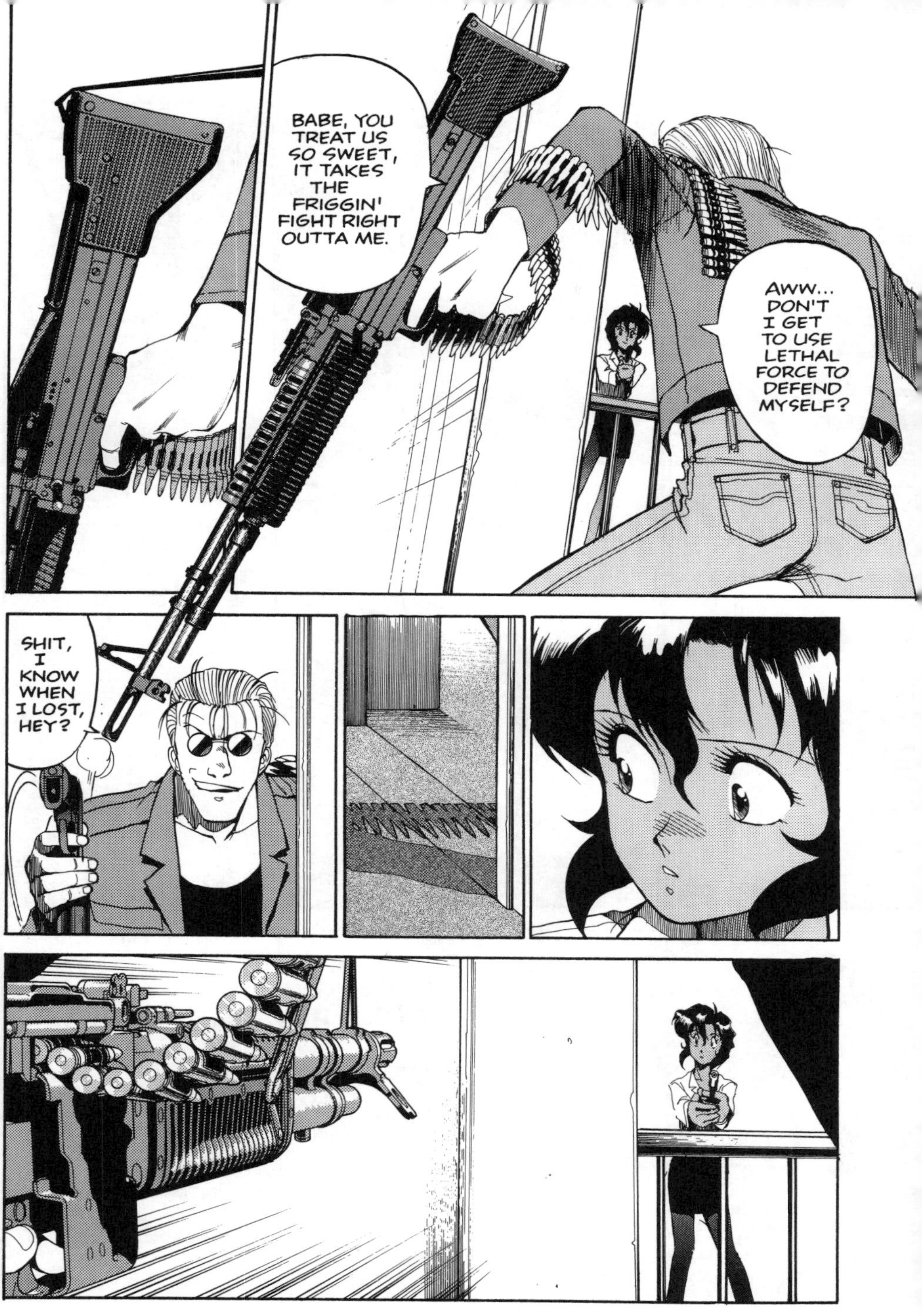
BABE, YOU TREAT US SO SWEET, IT TAKES THE FRIGGIN' FIGHT RIGHT OUTTA ME.
AWW... DON'T I GET TO USE LETHAL FORCE TO DEFEND MYSELF?
SHIT, I KNOW WHEN I LOST, HEY?

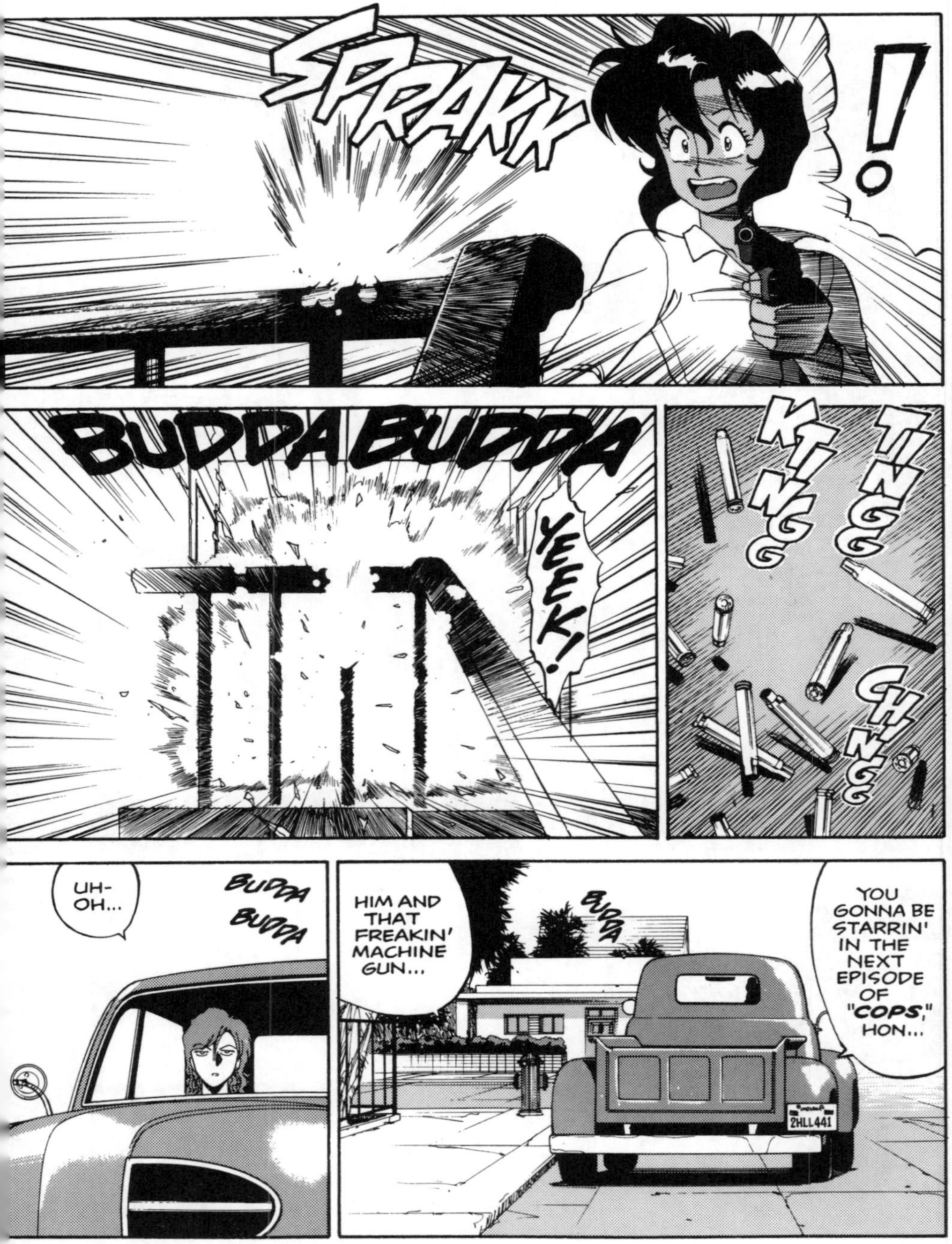
SPRAKK
!
BUDDA BUDDA
YEEEK!
KTINGG
TINGG
CHINGG
UH-OH...
BUDDA BUDDA
HIM AND THAT FREAKIN' MACHINE GUN...
BUDDA
YOU GONNA BE STARRIN' IN THE NEXT EPISODE OF "COPS," HON...

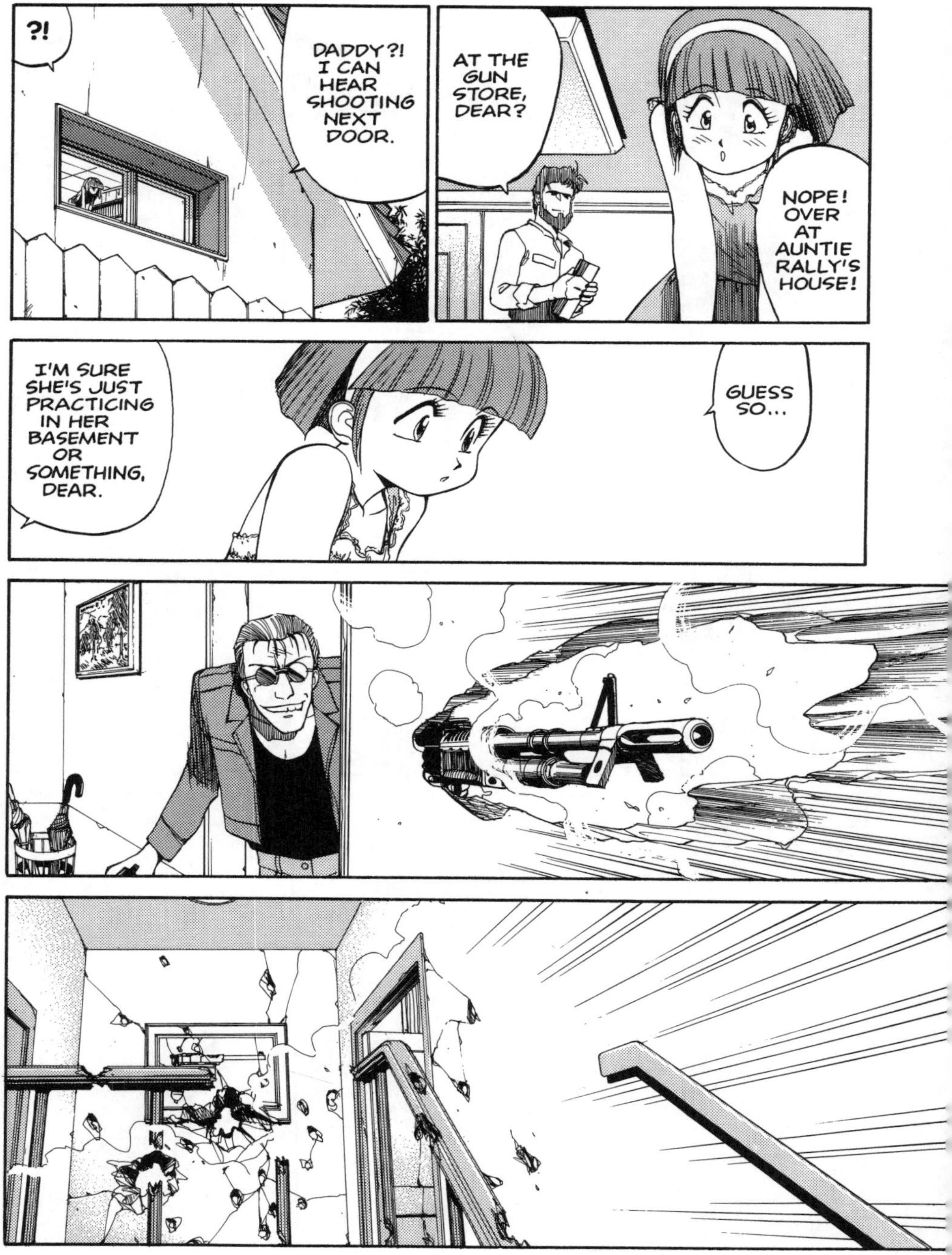
?!
DADDY?! I CAN HEAR SHOOTING NEXT DOOR.
AT THE GUN STORE, DEAR?
NOPE! OVER AT AUNTIE RALLY'S HOUSE!
I'M SURE SHE'S JUST PRACTICING IN HER BASEMENT OR SOMETHING, DEAR.
GUESS SO...

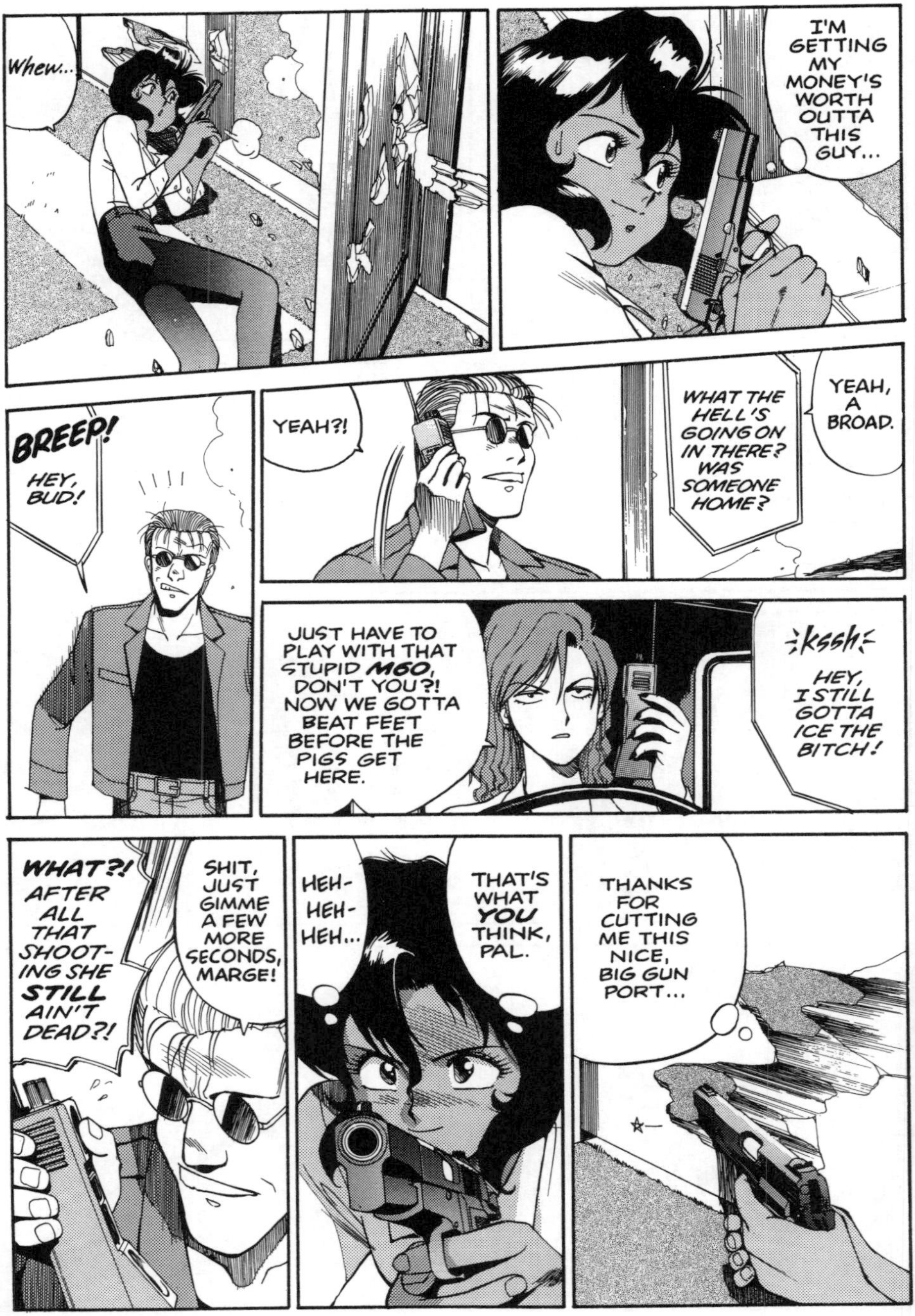
Whew...
I'M GETTING MY MONEY'S WORTH OUTTA THIS GUY...
BREEP!
HEY, BUD!
YEAH?!
WHAT THE HELL'S GOING ON IN THERE? WAS SOMEONE HOME?
YEAH, A BROAD.
JUST HAVE TO PLAY WITH THAT STUPID M60, DON'T YOU?! NOW WE GOTTA BEAT FEET BEFORE THE PIGS GET HERE.
kssh
HEY, I STILL GOTTA ICE THE BITCH!
WHAT?! AFTER ALL THAT SHOOT-ING SHE STILL AIN'T DEAD?!
SHIT, JUST GIMME A FEW MORE SECONDS, MARGE!
HEH-HEH-HEH...
THAT'S WHAT YOU THINK, PAL.
THANKS FOR CUTTING ME THIS NICE, BIG GUN PORT...

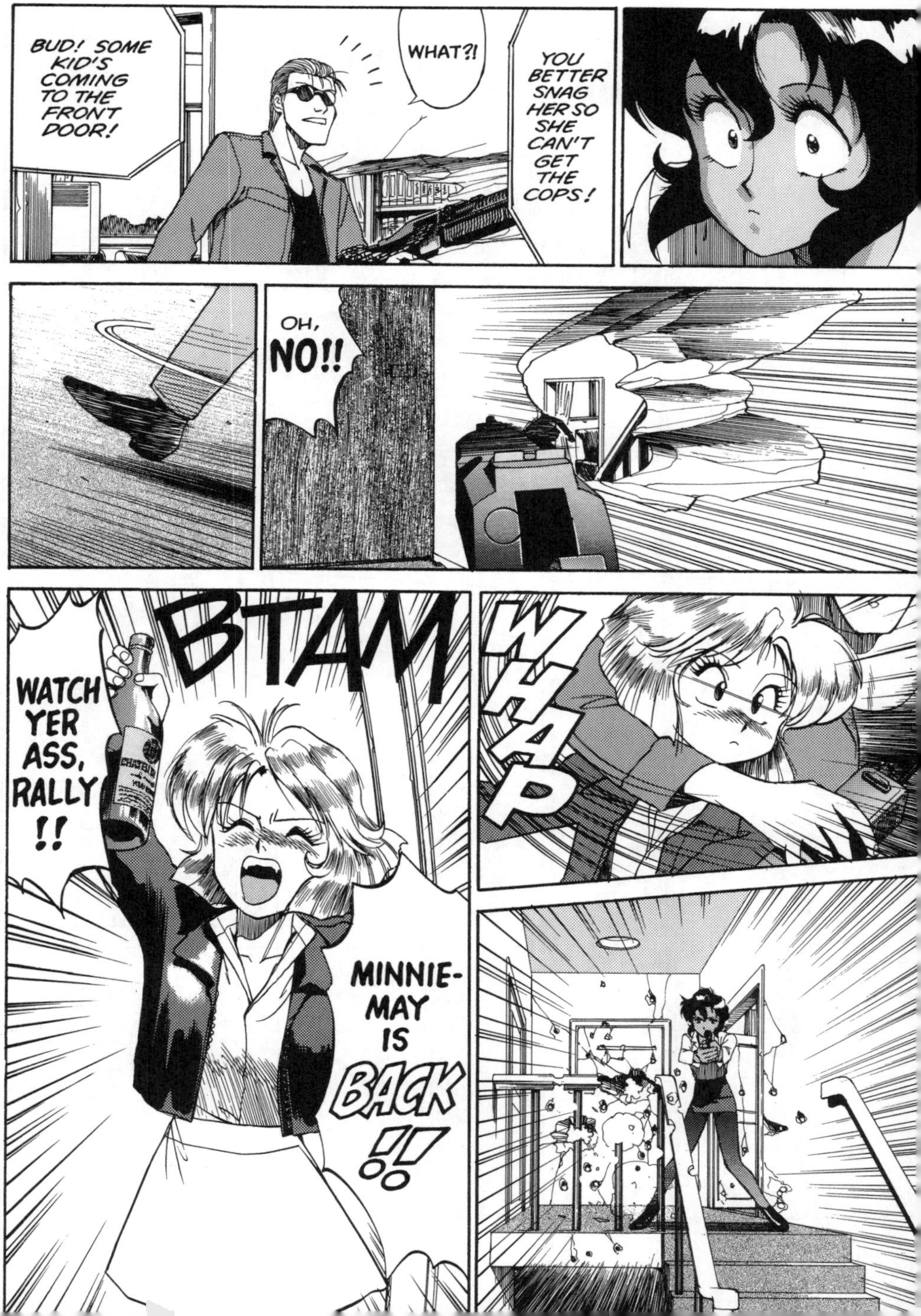
BUD! SOME KID'S COMING TO THE FRONT DOOR!
WHAT?!
YOU BETTER SNAG HER SO SHE CAN'T GET THE COPS!
OH, NO!!
BTAM
WATCH YER ASS, RALLY!!
MINNIE-MAY IS BACK!!
WHAP

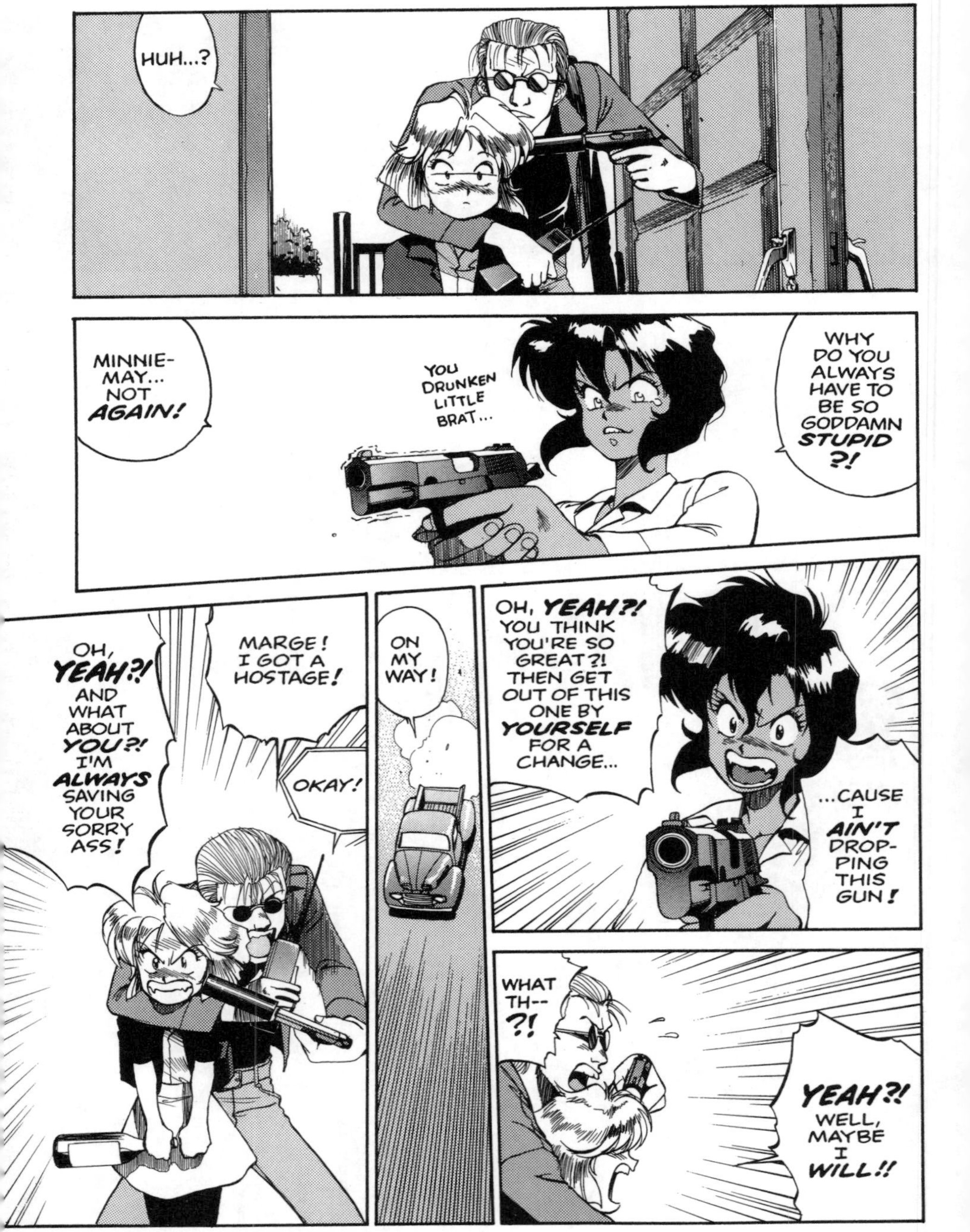
HUH...?
MINNIE-MAY... NOT AGAIN!
YOU DRUNKEN LITTLE BRAT...
WHY DO YOU ALWAYS HAVE TO BE SO GODDAMN STUPID?!
OH, YEAH?! AND WHAT ABOUT YOU?! I'M ALWAYS SAVING YOUR SORRY ASS!
MARGE! I GOT A HOSTAGE!
OKAY!
ON MY WAY!
OH, YEAH?! YOU THINK YOU'RE SO GREAT?! THEN GET OUT OF THIS ONE BY YOURSELF FOR A CHANGE...
...CAUSE I AIN'T DROPPING THIS GUN!
WHAT TH-- ?!
YEAH?! WELL, MAYBE I WILL!!

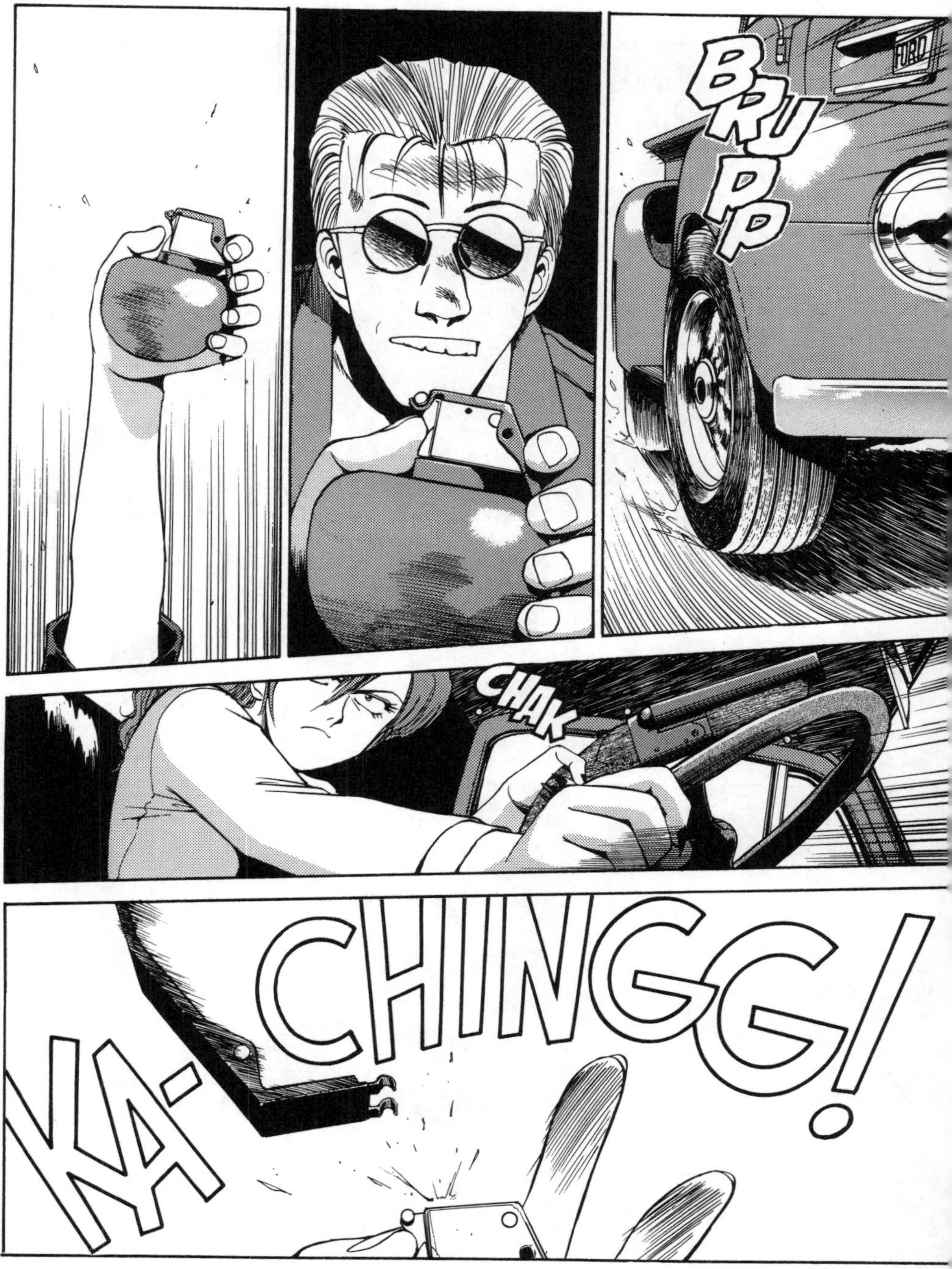
FORD
BRUPP
CHAK
KA-CHINGG!

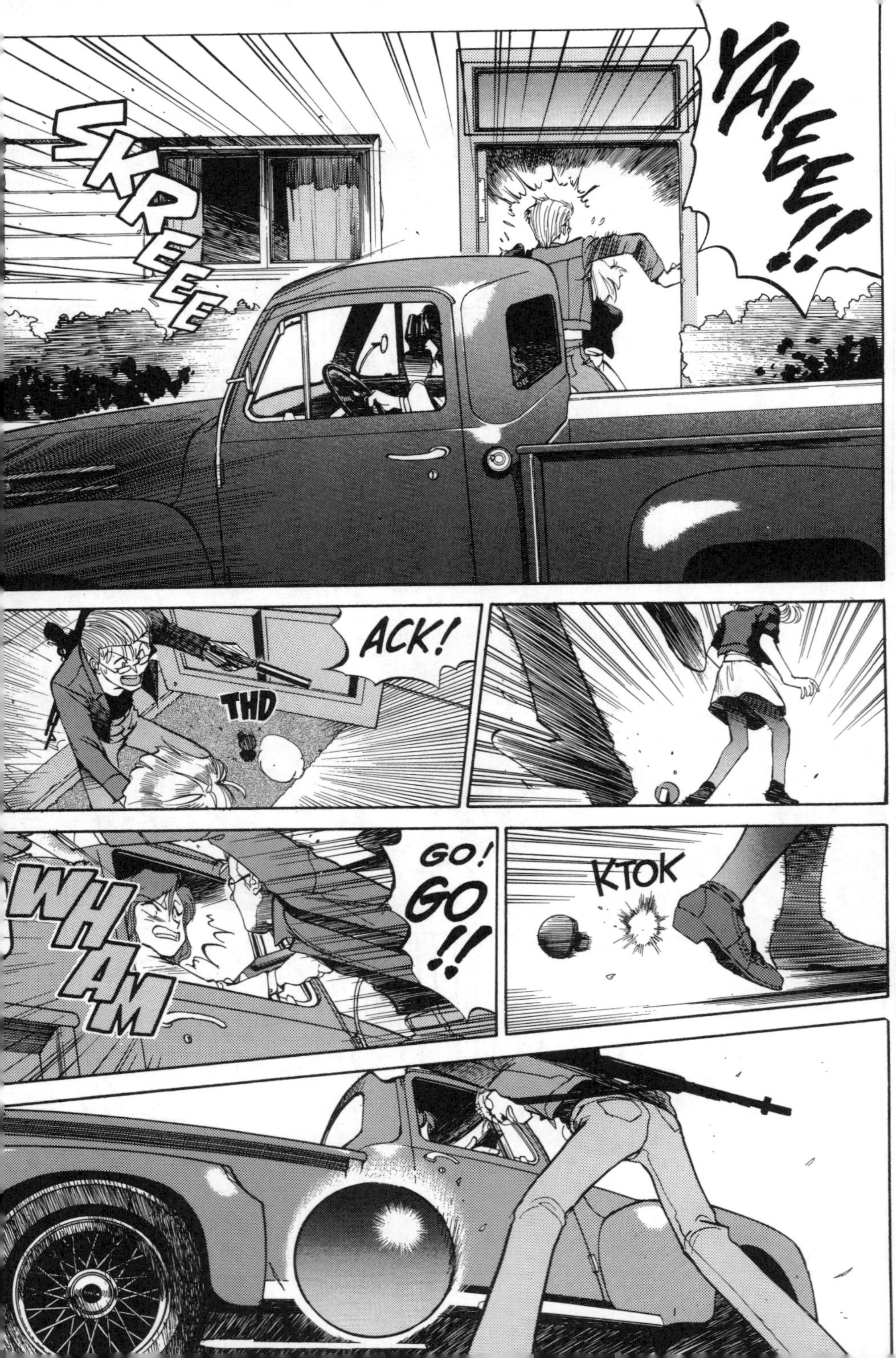
SKREEE
YAIEEE!!
ACK!
THD
WHAM
GO! GO!!
KTOK

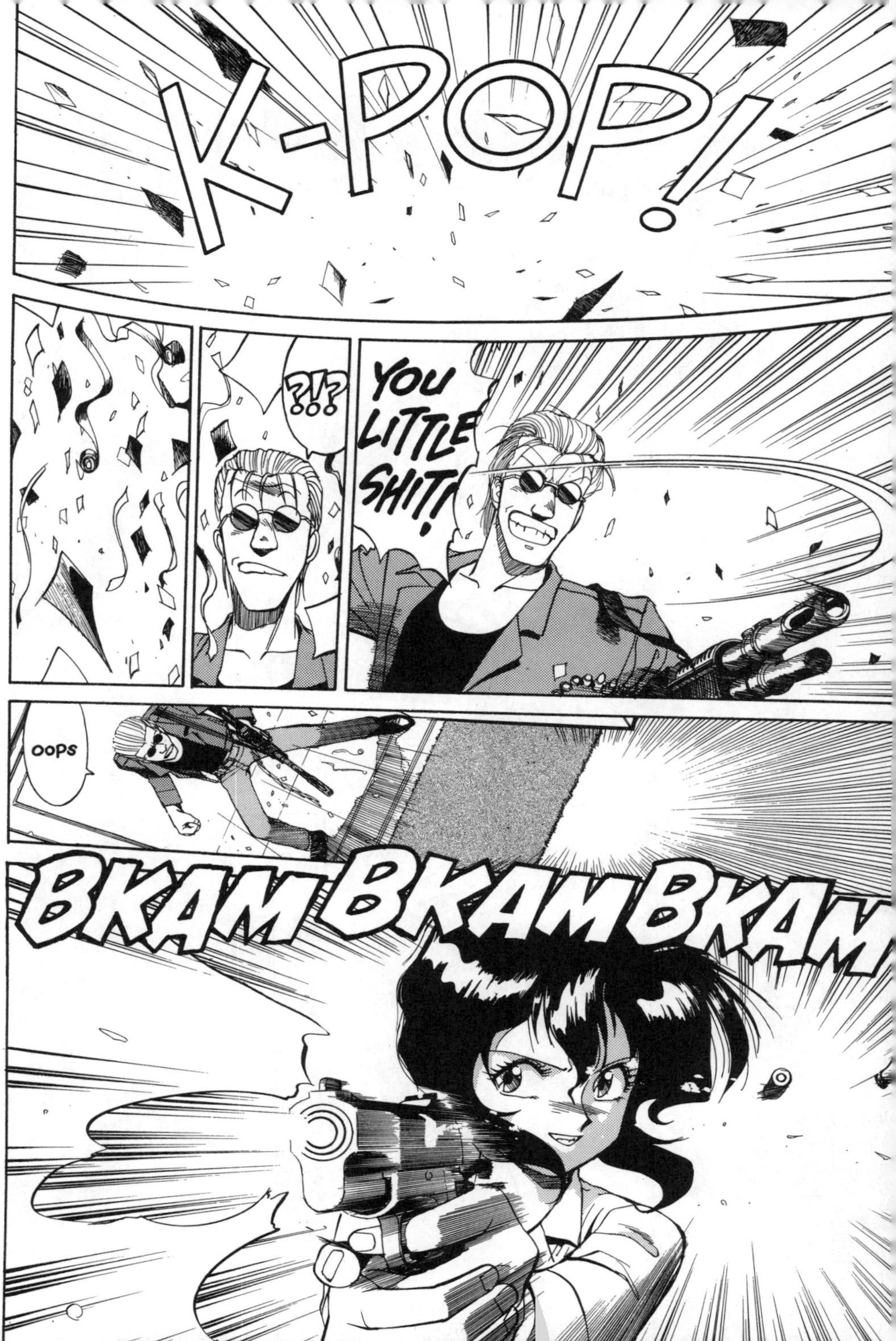
K-POP!
?!?
YOU LITTLE SHIT!
oops
BKAM BKAM BKAM

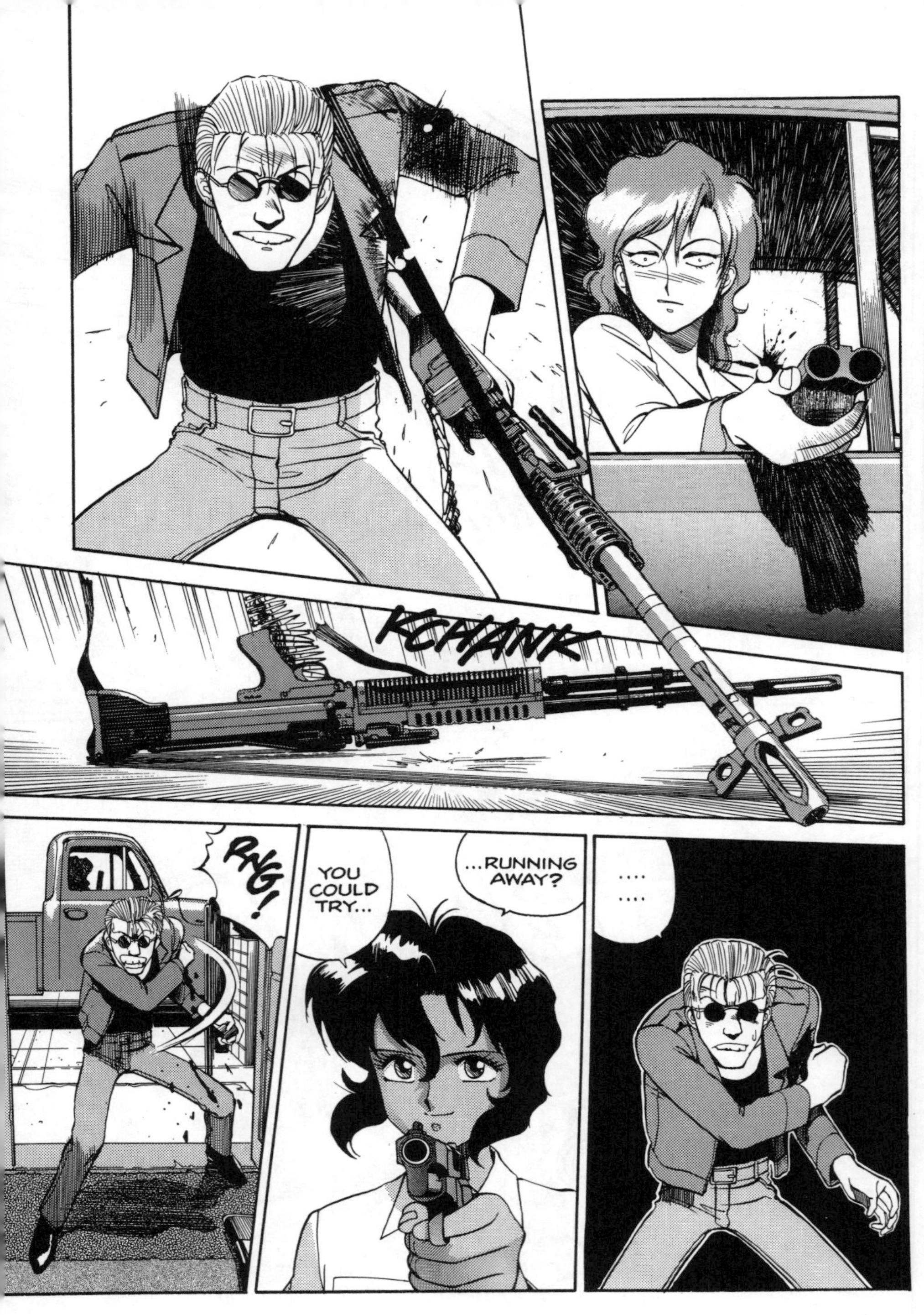
KCHANK
RNG!
YOU COULD TRY...
...RUNNING AWAY?
....
....

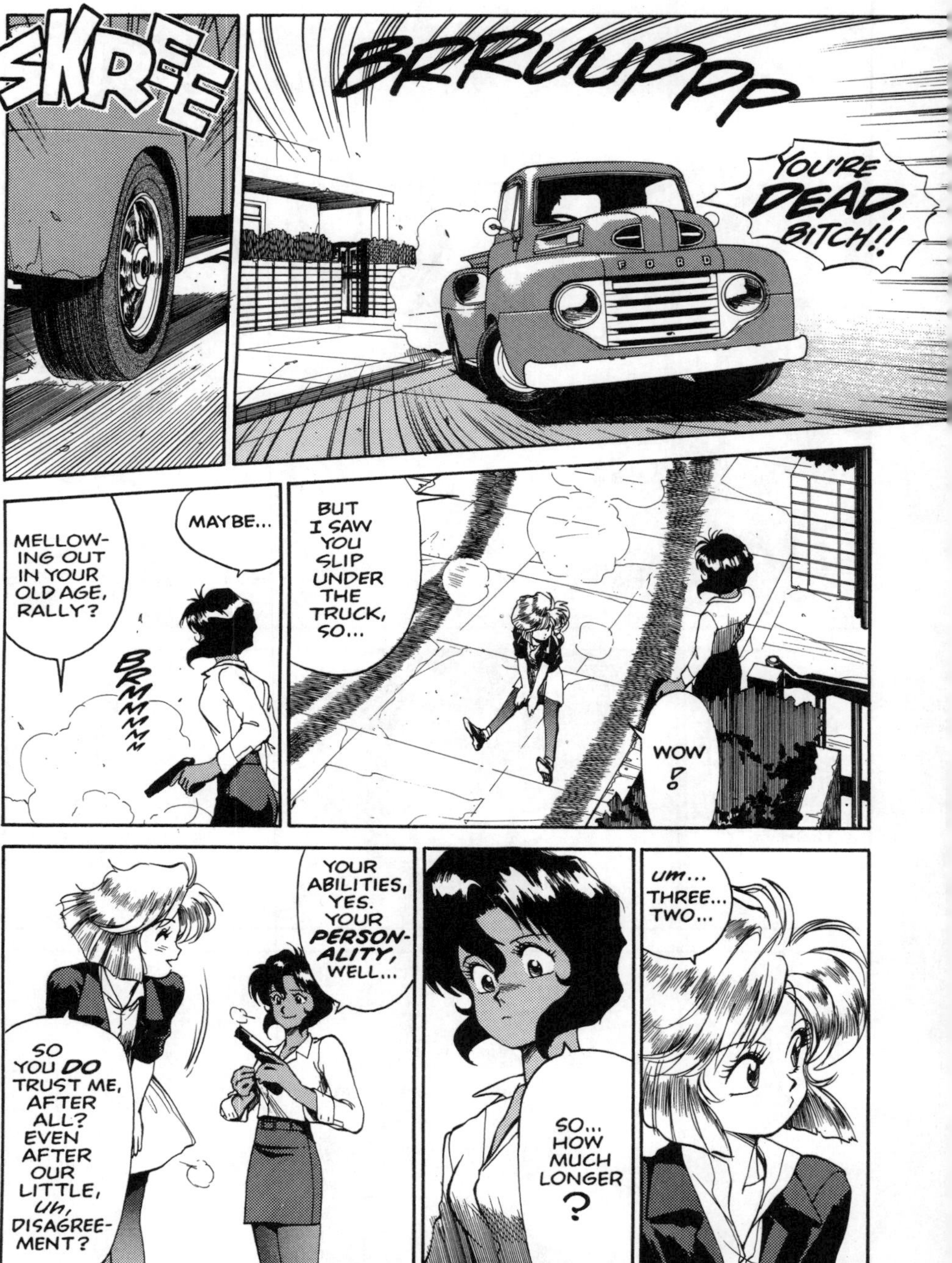
SKREEE
BRRUUPPP
YOU'RE DEAD, BITCH!!
FORD
MELLOWING OUT IN YOUR OLD AGE, RALLY?
MAYBE...
BRMMMM
BUT I SAW YOU SLIP UNDER THE TRUCK, SO...
WOW!
SO YOU DO TRUST ME, AFTER ALL? EVEN AFTER OUR LITTLE, uh, DISAGREEMENT?
YOUR ABILITIES, YES. YOUR PERSONALITY, WELL...
SO... HOW MUCH LONGER?
um... THREE... TWO...

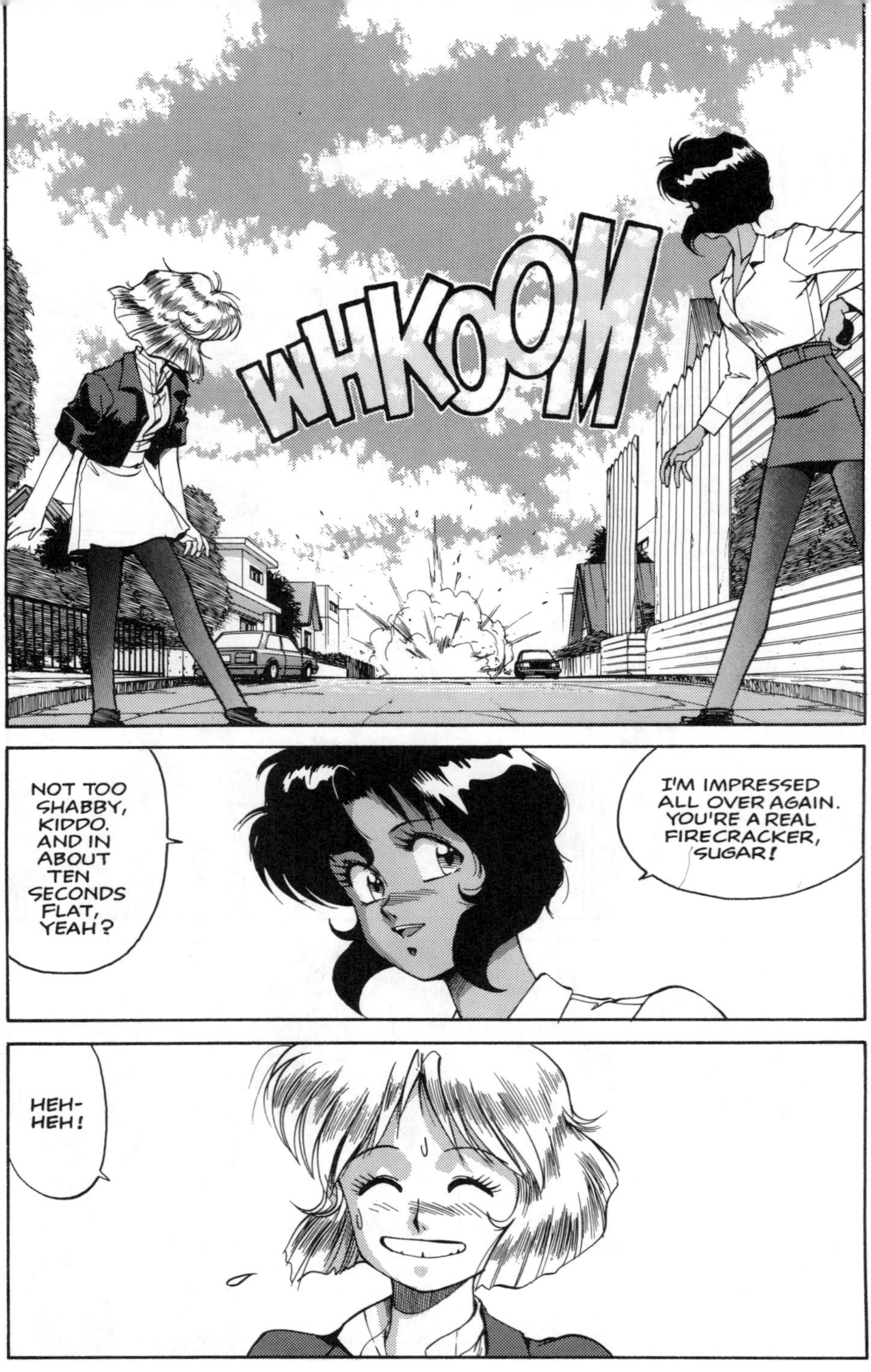
WHKOOM
NOT TOO SHABBY, KIDDO. AND IN ABOUT TEN SECONDS FLAT, YEAH?
I'M IMPRESSED ALL OVER AGAIN. YOU'RE A REAL FIRECRACKER, SUGAR!
HEH-HEH!

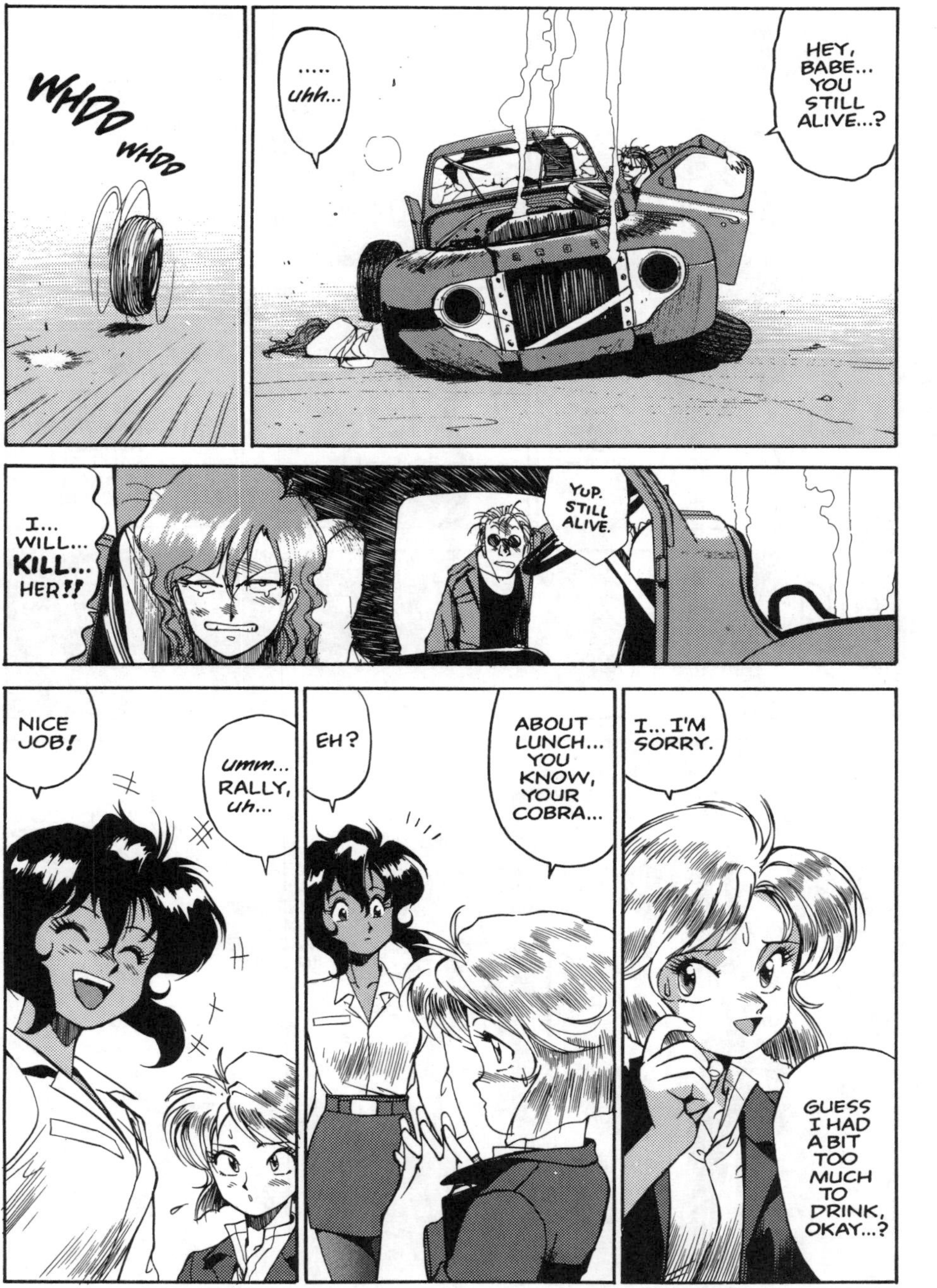
WHDO WHDO
..... uhh...
HEY, BABE... YOU STILL ALIVE...?
I... WILL... KILL... HER!!
YUP. STILL ALIVE.
NICE JOB!
umm... RALLY, uh...
EH?
ABOUT LUNCH... YOU KNOW, YOUR COBRA...
I... I'M SORRY.
GUESS I HAD A BIT TOO MUCH TO DRINK, OKAY...?

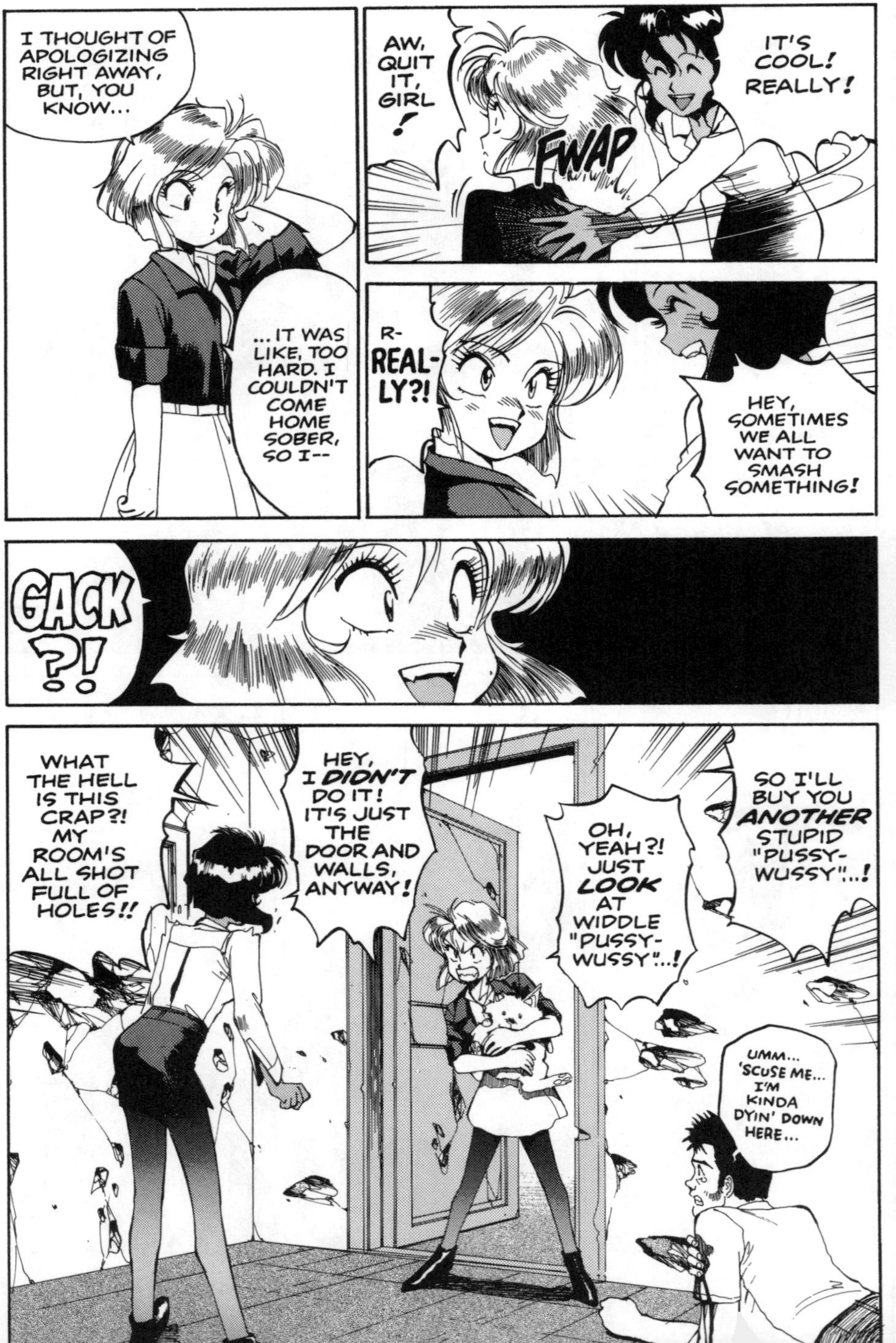
I THOUGHT OF APOLOGIZING RIGHT AWAY, BUT, YOU KNOW...
...IT WAS LIKE, TOO HARD. I COULDN'T COME HOME SOBER, SO I--
AW, QUIT IT, GIRL!
IT'S COOL! REALLY!
FWAP
R- REAL- LY?!
HEY, SOMETIMES WE ALL WANT TO SMASH SOMETHING!
GACK ?!
WHAT THE HELL IS THIS CRAP?! MY ROOM'S ALL SHOT FULL OF HOLES!!
HEY, I DIDN'T DO IT! IT'S JUST THE DOOR AND WALLS, ANYWAY!
OH, YEAH?! JUST LOOK AT WIDDLE "PUSSY-WUSSY"...!
SO I'LL BUY YOU ANOTHER STUPID "PUSSY-WUSSY"...!
UMM... 'SCUSE ME... I'M KINDA DYIN' DOWN HERE...

MUZZLE and EDGE

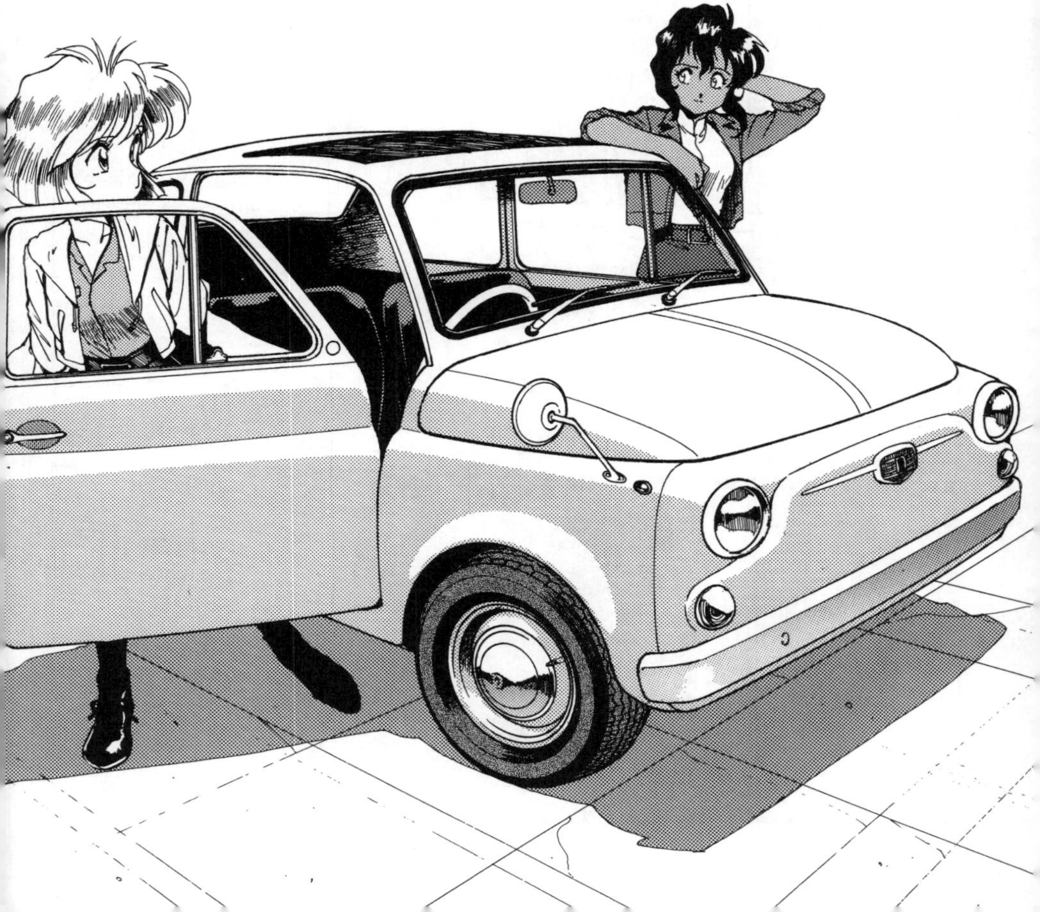

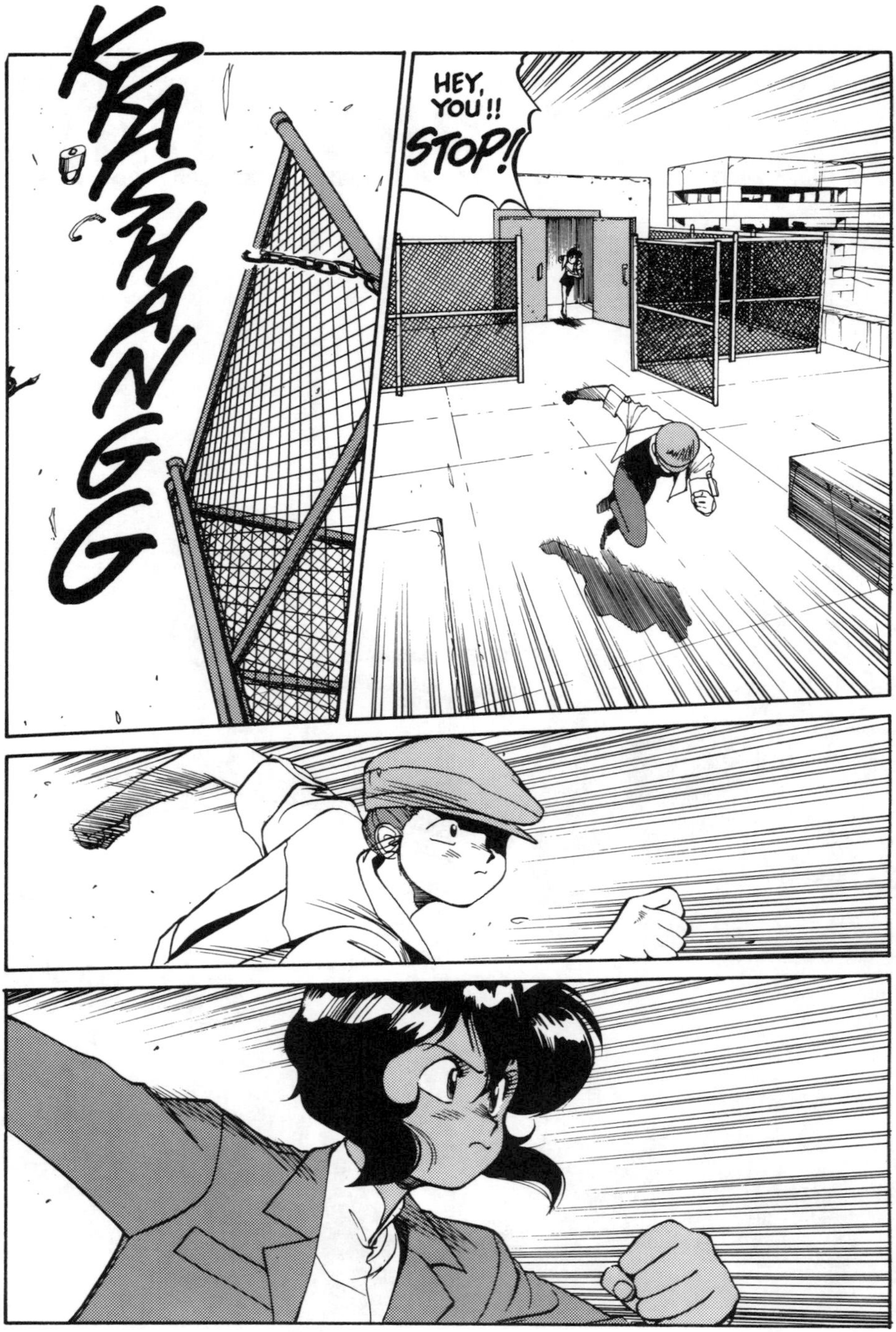
KRASHANGG
HEY, YOU!! STOP!!

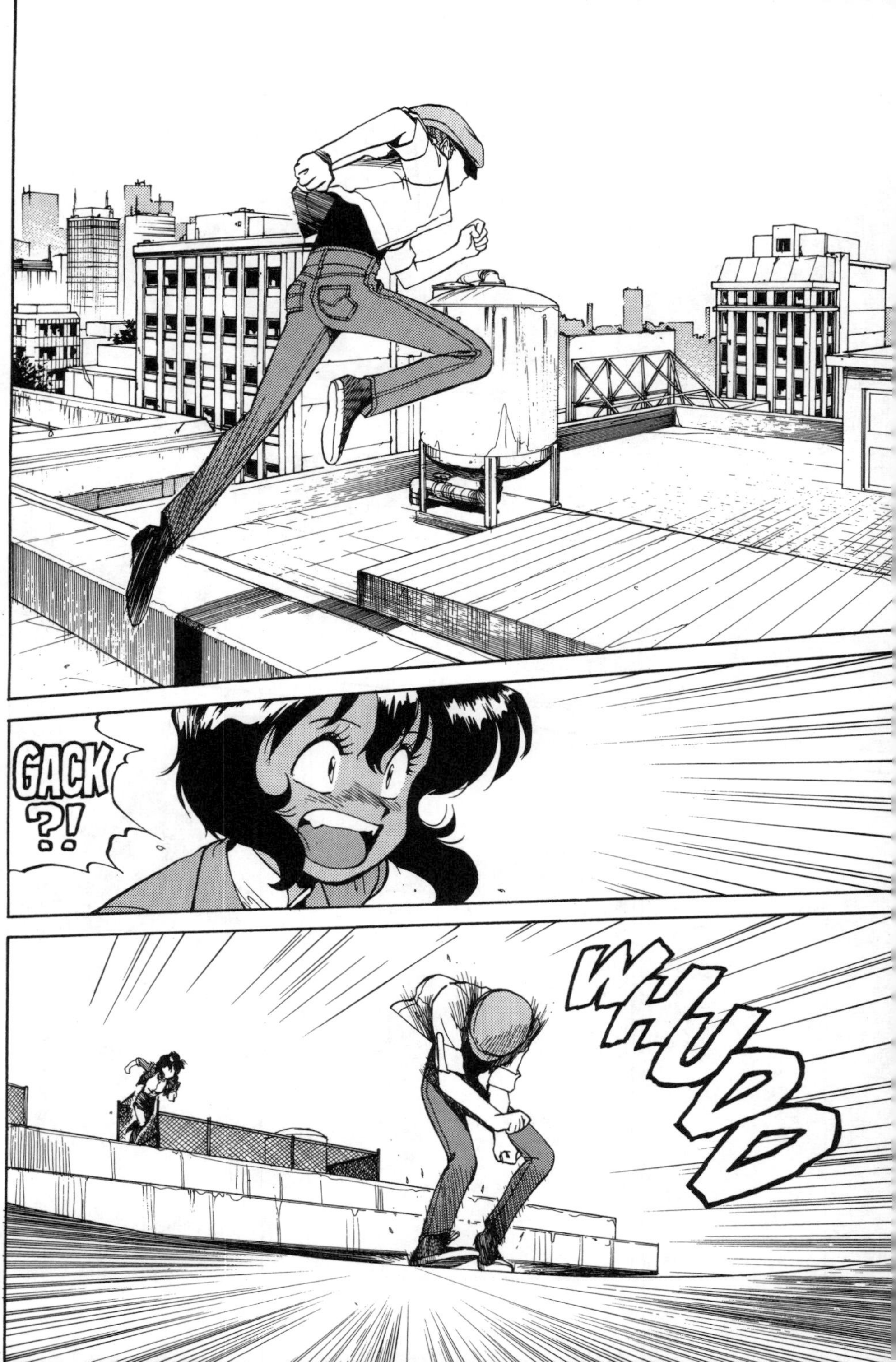
GACK ?!
WHUDD

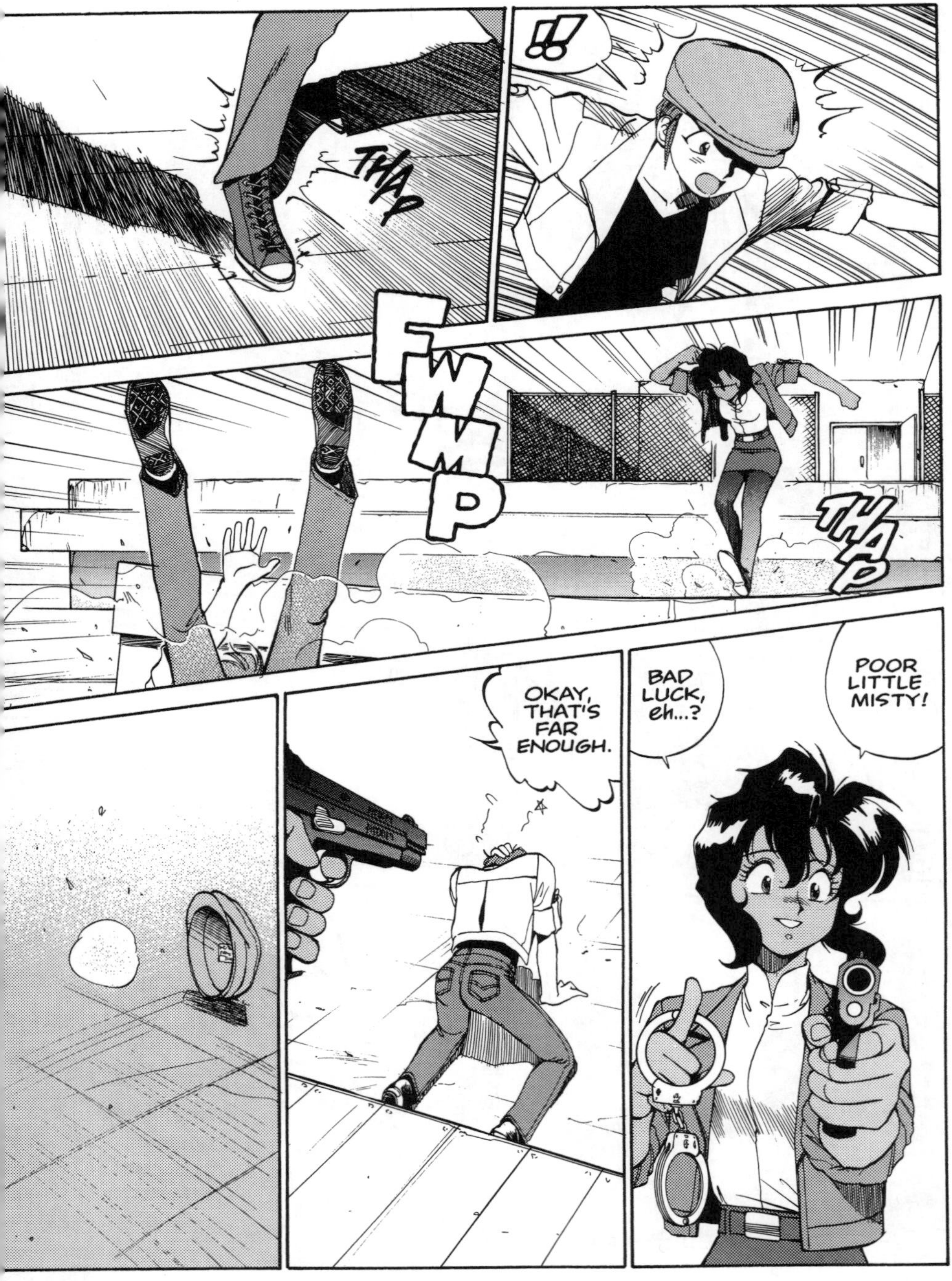
THAP
!!
FWMP
THAP
OKAY, THAT'S FAR ENOUGH.
BAD LUCK, eh...?
POOR LITTLE MISTY!

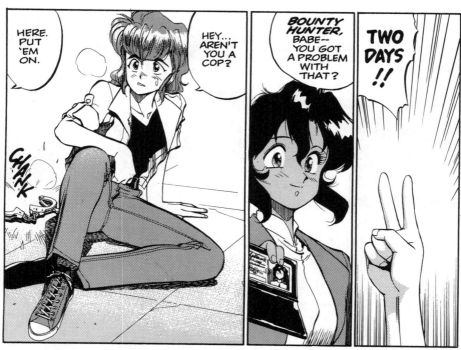

HERE. PUT 'EM ON.

HEY... AREN'T YOU A COP?

BOUNTY HUNTER, BABE-- YOU GOT A PROBLEM WITH THAT?

TWO DAYS !!

GHANK

HUH?

ALL YOU HAVE TO DO IS DELIVER ME BY YOUR DEADLINE, RIGHT? SO JUST WAIT *TWO DAYS!*

THE GUY WHO DID IT IS STILL OUT THERE! I DIDN'T DO THIS ONE, I *SWEAR!!*

LOOK-- I KNOW WHO *REALLY* DID IT. JUST GIMME 48 HOURS, AND I CAN NAIL HIM !!

YEAH, SURE YOU COULD. *NOW GET THOSE BRACELETS ON!!*

CHAK

....
....

BREEP!!

HI, MINNIE-MAY HERE! ♡

WHA--?! PULL UP NEXT DOOR?

YOU JUMPED BETWEEN THE BUILD-INGS?!

ARE YOU *NUTS?!*

GEEZ, ANY-THING FOR A BUCK...

'BOUT 8 FEET, I'D SAY...

LOOK, MISTY, THIS DOESN'T MAKE SENSE. YOU HAVE A LAWYER...HE'S ALREADY CALLED IN YOUR BAIL BOND. AFTER A BIT OF PAPERWORK, YOU CAN WALK.

YOU'D BE BACK ON THE STREET IN TWO HOURS-- SO WHY DIDN'T YOU GO TO HIM?

ARE YOU CRAZY?! HILLS IS THE *MAN!!*

HE'S THE ONE WHO SET ME UP!!

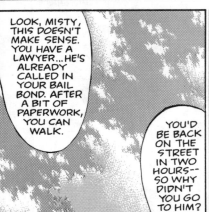

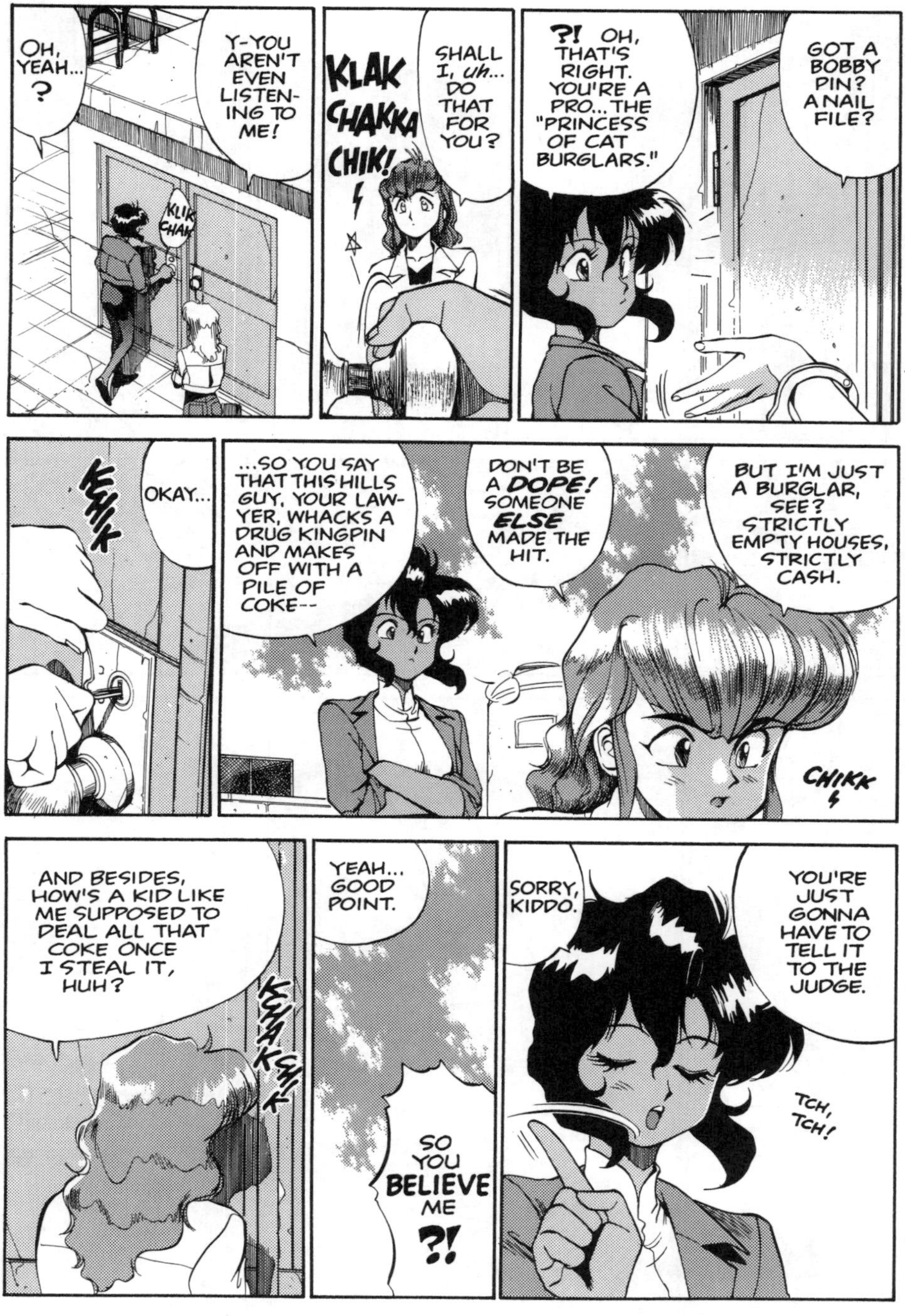
OH, YEAH... ?
Y-YOU AREN'T EVEN LISTENING TO ME!
KLIK CHAK
KLAK CHAKKA CHIK!
SHALL I, *uh*... DO THAT FOR YOU?
?! OH, THAT'S RIGHT. YOU'RE A PRO... THE "PRINCESS OF CAT BURGLARS."
GOT A BOBBY PIN? A NAIL FILE?
KCHIK
OKAY...
...SO YOU SAY THAT THIS HILLS GUY, YOUR LAWYER, WHACKS A DRUG KINGPIN AND MAKES OFF WITH A PILE OF COKE--
DON'T BE A **DOPE!** SOMEONE **ELSE** MADE THE HIT.
BUT I'M JUST A BURGLAR, SEE? STRICTLY EMPTY HOUSES, STRICTLY CASH.
CHIKK
AND BESIDES, HOW'S A KID LIKE ME SUPPOSED TO DEAL ALL THAT COKE ONCE I STEAL IT, HUH?
KCHAKCHIK
YEAH... GOOD POINT.
SO YOU **BELIEVE** ME ?!
SORRY, KIDDO.
YOU'RE JUST GONNA HAVE TO TELL IT TO THE JUDGE.
TCH, TCH!

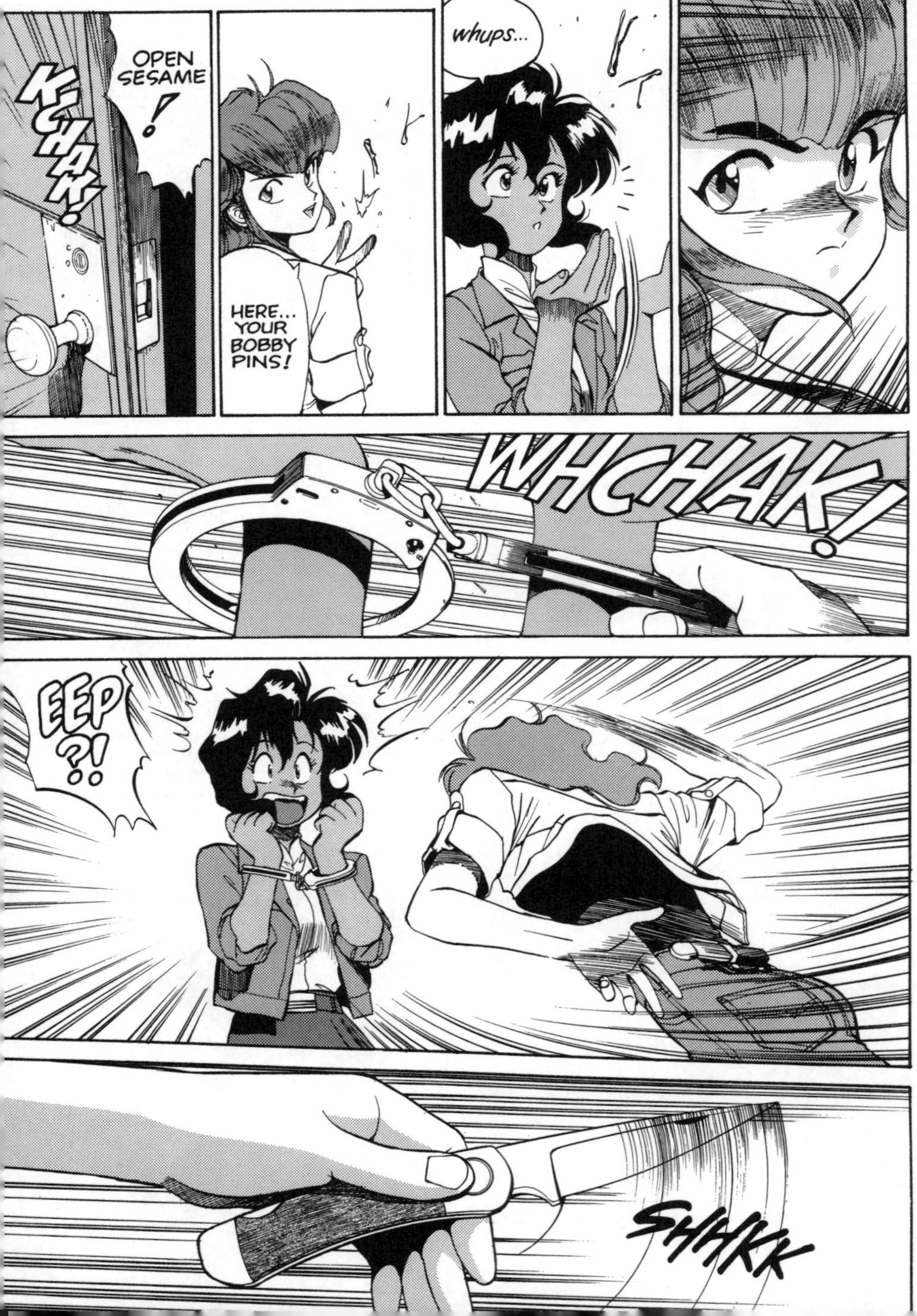
K-CHAK!
OPEN SESAME!
HERE... YOUR BOBBY PINS!
whups...
WHCHAK!
EEP ?!
SHHKK

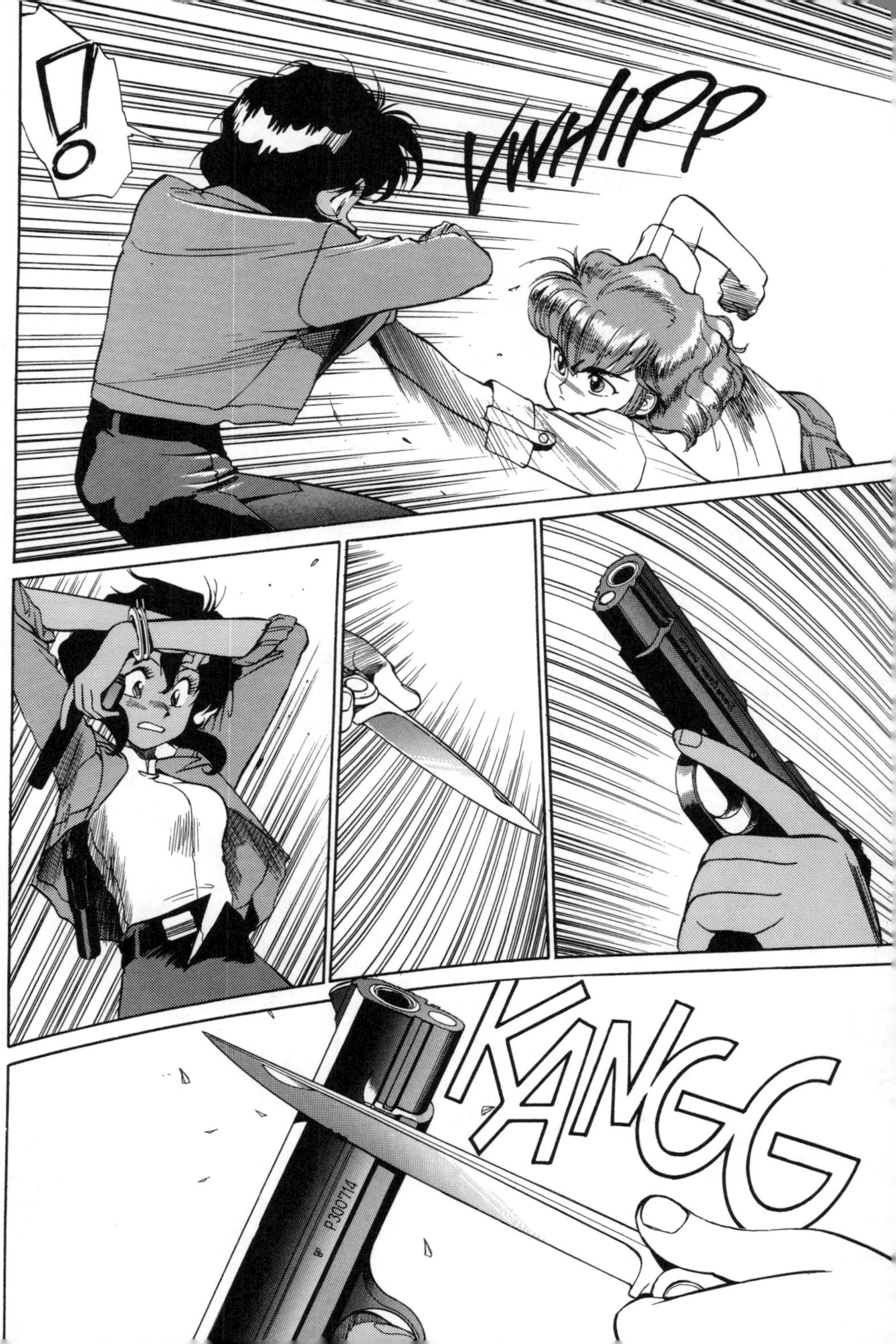
!
VWHIPP
KANGG
P300714

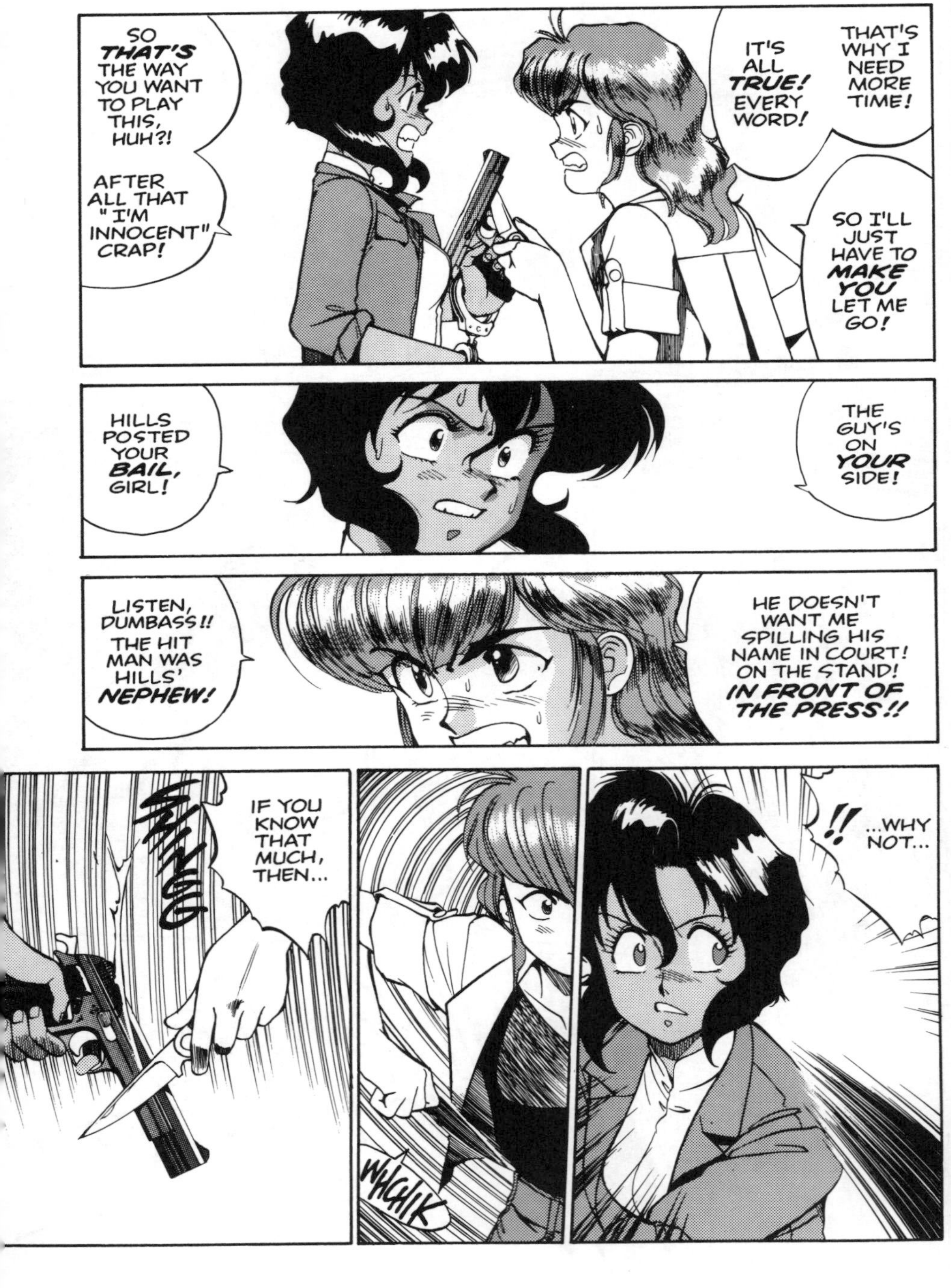
SO THAT'S THE WAY YOU WANT TO PLAY THIS, HUH?!
AFTER ALL THAT "I'M INNOCENT" CRAP!
IT'S ALL TRUE! EVERY WORD!
THAT'S WHY I NEED MORE TIME!
SO I'LL JUST HAVE TO MAKE YOU LET ME GO!
HILLS POSTED YOUR BAIL, GIRL!
THE GUY'S ON YOUR SIDE!
LISTEN, DUMBASS!! THE HIT MAN WAS HILLS' NEPHEW!
HE DOESN'T WANT ME SPILLING HIS NAME IN COURT! ON THE STAND! IN FRONT OF THE PRESS!!
SHINGG
IF YOU KNOW THAT MUCH, THEN...
WHCHIK
!!
...WHY NOT...

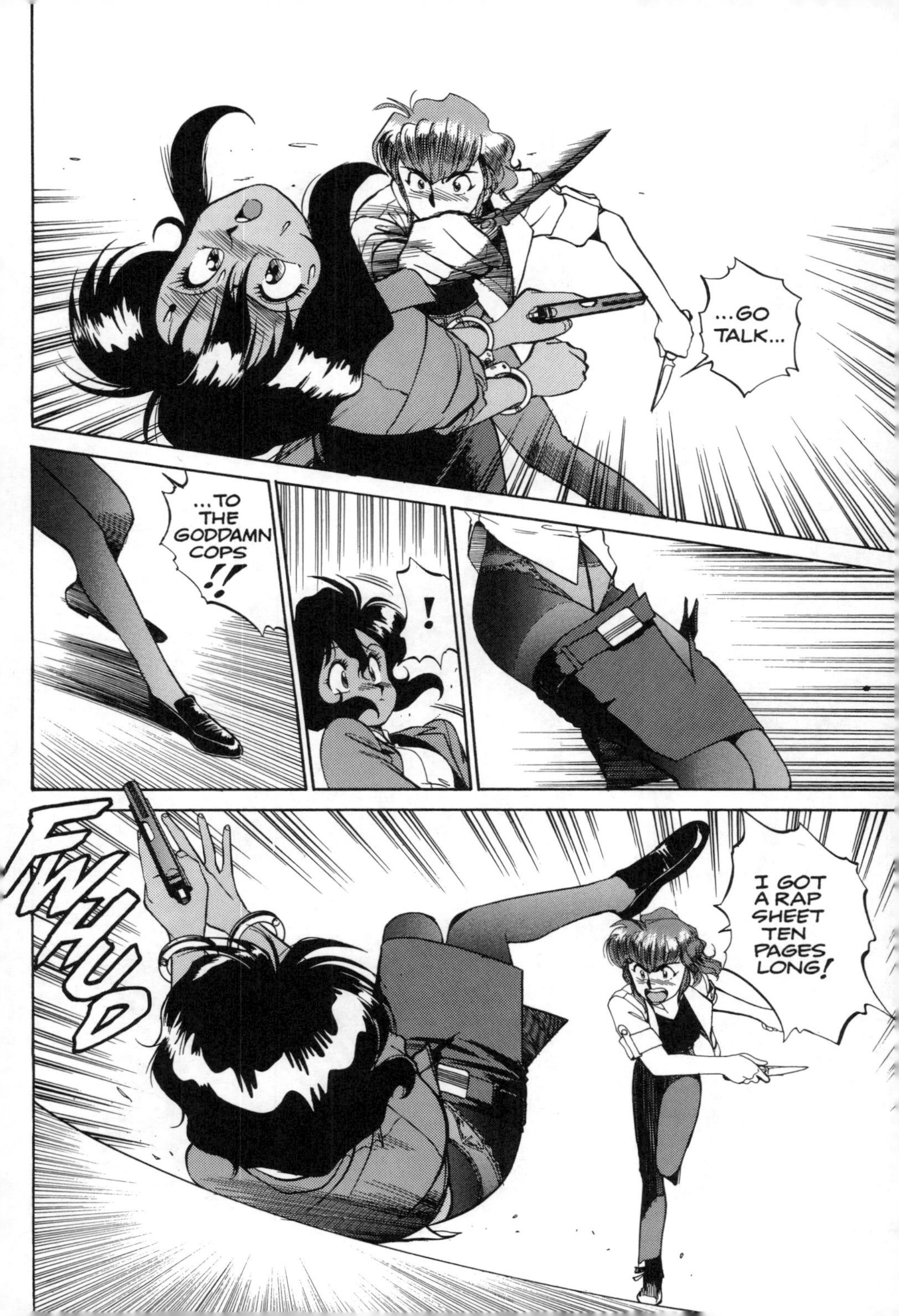
...GO TALK...
...TO THE GODDAMN COPS!!
!
FWHUD
I GOT A RAP SHEET TEN PAGES LONG!

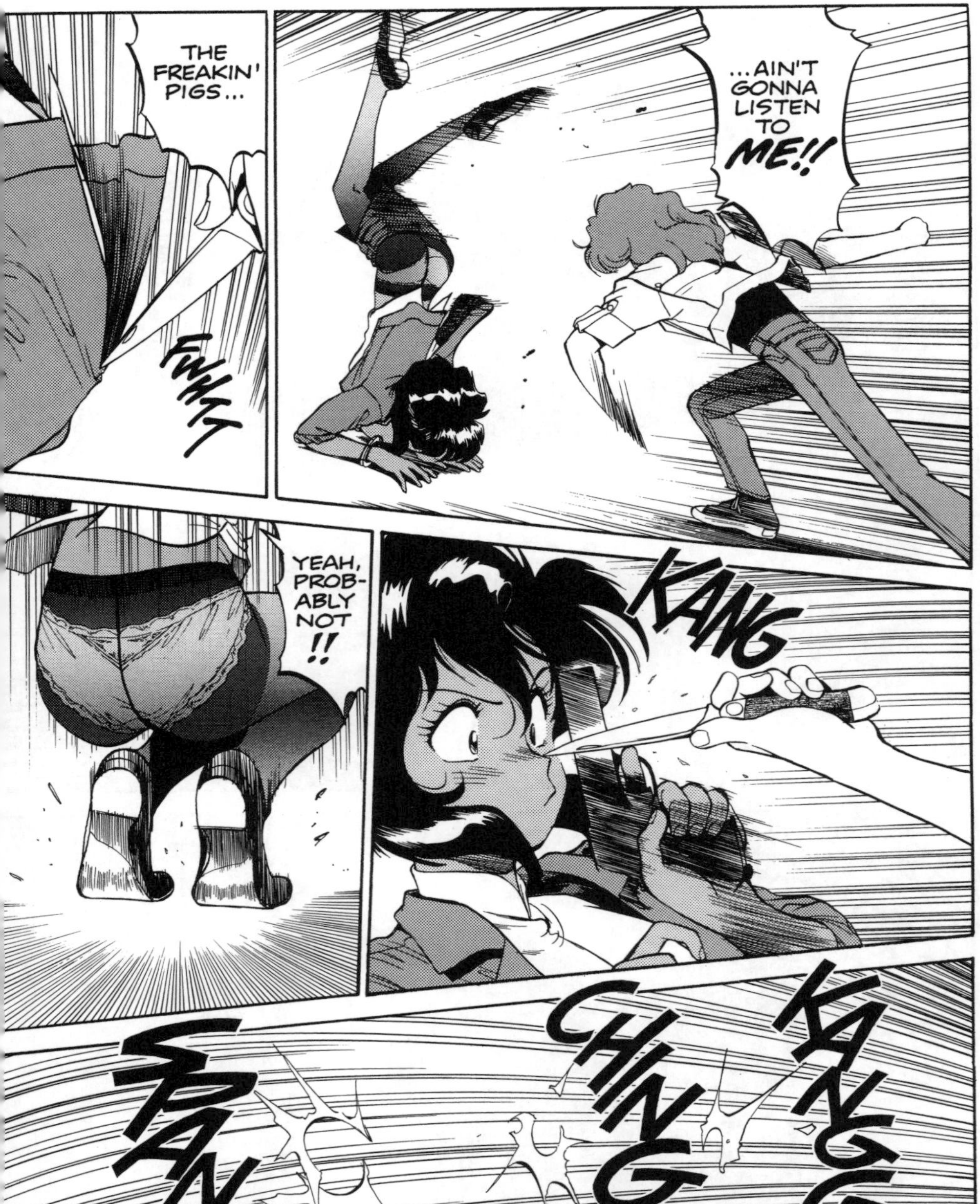
THE FREAKIN' PIGS...
FWHTT
...AIN'T GONNA LISTEN TO ME!!
YEAH, PROBABLY NOT!!
KANG
SPANG
CHING
KANG

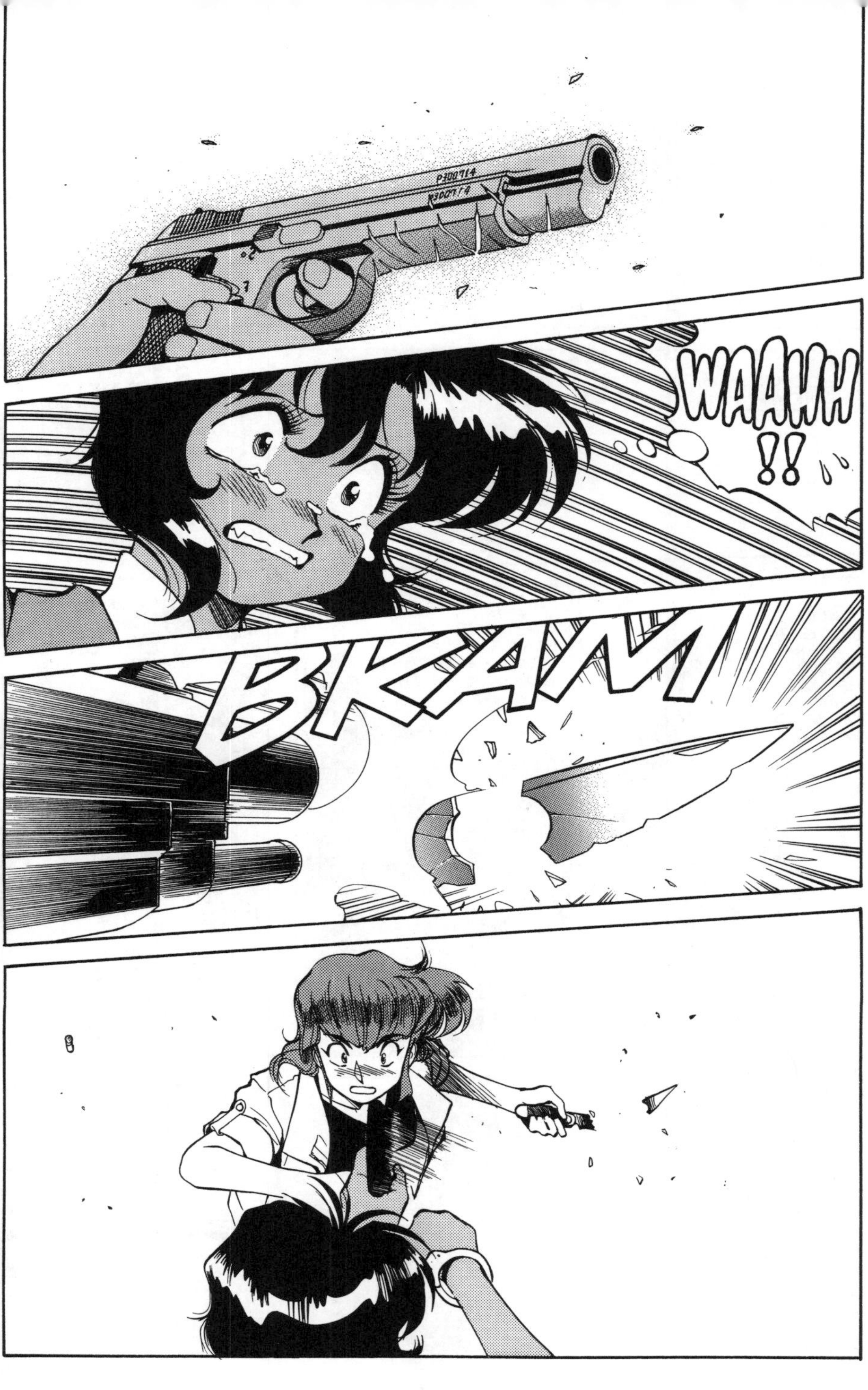
WAAHH !!
BKAM

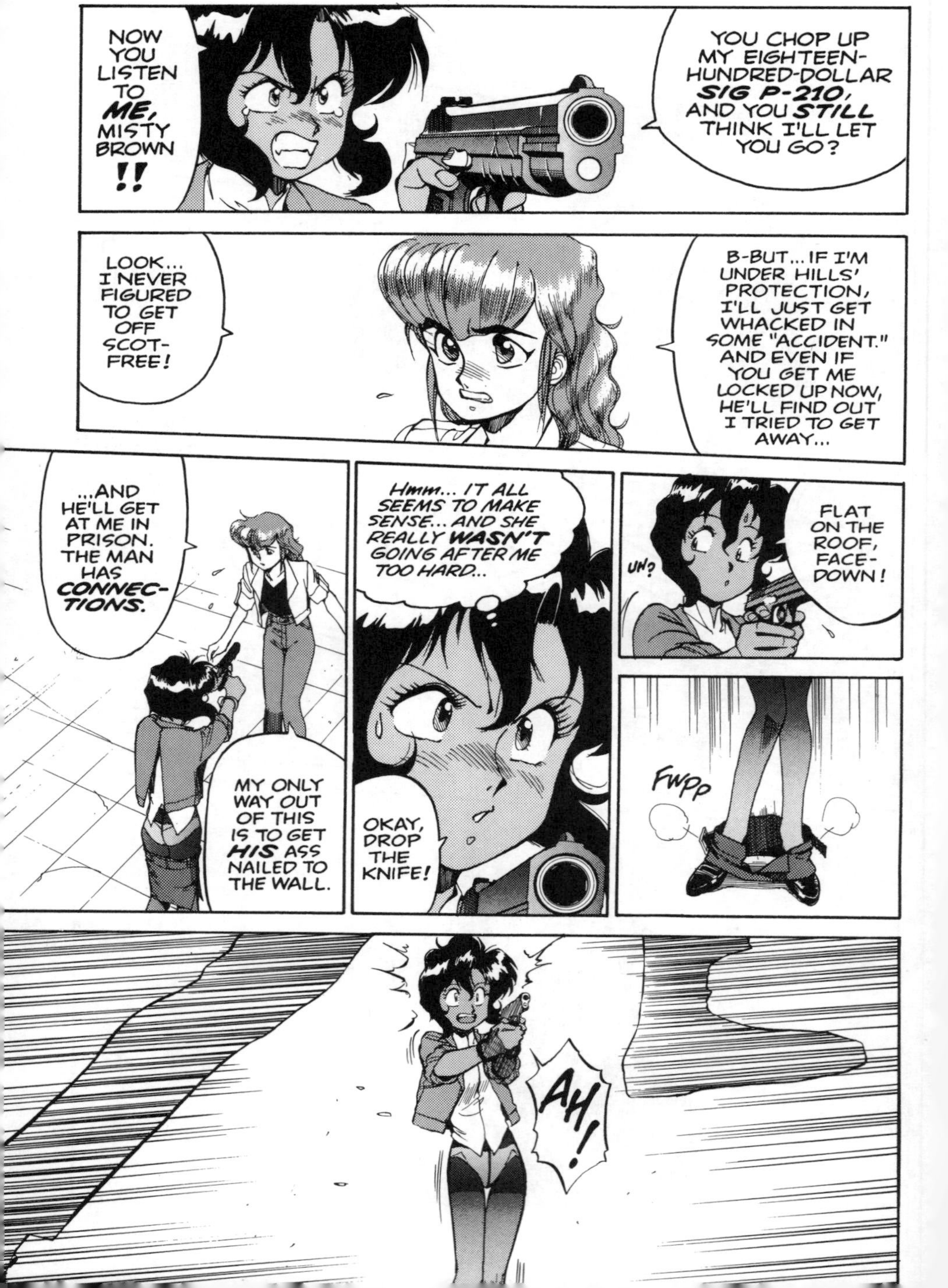
NOW YOU LISTEN TO ME, MISTY BROWN!!
YOU CHOP UP MY EIGHTEEN-HUNDRED-DOLLAR SIG P-210, AND YOU STILL THINK I'LL LET YOU GO?
LOOK... I NEVER FIGURED TO GET OFF SCOT-FREE!
B-BUT... IF I'M UNDER HILLS' PROTECTION, I'LL JUST GET WHACKED IN SOME "ACCIDENT." AND EVEN IF YOU GET ME LOCKED UP NOW, HE'LL FIND OUT I TRIED TO GET AWAY...
...AND HE'LL GET AT ME IN PRISON. THE MAN HAS CONNECTIONS.
MY ONLY WAY OUT OF THIS IS TO GET HIS ASS NAILED TO THE WALL.
Hmm... IT ALL SEEMS TO MAKE SENSE... AND SHE REALLY WASN'T GOING AFTER ME TOO HARD...
OKAY, DROP THE KNIFE!
UH?
FLAT ON THE ROOF, FACE-DOWN!
FWPP
AH!

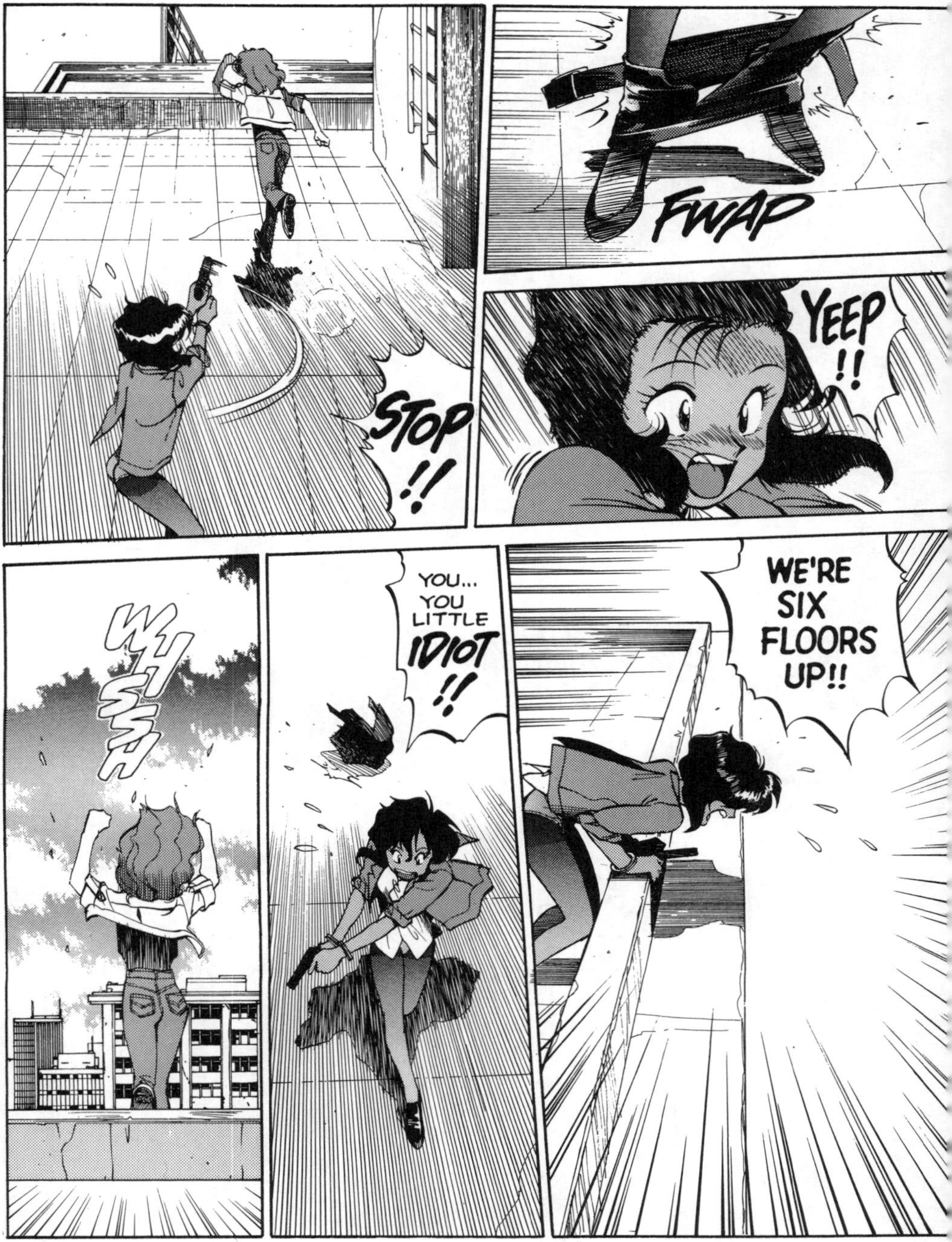
STOP !!
FWAP
YEEP !!
WHSSH
YOU... YOU LITTLE IDIOT !!
WE'RE SIX FLOORS UP!!

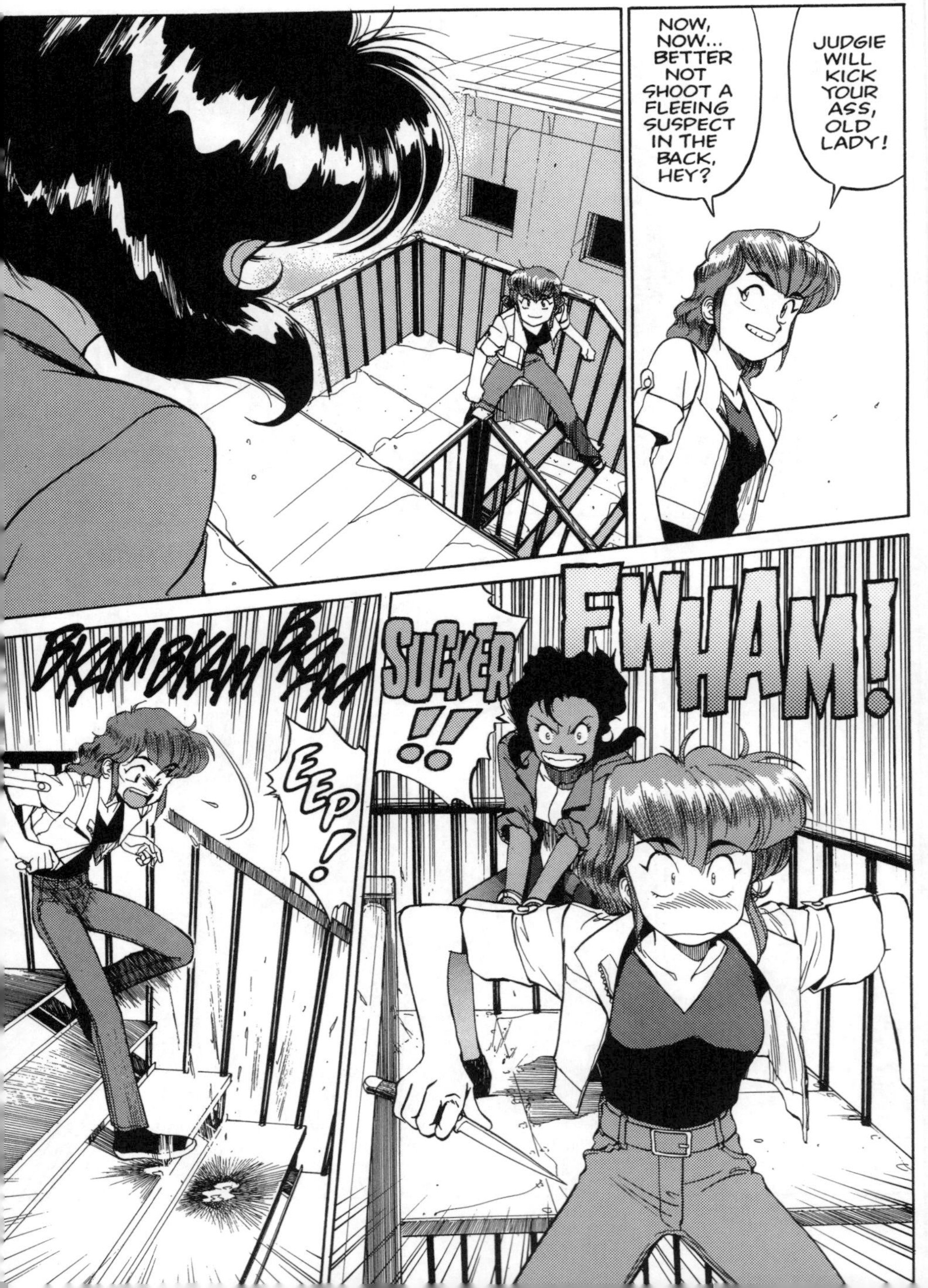
NOW, NOW... BETTER NOT SHOOT A FLEEING SUSPECT IN THE BACK, HEY?
JUDGIE WILL KICK YOUR ASS, OLD LADY!
BKAM BKAM BKAM
EEP!
SUCKER !!
FWHAM!

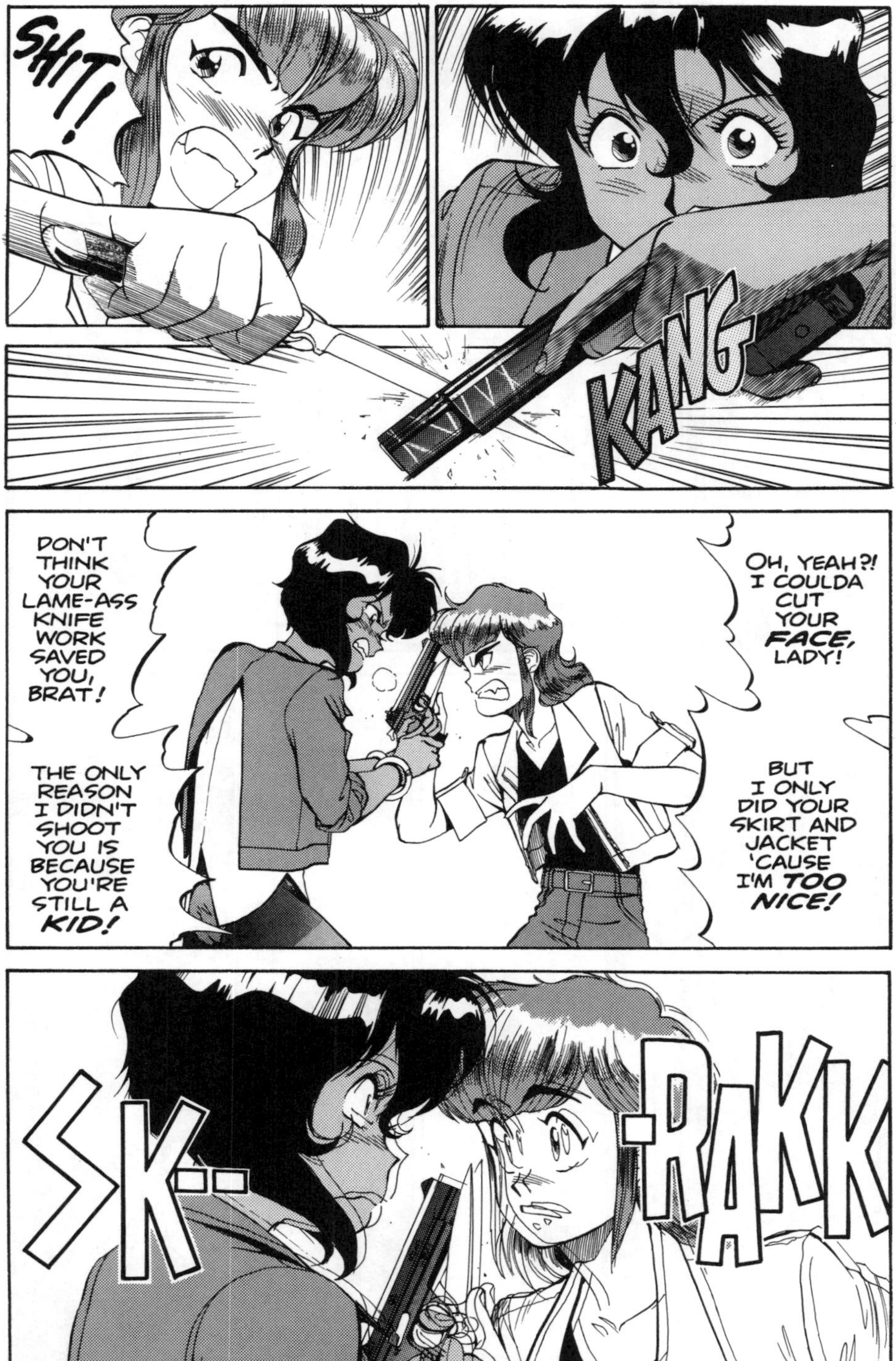
SHIT!!
KANG
DON'T THINK YOUR LAME-ASS KNIFE WORK SAVED YOU, BRAT!
THE ONLY REASON I DIDN'T SHOOT YOU IS BECAUSE YOU'RE STILL A KID!
OH, YEAH?! I COULDA CUT YOUR FACE, LADY!
BUT I ONLY DID YOUR SKIRT AND JACKET 'CAUSE I'M TOO NICE!
SK...-RAKK

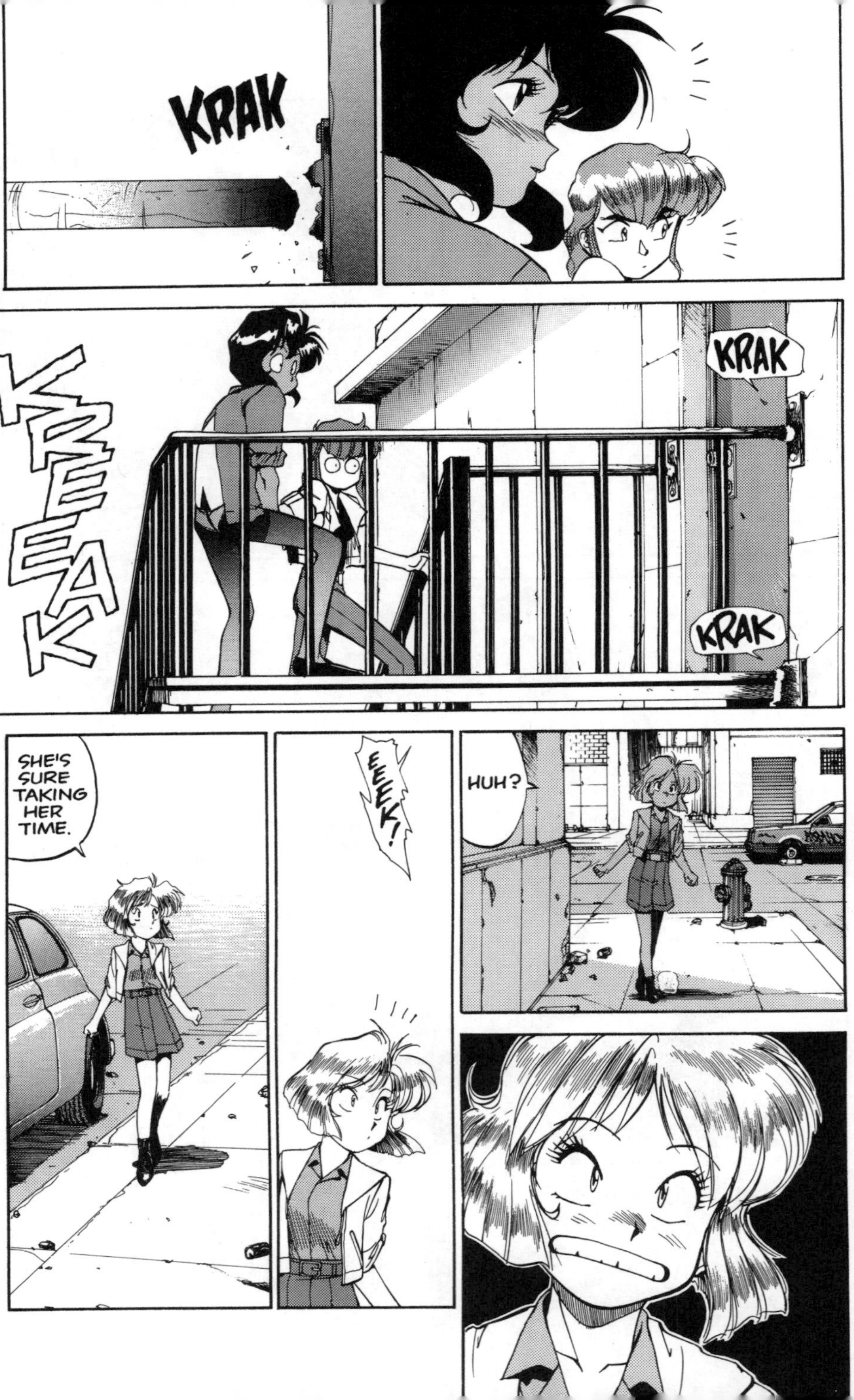
KRAK
KREEAK
KRAK
KRAK
SHE'S SURE TAKING HER TIME.
EEEEK!
HUH?

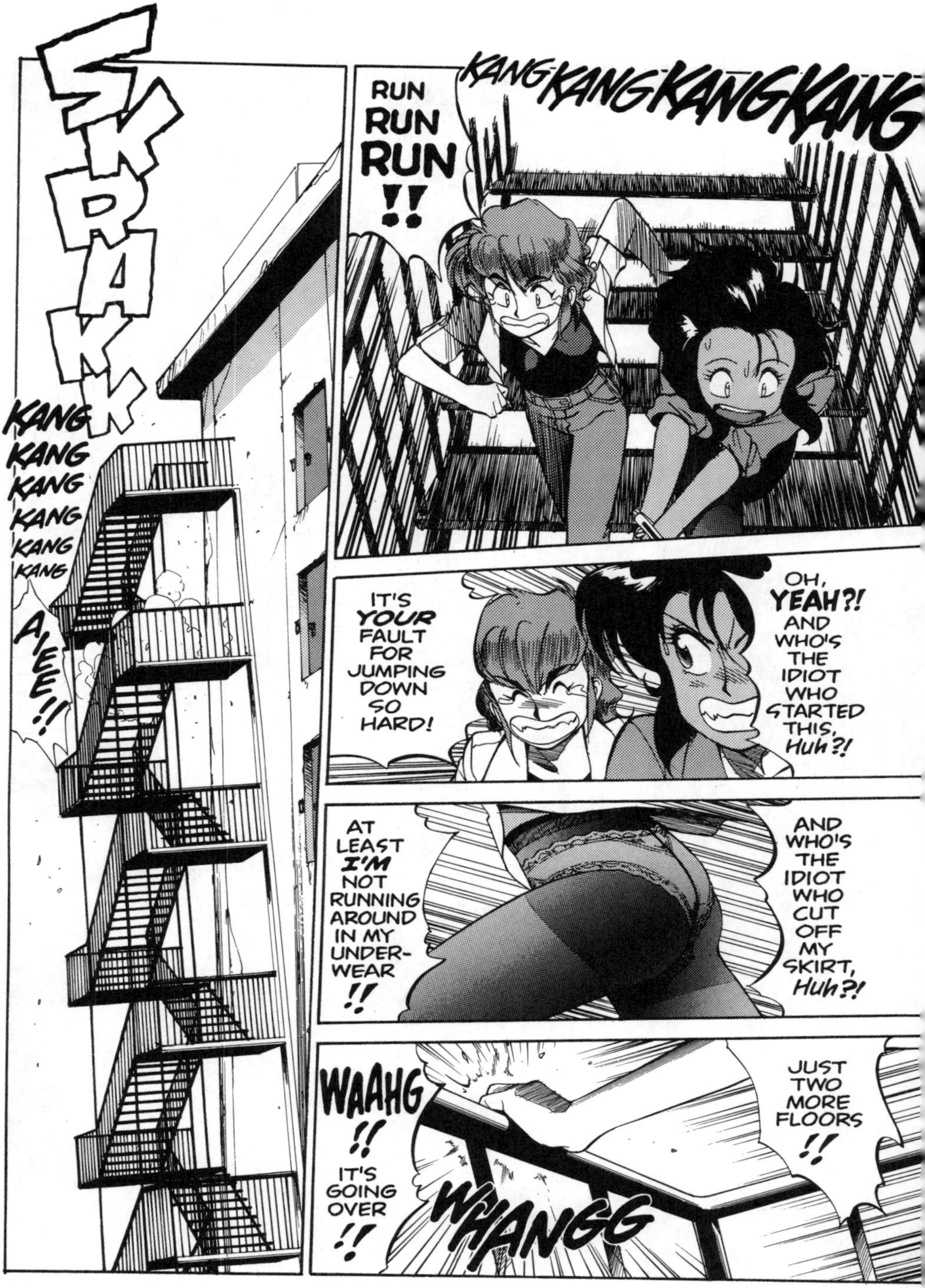
SKRAKK
KANG KANG KANG KANG KANG KANG
AIEEE!!
KANG-KANG-KANG-KANG-KANG
RUN RUN RUN!!
IT'S YOUR FAULT FOR JUMPING DOWN SO HARD!
OH, YEAH?! AND WHO'S THE IDIOT WHO STARTED THIS, HUH?!
AT LEAST I'M NOT RUNNING AROUND IN MY UNDER-WEAR!!
AND WHO'S THE IDIOT WHO CUT OFF MY SKIRT, HUH?!
WAAHG!!
IT'S GOING OVER!!
WHANGG
JUST TWO MORE FLOORS!!

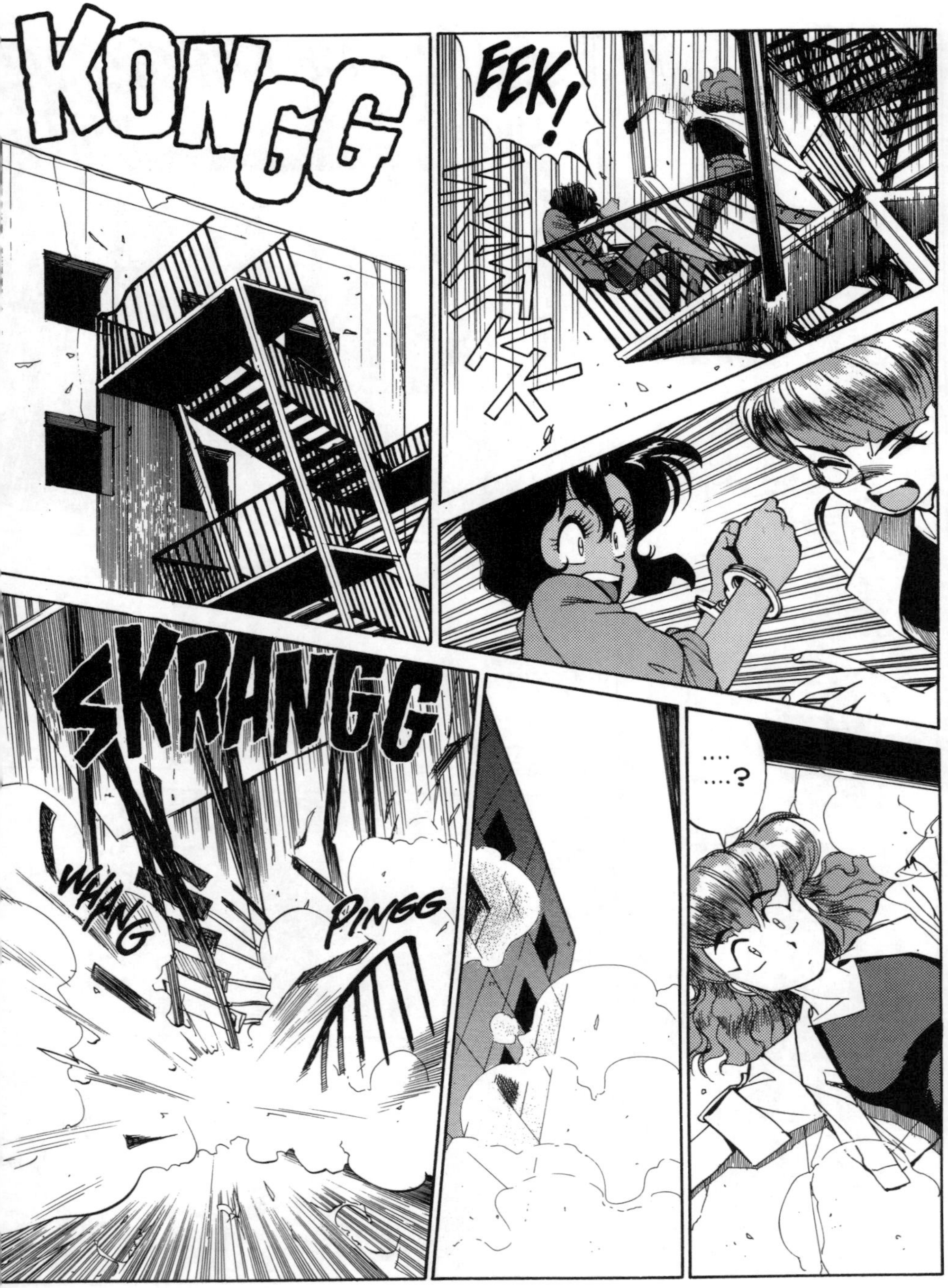
KONGG
EEK!
SKRANGG
WHANG
PINGG
....
....?

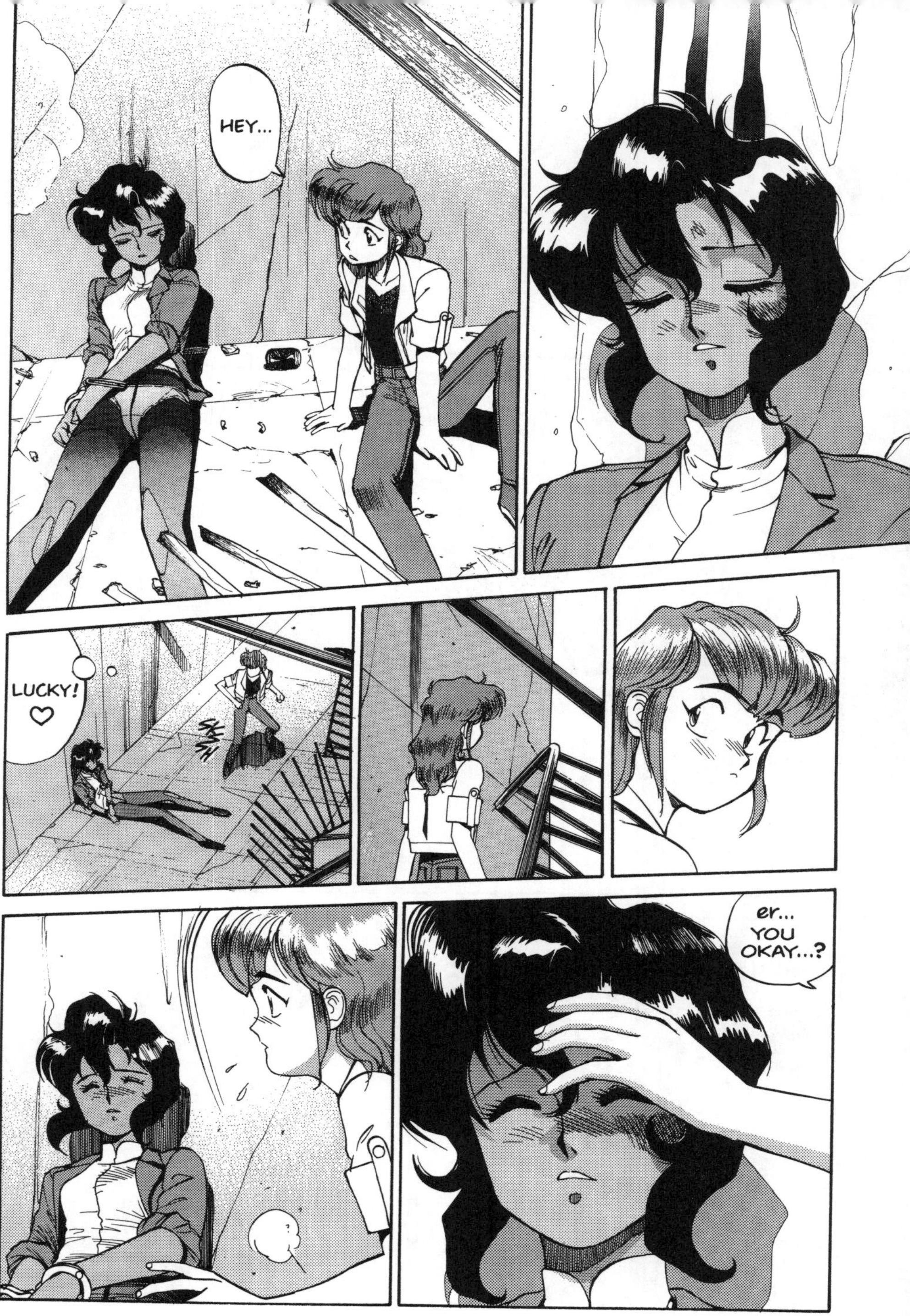
HEY...
LUCKY! ♡
er... YOU OKAY...?

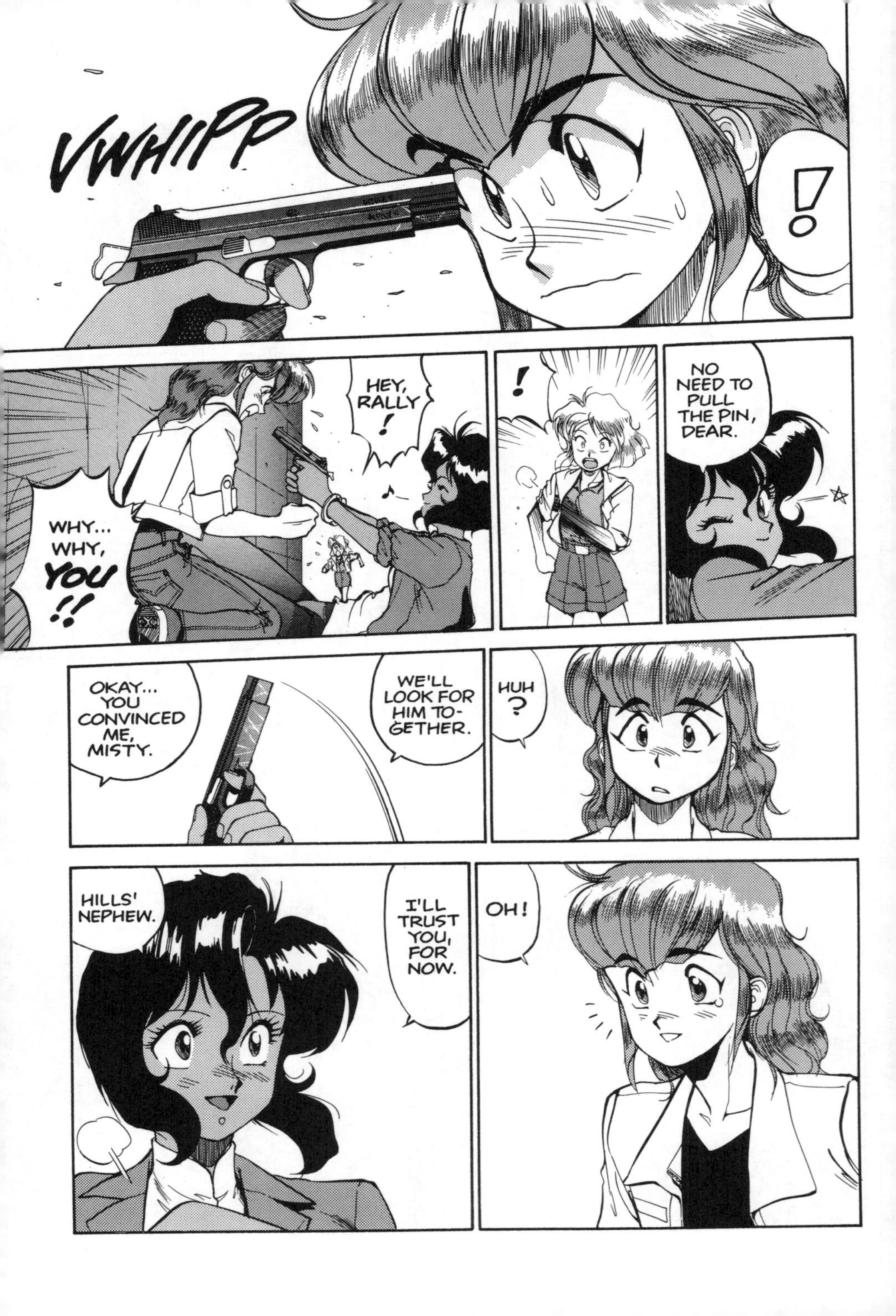
VWHIPP
!
WHY... WHY, YOU!!
HEY, RALLY!
!
NO NEED TO PULL THE PIN, DEAR.
OKAY... YOU CONVINCED ME, MISTY.
WE'LL LOOK FOR HIM TOGETHER.
HUH?
HILLS' NEPHEW.
I'LL TRUST YOU, FOR NOW.
OH!

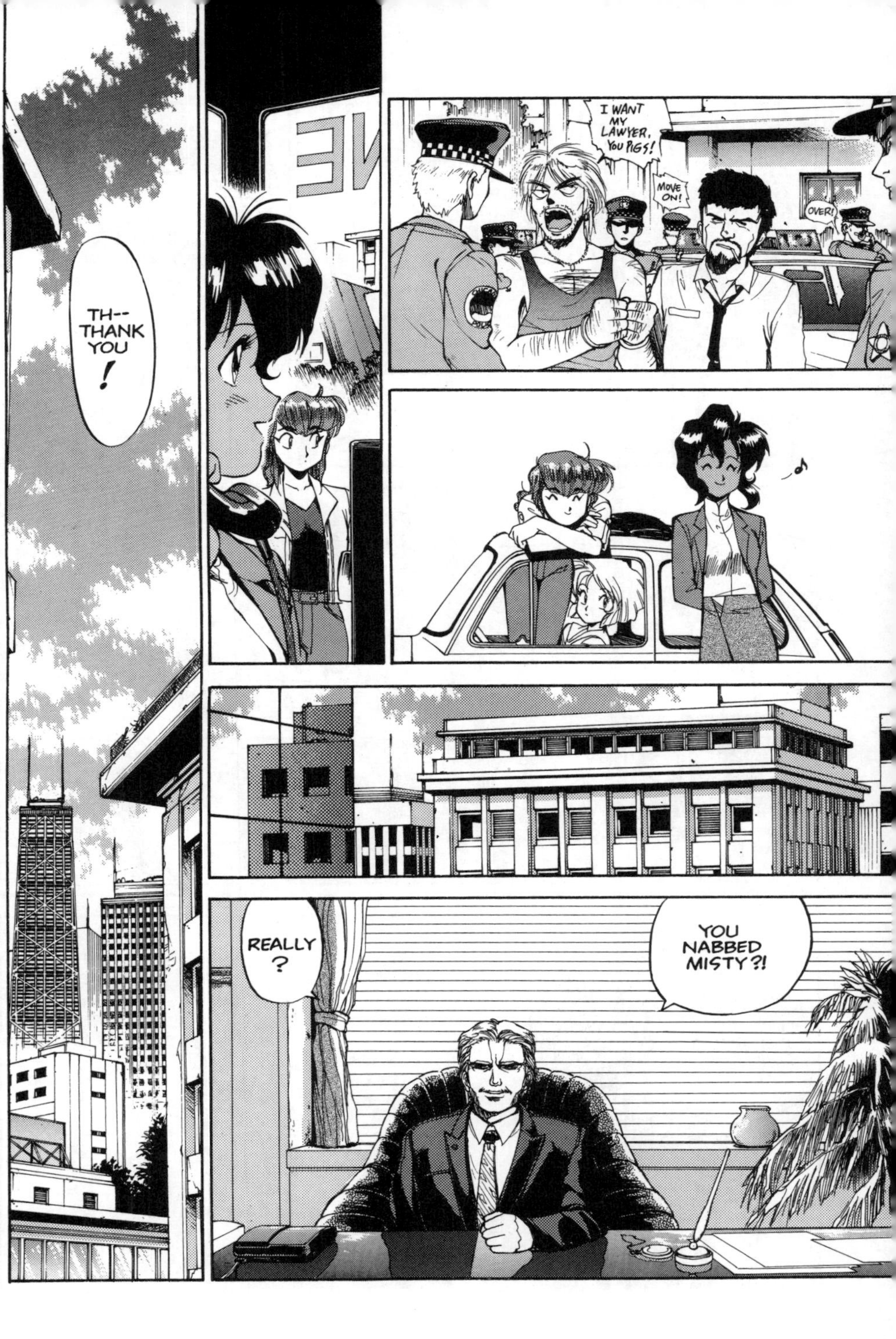
TH-- THANK YOU!
I WANT MY LAWYER, YOU PIGS!
MOVE ON!
OVER!
REALLY?
YOU NABBED MISTY?!

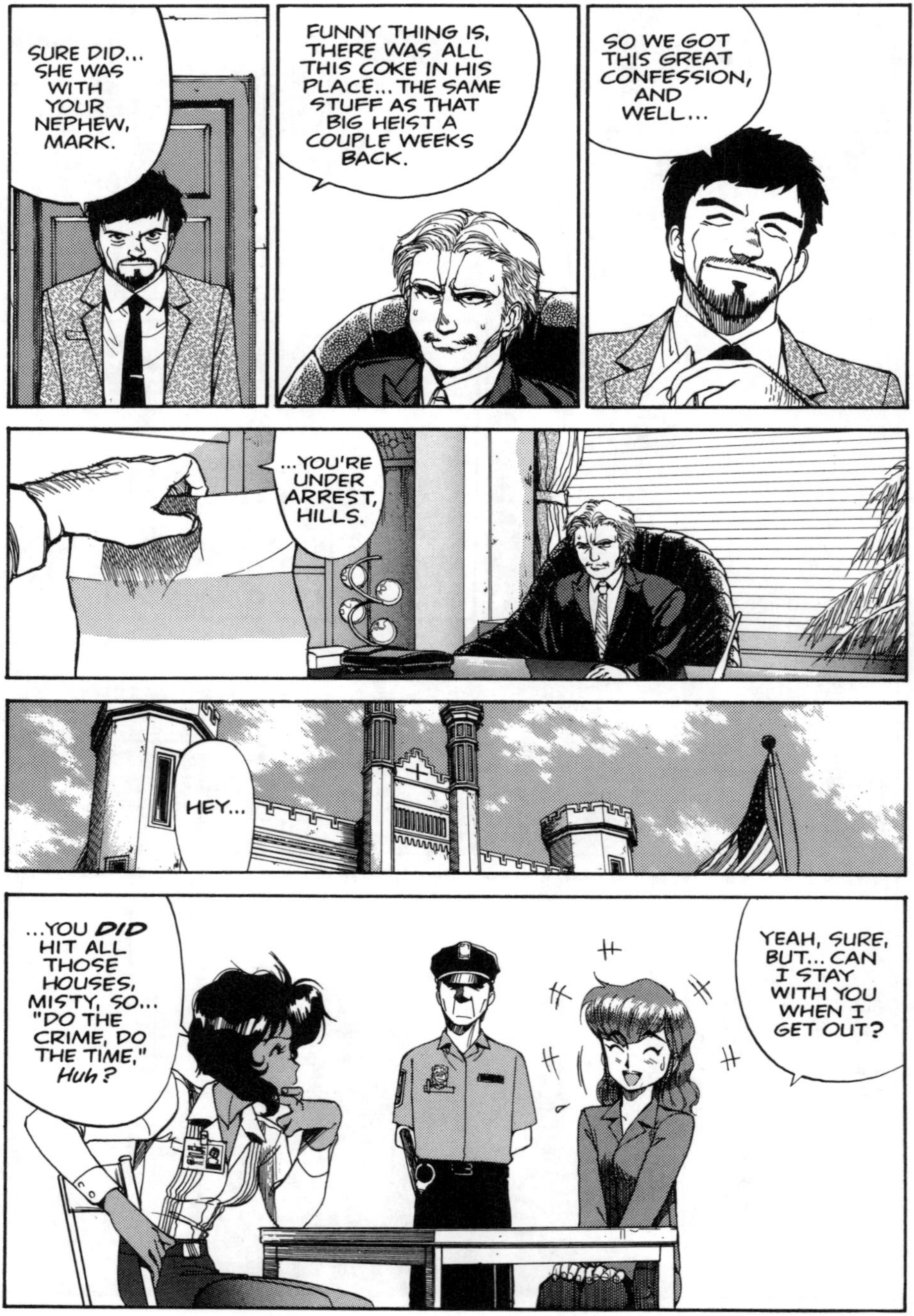
SURE DID... SHE WAS WITH YOUR NEPHEW, MARK.
FUNNY THING IS, THERE WAS ALL THIS COKE IN HIS PLACE... THE SAME STUFF AS THAT BIG HEIST A COUPLE WEEKS BACK.
SO WE GOT THIS GREAT CONFESSION, AND WELL...
...YOU'RE UNDER ARREST, HILLS.
HEY...
...YOU DID HIT ALL THOSE HOUSES, MISTY, SO... "DO THE CRIME, DO THE TIME," Huh?
YEAH, SURE, BUT... CAN I STAY WITH YOU WHEN I GET OUT?

MAGNUM PRIMER

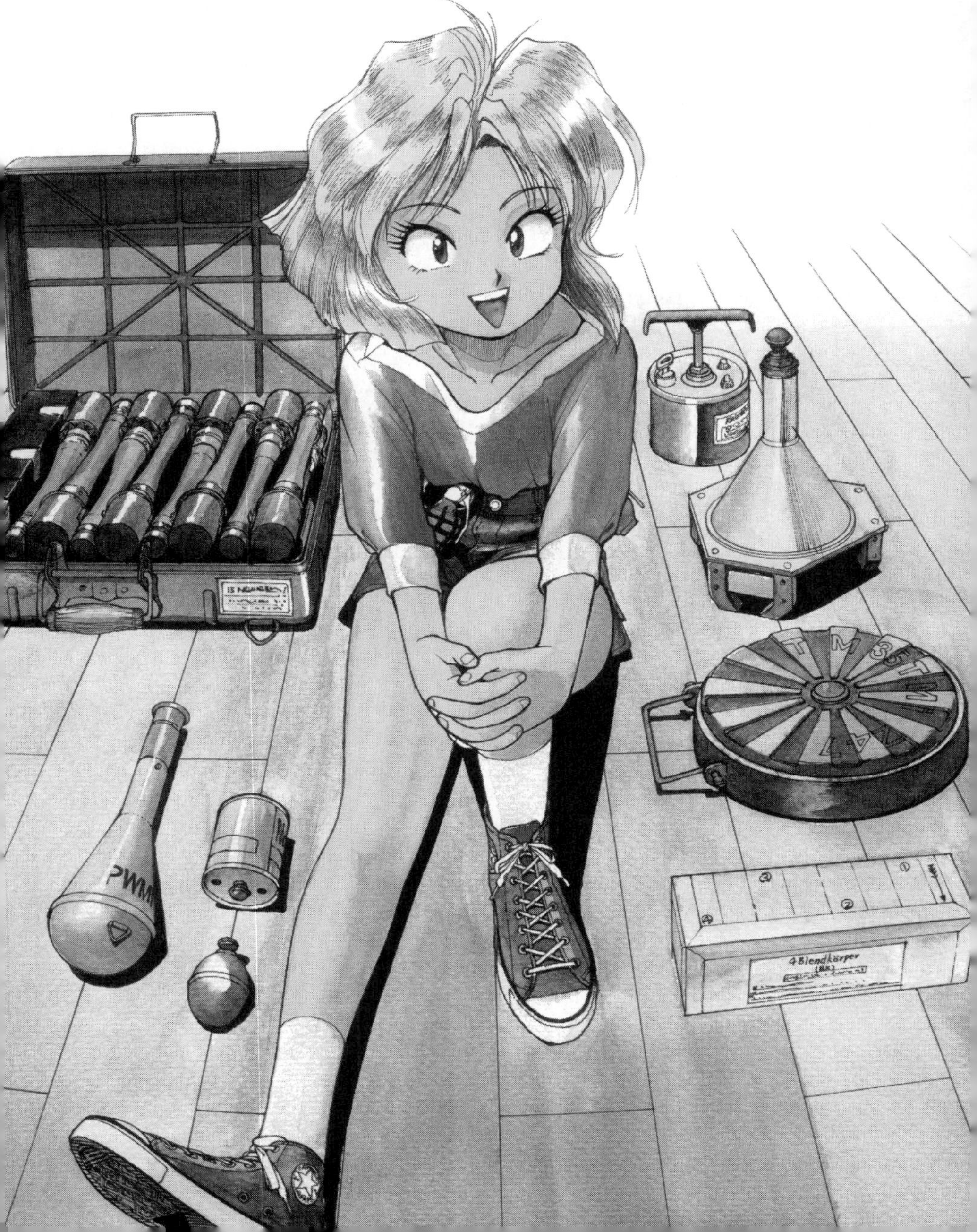
PWM
4 Blendkörper

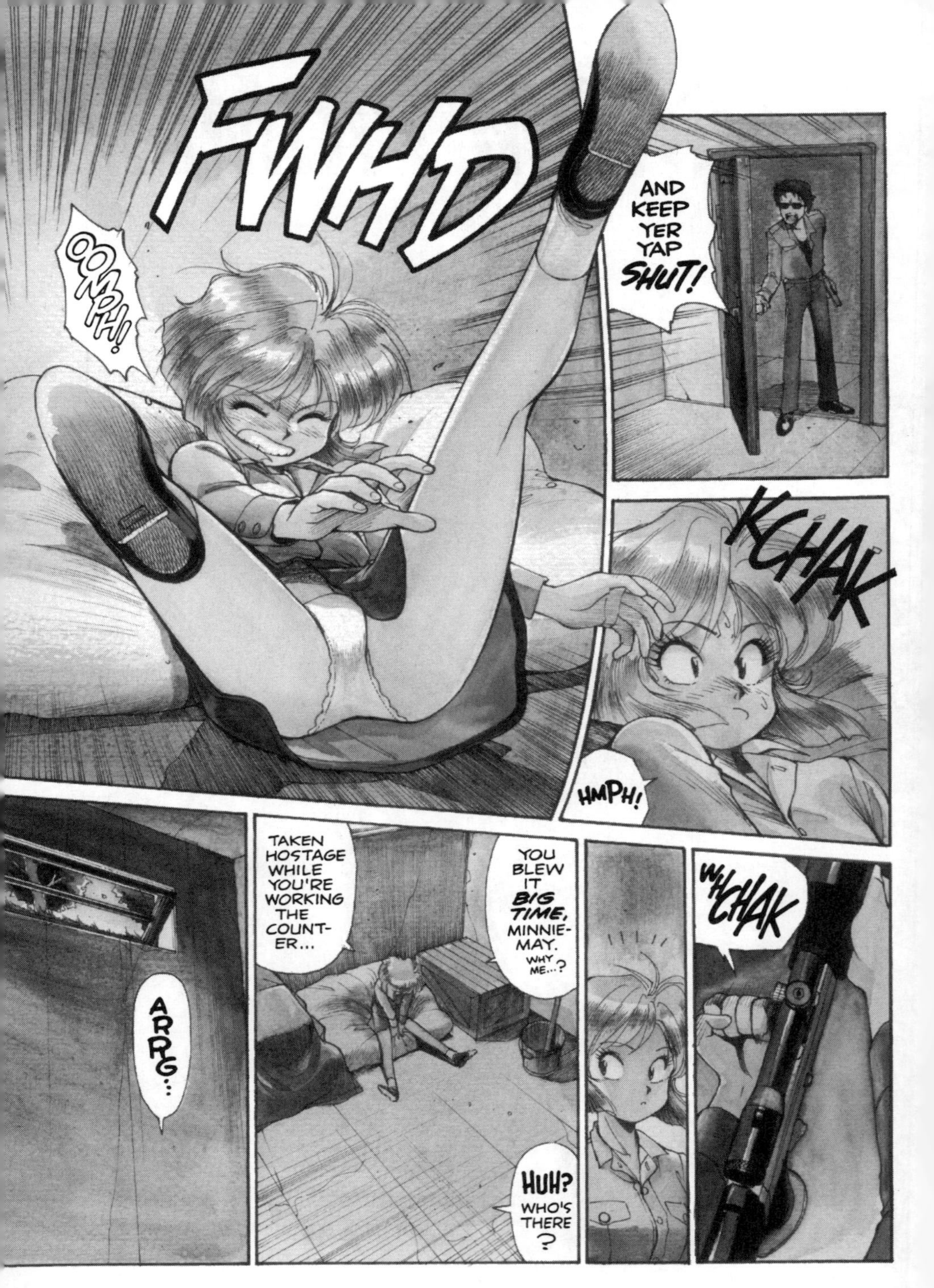

FWHD
OOMPH!
AND KEEP YER YAP SHUT!
KCHAK
HMPH!
ARRG...
TAKEN HOSTAGE WHILE YOU'RE WORKING THE COUNTER...
YOU BLEW IT BIG TIME, MINNIE-MAY.
WHY ME...?
HUH? WHO'S THERE?
WHCHAK

MAN, LOOK AT THIS BABY! AN *SG 550!*

YEAH... FOR A PISSANT LITTLE GUN SHOP ON THE EDGE OF TOWN, THEY'VE GOT A SHIT-LOAD OF GREAT STUFF.

HEH HEH... I GOT *ME* A HECKLER AND KOCH!

HEY, HEY-- YOU GUYS... GET A LOAD OF THE KID'S JACKET!

WHAT?

CHECK IT OUT!

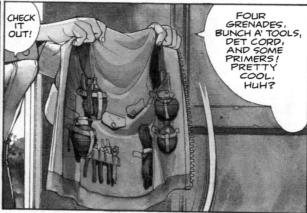

FOUR GRENADES, BUNCH A' TOOLS, DET CORD, AND SOME PRIMERS! PRETTY COOL, HUH?

WHAT THE HELL? SHE IN THE SAME BUSINESS WE ARE?

HEY! THIS THING'S FULL AUTO!

?!

THE JOINT'S BLACK MARKET...?

WHAT THE HELL KIND OF PLACE *IS* IT? "GUNSMITH CATS"... WEIRD.

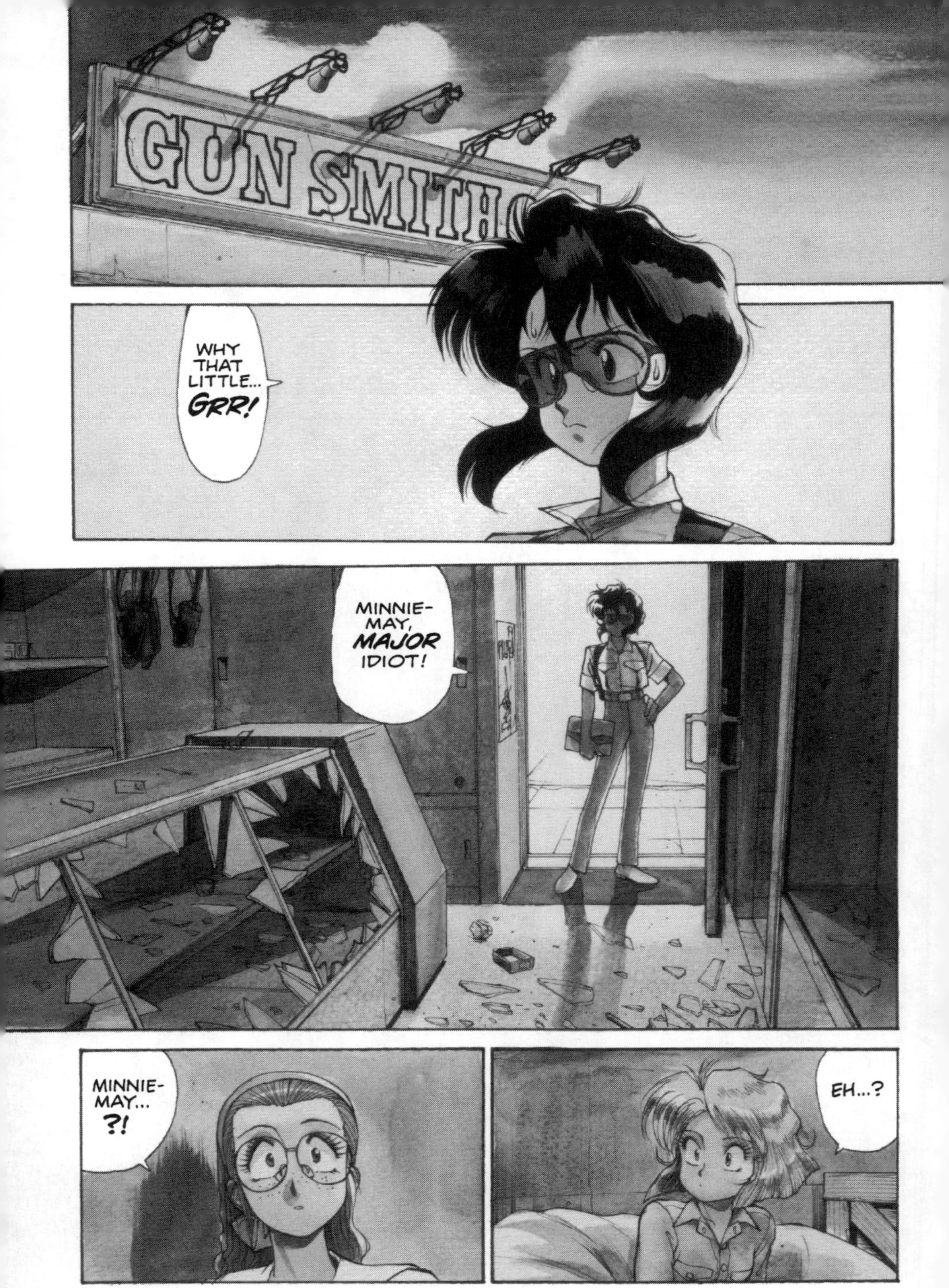
GUN SMITH
WHY THAT LITTLE... GRR!
MINNIE-MAY, MAJOR IDIOT!
MINNIE-MAY... ?!
EH...?

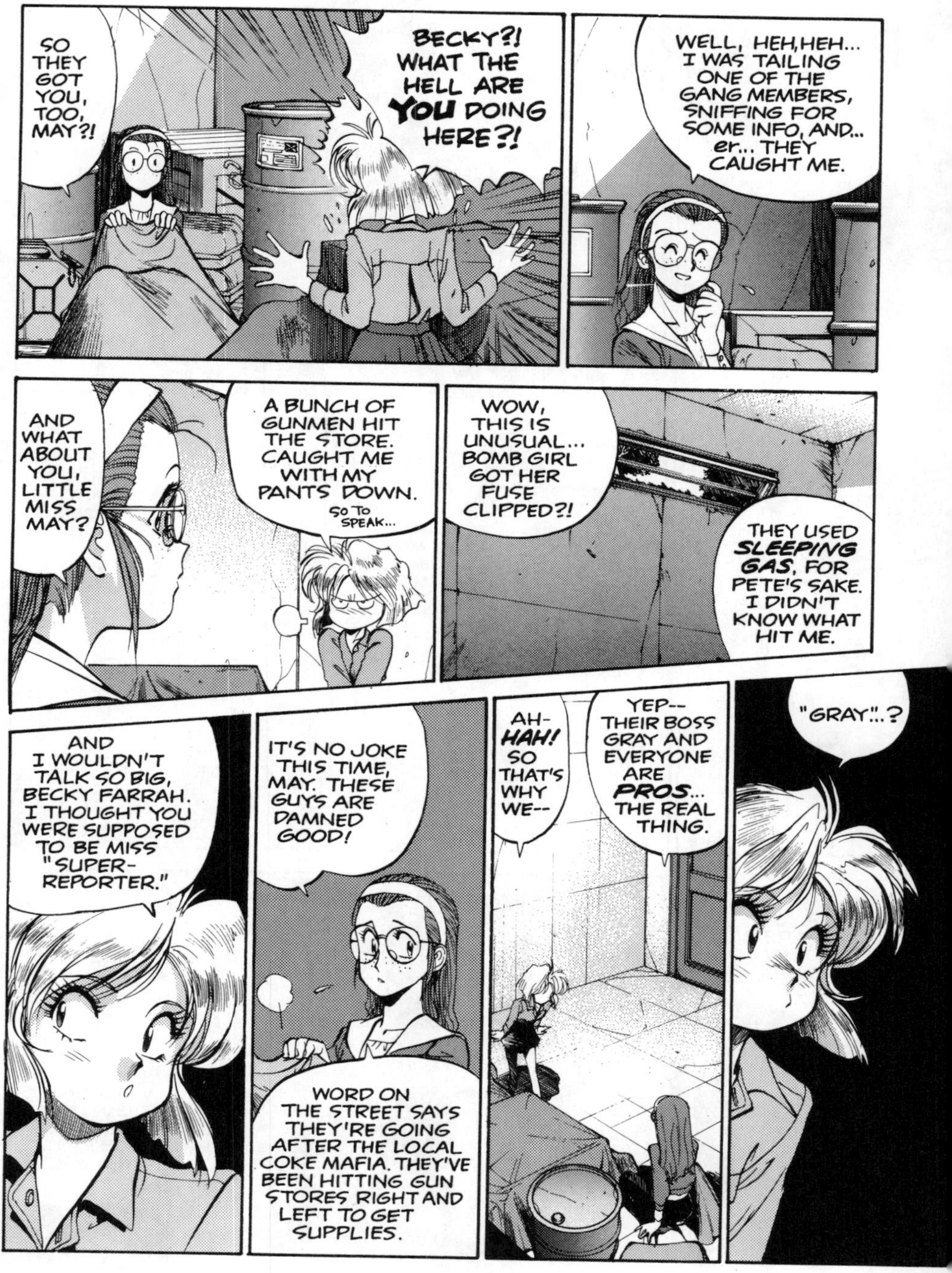
SO THEY GOT YOU, TOO, MAY?!
BECKY?! WHAT THE HELL ARE YOU DOING HERE?!
WELL, HEH, HEH... I WAS TAILING ONE OF THE GANG MEMBERS, SNIFFING FOR SOME INFO, AND... er... THEY CAUGHT ME.
AND WHAT ABOUT YOU, LITTLE MISS MAY?
A BUNCH OF GUNMEN HIT THE STORE. CAUGHT ME WITH MY PANTS DOWN.
SO TO SPEAK...
WOW, THIS IS UNUSUAL... BOMB GIRL GOT HER FUSE CLIPPED?!
THEY USED SLEEPING GAS, FOR PETE'S SAKE. I DIDN'T KNOW WHAT HIT ME.
AND I WOULDN'T TALK SO BIG, BECKY FARRAH. I THOUGHT YOU WERE SUPPOSED TO BE MISS "SUPER-REPORTER."
IT'S NO JOKE THIS TIME, MAY. THESE GUYS ARE DAMNED GOOD!
WORD ON THE STREET SAYS THEY'RE GOING AFTER THE LOCAL COKE MAFIA. THEY'VE BEEN HITTING GUN STORES RIGHT AND LEFT TO GET SUPPLIES.
AH-HAH! SO THAT'S WHY WE--
YEP-- THEIR BOSS GRAY AND EVERYONE ARE PROS... THE REAL THING.
"GRAY"...?

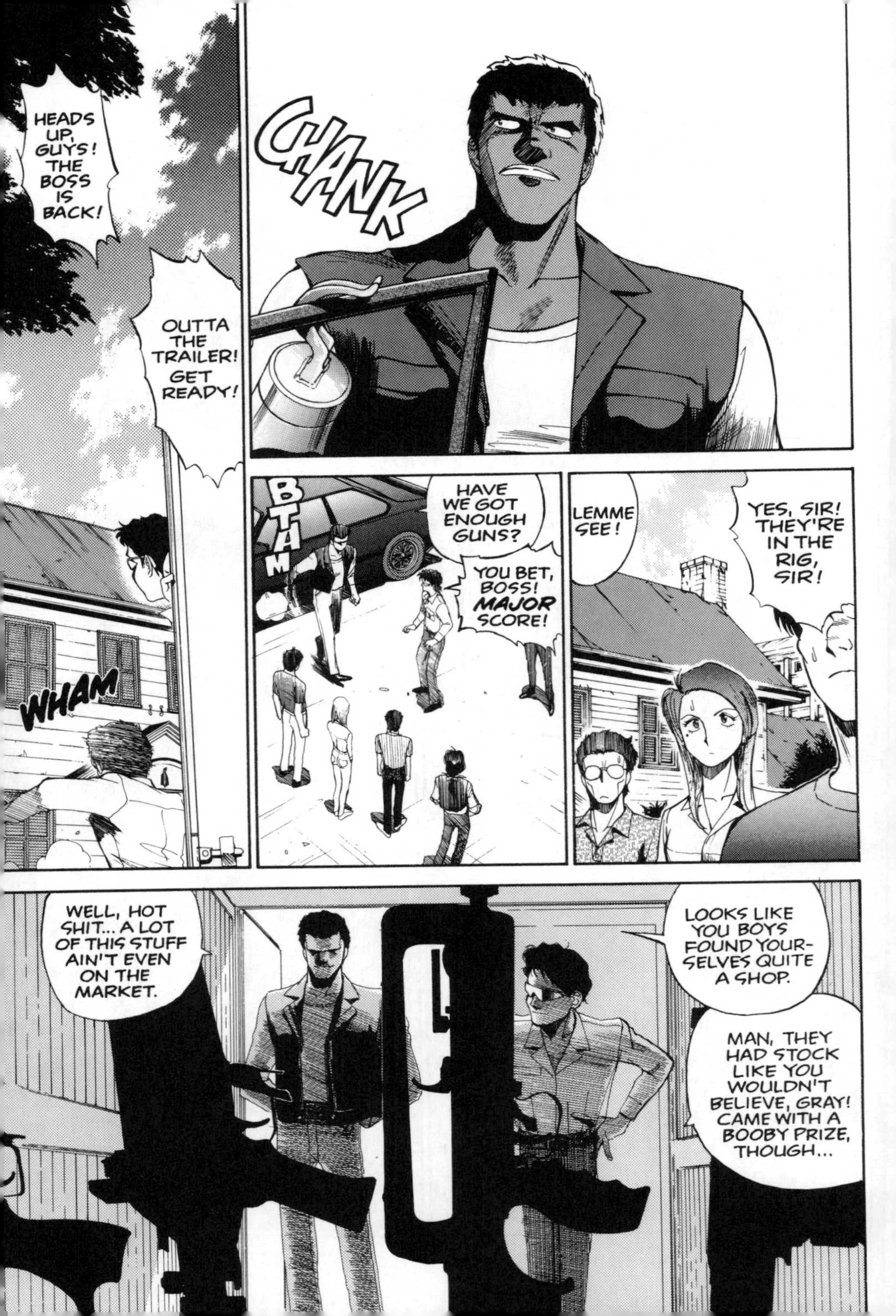
HEADS UP, GUYS! THE BOSS IS BACK!
CHANK
OUTTA THE TRAILER! GET READY!
WHAM
BTAM
HAVE WE GOT ENOUGH GUNS?
YOU BET, BOSS! MAJOR SCORE!
LEMME SEE!
YES, SIR! THEY'RE IN THE RIG, SIR!
WELL, HOT SHIT... A LOT OF THIS STUFF AIN'T EVEN ON THE MARKET.
LOOKS LIKE YOU BOYS FOUND YOURSELVES QUITE A SHOP.
MAN, THEY HAD STOCK LIKE YOU WOULDN'T BELIEVE, GRAY! CAME WITH A BOOBY PRIZE, THOUGH...

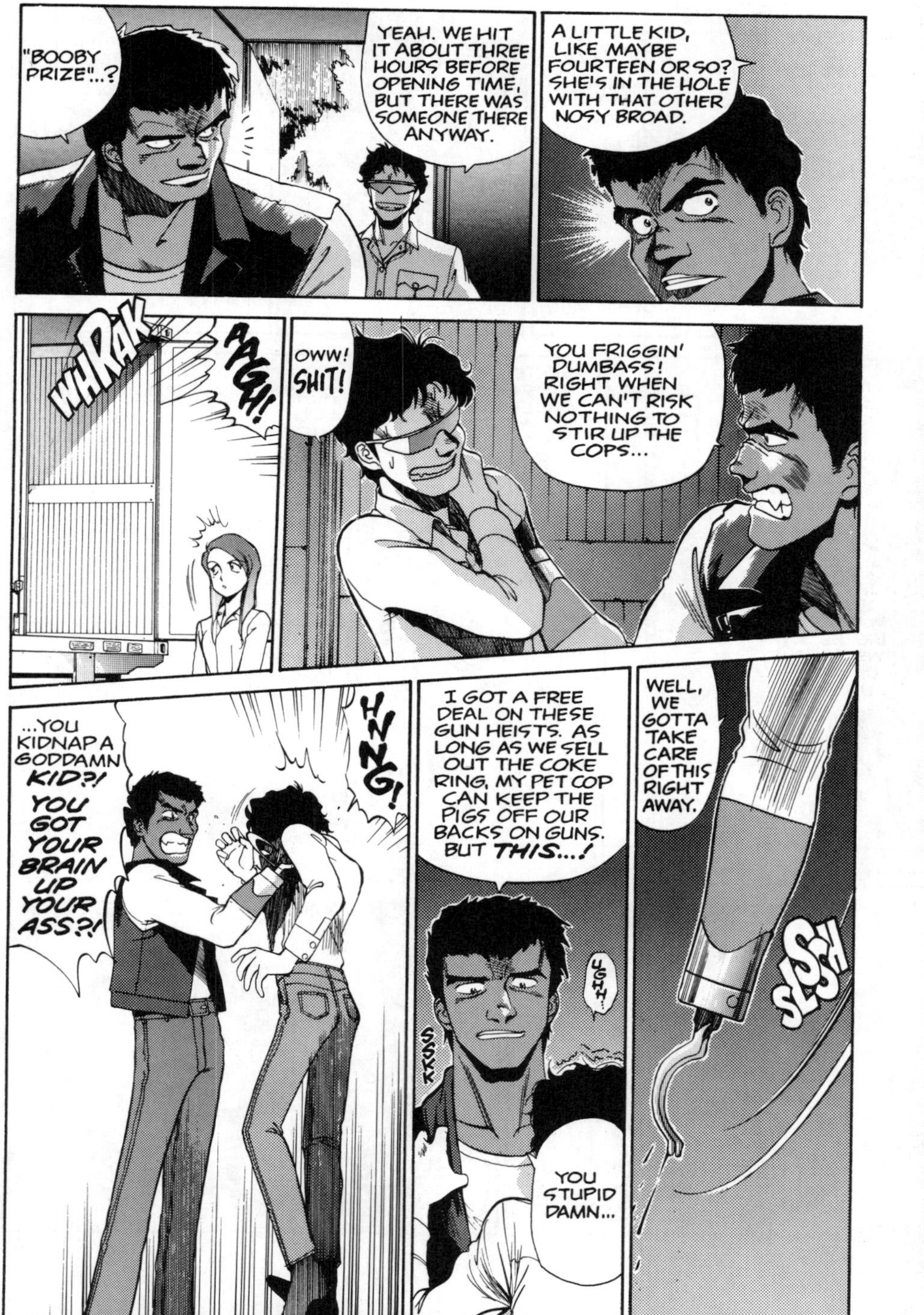
"BOOBY PRIZE"...?
YEAH. WE HIT IT ABOUT THREE HOURS BEFORE OPENING TIME, BUT THERE WAS SOMEONE THERE ANYWAY.
A LITTLE KID, LIKE MAYBE FOURTEEN OR SO? SHE'S IN THE HOLE WITH THAT OTHER NOSY BROAD.
WHRAK
AAGH!
OWW! SHIT!
YOU FRIGGIN' DUMBASS! RIGHT WHEN WE CAN'T RISK NOTHING TO STIR UP THE COPS...
...YOU KIDNAP A GODDAMN KID?! YOU GOT YOUR BRAIN UP YOUR ASS?!
HNNG!
I GOT A FREE DEAL ON THESE GUN HEISTS. AS LONG AS WE SELL OUT THE COKE RING, MY PET COP CAN KEEP THE PIGS OFF OUR BACKS ON GUNS. BUT THIS...!
UGHH...
SSSKK
YOU STUPID DAMN...
WELL, WE GOTTA TAKE CARE OF THIS RIGHT AWAY.
SLOSH

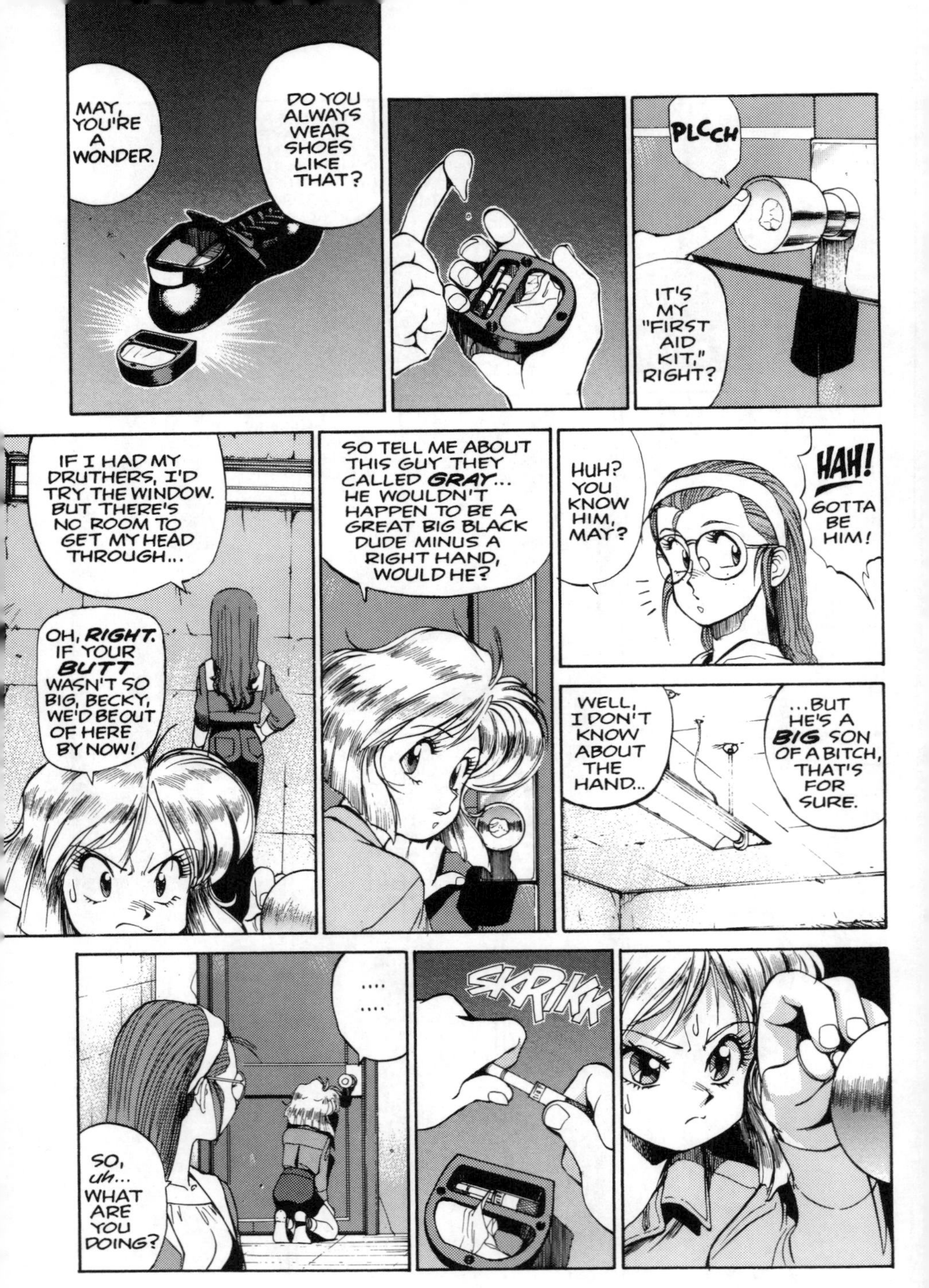
MAY, YOU'RE A WONDER.
DO YOU ALWAYS WEAR SHOES LIKE THAT?
PLCCH
IT'S MY "FIRST AID KIT," RIGHT?
IF I HAD MY DRUTHERS, I'D TRY THE WINDOW. BUT THERE'S NO ROOM TO GET MY HEAD THROUGH...
OH, RIGHT. IF YOUR BUTT WASN'T SO BIG, BECKY, WE'D BE OUT OF HERE BY NOW!
SO TELL ME ABOUT THIS GUY THEY CALLED GRAY... HE WOULDN'T HAPPEN TO BE A GREAT BIG BLACK DUDE MINUS A RIGHT HAND, WOULD HE?
HUH? YOU KNOW HIM, MAY?
HAH!
GOTTA BE HIM!
WELL, I DON'T KNOW ABOUT THE HAND...
...BUT HE'S A BIG SON OF A BITCH, THAT'S FOR SURE.
....
....
SO, uh... WHAT ARE YOU DOING?
SKRIKK

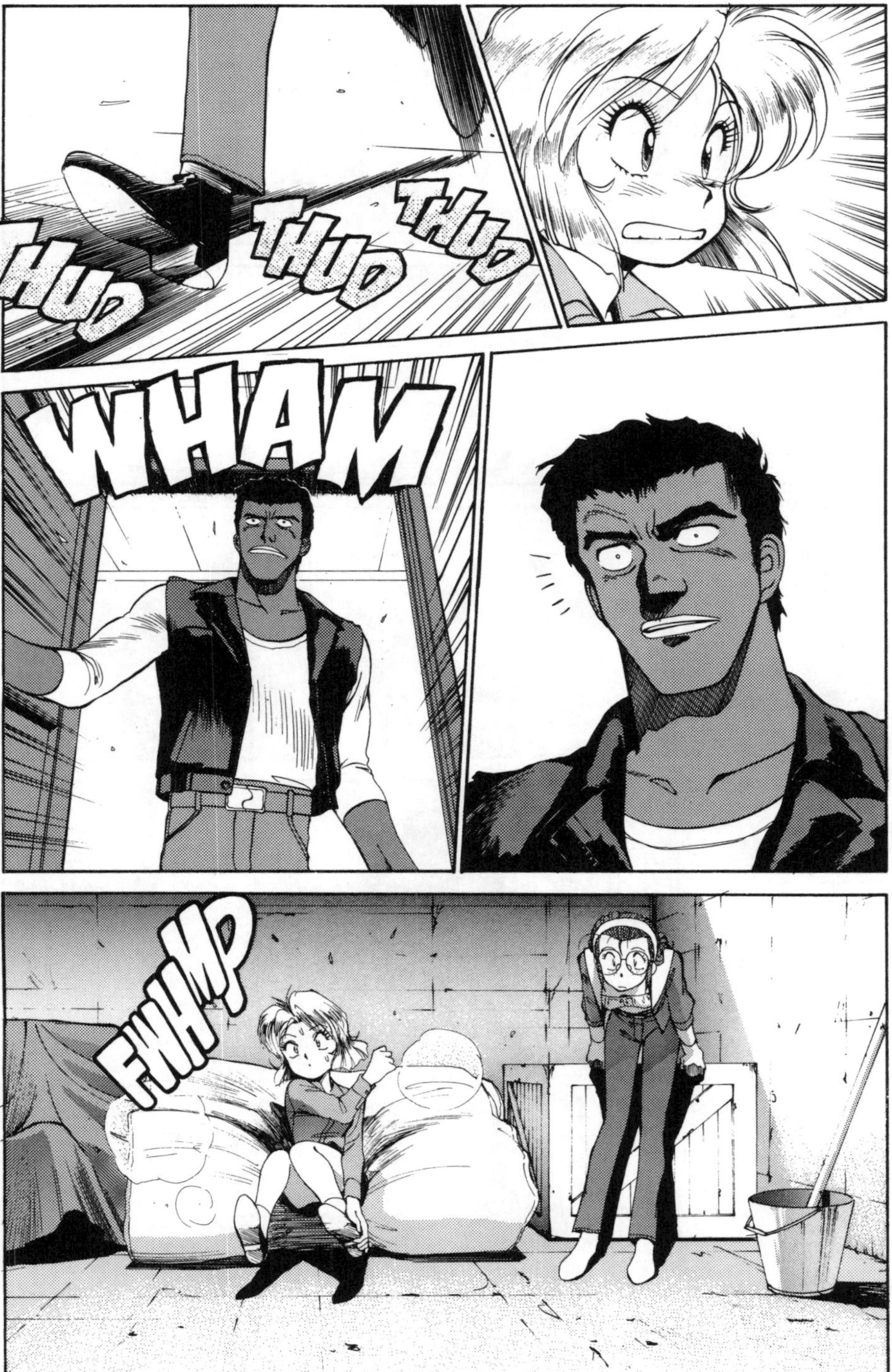
THUD
THUD
THUD
WHAM
FWHMP

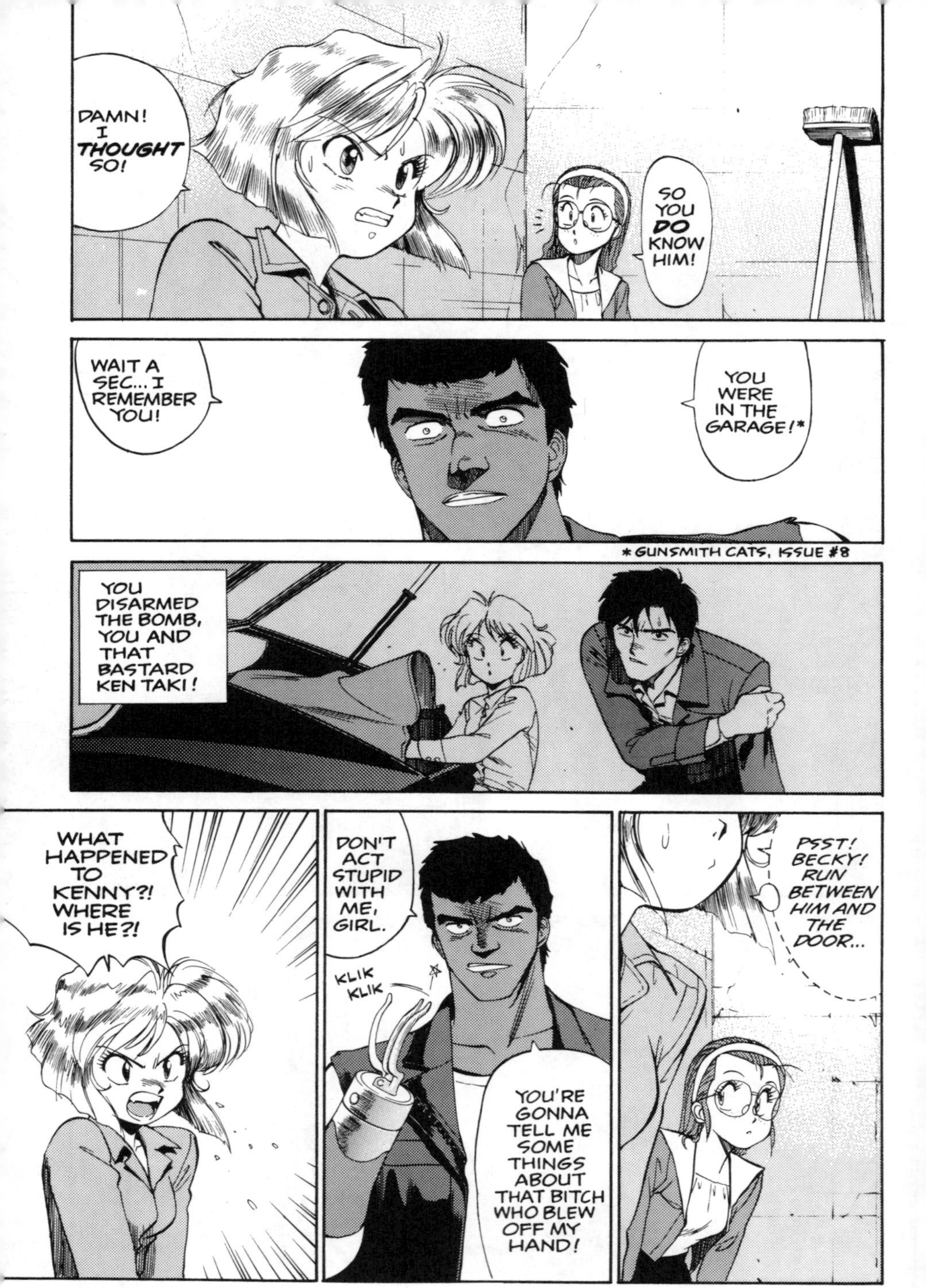
DAMN! I **THOUGHT** SO!
SO YOU **DO** KNOW HIM!
WAIT A SEC... I REMEMBER YOU!
YOU WERE IN THE GARAGE!*
*GUNSMITH CATS, ISSUE #8
YOU DISARMED THE BOMB, YOU AND THAT BASTARD KEN TAKI!
WHAT HAPPENED TO KENNY?! WHERE IS HE?!
DON'T ACT STUPID WITH ME, GIRL.
KLIK KLIK
YOU'RE GONNA TELL ME SOME THINGS ABOUT THAT BITCH WHO BLEW OFF MY HAND!
PSST! BECKY! RUN BETWEEN HIM AND THE DOOR...

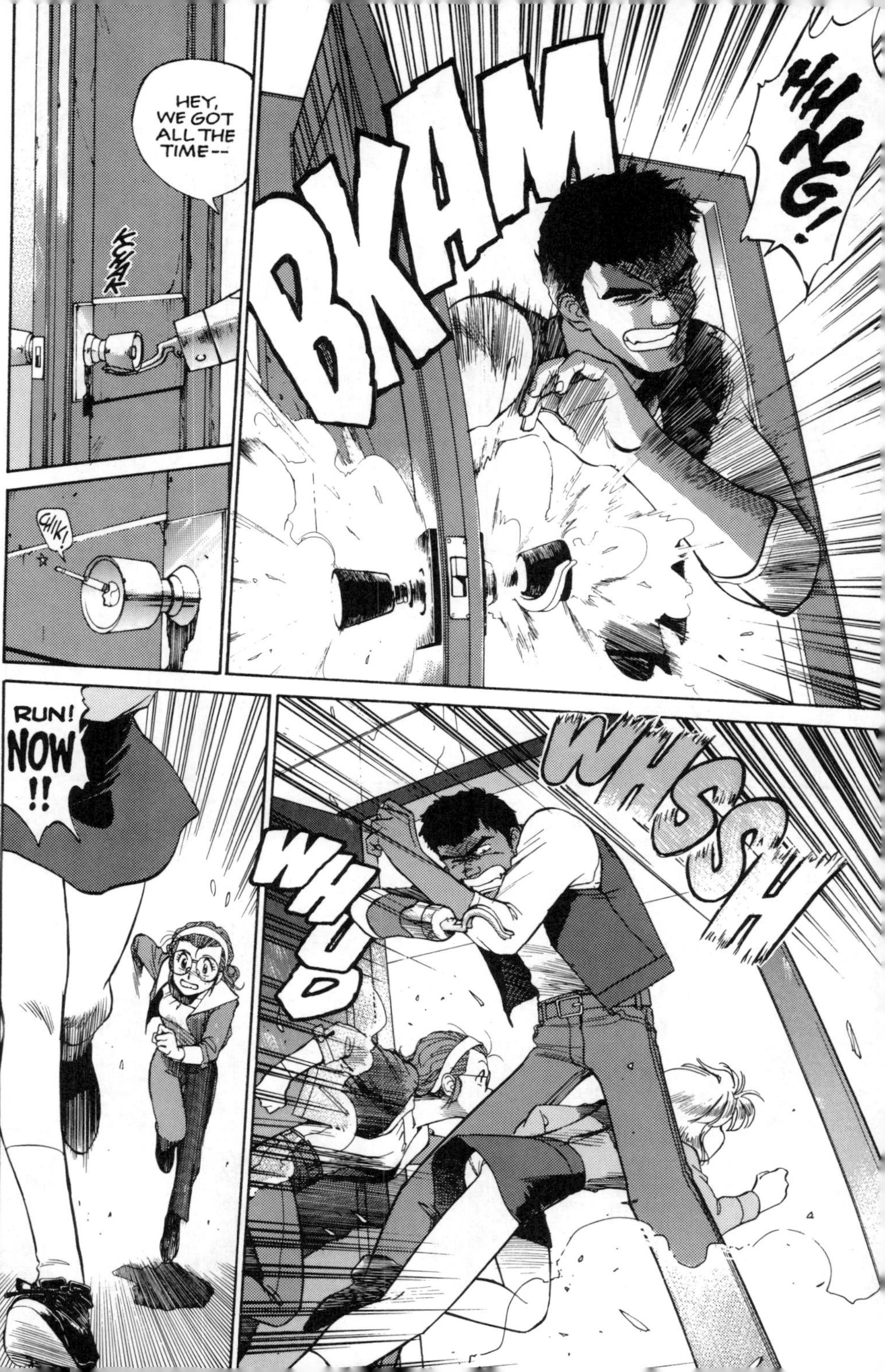
HEY, WE GOT ALL THE TIME--
KCHAK
CHIK!
BKAM
HHNG!
RUN! NOW!!
WHSSH
WHUD

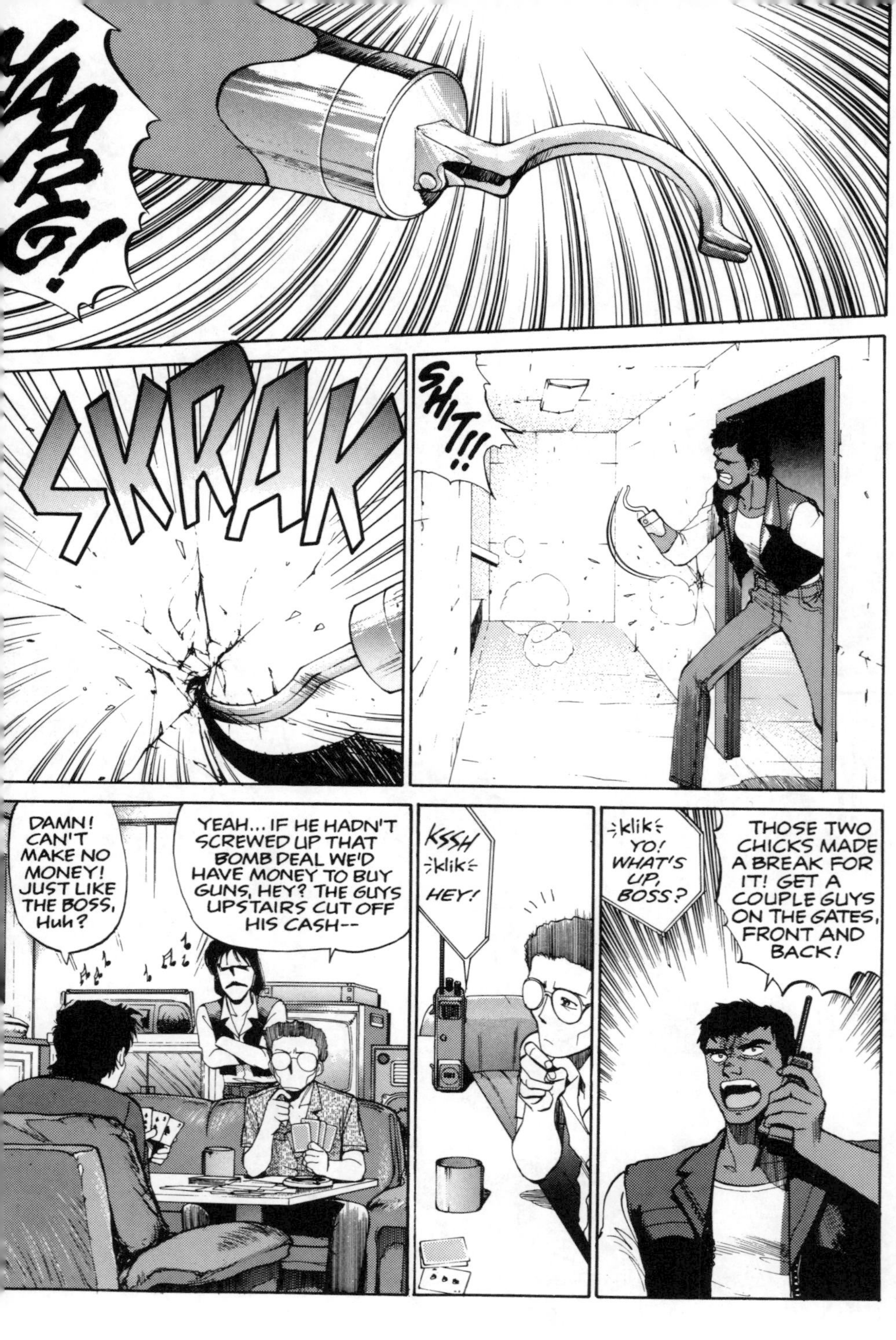
YARGG!
SKRAK
SHIT!!
DAMN! CAN'T MAKE NO MONEY! JUST LIKE THE BOSS, Huh?
YEAH... IF HE HADN'T SCREWED UP THAT BOMB DEAL WE'D HAVE MONEY TO BUY GUNS, HEY? THE GUYS UPSTAIRS CUT OFF HIS CASH--
KSSH
klik
HEY!
klik
YO! WHAT'S UP, BOSS?
THOSE TWO CHICKS MADE A BREAK FOR IT! GET A COUPLE GUYS ON THE GATES, FRONT AND BACK!

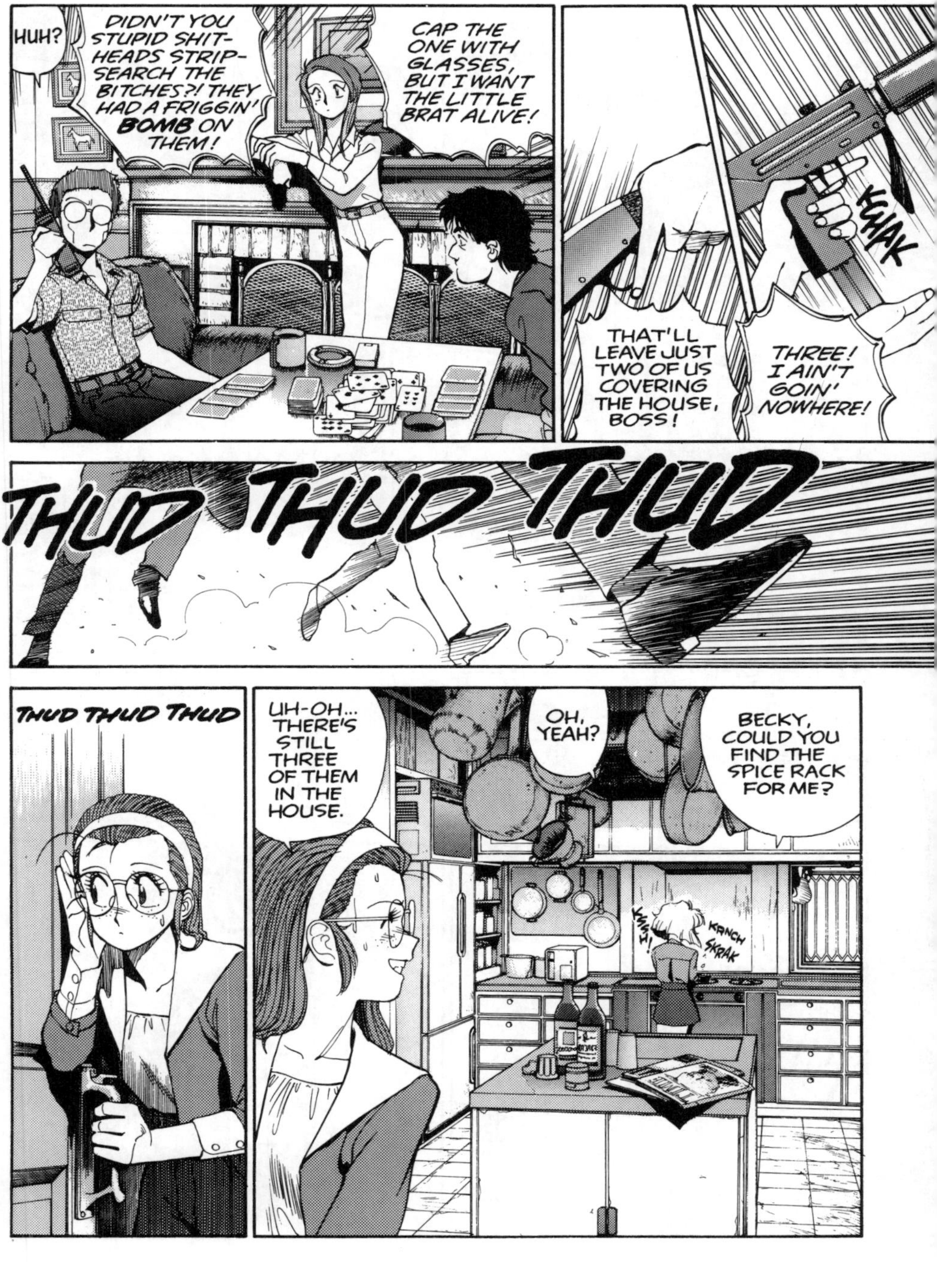
HUH?
DIDN'T YOU STUPID SHIT-HEADS STRIP-SEARCH THE BITCHES?! THEY HAD A FRIGGIN' **BOMB** ON THEM!
CAP THE ONE WITH GLASSES, BUT I WANT THE LITTLE BRAT ALIVE!
KCHAK
THAT'LL LEAVE JUST TWO OF US COVERING THE HOUSE, BOSS!
THREE! I AIN'T GOIN' NOWHERE!
THUD THUD THUD
THUD THUD THUD
UH-OH... THERE'S STILL THREE OF THEM IN THE HOUSE.
OH, YEAH?
BECKY, COULD YOU FIND THE SPICE RACK FOR ME?
KWISH!
KRNCH
SKRAK

I NEED PEPPER OR TABASCO SAUCE, IF THEY'VE GOT IT.

KSSH!

OOH, YUMMY! STIR-FRIED GLASS?

JUST A LITTLE SOMETHING TO LIGHT UP THEIR LIVES! ♥

SKRSSH

THUNK

SPICE ISLAND
JAVA
BLACK PEPPER

TABASCO

WHAM!

KRAK

BASTARDS! THEY'VE JAMMED A POLE ACROSS THE DOOR!

WHAM!

B-BE CAREFUL, MAN! HE SAID SHE HAD SOME BOMBS!

HELL, SINCE WHEN DOES SOME KID WITH FIRE-WORKS...

KCHIK

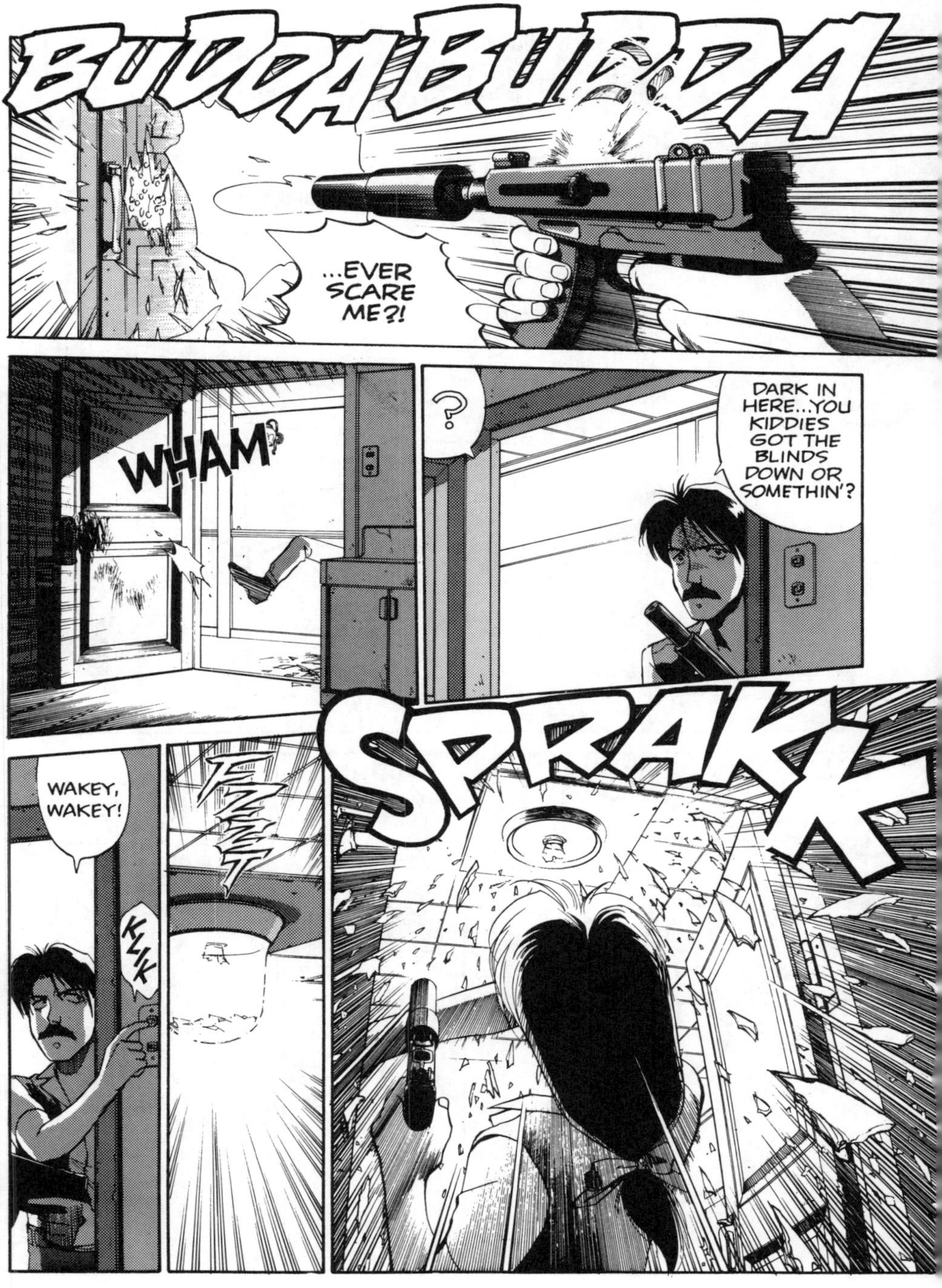
BUDDABUDDA
...EVER SCARE ME?!
WHAM
?
DARK IN HERE...YOU KIDDIES GOT THE BLINDS DOWN OR SOMETHIN'?
WAKEY, WAKEY!
KLIK
FZZZT
SPRAKK

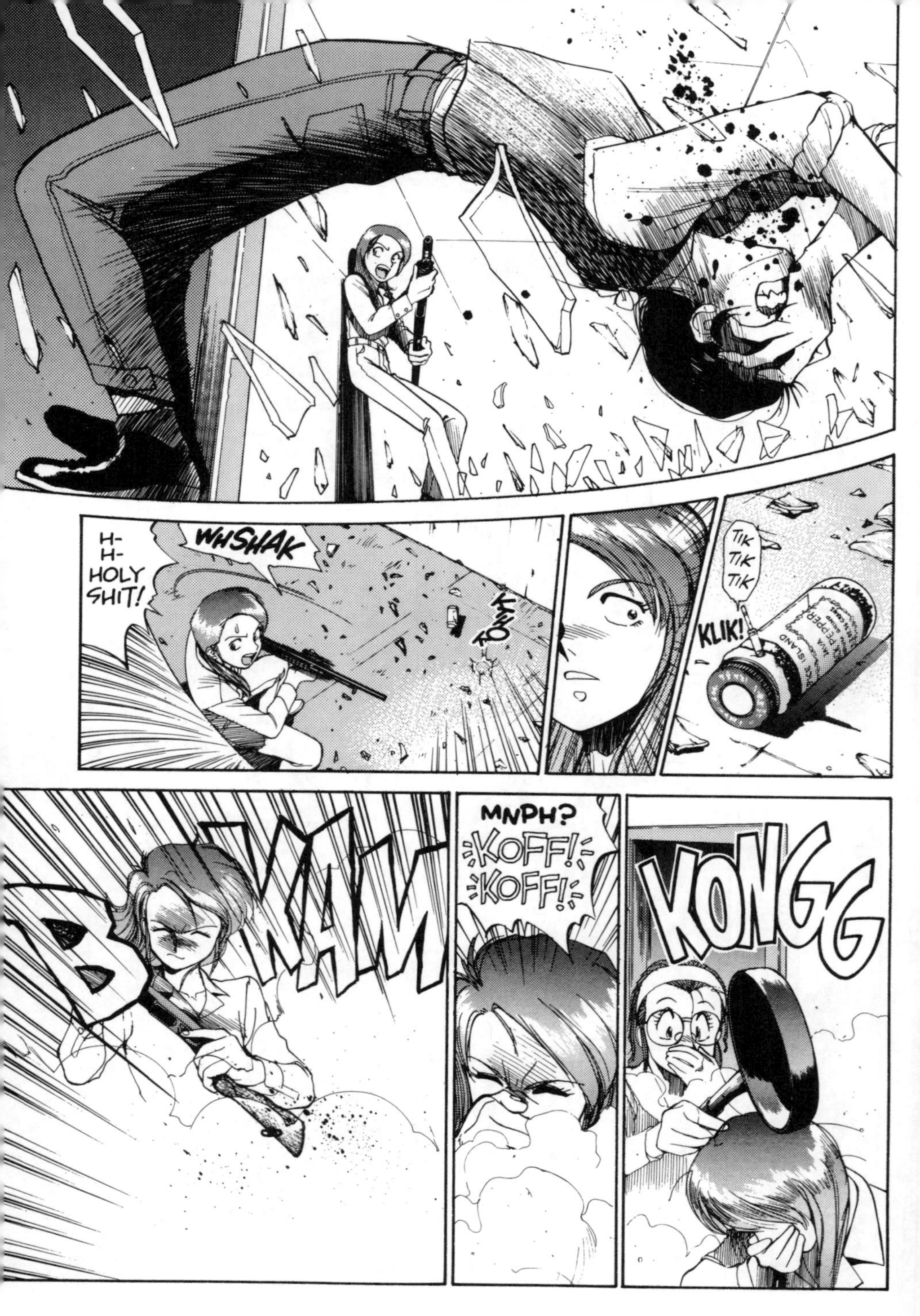
H-H-HOLY SHIT!
WHSHAK
TIK TIK TIK
KLIK!
BWAM
MNPH?
KOFF! KOFF!
KONGG

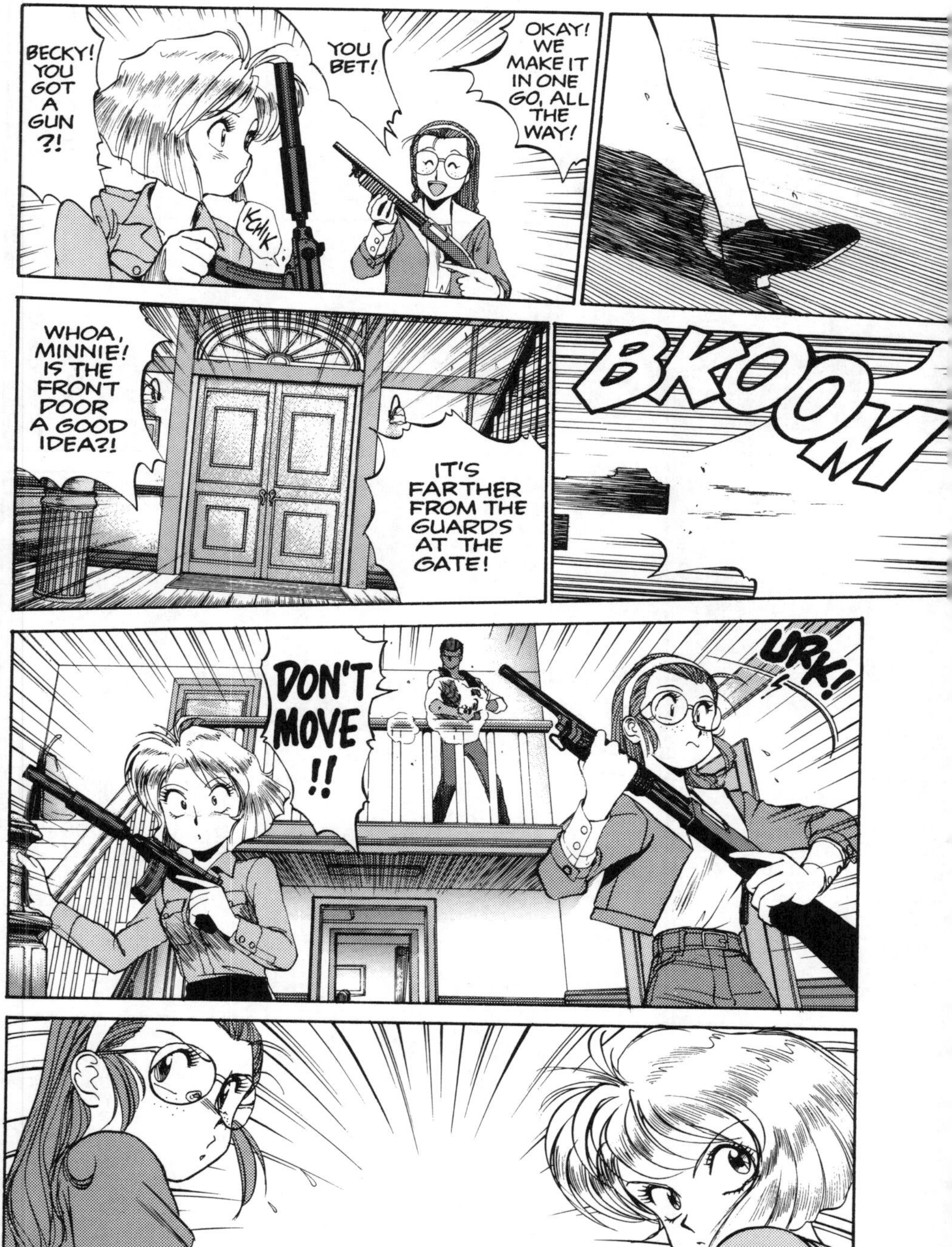
BECKY! YOU GOT A GUN ?!
KCHIK
YOU BET!
OKAY! WE MAKE IT IN ONE GO, ALL THE WAY!
WHOA, MINNIE! IS THE FRONT DOOR A GOOD IDEA?!
IT'S FARTHER FROM THE GUARDS AT THE GATE!
BKOOM
DON'T MOVE !!
URK!

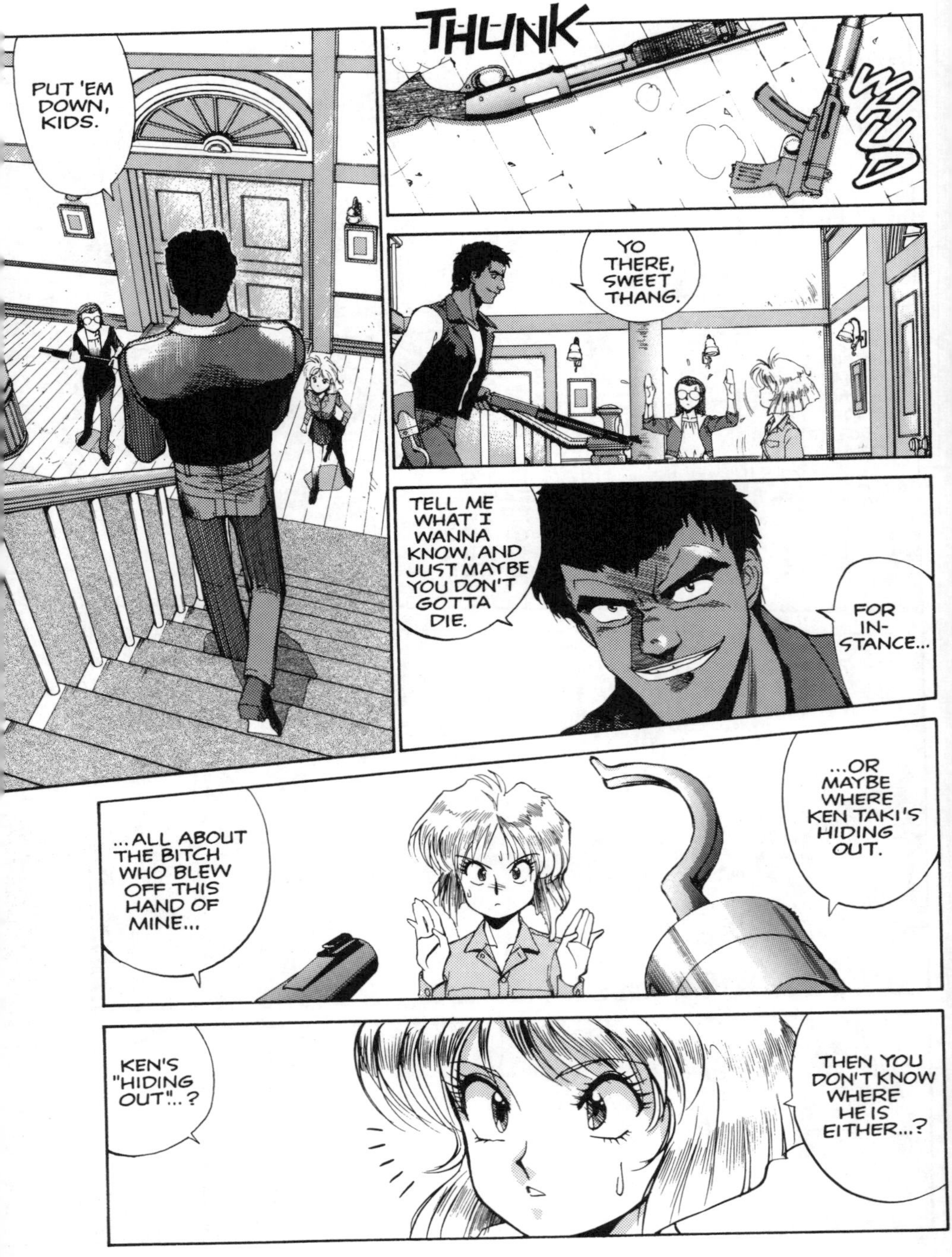
PUT 'EM DOWN, KIDS.
THUNK
WHUD
YO THERE, SWEET THANG.
TELL ME WHAT I WANNA KNOW, AND JUST MAYBE YOU DON'T GOTTA DIE.
FOR IN-STANCE...
...ALL ABOUT THE BITCH WHO BLEW OFF THIS HAND OF MINE...
...OR MAYBE WHERE KEN TAKI'S HIDING OUT.
KEN'S "HIDING OUT"...?
THEN YOU DON'T KNOW WHERE HE IS EITHER...?

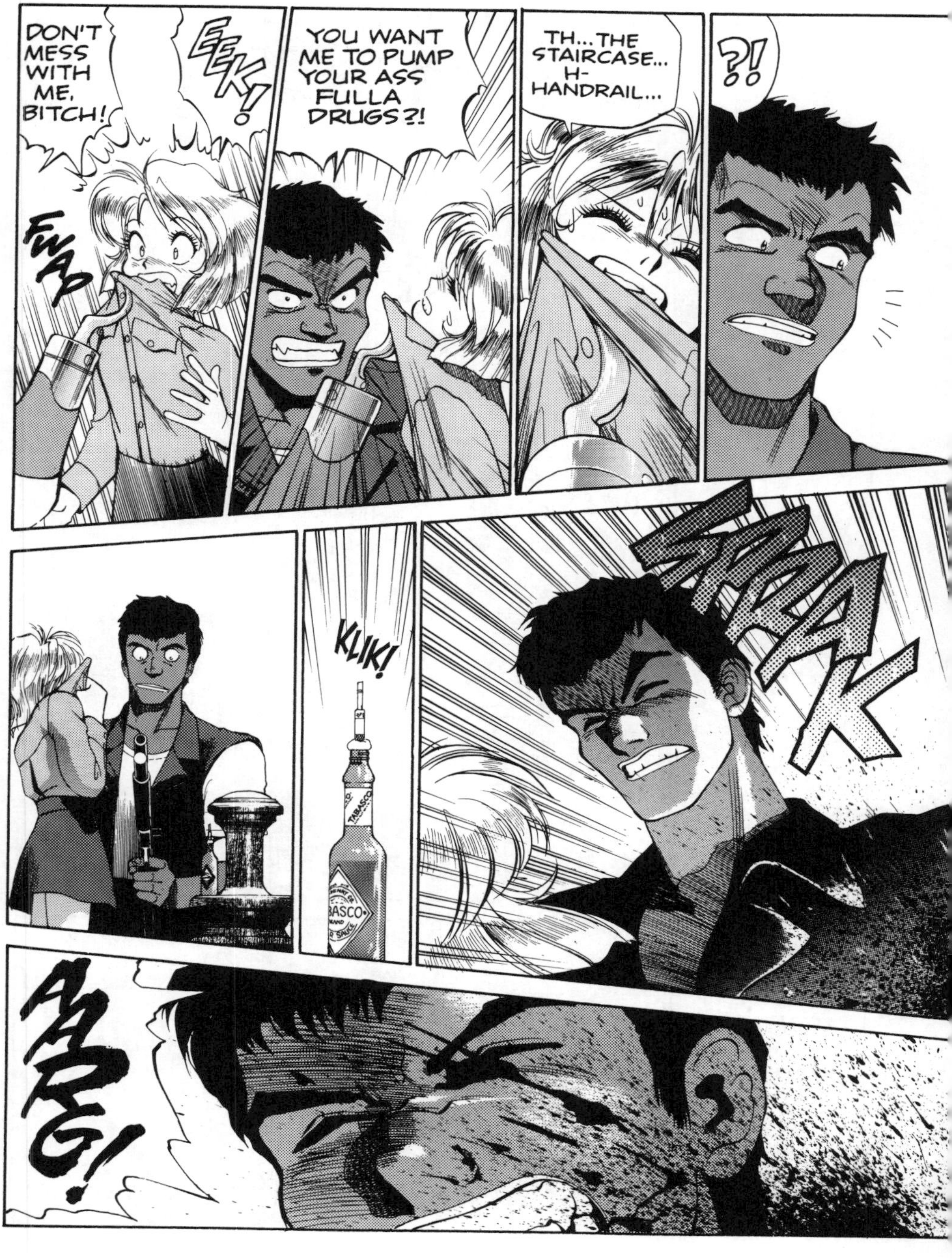
DON'T MESS WITH ME, BITCH!
EEEK!
FWAP
YOU WANT ME TO PUMP YOUR ASS FULLA DRUGS?!
TH... THE STAIRCASE... H-HANDRAIL...
?!
KLIK!
TABASCO
SMAAAK
AARG!

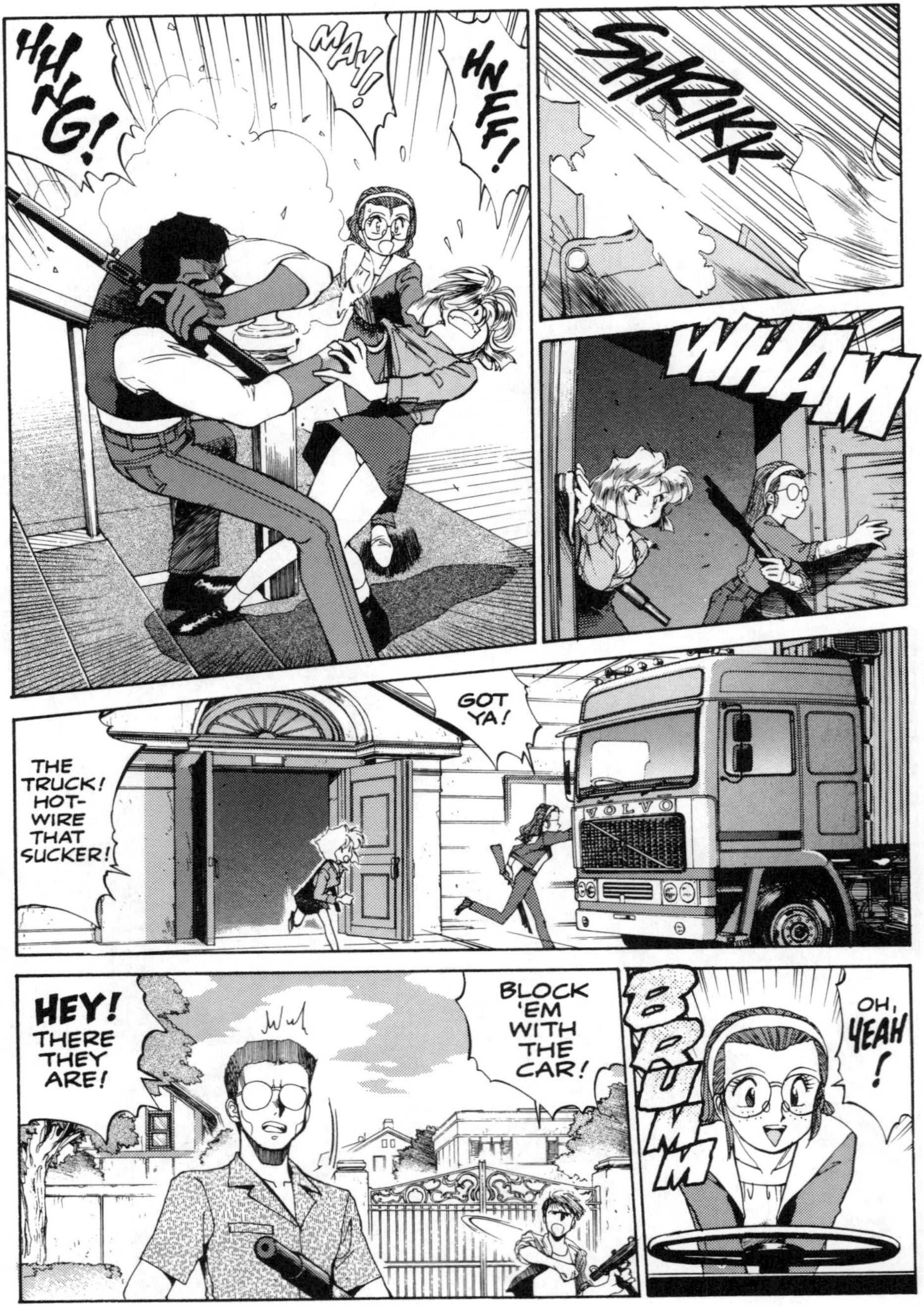

HHNG!
MAN!!
HNFF!
SHRIKK
WHAM
THE TRUCK! HOT-WIRE THAT SUCKER!
GOT YA!
VOLVO
HEY! THERE THEY ARE!
BLOCK 'EM WITH THE CAR!
BRUMM
OH, YEAH!

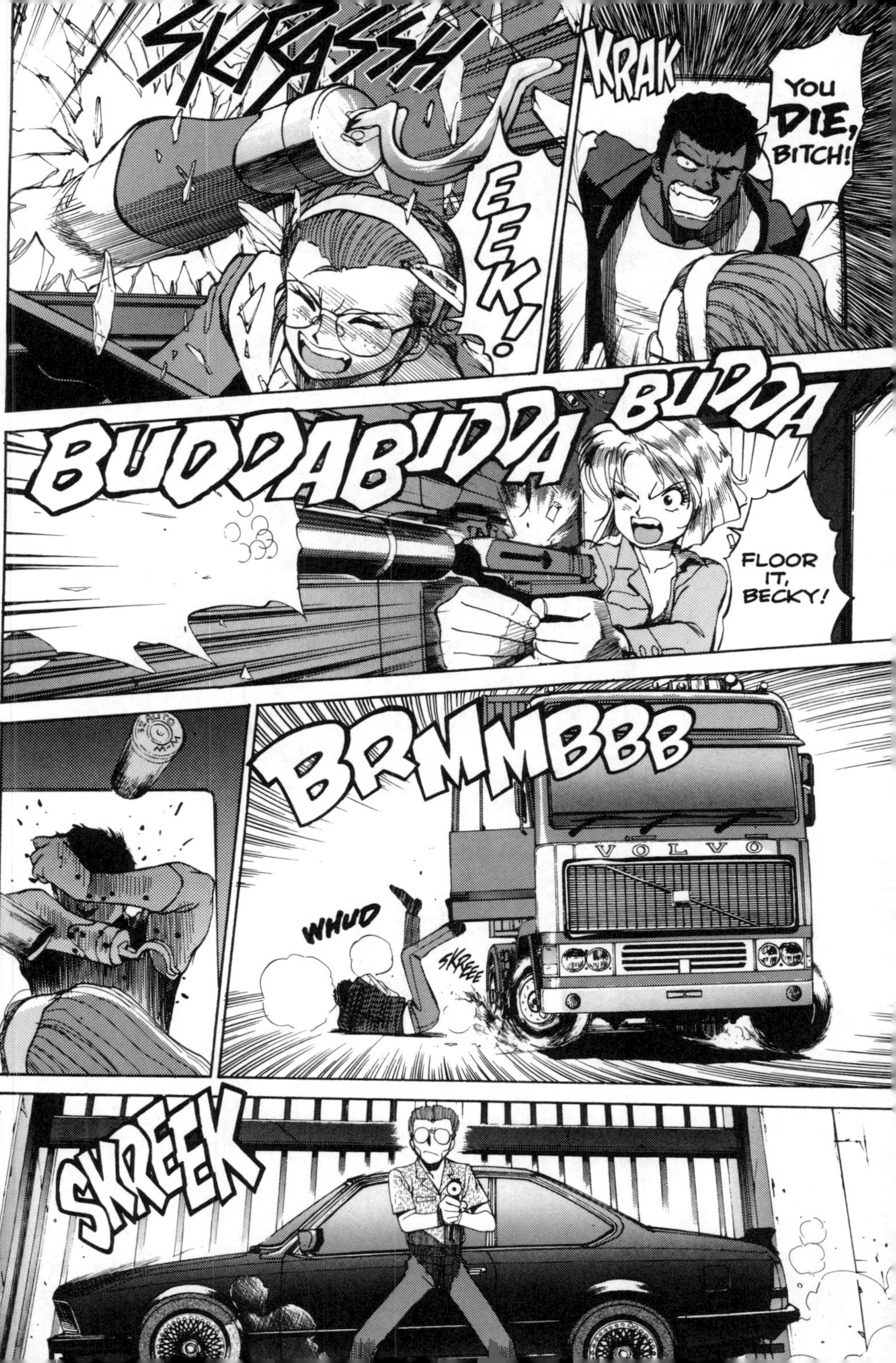
SKRASSH
EEEK!
KRAK
YOU DIE, BITCH!
BUDDABUDDA BUDDA
FLOOR IT, BECKY!
BRMMBBB
VOLVO
WHUD
SKREEE
SKREEK

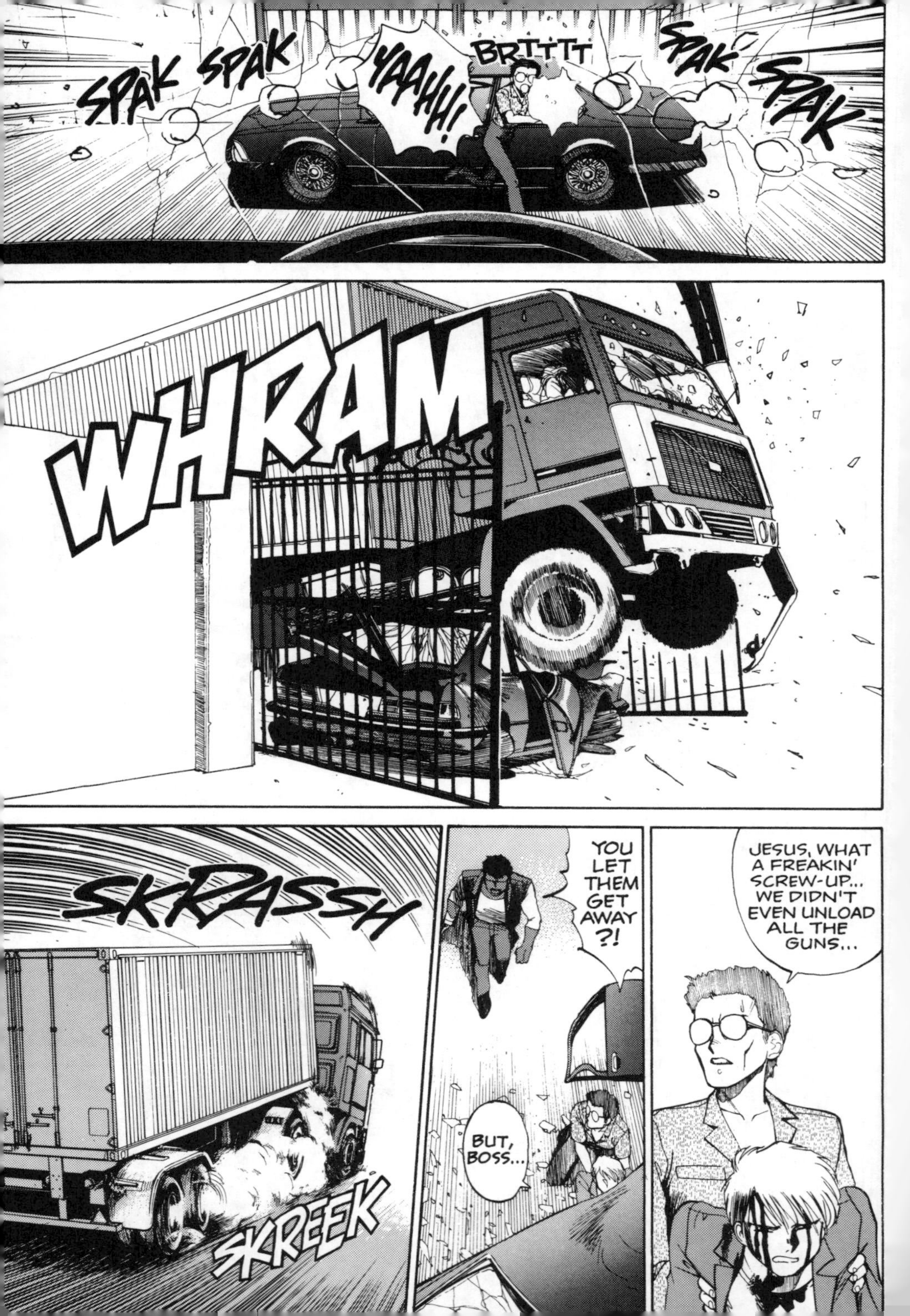
SPAK SPAK
YAAHH!!
BRTTTT
SPAK
SPAK
WHRAM
SKRASSH
SKREEK
YOU LET THEM GET AWAY?!
BUT, BOSS...
JESUS, WHAT A FREAKIN' SCREW-UP... WE DIDN'T EVEN UNLOAD ALL THE GUNS...

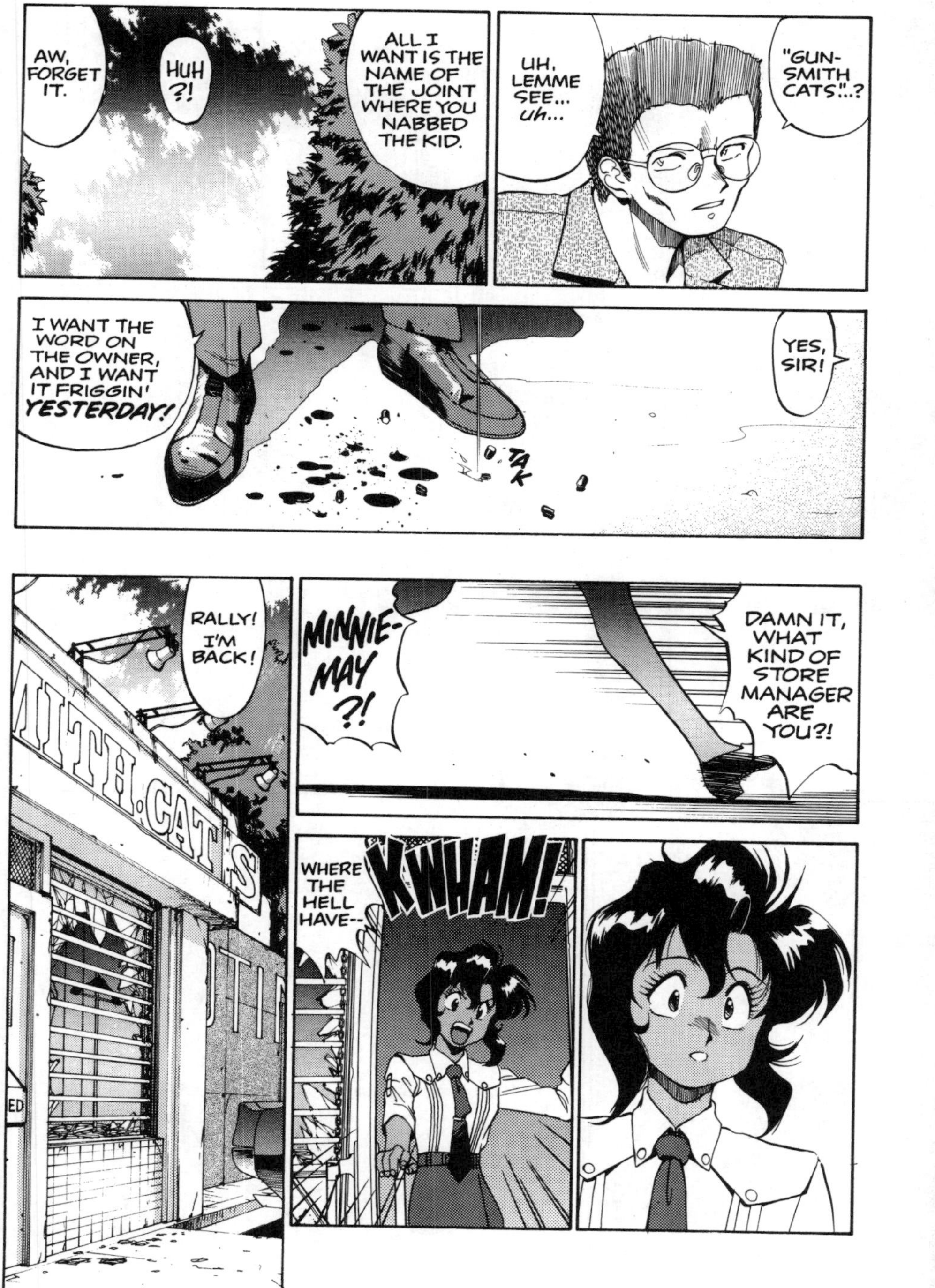

AW, FORGET IT.
HUH ?!
ALL I WANT IS THE NAME OF THE JOINT WHERE YOU NABBED THE KID.
UH, LEMME SEE... uh...
"GUN-SMITH CATS"..?
I WANT THE WORD ON THE OWNER, AND I WANT IT FRIGGIN' YESTERDAY!
YES, SIR!
TAK
RALLY! I'M BACK!
MINNIE-MAY ?!
DAMN IT, WHAT KIND OF STORE MANAGER ARE YOU?!
WHERE THE HELL HAVE--
KWHAM!

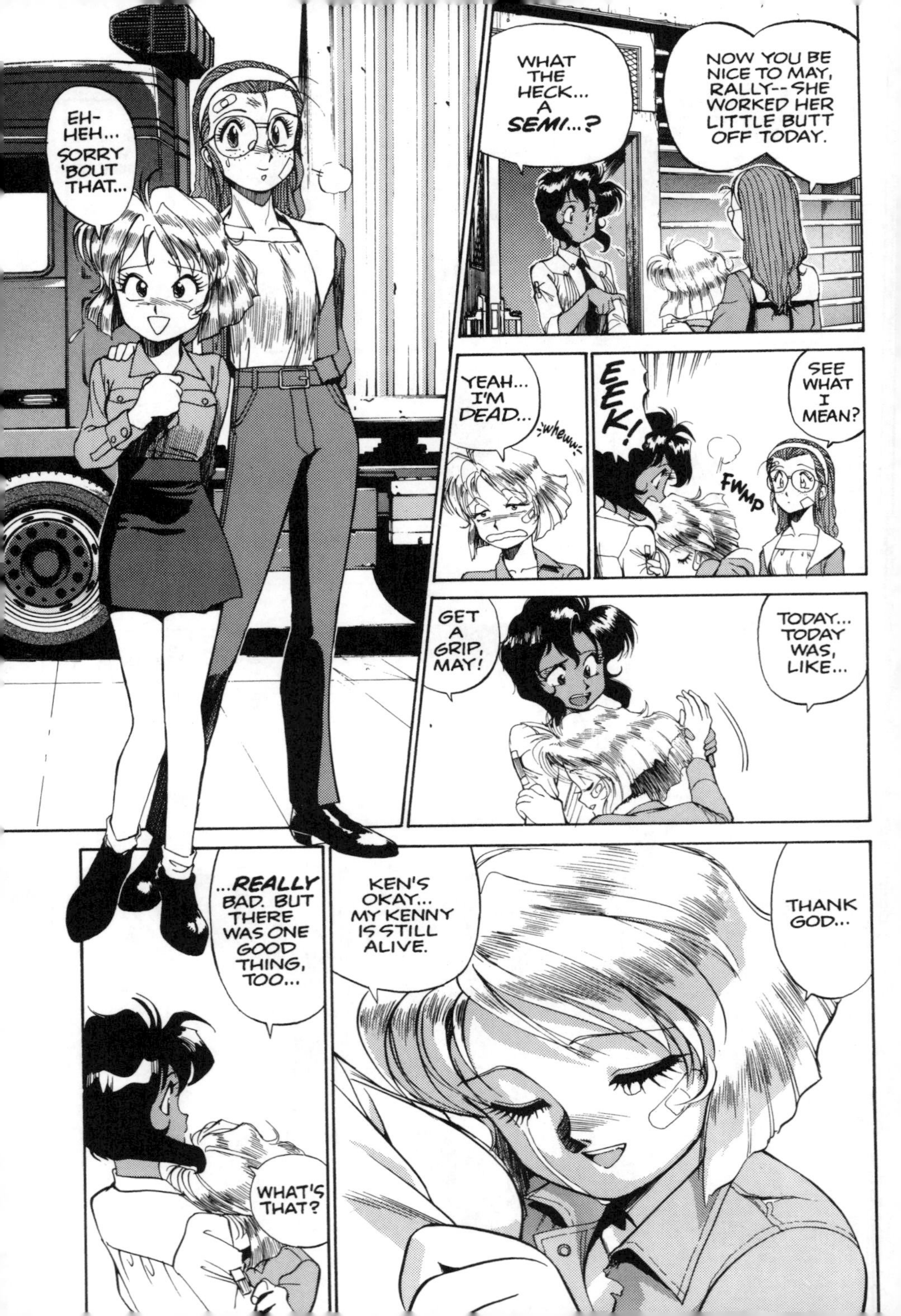
EH-HEH... SORRY 'BOUT THAT...
WHAT THE HECK... A *SEMI*...?
NOW YOU BE NICE TO MAY, RALLY-- SHE WORKED HER LITTLE BUTT OFF TODAY.
YEAH... I'M DEAD...
whewww
EEK!
FWMP
SEE WHAT I MEAN?
GET A GRIP, MAY!
TODAY... TODAY WAS, LIKE...
...*REALLY* BAD. BUT THERE WAS ONE GOOD THING, TOO...
WHAT'S THAT?
KEN'S OKAY... MY KENNY IS STILL ALIVE.
THANK GOD...

SIGHT IN

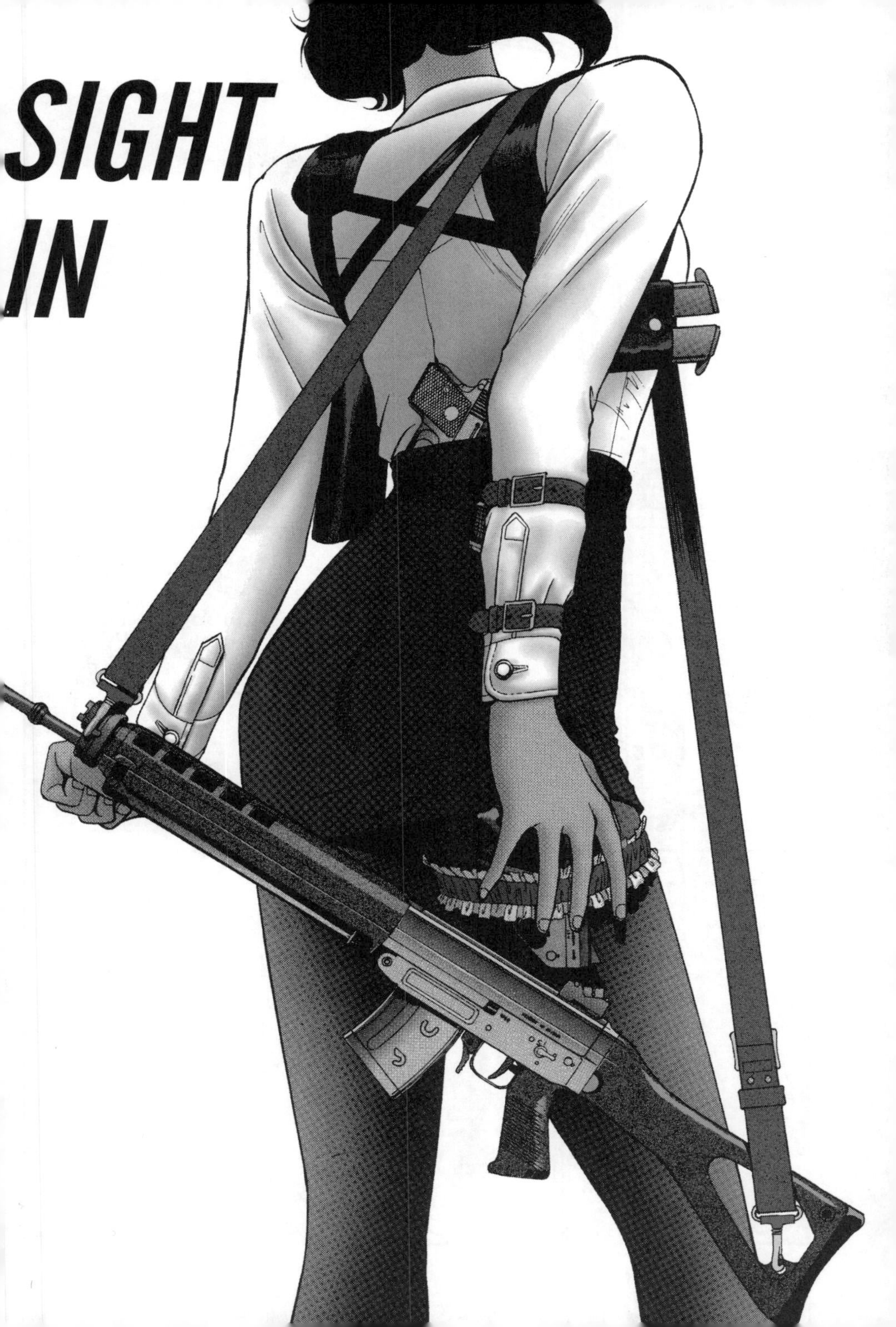

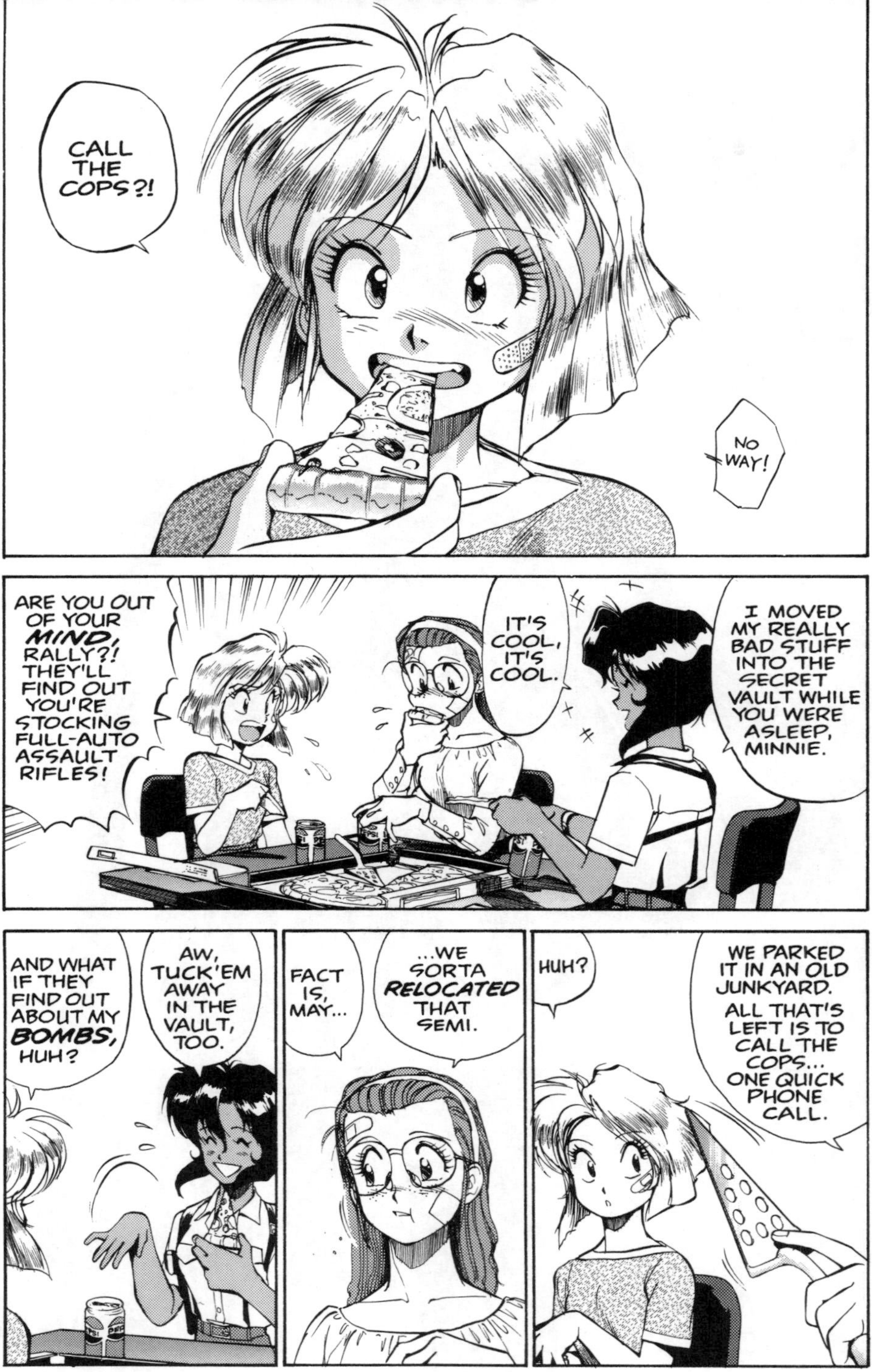
CALL THE COPS?!
NO WAY!
ARE YOU OUT OF YOUR MIND, RALLY?! THEY'LL FIND OUT YOU'RE STOCKING FULL-AUTO ASSAULT RIFLES!
IT'S COOL, IT'S COOL.
I MOVED MY REALLY BAD STUFF INTO THE SECRET VAULT WHILE YOU WERE ASLEEP, MINNIE.
AND WHAT IF THEY FIND OUT ABOUT MY BOMBS, HUH?
AW, TUCK'EM AWAY IN THE VAULT, TOO.
FACT IS, MAY...
...WE SORTA RELOCATED THAT SEMI.
HUH?
WE PARKED IT IN AN OLD JUNKYARD.
ALL THAT'S LEFT IS TO CALL THE COPS... ONE QUICK PHONE CALL.

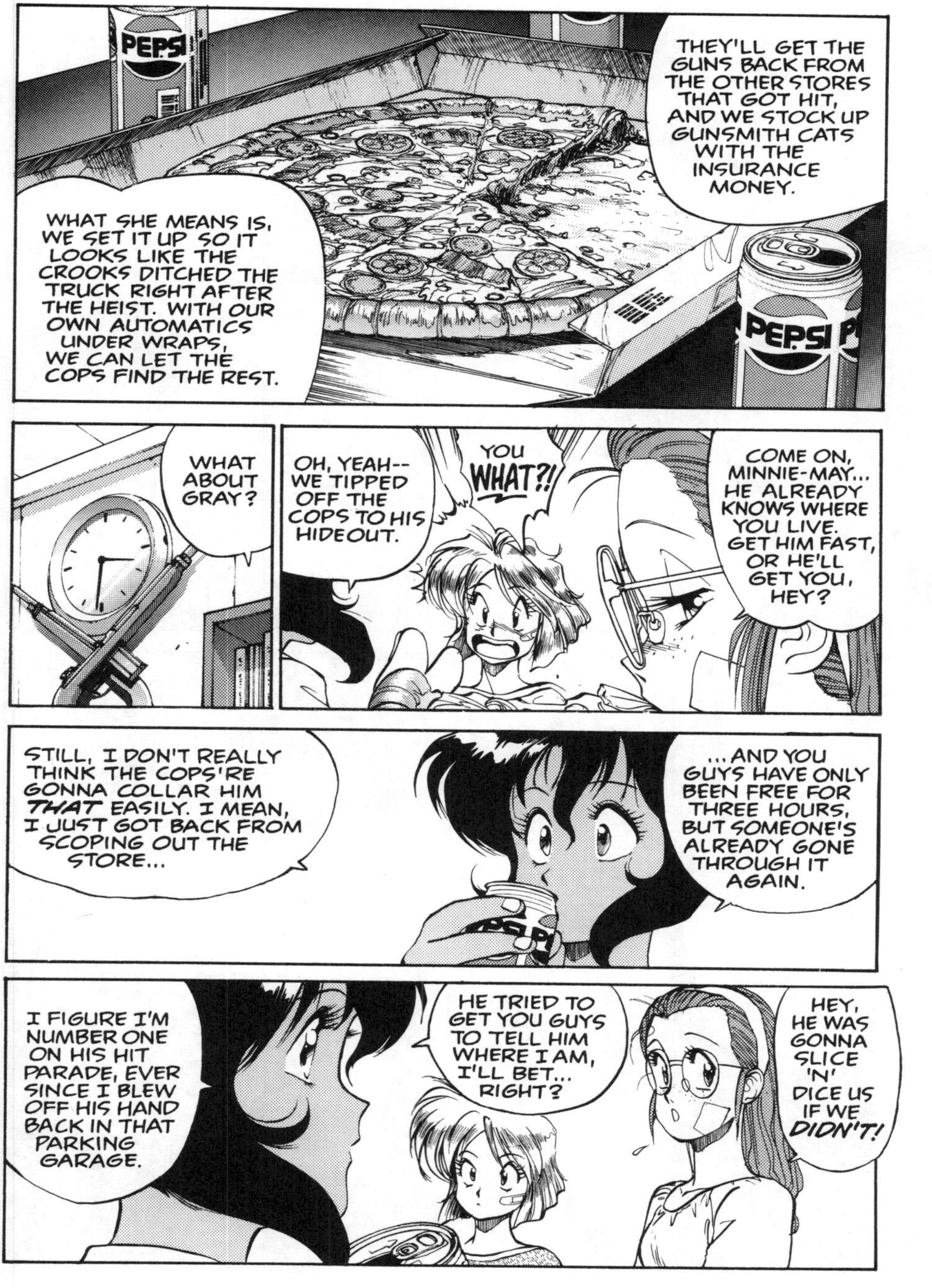
PEPSI
WHAT SHE MEANS IS, WE SET IT UP SO IT LOOKS LIKE THE CROOKS DITCHED THE TRUCK RIGHT AFTER THE HEIST. WITH OUR OWN AUTOMATICS UNDER WRAPS, WE CAN LET THE COPS FIND THE REST.
THEY'LL GET THE GUNS BACK FROM THE OTHER STORES THAT GOT HIT, AND WE STOCK UP GUNSMITH CATS WITH THE INSURANCE MONEY.
PEPSI
WHAT ABOUT GRAY?
OH, YEAH-- WE TIPPED OFF THE COPS TO HIS HIDEOUT.
YOU WHAT?!
COME ON, MINNIE-MAY... HE ALREADY KNOWS WHERE YOU LIVE. GET HIM FAST, OR HE'LL GET YOU, HEY?
STILL, I DON'T REALLY THINK THE COPS'RE GONNA COLLAR HIM *THAT* EASILY. I MEAN, I JUST GOT BACK FROM SCOPING OUT THE STORE...
...AND YOU GUYS HAVE ONLY BEEN FREE FOR THREE HOURS, BUT SOMEONE'S ALREADY GONE THROUGH IT AGAIN.
I FIGURE I'M NUMBER ONE ON HIS HIT PARADE, EVER SINCE I BLEW OFF HIS HAND BACK IN THAT PARKING GARAGE.
HE TRIED TO GET YOU GUYS TO TELL HIM WHERE I AM, I'LL BET... RIGHT?
HEY, HE WAS GONNA SLICE 'N' DICE US IF WE *DIDN'T*!

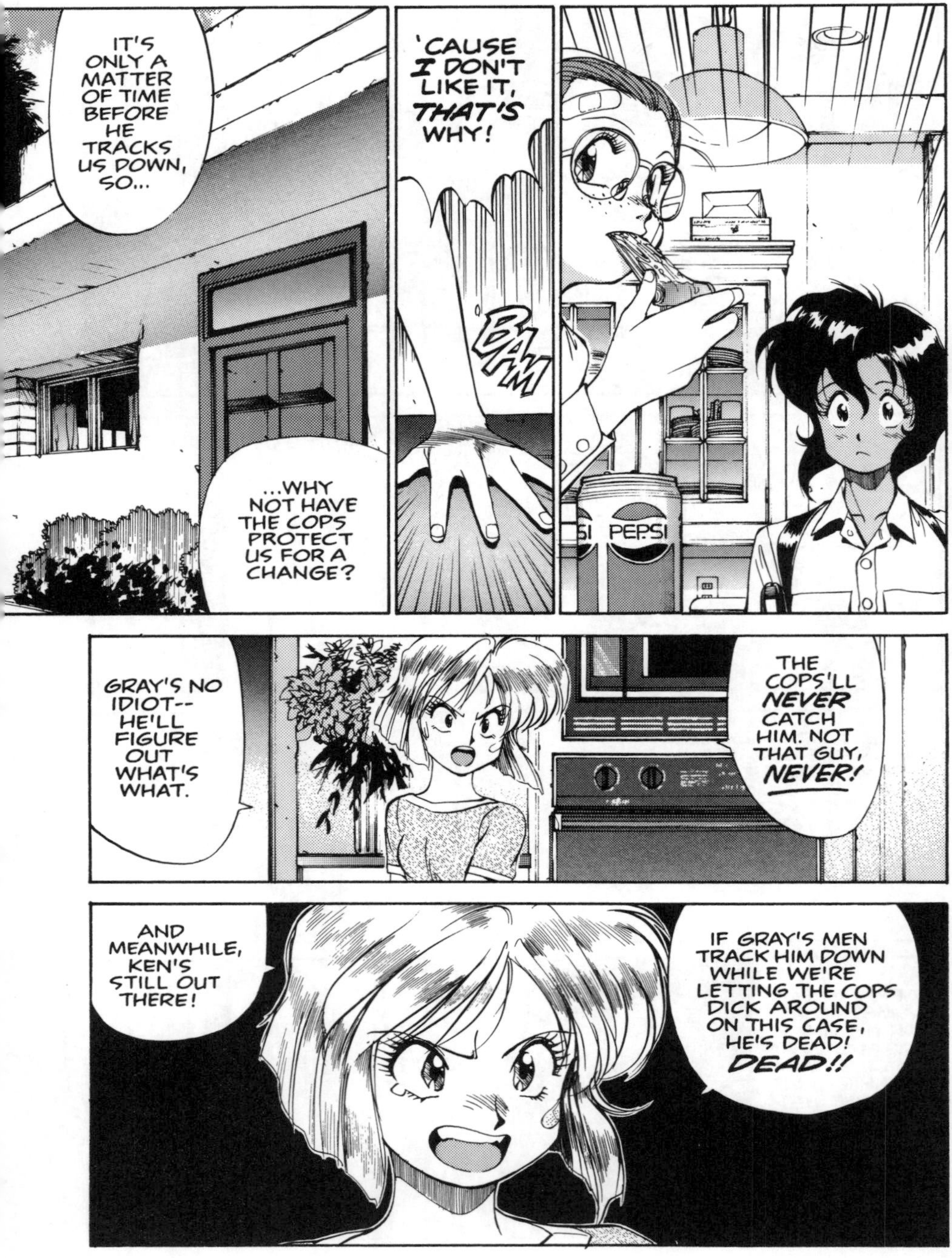
IT'S ONLY A MATTER OF TIME BEFORE HE TRACKS US DOWN, SO...
...WHY NOT HAVE THE COPS PROTECT US FOR A CHANGE?
'CAUSE *I* DON'T LIKE IT, *THAT'S* WHY!
BAM
SI PEPSI
GRAY'S NO IDIOT-- HE'LL FIGURE OUT WHAT'S WHAT.
THE COPS'LL *NEVER* CATCH HIM. NOT THAT GUY, *NEVER!*
AND MEANWHILE, KEN'S STILL OUT THERE!
IF GRAY'S MEN TRACK HIM DOWN WHILE WE'RE LETTING THE COPS DICK AROUND ON THIS CASE, HE'S DEAD! *DEAD!!*

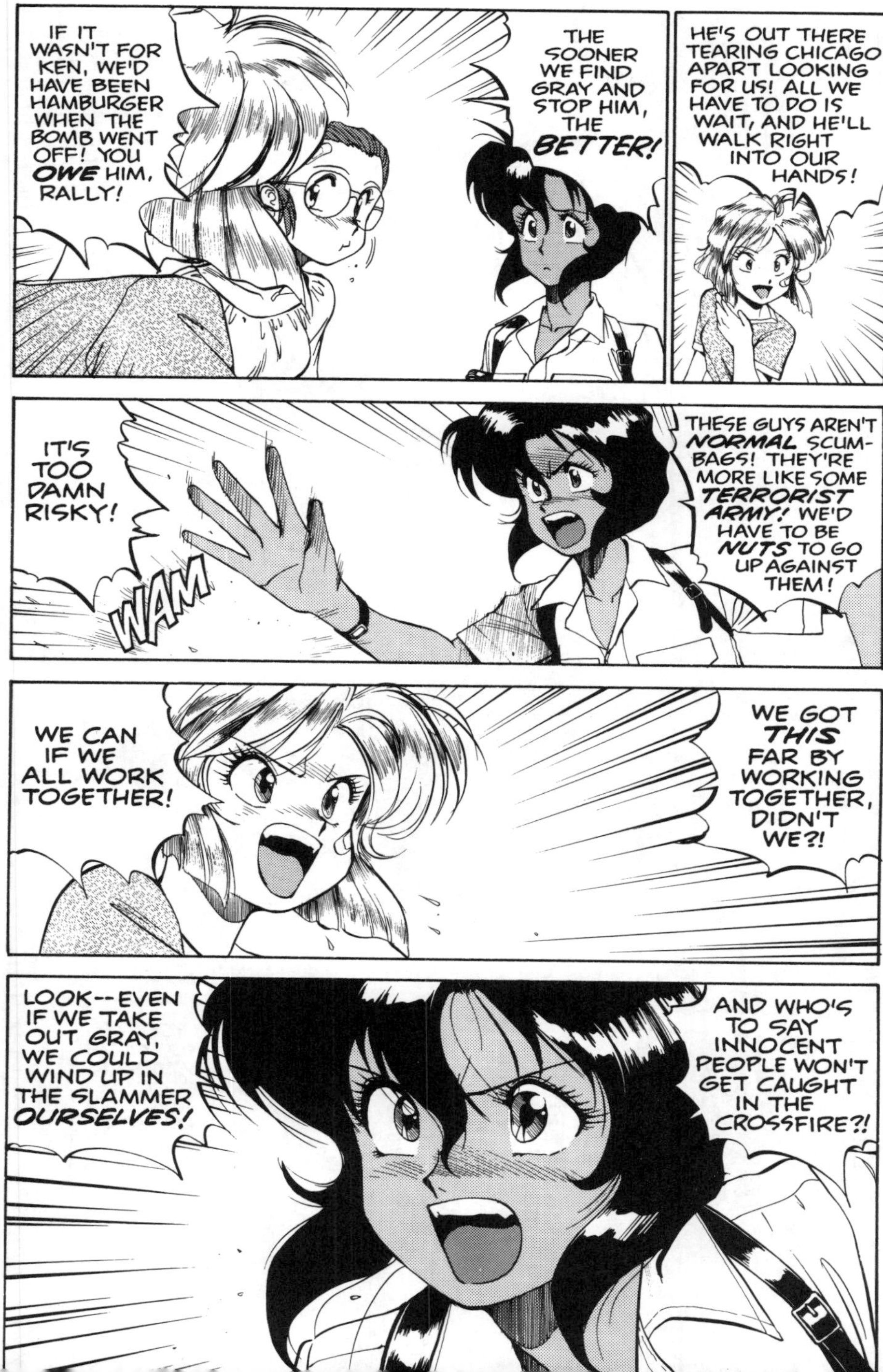
IF IT WASN'T FOR KEN, WE'D HAVE BEEN HAMBURGER WHEN THE BOMB WENT OFF! YOU OWE HIM, RALLY!
THE SOONER WE FIND GRAY AND STOP HIM, THE BETTER!
HE'S OUT THERE TEARING CHICAGO APART LOOKING FOR US! ALL WE HAVE TO DO IS WAIT, AND HE'LL WALK RIGHT INTO OUR HANDS!
IT'S TOO DAMN RISKY!
THESE GUYS AREN'T NORMAL SCUM-BAGS! THEY'RE MORE LIKE SOME TERRORIST ARMY! WE'D HAVE TO BE NUTS TO GO UP AGAINST THEM!
WAM
WE CAN IF WE ALL WORK TOGETHER!
WE GOT THIS FAR BY WORKING TOGETHER, DIDN'T WE?!
LOOK--EVEN IF WE TAKE OUT GRAY, WE COULD WIND UP IN THE SLAMMER OURSELVES!
AND WHO'S TO SAY INNOCENT PEOPLE WON'T GET CAUGHT IN THE CROSSFIRE?!

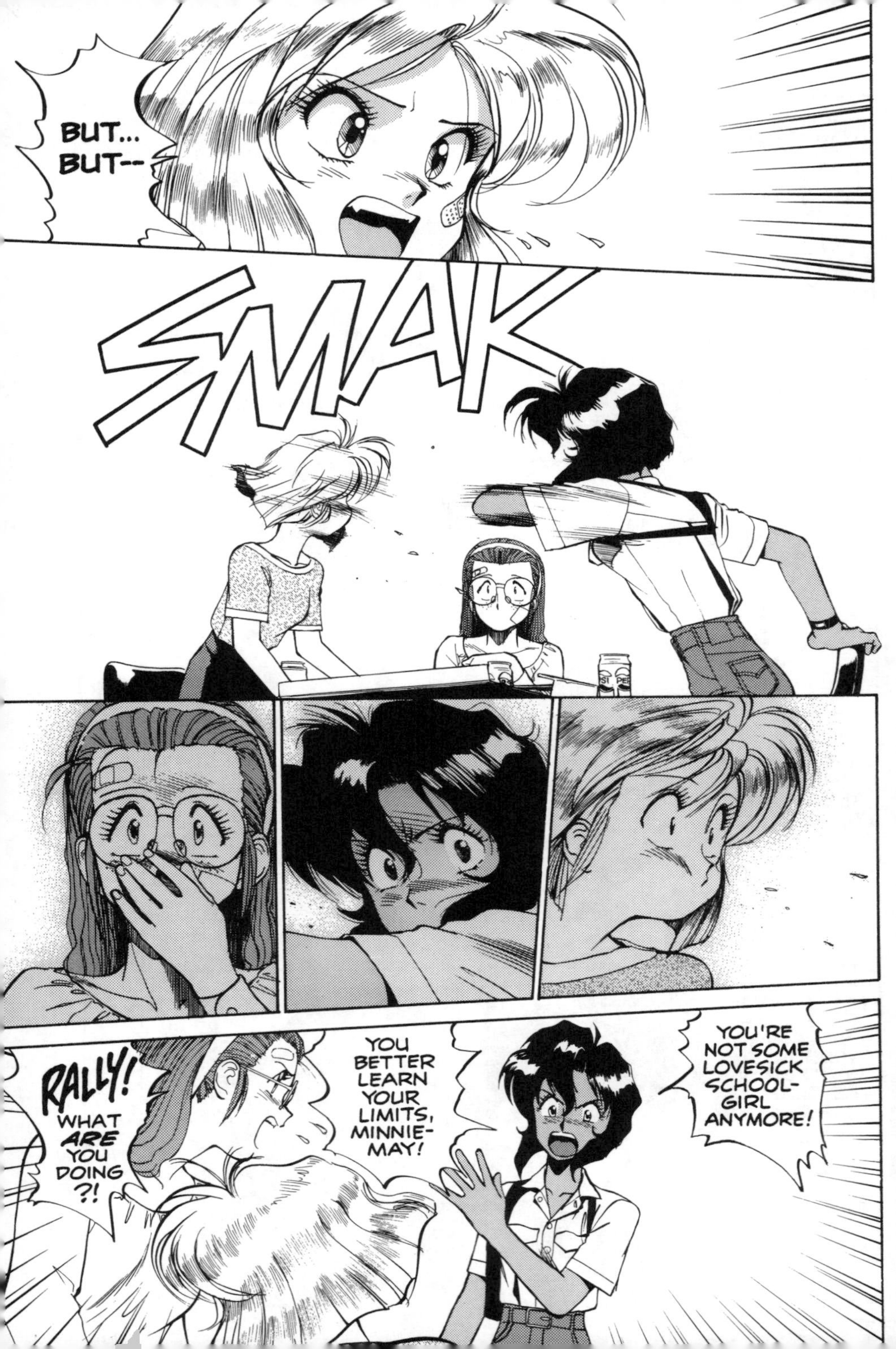

BUT... BUT--
SMAK
RALLY! WHAT ARE YOU DOING ?!
YOU BETTER LEARN YOUR LIMITS, MINNIE-MAY!
YOU'RE NOT SOME LOVESICK SCHOOL-GIRL ANYMORE!

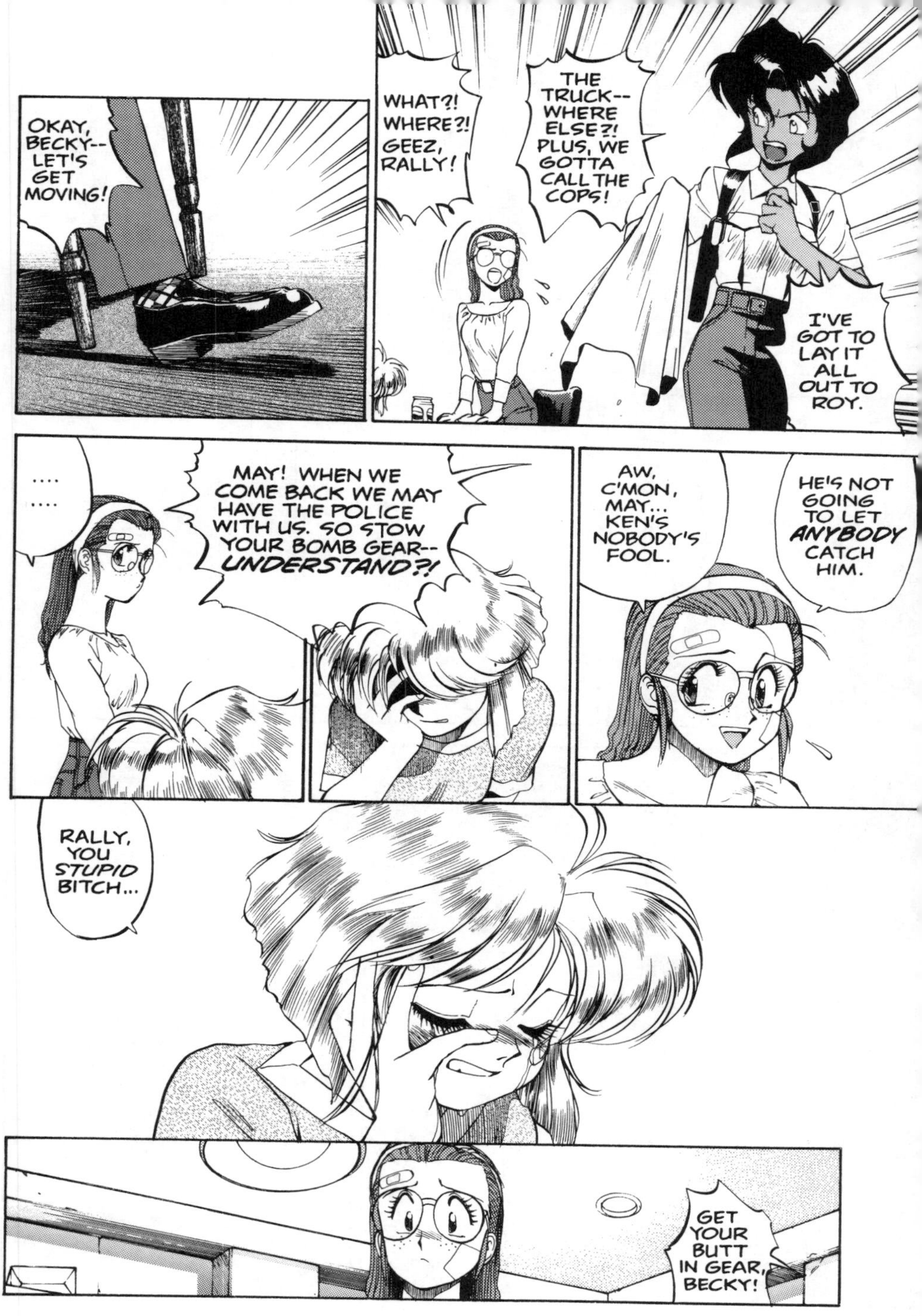
OKAY, BECKY-- LET'S GET MOVING!
WHAT?! WHERE?! GEEZ, RALLY!
THE TRUCK-- WHERE ELSE?! PLUS, WE GOTTA CALL THE COPS!
I'VE GOT TO LAY IT ALL OUT TO ROY.
....
MAY! WHEN WE COME BACK WE MAY HAVE THE POLICE WITH US. SO STOW YOUR BOMB GEAR-- *UNDERSTAND?!*
AW, C'MON, MAY... KEN'S NOBODY'S FOOL.
HE'S NOT GOING TO LET *ANYBODY* CATCH HIM.
RALLY, YOU *STUPID* BITCH...
GET YOUR BUTT IN GEAR, BECKY!

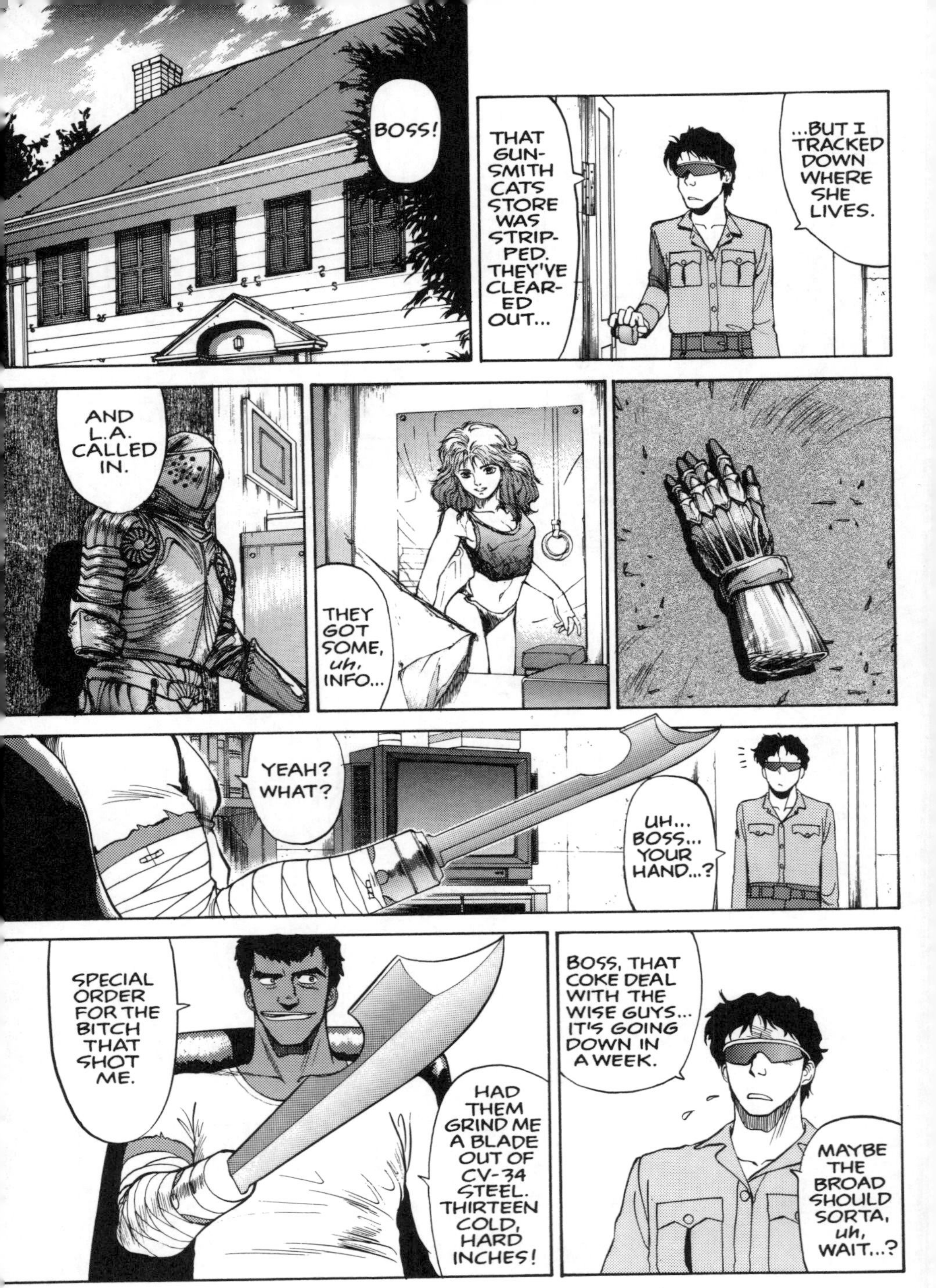
BOSS!
THAT GUN-SMITH CATS STORE WAS STRIP-PED. THEY'VE CLEAR-ED OUT...
...BUT I TRACKED DOWN WHERE SHE LIVES.
AND L.A. CALLED IN.
THEY GOT SOME, uh, INFO...
YEAH? WHAT?
UH... BOSS... YOUR HAND...?
SPECIAL ORDER FOR THE BITCH THAT SHOT ME.
HAD THEM GRIND ME A BLADE OUT OF CV-34 STEEL. THIRTEEN COLD, HARD INCHES!
BOSS, THAT COKE DEAL WITH THE WISE GUYS... IT'S GOING DOWN IN A WEEK.
MAYBE THE BROAD SHOULD SORTA, uh, WAIT...?

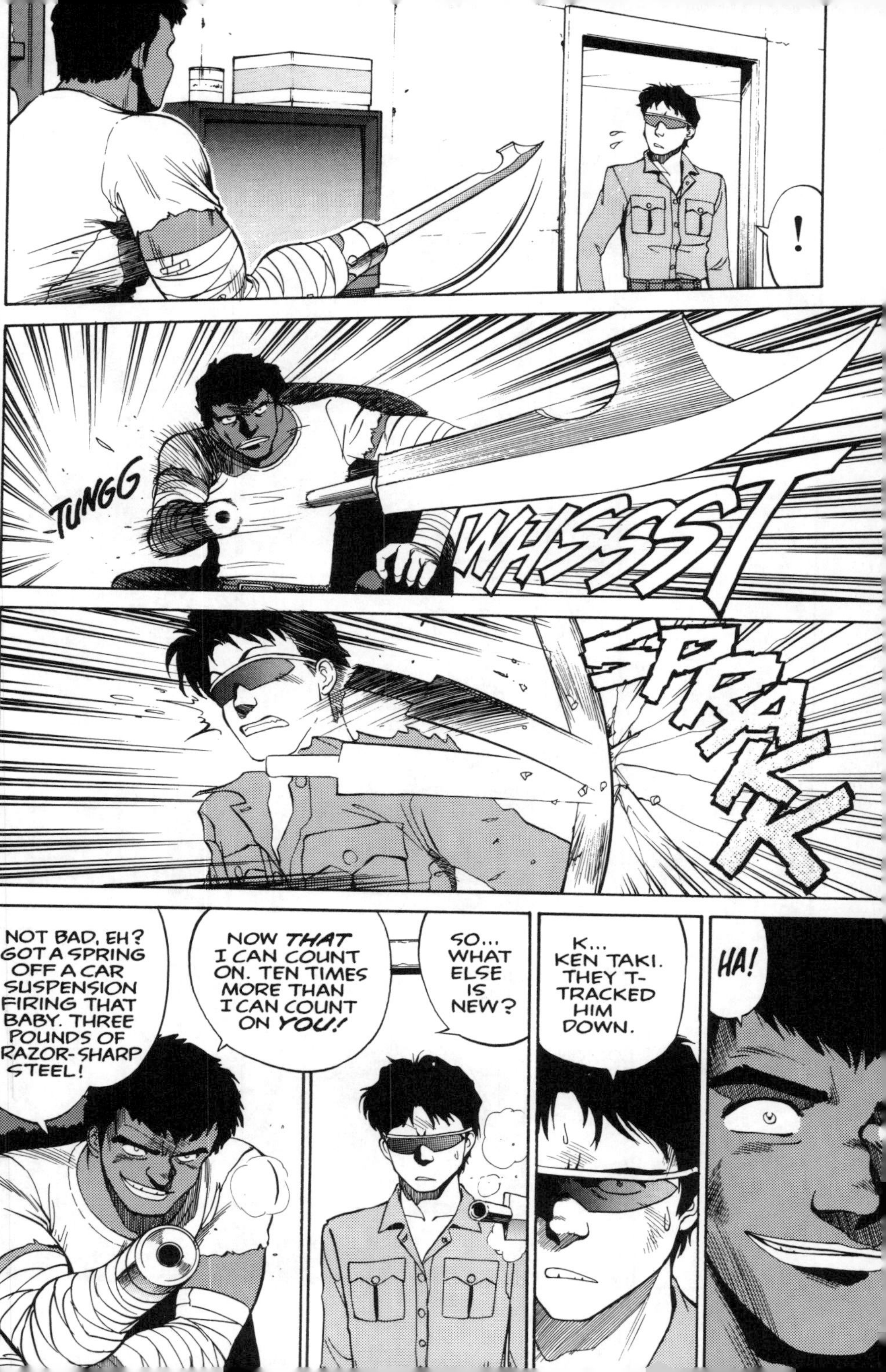
!
TUNGG
WHSSSST
SPRAKK
NOT BAD, EH? GOT A SPRING OFF A CAR SUSPENSION FIRING THAT BABY. THREE POUNDS OF RAZOR-SHARP STEEL!
NOW THAT I CAN COUNT ON. TEN TIMES MORE THAN I CAN COUNT ON YOU!
SO... WHAT ELSE IS NEW?
K... KEN TAKI. THEY T-TRACKED HIM DOWN.
HA!

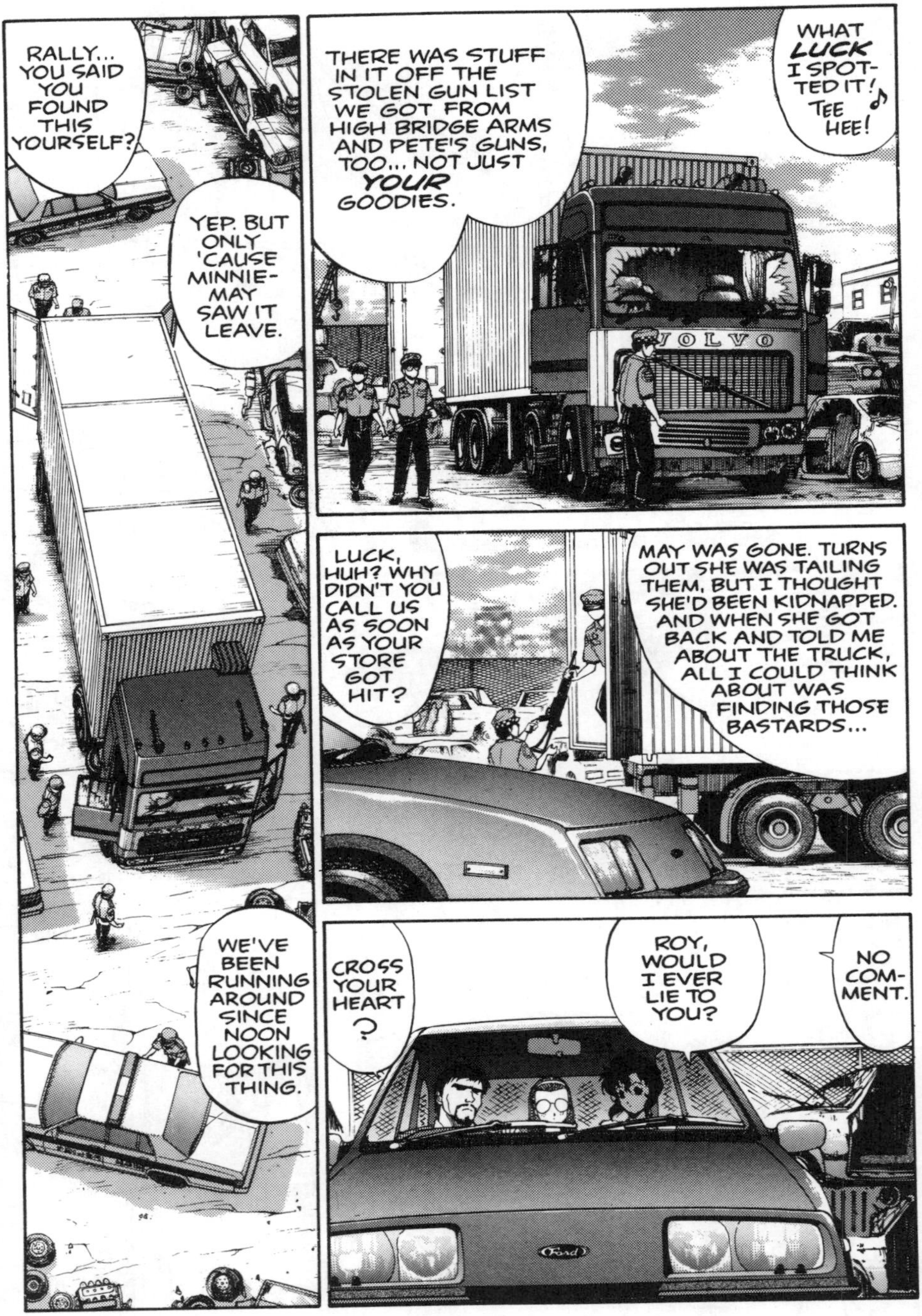
RALLY... YOU SAID YOU FOUND THIS YOURSELF?
YEP. BUT ONLY 'CAUSE MINNIE-MAY SAW IT LEAVE.
WE'VE BEEN RUNNING AROUND SINCE NOON LOOKING FOR THIS THING.
THERE WAS STUFF IN IT OFF THE STOLEN GUN LIST WE GOT FROM HIGH BRIDGE ARMS AND PETE'S GUNS, TOO... NOT JUST YOUR GOODIES.
WHAT LUCK I SPOTTED IT! ♪ TEE HEE!
VOLVO
LUCK, HUH? WHY DIDN'T YOU CALL US AS SOON AS YOUR STORE GOT HIT?
MAY WAS GONE. TURNS OUT SHE WAS TAILING THEM, BUT I THOUGHT SHE'D BEEN KIDNAPPED. AND WHEN SHE GOT BACK AND TOLD ME ABOUT THE TRUCK, ALL I COULD THINK ABOUT WAS FINDING THOSE BASTARDS...
CROSS YOUR HEART?
ROY, WOULD I EVER LIE TO YOU?
NO COMMENT.
Ford

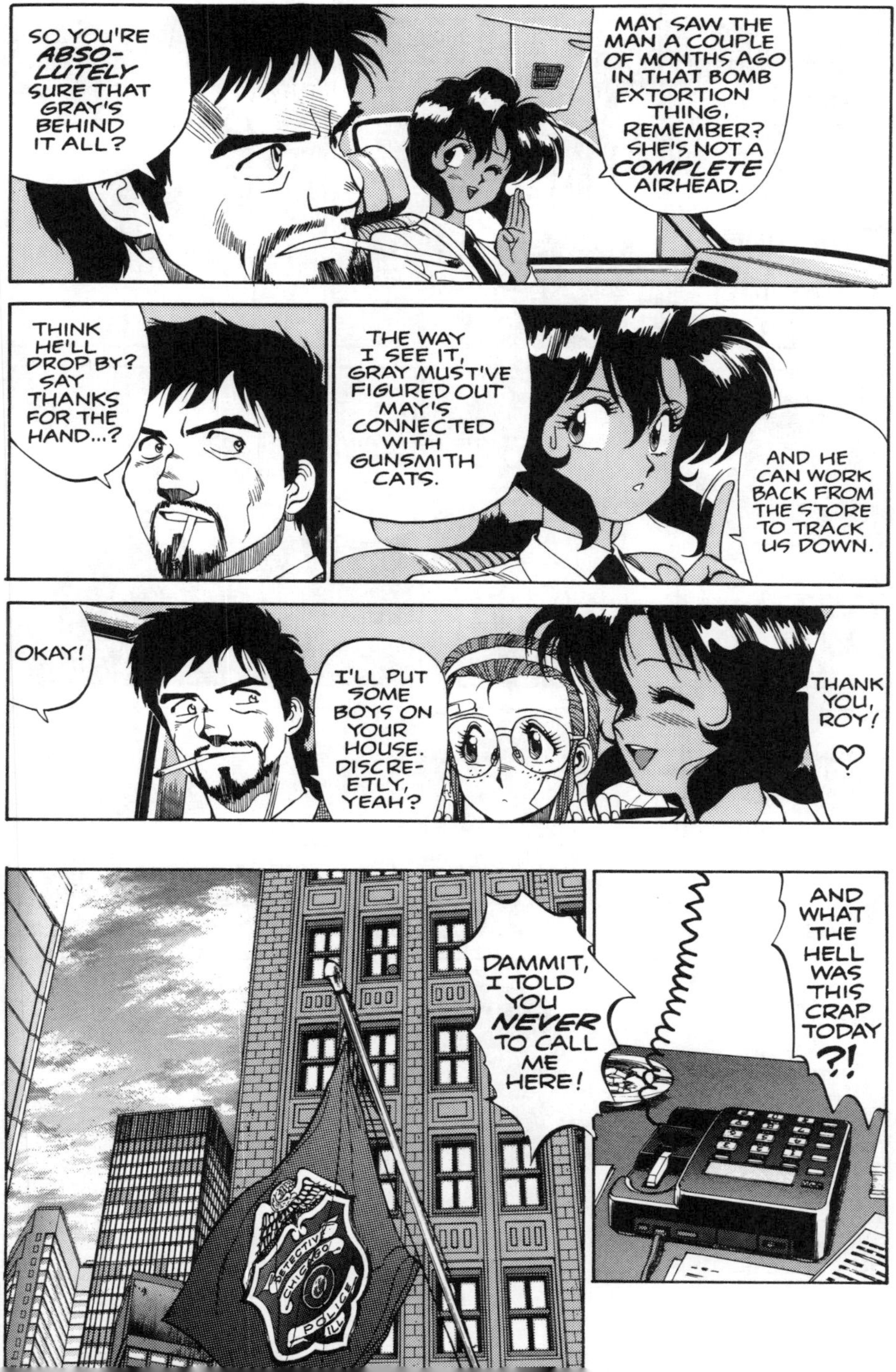
SO YOU'RE ABSOLUTELY SURE THAT GRAY'S BEHIND IT ALL?
MAY SAW THE MAN A COUPLE OF MONTHS AGO IN THAT BOMB EXTORTION THING, REMEMBER? SHE'S NOT A COMPLETE AIRHEAD.
THINK HE'LL DROP BY? SAY THANKS FOR THE HAND...?
THE WAY I SEE IT, GRAY MUST'VE FIGURED OUT MAY'S CONNECTED WITH GUNSMITH CATS.
AND HE CAN WORK BACK FROM THE STORE TO TRACK US DOWN.
OKAY!
I'LL PUT SOME BOYS ON YOUR HOUSE. DISCRE-ETLY, YEAH?
THANK YOU, ROY! ♡
DAMMIT, I TOLD YOU NEVER TO CALL ME HERE!
AND WHAT THE HELL WAS THIS CRAP TODAY ?!

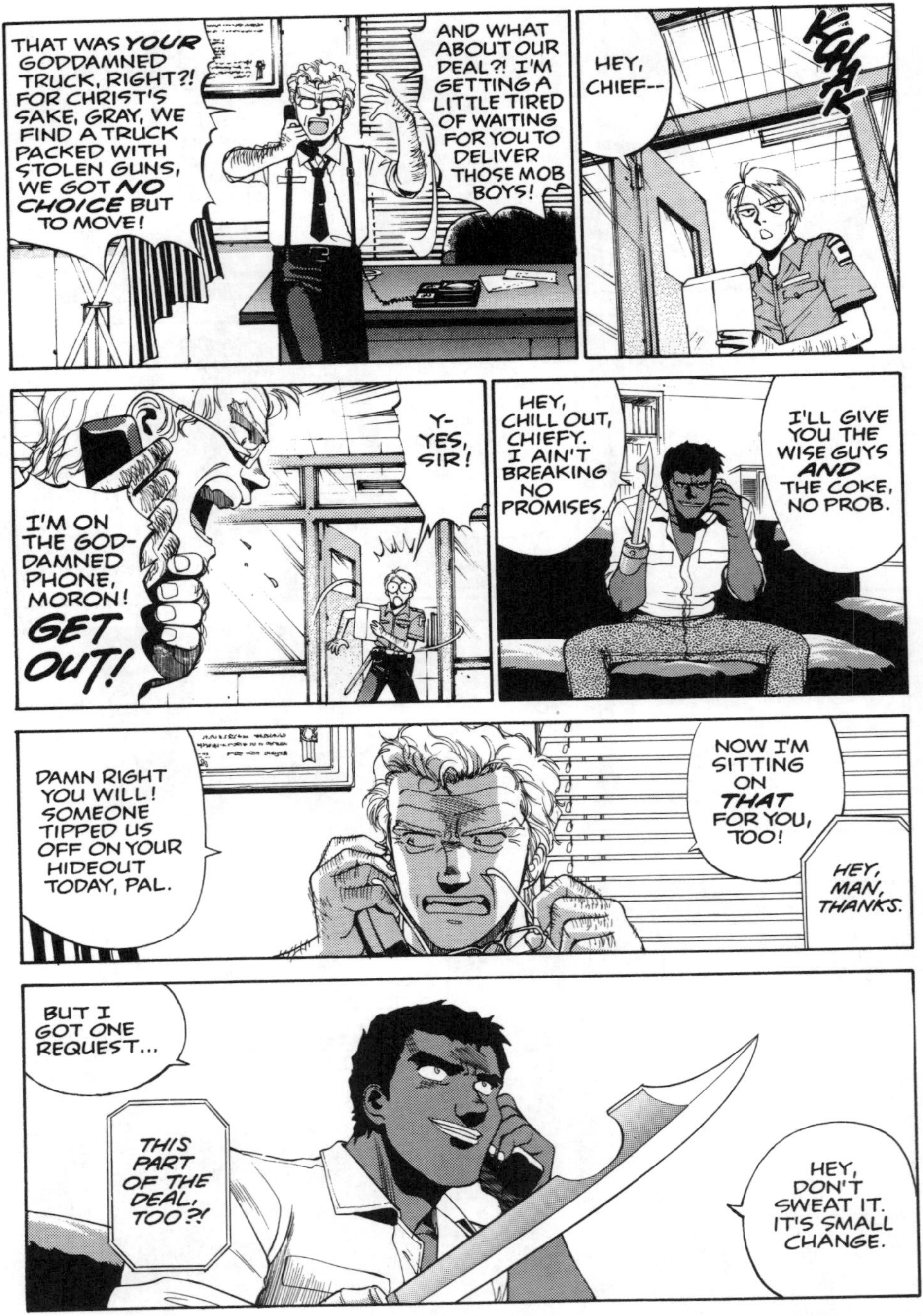
THAT WAS YOUR GODDAMNED TRUCK, RIGHT?! FOR CHRIST'S SAKE, GRAY, WE FIND A TRUCK PACKED WITH STOLEN GUNS, WE GOT NO CHOICE BUT TO MOVE!
AND WHAT ABOUT OUR DEAL?! I'M GETTING A LITTLE TIRED OF WAITING FOR YOU TO DELIVER THOSE MOB BOYS!
KCHAK
HEY, CHIEF--
I'M ON THE GOD-DAMNED PHONE, MORON! GET OUT!
Y-YES, SIR!
HEY, CHILL OUT, CHIEFY. I AIN'T BREAKING NO PROMISES.
I'LL GIVE YOU THE WISE GUYS AND THE COKE, NO PROB.
DAMN RIGHT YOU WILL! SOMEONE TIPPED US OFF ON YOUR HIDEOUT TODAY, PAL.
NOW I'M SITTING ON THAT FOR YOU, TOO!
HEY, MAN, THANKS.
BUT I GOT ONE REQUEST...
THIS PART OF THE DEAL, TOO?!
HEY, DON'T SWEAT IT. IT'S SMALL CHANGE.

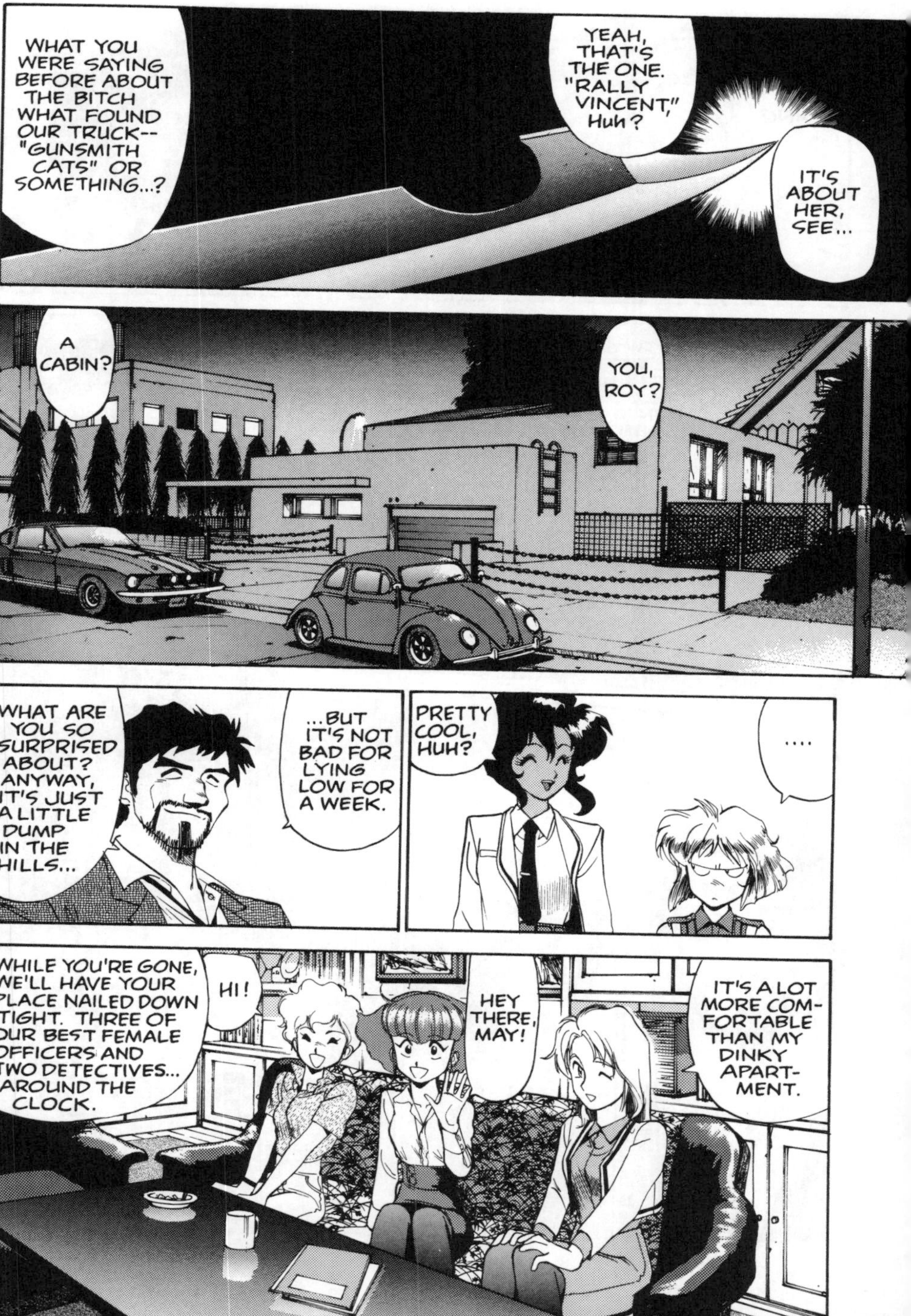
WHAT YOU WERE SAYING BEFORE ABOUT THE BITCH WHAT FOUND OUR TRUCK-- "GUNSMITH CATS" OR SOMETHING...?
YEAH, THAT'S THE ONE. "RALLY VINCENT," Huh?
IT'S ABOUT HER, SEE...
A CABIN?
YOU, ROY?
WHAT ARE YOU SO SURPRISED ABOUT? ANYWAY, IT'S JUST A LITTLE DUMP IN THE HILLS...
...BUT IT'S NOT BAD FOR LYING LOW FOR A WEEK.
PRETTY COOL, HUH?
....
WHILE YOU'RE GONE, WE'LL HAVE YOUR PLACE NAILED DOWN TIGHT. THREE OF OUR BEST FEMALE OFFICERS AND TWO DETECTIVES... AROUND THE CLOCK.
HI!
HEY THERE, MAY!
IT'S A LOT MORE COMFORTABLE THAN MY DINKY APARTMENT.

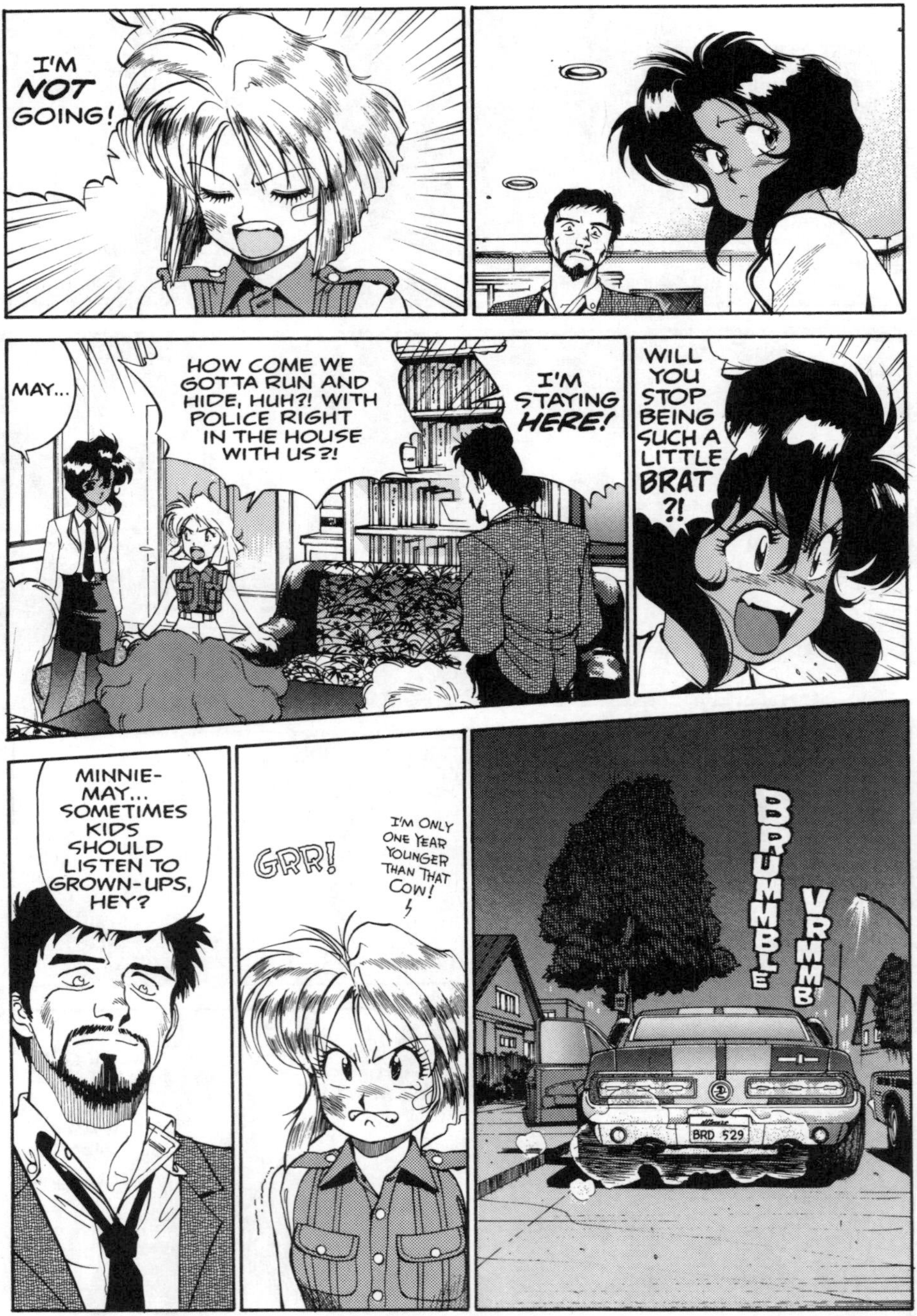
I'M NOT GOING!
MAY...
HOW COME WE GOTTA RUN AND HIDE, HUH?! WITH POLICE RIGHT IN THE HOUSE WITH US?!
I'M STAYING HERE!
WILL YOU STOP BEING SUCH A LITTLE BRAT?!
MINNIE-MAY... SOMETIMES KIDS SHOULD LISTEN TO GROWN-UPS, HEY?
GRR!
I'M ONLY ONE YEAR YOUNGER THAN THAT COW!
BRUMMBLE
VRMMB
BRD 529

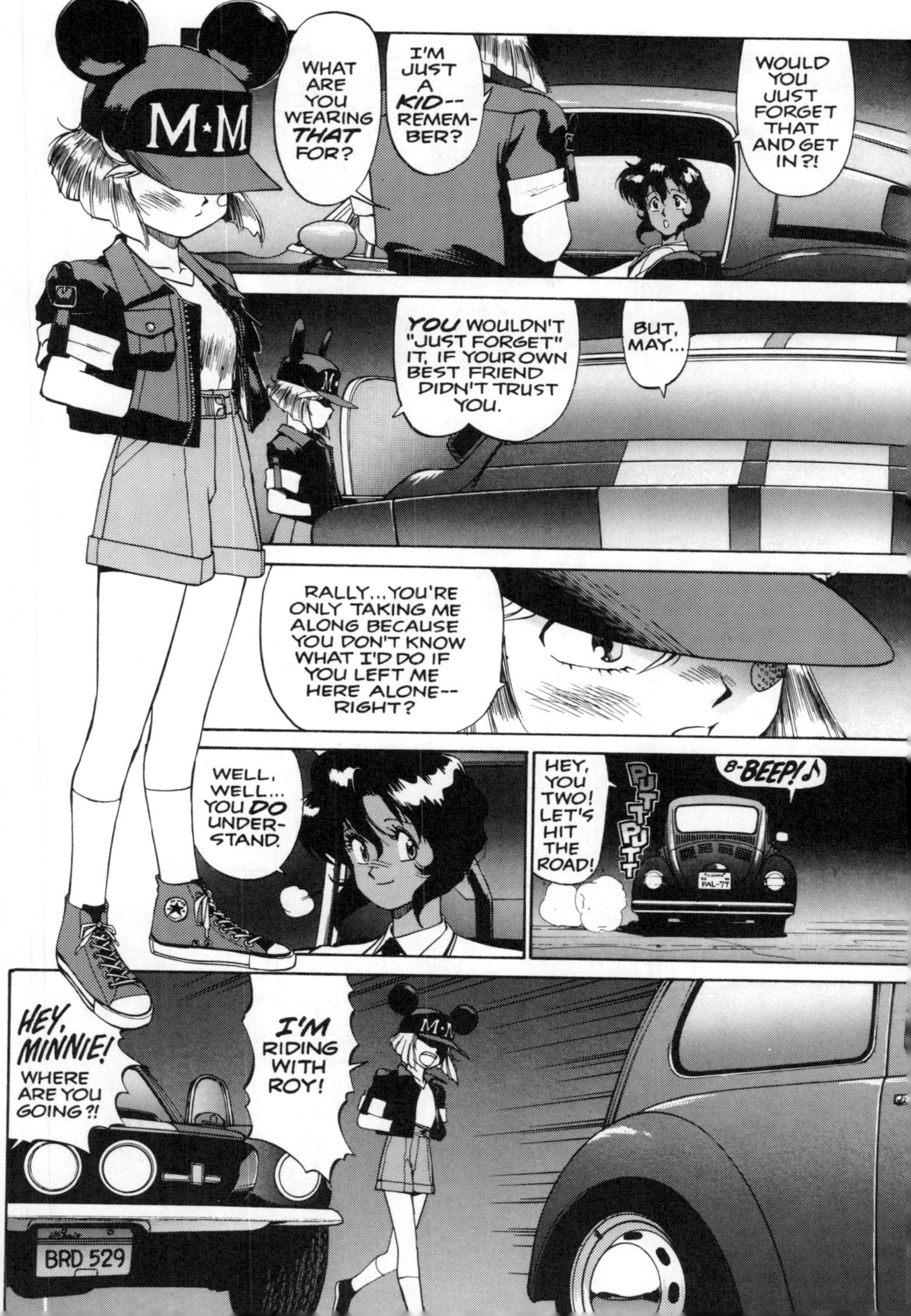
M·M
WHAT ARE YOU WEARING THAT FOR?
I'M JUST A KID-- REMEMBER?
WOULD YOU JUST FORGET THAT AND GET IN?!
YOU WOULDN'T "JUST FORGET" IT, IF YOUR OWN BEST FRIEND DIDN'T TRUST YOU.
BUT, MAY...
RALLY... YOU'RE ONLY TAKING ME ALONG BECAUSE YOU DON'T KNOW WHAT I'D DO IF YOU LEFT ME HERE ALONE-- RIGHT?
WELL, WELL... YOU DO UNDERSTAND.
HEY, YOU TWO! LET'S HIT THE ROAD!
PUTT PUTT PUTT
B-BEEP!♪
FAL-77
HEY, MINNIE! WHERE ARE YOU GOING?!
I'M RIDING WITH ROY!
M·M
BRD 529

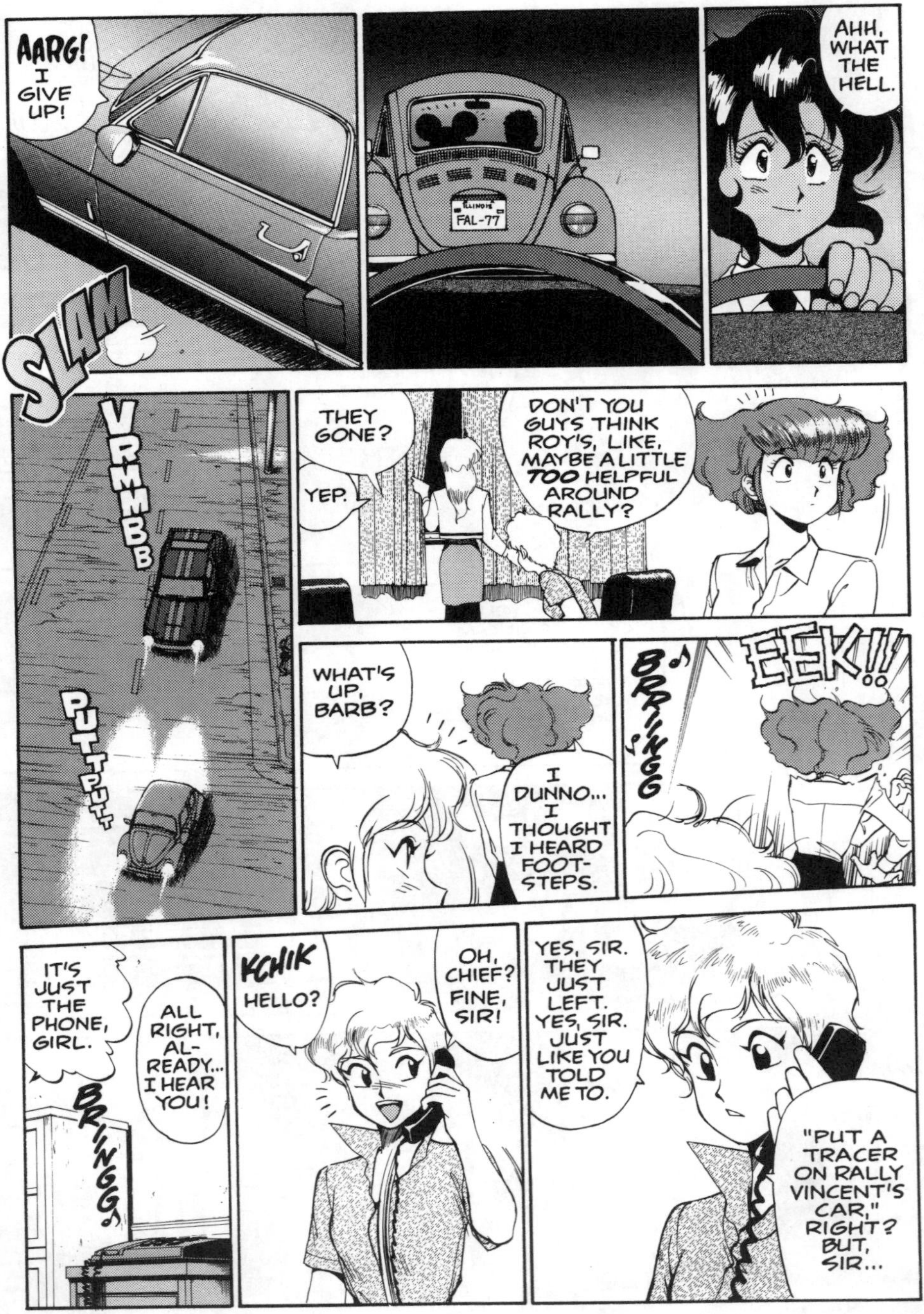
AARG! I GIVE UP!
SLAM
ILLINOIS
FAL-77
AHH, WHAT THE HELL.
VRMMBB
PUTT PUTT
THEY GONE?
YEP.
DON'T YOU GUYS THINK ROY'S, LIKE, MAYBE A LITTLE *TOO* HELPFUL AROUND RALLY?
WHAT'S UP, BARB?
I DUNNO... I THOUGHT I HEARD FOOT-STEPS.
BRRIINGG
EEK!!
IT'S JUST THE PHONE, GIRL.
ALL RIGHT, AL-READY... I HEAR YOU!
BRINGG
KCHIK
HELLO?
OH, CHIEF? FINE, SIR!
YES, SIR. THEY JUST LEFT. YES, SIR. JUST LIKE YOU TOLD ME TO.
"PUT A TRACER ON RALLY VINCENT'S CAR," RIGHT? BUT, SIR...

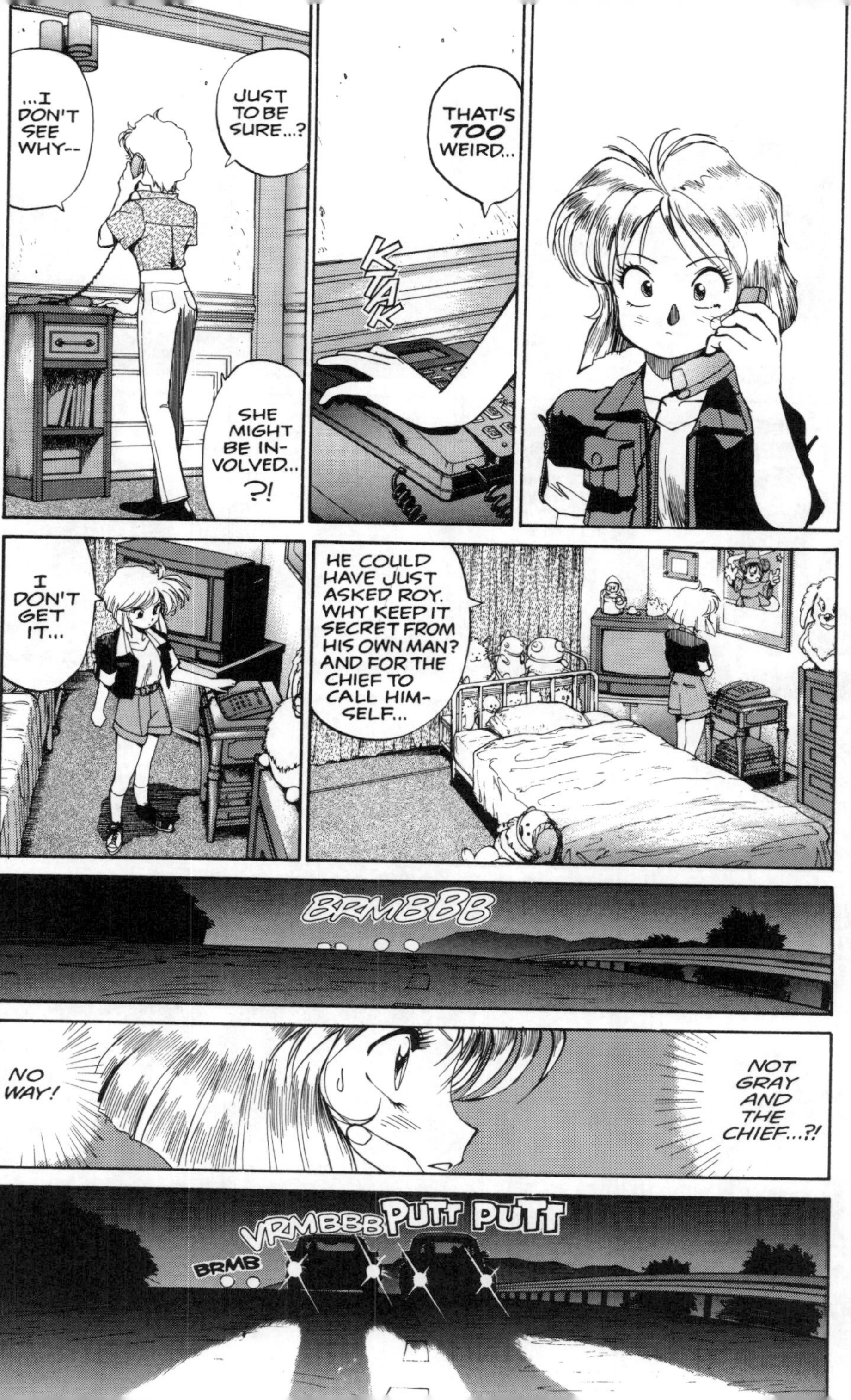
...I DON'T SEE WHY--
JUST TO BE SURE...?
SHE MIGHT BE IN-VOLVED...
?!
THAT'S TOO WEIRD...
KTAK
I DON'T GET IT...
HE COULD HAVE JUST ASKED ROY. WHY KEEP IT SECRET FROM HIS OWN MAN? AND FOR THE CHIEF TO CALL HIM-SELF...
BRMBBB
NO WAY!
NOT GRAY AND THE CHIEF...?!
BRMB
VRMBBB
PUTT PUTT

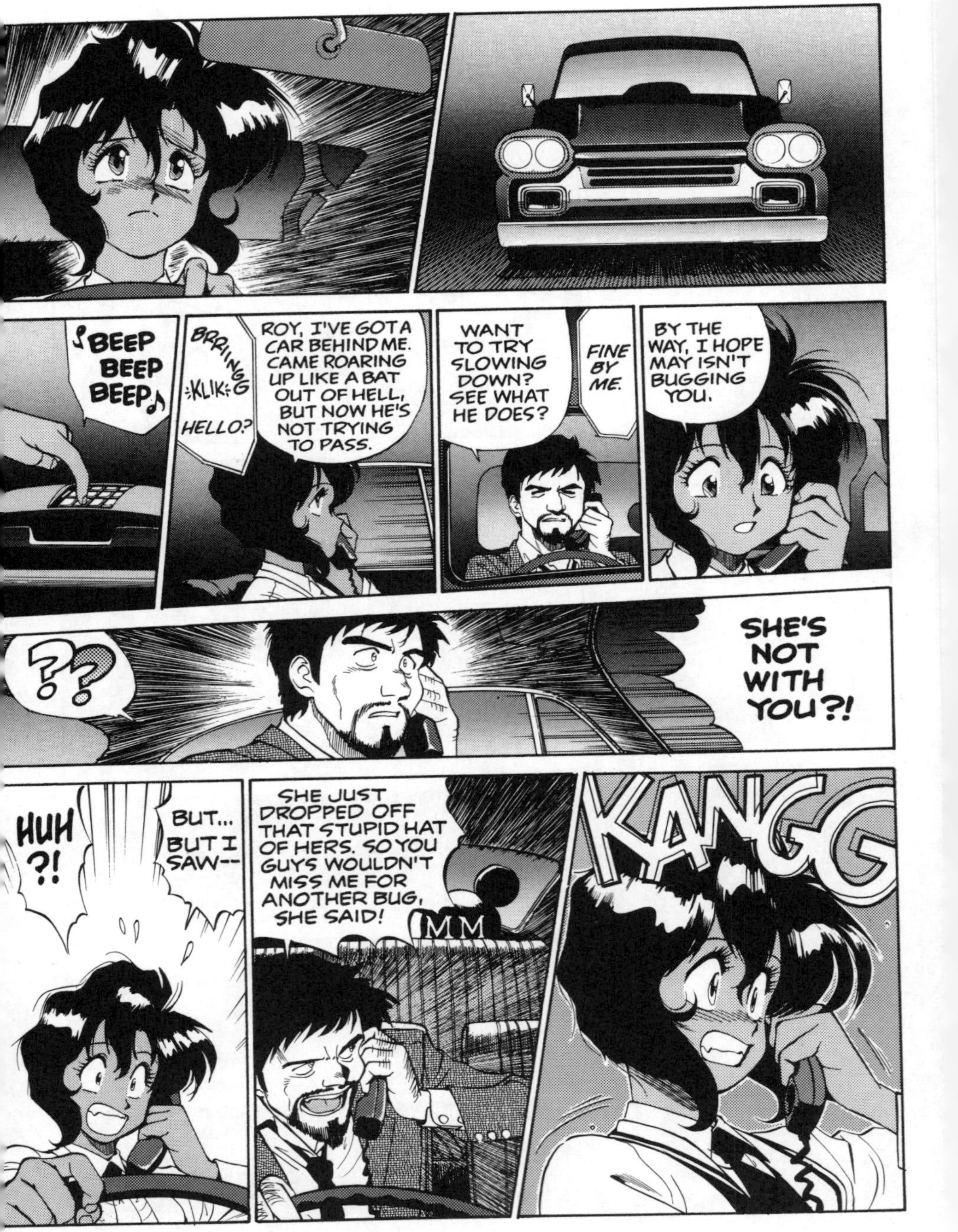

BEEP BEEP BEEP
BRRINGG
KLIK
HELLO?
ROY, I'VE GOT A CAR BEHIND ME. CAME ROARING UP LIKE A BAT OUT OF HELL, BUT NOW HE'S NOT TRYING TO PASS.
WANT TO TRY SLOWING DOWN? SEE WHAT HE DOES?
FINE BY ME.
BY THE WAY, I HOPE MAY ISN'T BUGGING YOU.
??
SHE'S NOT WITH YOU?!
HUH ?!
BUT... BUT I SAW--
SHE JUST DROPPED OFF THAT STUPID HAT OF HERS. SO YOU GUYS WOULDN'T MISS ME FOR ANOTHER BUG, SHE SAID!
MM
KANGG

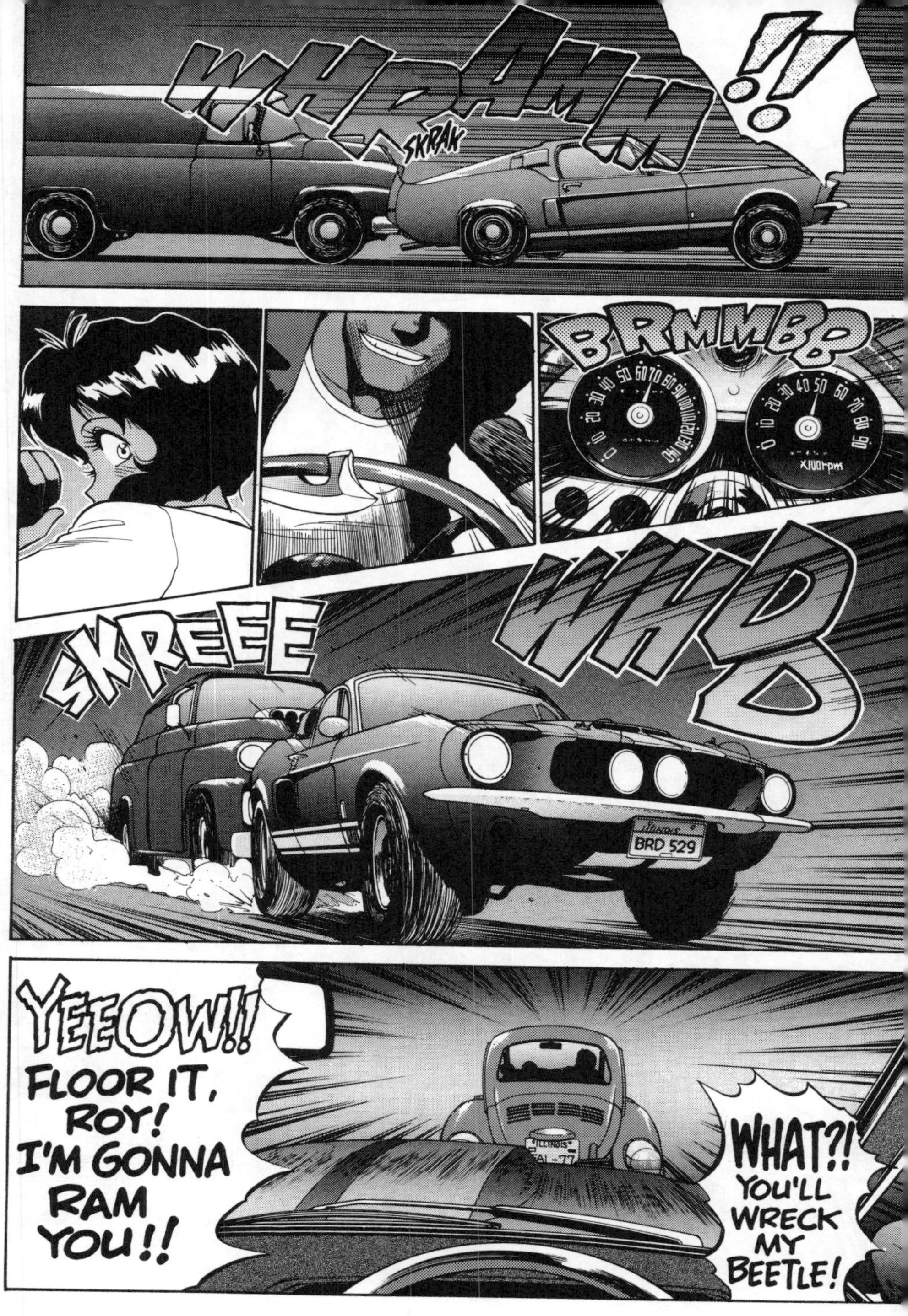
SKRAK
!!
BRMMBB
x1000rpm
SKREEE
BRD 529
YEEOW!!
FLOOR IT, ROY! I'M GONNA RAM YOU!!
WHAT?!
YOU'LL WRECK MY BEETLE!

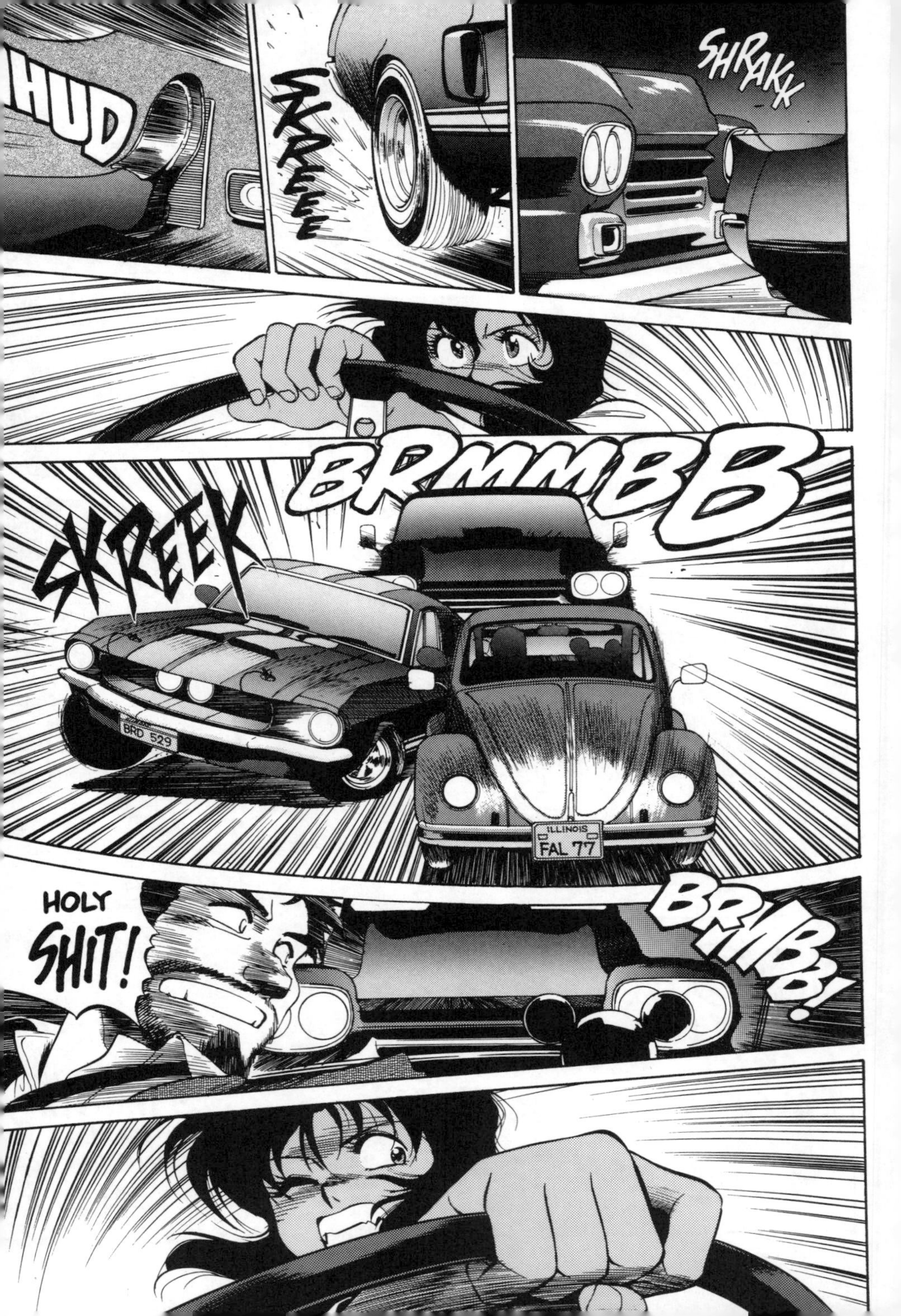
HUD
SKREEEE
SHIRAKK
BRMMBB
SKREEK
BRD 529
ILLINOIS
FAL 77
HOLY SHIT!
BRMBB!

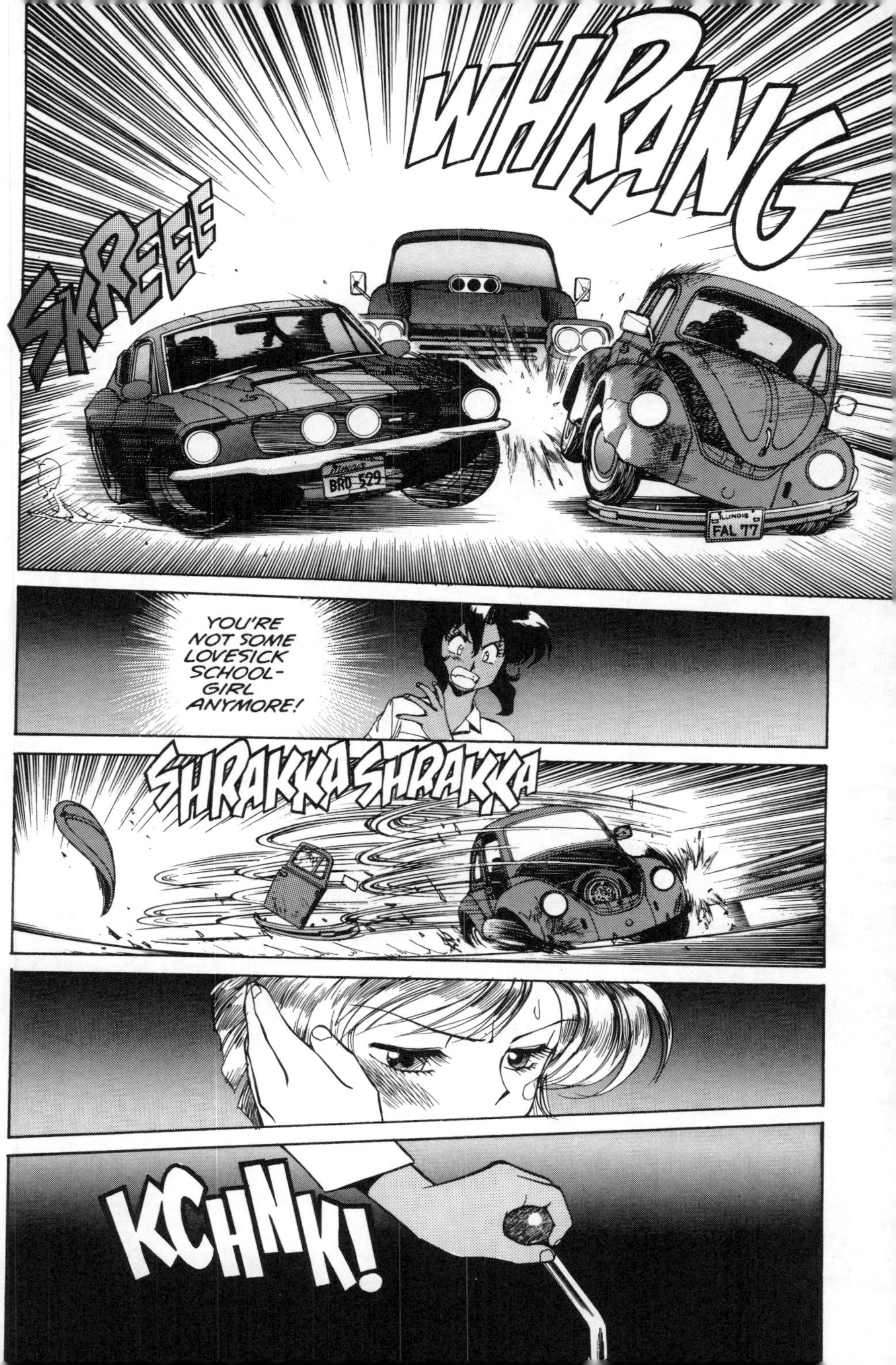
SKREEE
WHRANG
BRD 529
FAL 77
YOU'RE NOT SOME LOVESICK SCHOOL-GIRL ANYMORE!
SHRAKKA SHRAKKA
KCHNK!

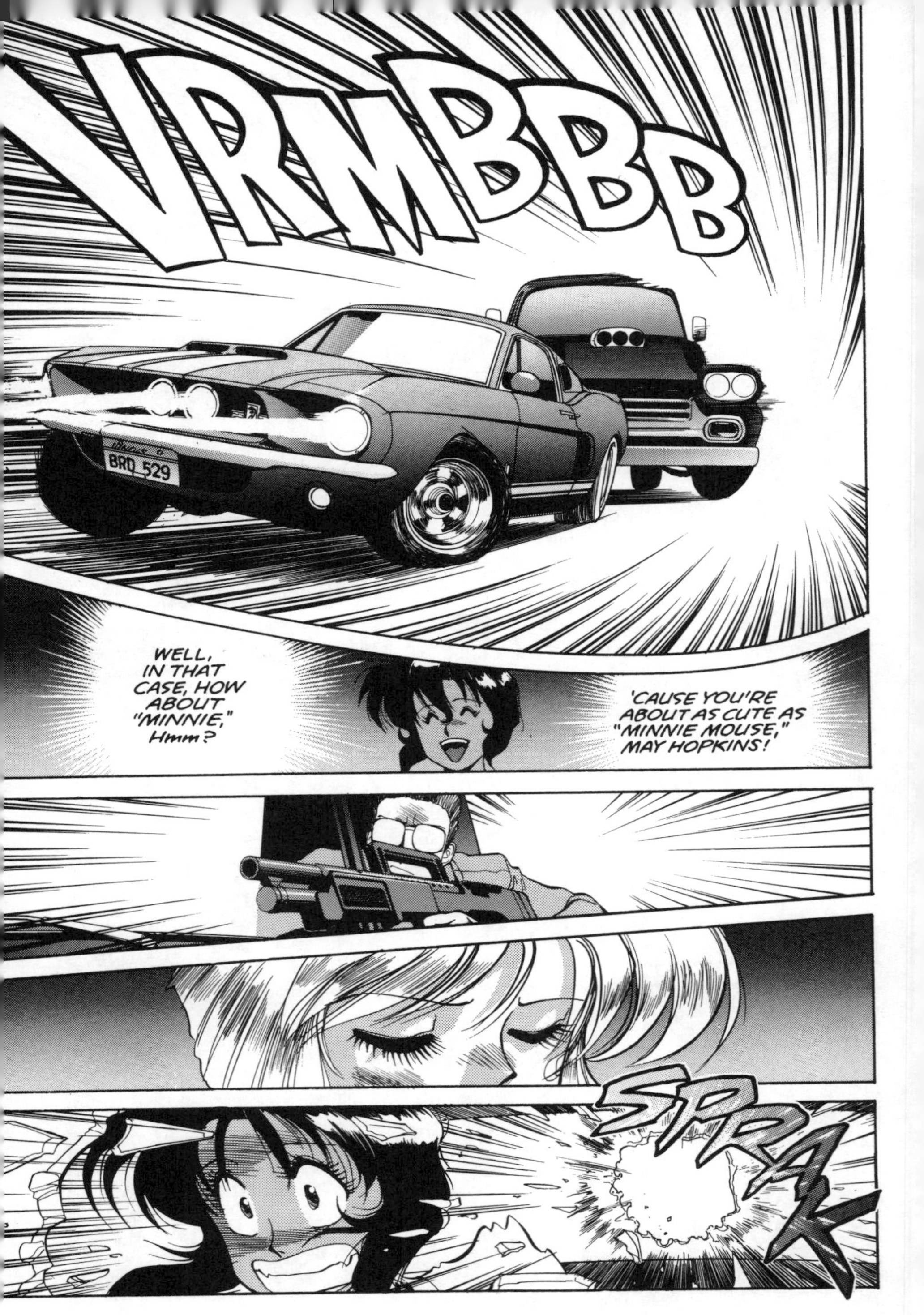
VRMBBB
BRD 529
WELL, IN THAT CASE, HOW ABOUT "MINNIE," Hmm?
'CAUSE YOU'RE ABOUT AS CUTE AS "MINNIE MOUSE," MAY HOPKINS!
SPRAK

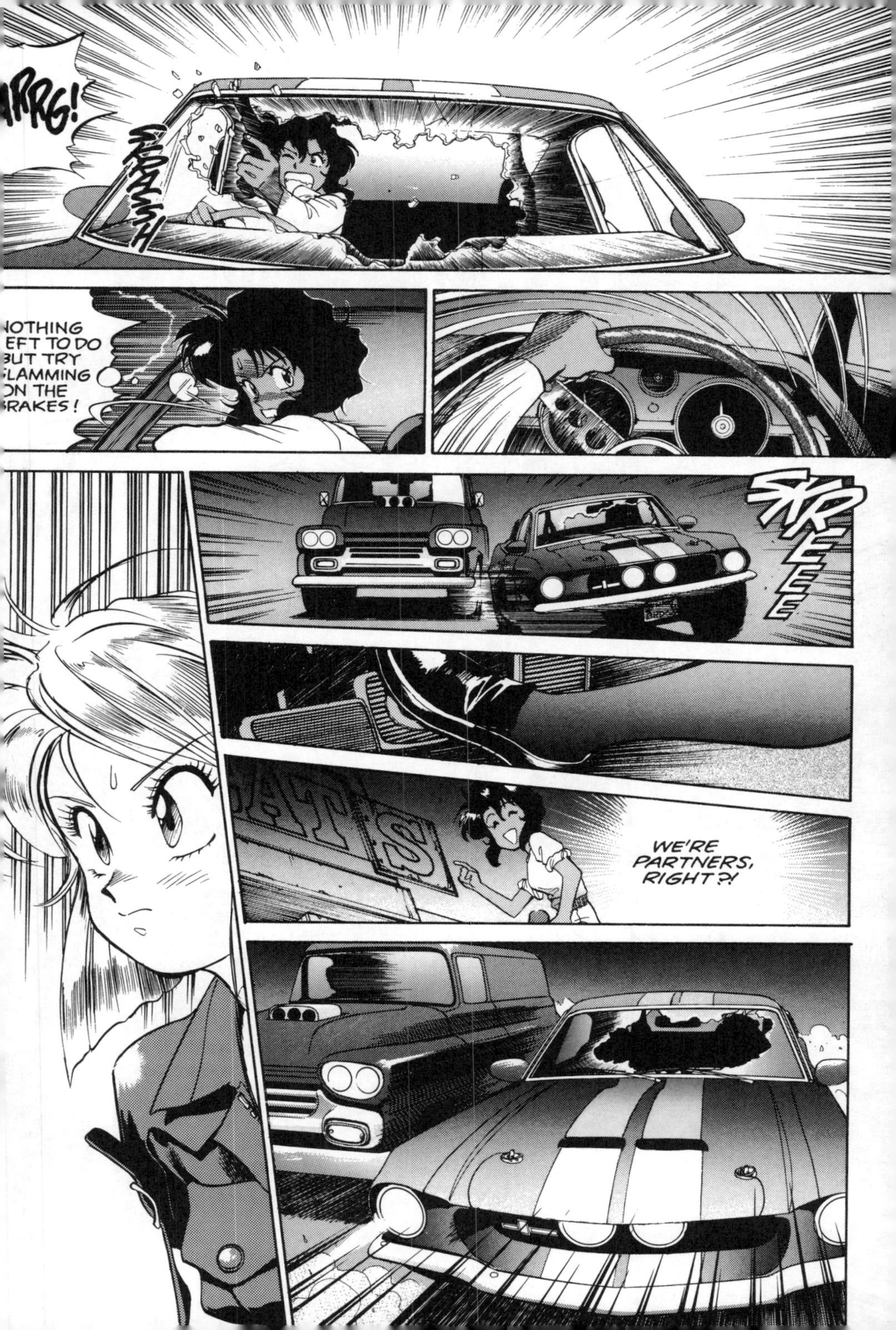
RRG!
SKRASSH
NOTHING EFT TO DO BUT TRY LAMMING ON THE RAKES!
SKREEEE
WE'RE PARTNERS, RIGHT?!

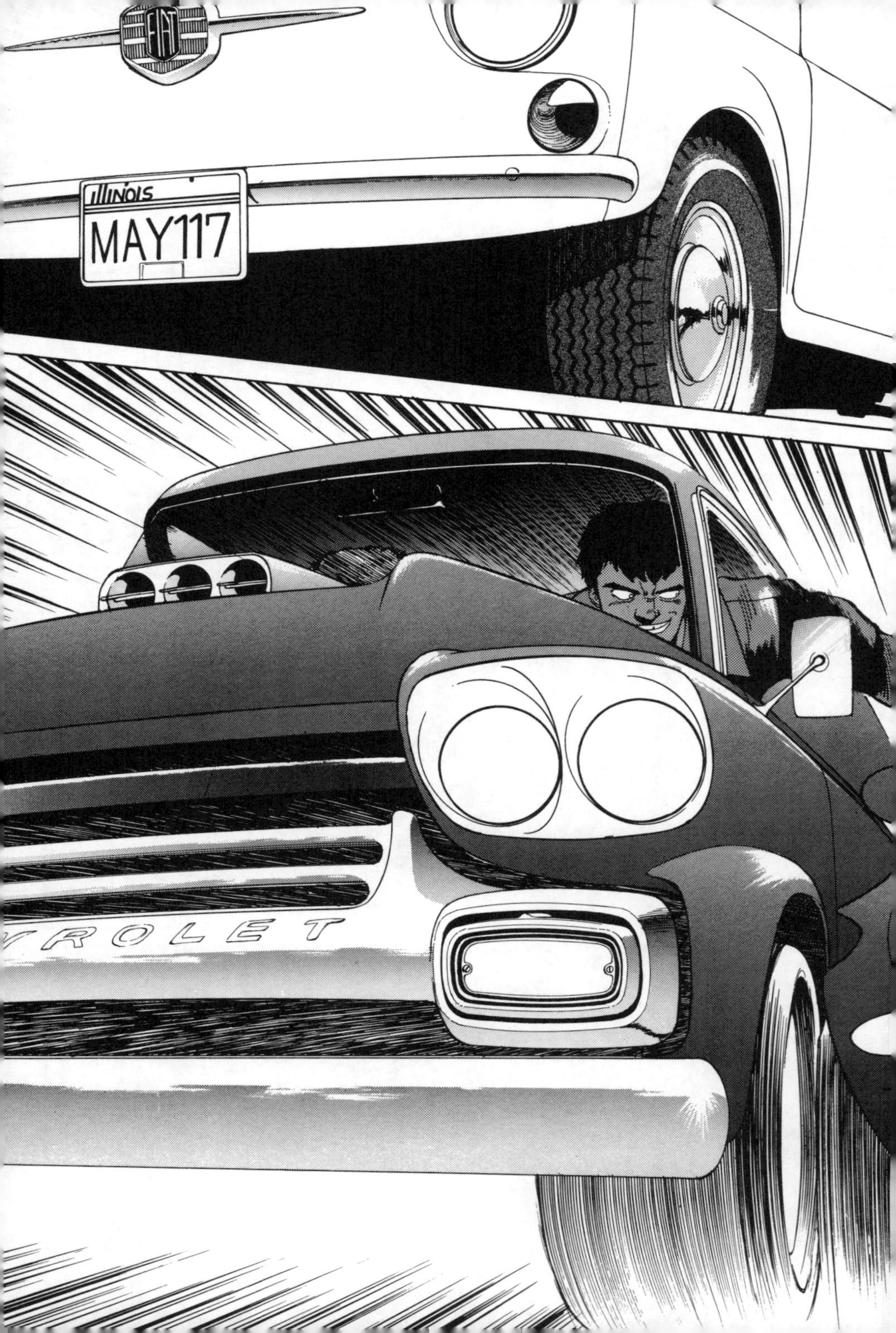
FIAT
ILLINOIS
MAY117
VROLET

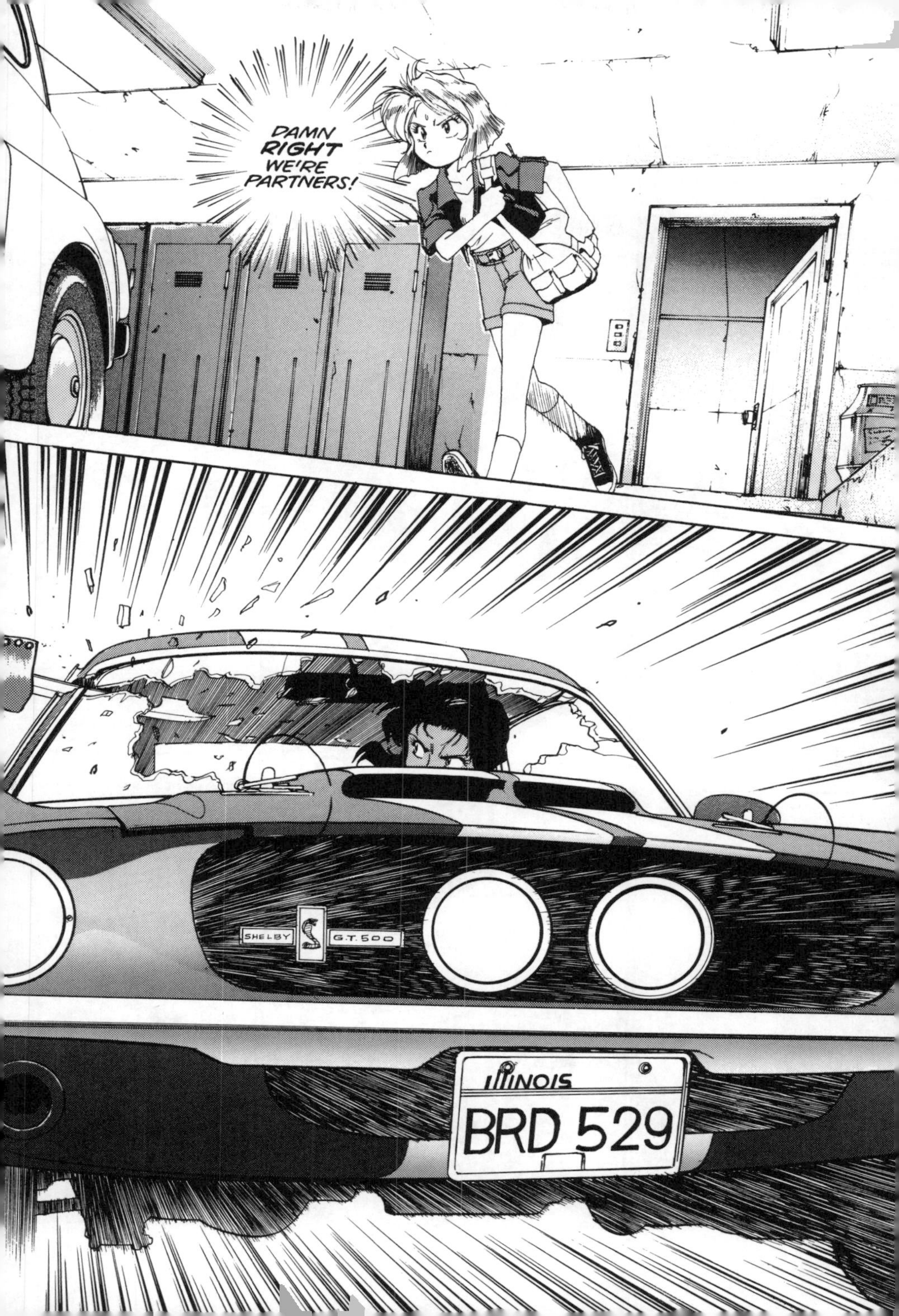
DAMN RIGHT WE'RE PARTNERS!
SHELBY G.T.500
ILLINOIS
BRD 529

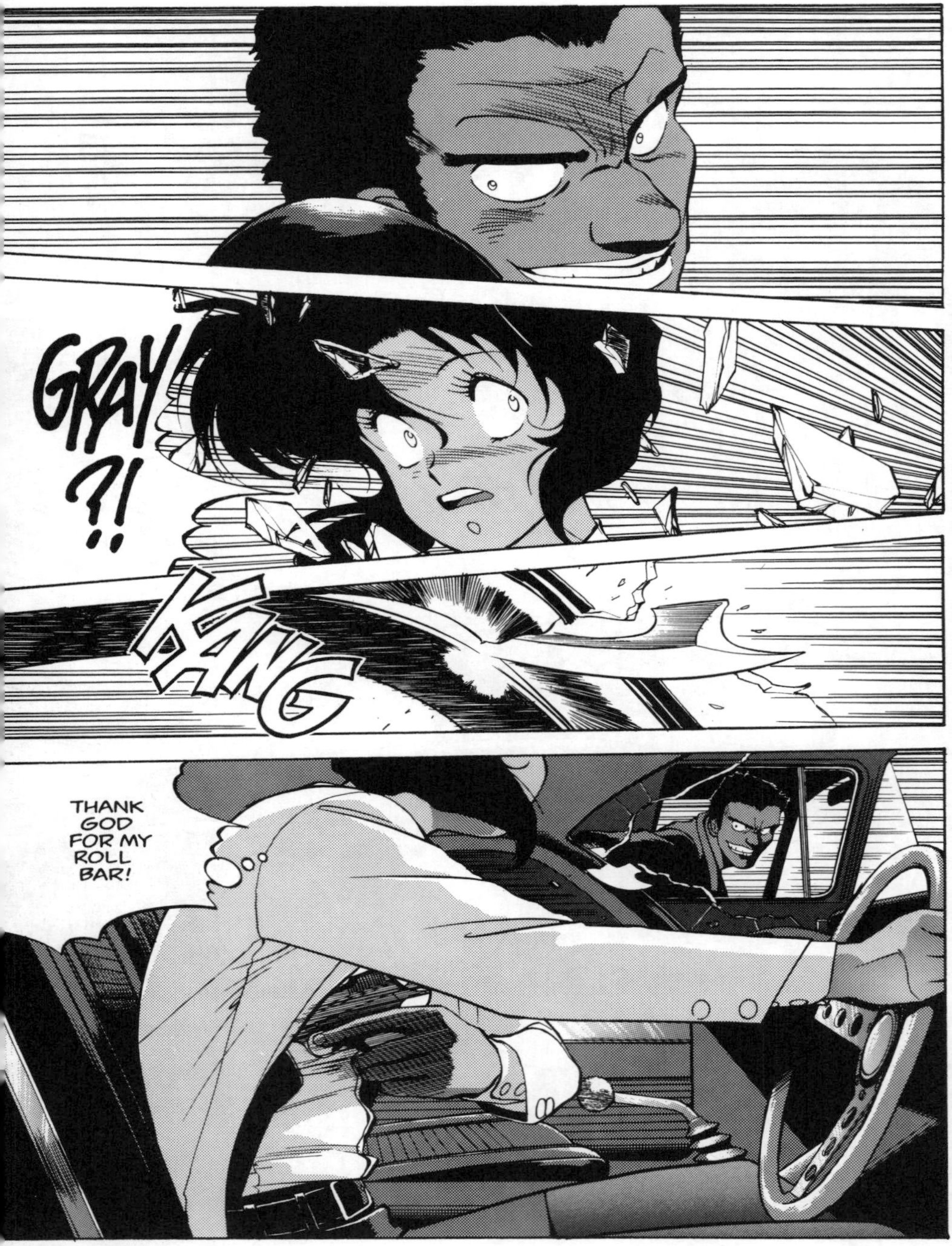
GRAY ?!
KANG
THANK GOD FOR MY ROLL BAR!

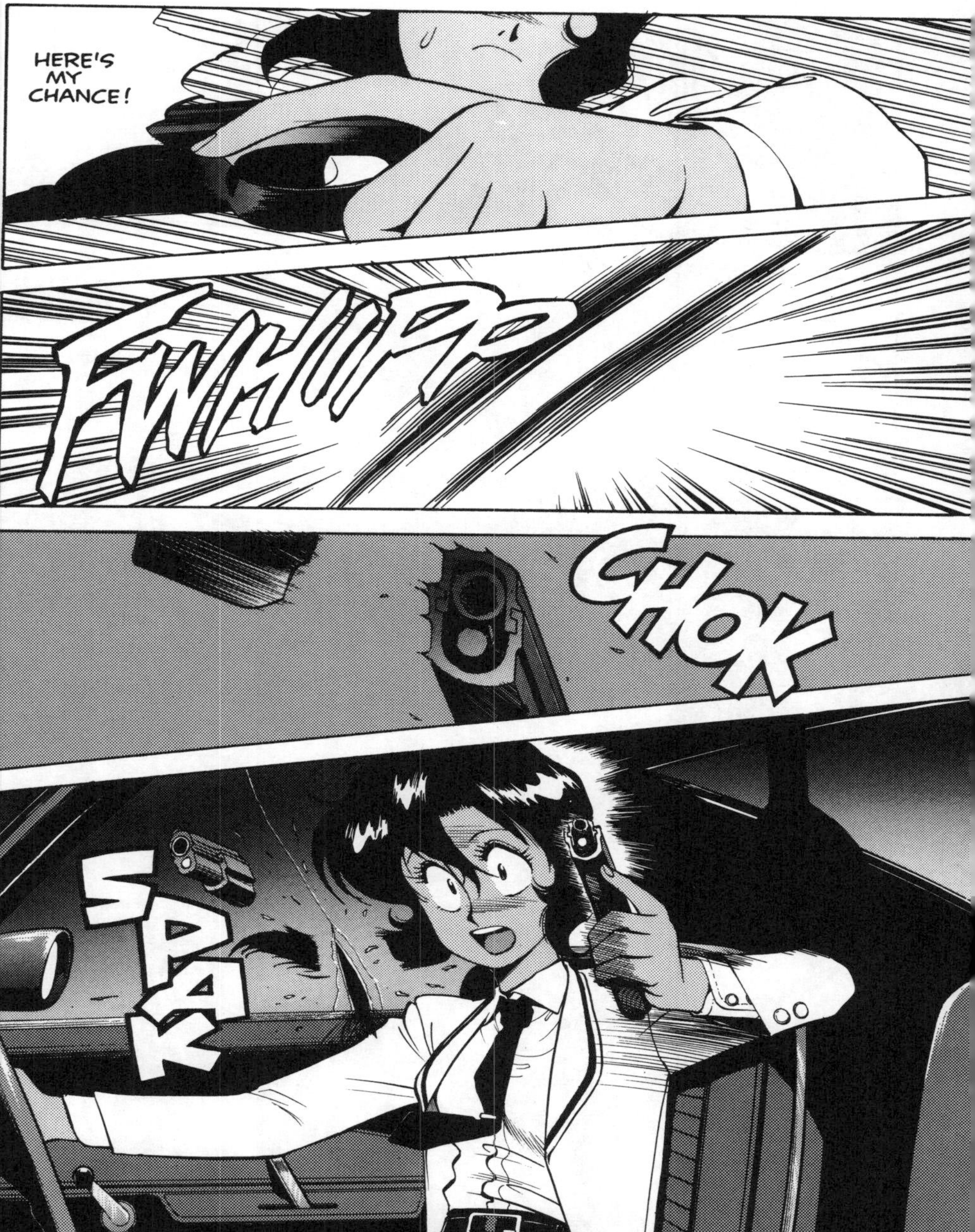
HERE'S MY CHANCE!
FWHIPP
CHOK
SPAK

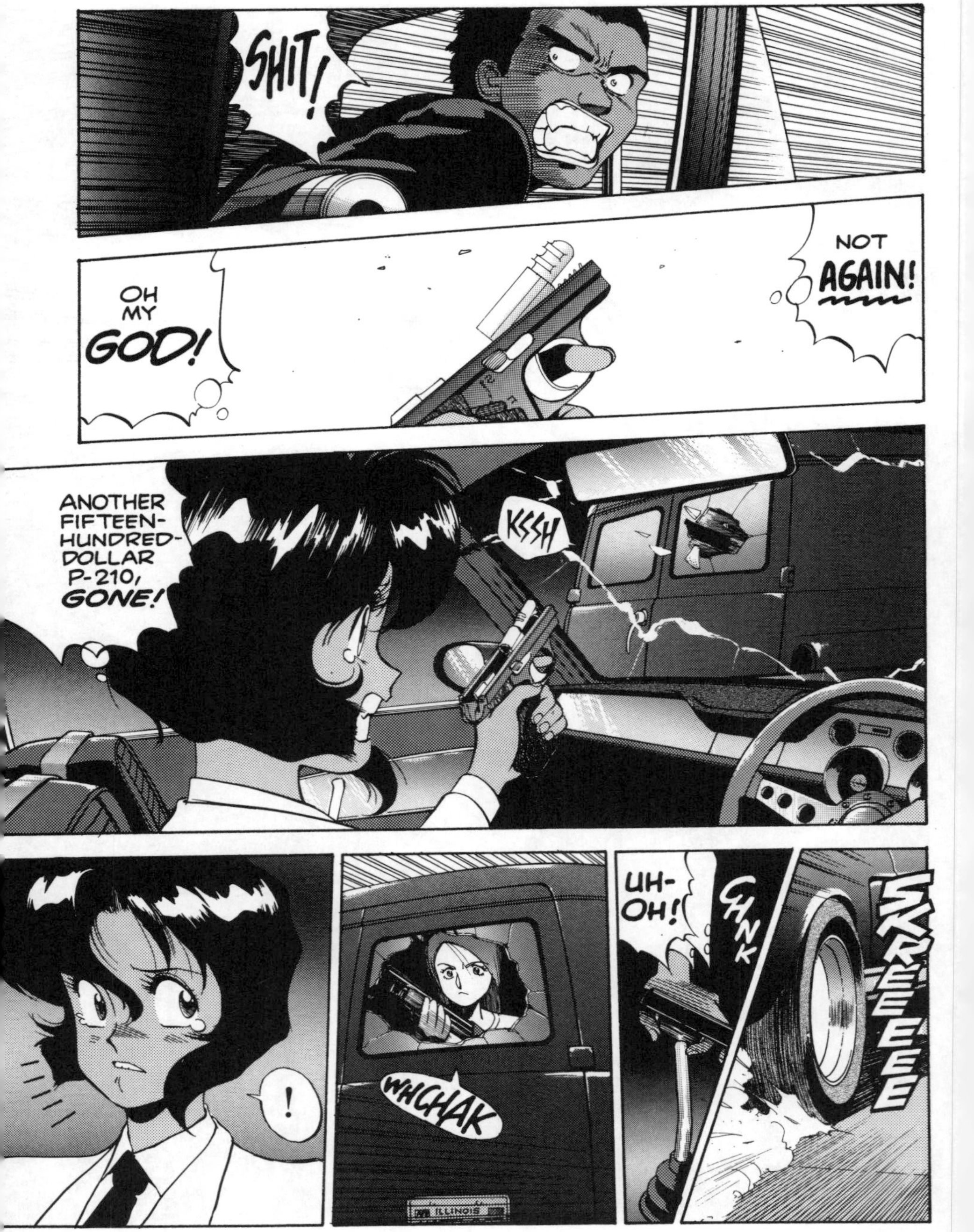
SHIT!
OH MY GOD!
NOT AGAIN!
ANOTHER FIFTEEN-HUNDRED-DOLLAR P-210, GONE!
KSSH
!
WHCHAK
ILLINOIS
UH-OH!
CHNK
SKREEEEE

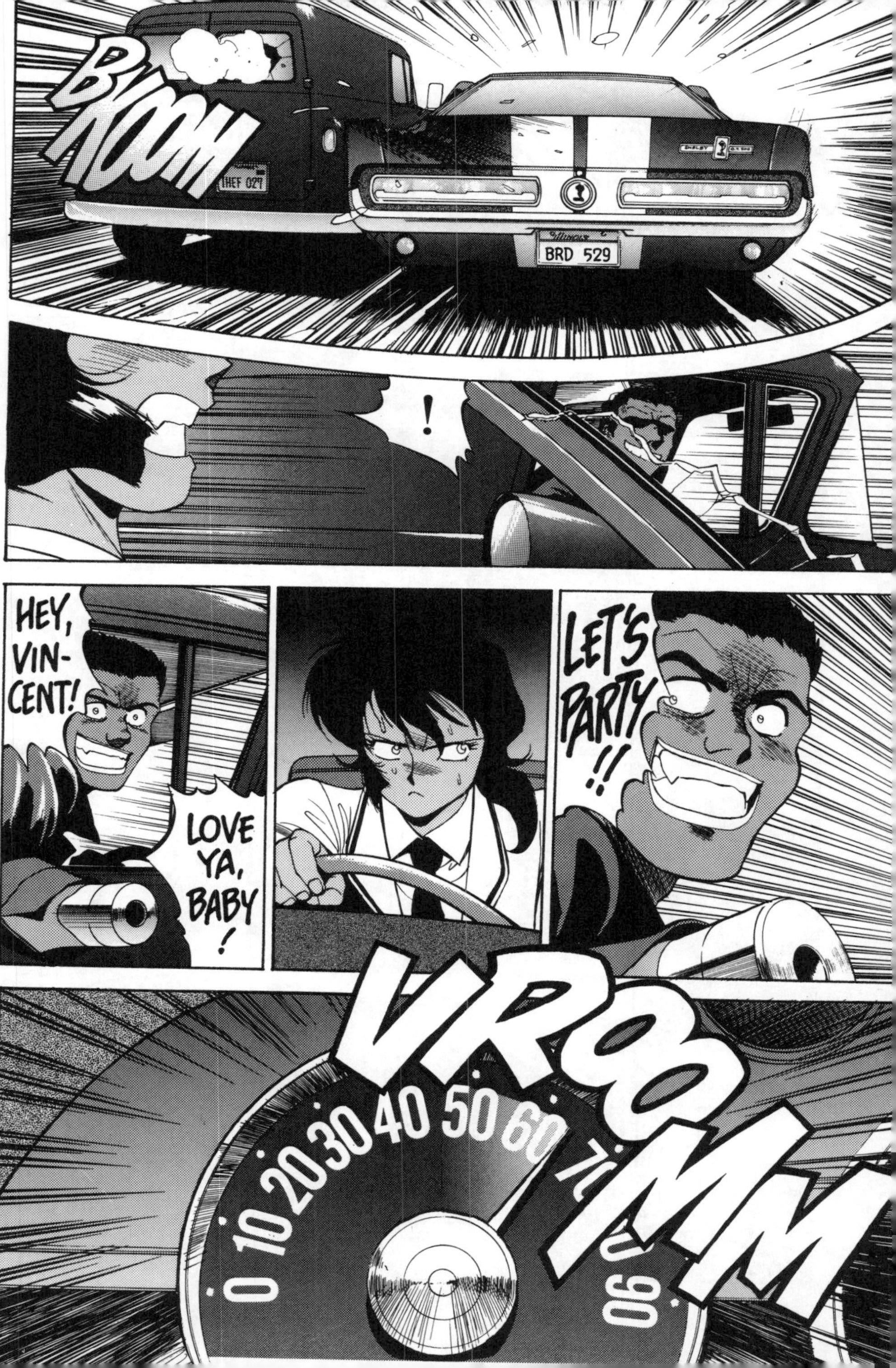
BOOM
THEF 027
BRD 529
!
HEY, VIN-CENT!
LOVE YA, BABY!
LET'S PARTY!!
VROOMM
0 10 20 30 40 50 60 70
90

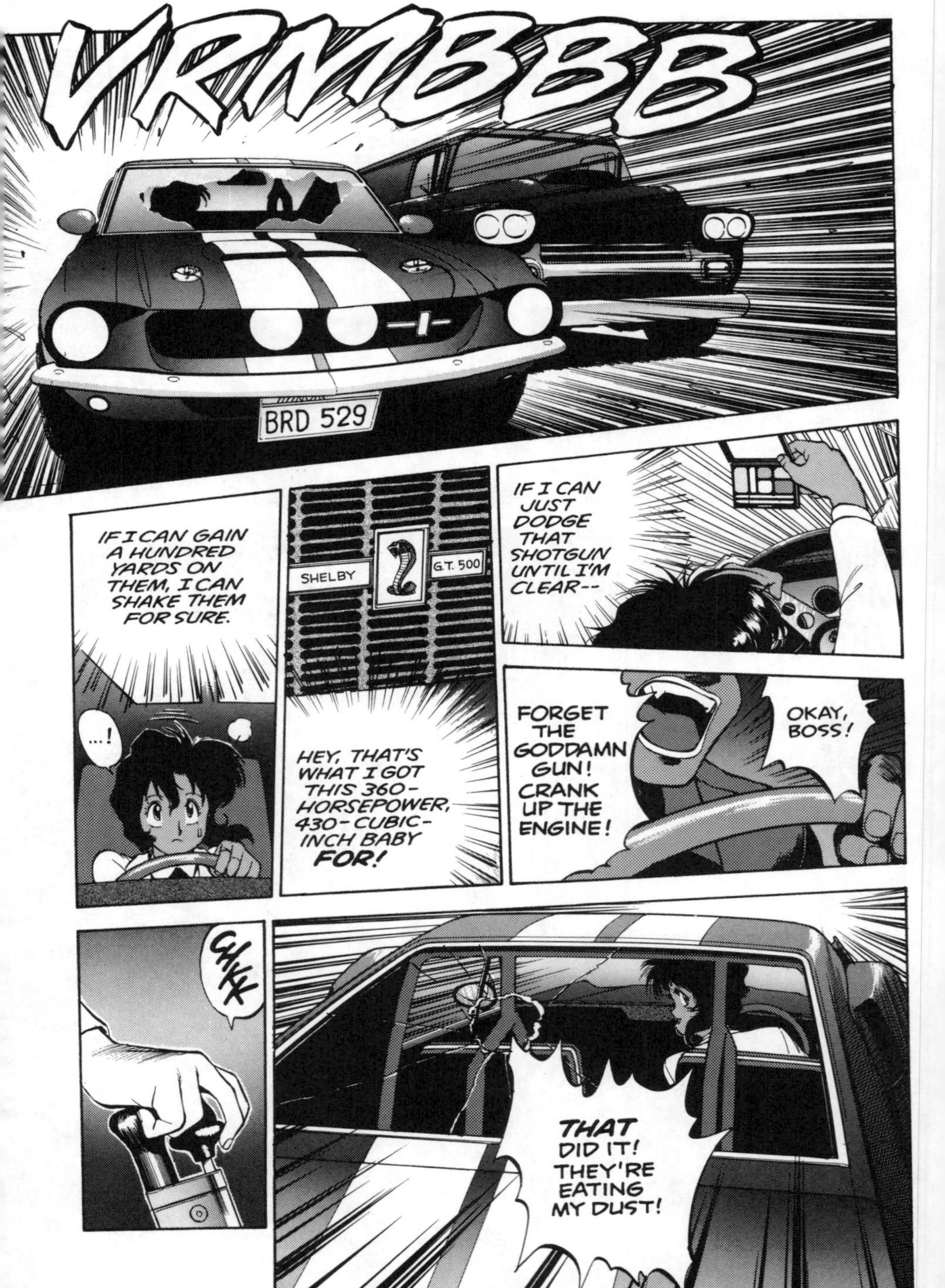
VRMBBB
BRD 529
IF I CAN GAIN A HUNDRED YARDS ON THEM, I CAN SHAKE THEM FOR SURE.
SHELBY
G.T. 500
IF I CAN JUST DODGE THAT SHOTGUN UNTIL I'M CLEAR--
...!
HEY, THAT'S WHAT I GOT THIS 360-HORSEPOWER, 430-CUBIC-INCH BABY FOR!
FORGET THE GODDAMN GUN! CRANK UP THE ENGINE!
OKAY, BOSS!
CHKK
THAT DID IT! THEY'RE EATING MY DUST!

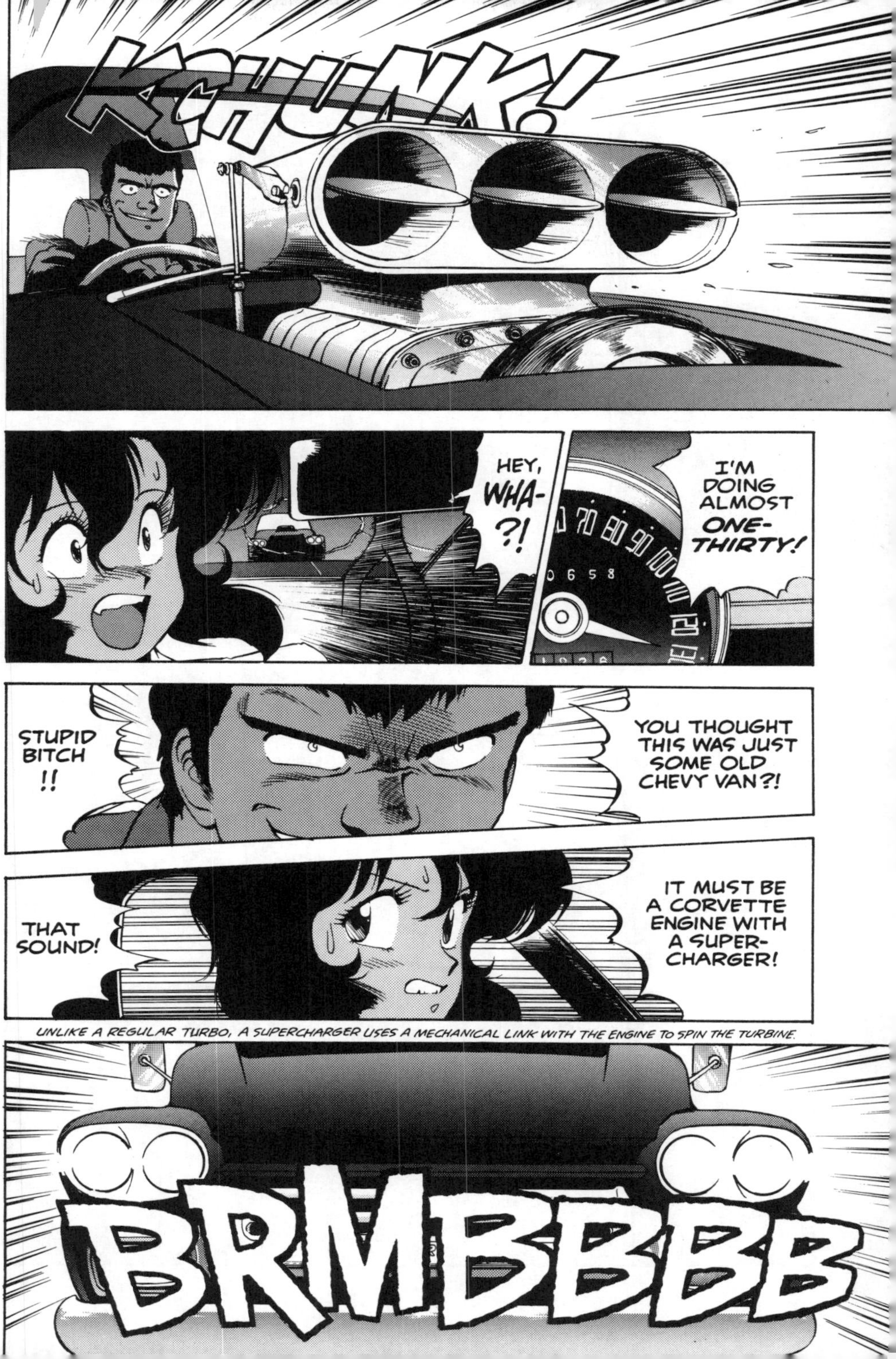
K'CHUNK!
HEY, WHA-?!
I'M DOING ALMOST ONE-THIRTY!
STUPID BITCH !!
YOU THOUGHT THIS WAS JUST SOME OLD CHEVY VAN?!
THAT SOUND!
IT MUST BE A CORVETTE ENGINE WITH A SUPER-CHARGER!
UNLIKE A REGULAR TURBO, A SUPERCHARGER USES A MECHANICAL LINK WITH THE ENGINE TO SPIN THE TURBINE.
BRMBBBB

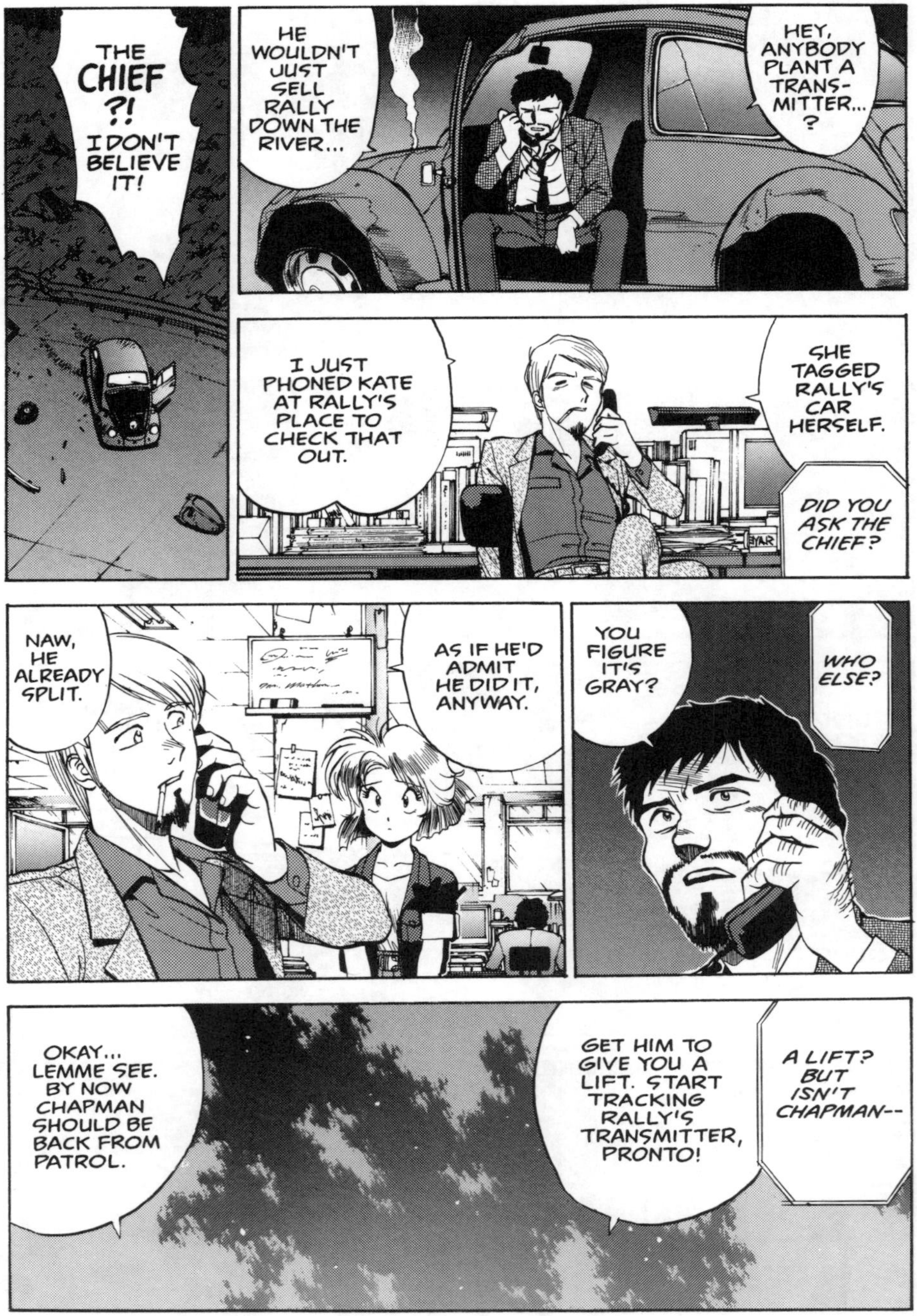
THE CHIEF?! I DON'T BELIEVE IT!
HE WOULDN'T JUST SELL RALLY DOWN THE RIVER...
HEY, ANYBODY PLANT A TRANSMITTER...?
I JUST PHONED KATE AT RALLY'S PLACE TO CHECK THAT OUT.
SHE TAGGED RALLY'S CAR HERSELF.
DID YOU ASK THE CHIEF?
NAW, HE ALREADY SPLIT.
AS IF HE'D ADMIT HE DID IT, ANYWAY.
YOU FIGURE IT'S GRAY?
WHO ELSE?
OKAY... LEMME SEE. BY NOW CHAPMAN SHOULD BE BACK FROM PATROL.
GET HIM TO GIVE YOU A LIFT. START TRACKING RALLY'S TRANSMITTER, PRONTO!
A LIFT? BUT ISN'T CHAPMAN--

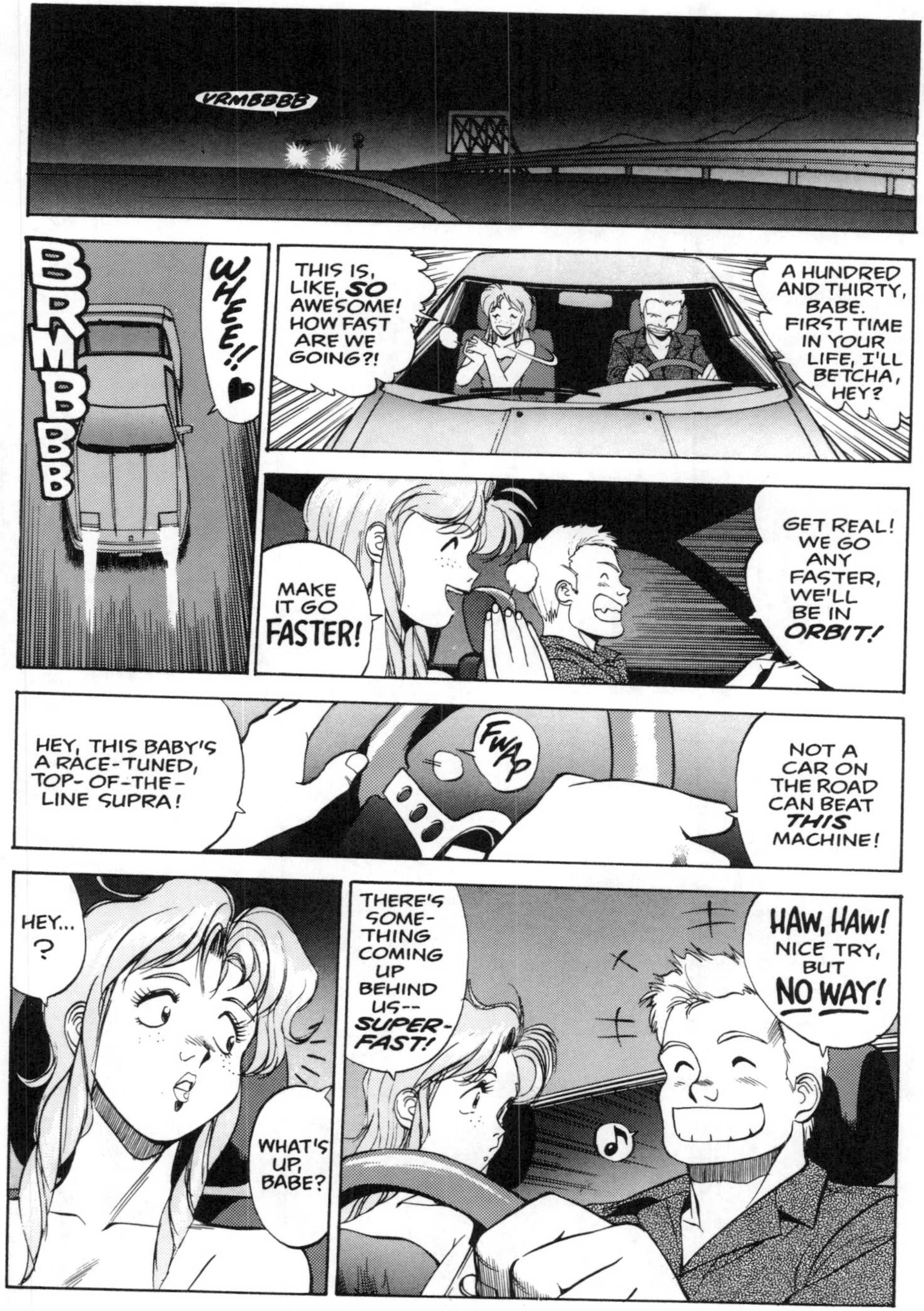
VRMBBBB
BRMBBBB
WHEE!! ♥
THIS IS, LIKE, SO AWESOME! HOW FAST ARE WE GOING?!
A HUNDRED AND THIRTY, BABE. FIRST TIME IN YOUR LIFE, I'LL BETCHA, HEY?
MAKE IT GO FASTER!
GET REAL! WE GO ANY FASTER, WE'LL BE IN ORBIT!
HEY, THIS BABY'S A RACE-TUNED, TOP-OF-THE-LINE SUPRA!
FWAP
NOT A CAR ON THE ROAD CAN BEAT THIS MACHINE!
HEY... ?
WHAT'S UP, BABE?
THERE'S SOME-THING COMING UP BEHIND US-- SUPER-FAST!
HAW, HAW! NICE TRY, BUT NO WAY!

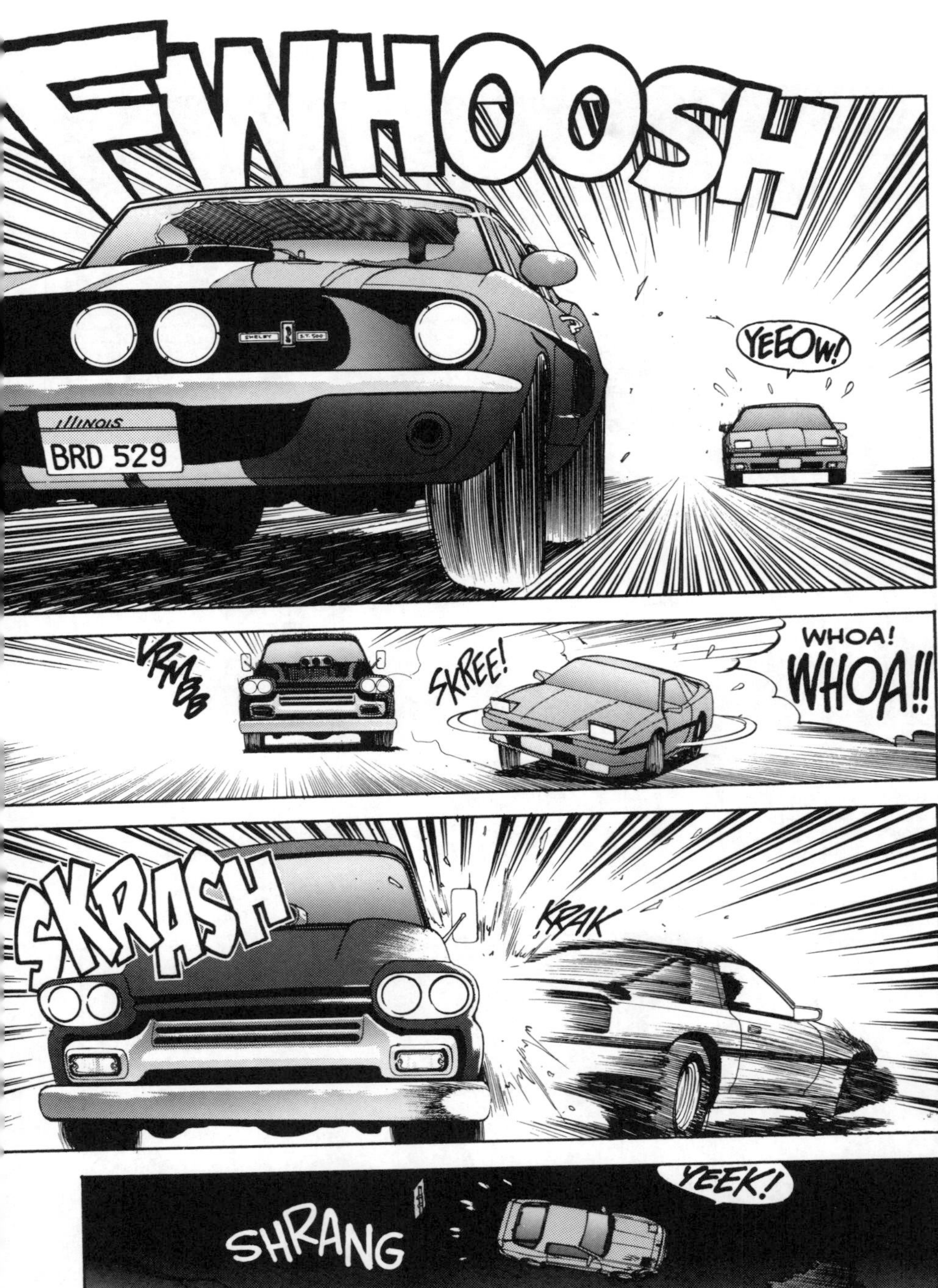
FWHOOSH
ILLINOIS
BRD 529
YEEOW!
VRMBB
SKREE!
WHOA!
WHOA!!
SKRASH
KRAK
YEEK!
SHRANG

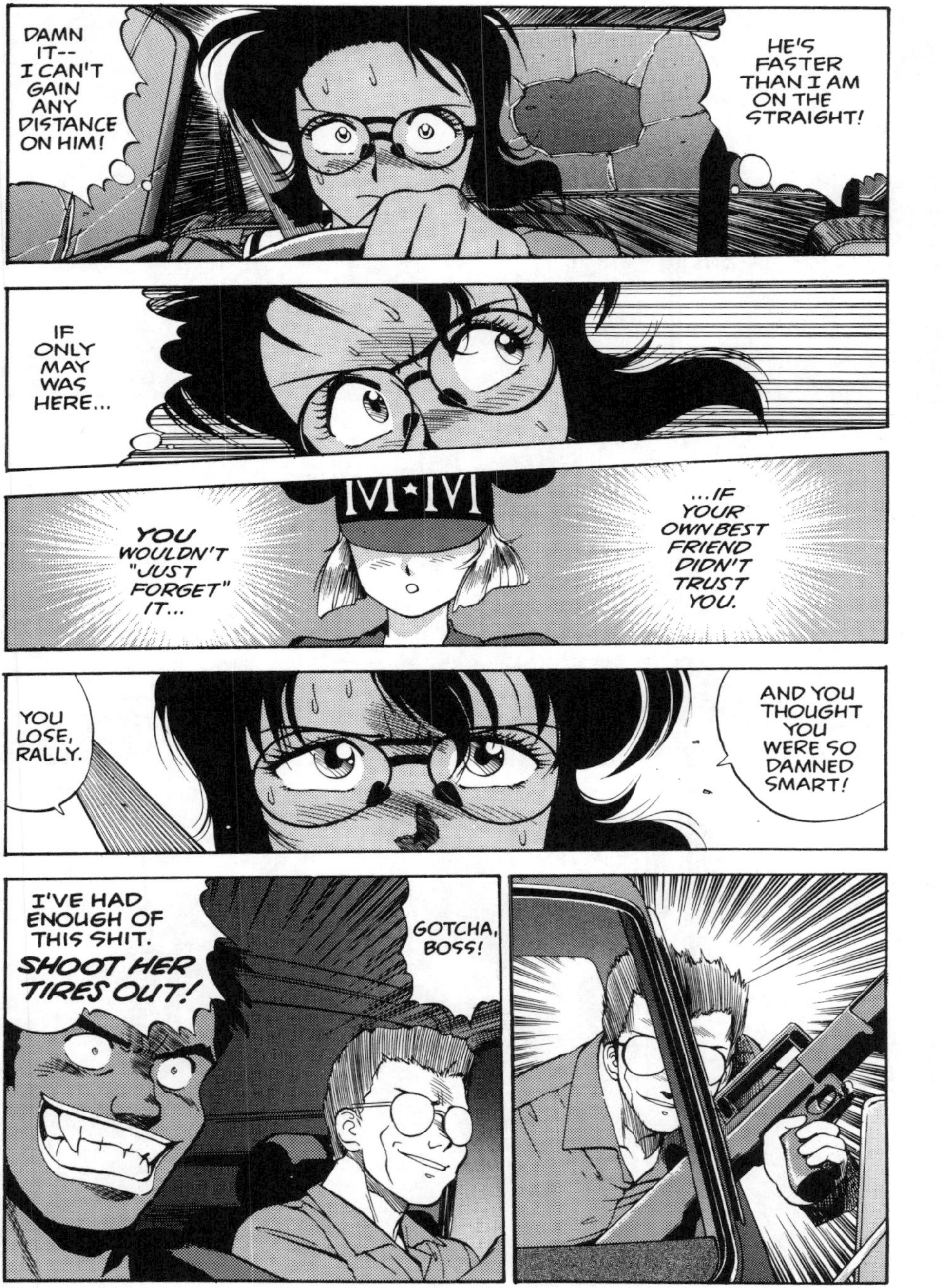
DAMN IT-- I CAN'T GAIN ANY DISTANCE ON HIM!
HE'S FASTER THAN I AM ON THE STRAIGHT!
IF ONLY MAY WAS HERE...
YOU WOULDN'T "JUST FORGET" IT...
...IF YOUR OWN BEST FRIEND DIDN'T TRUST YOU.
YOU LOSE, RALLY.
AND YOU THOUGHT YOU WERE SO DAMNED SMART!
I'VE HAD ENOUGH OF THIS SHIT. SHOOT HER TIRES OUT!
GOTCHA, BOSS!

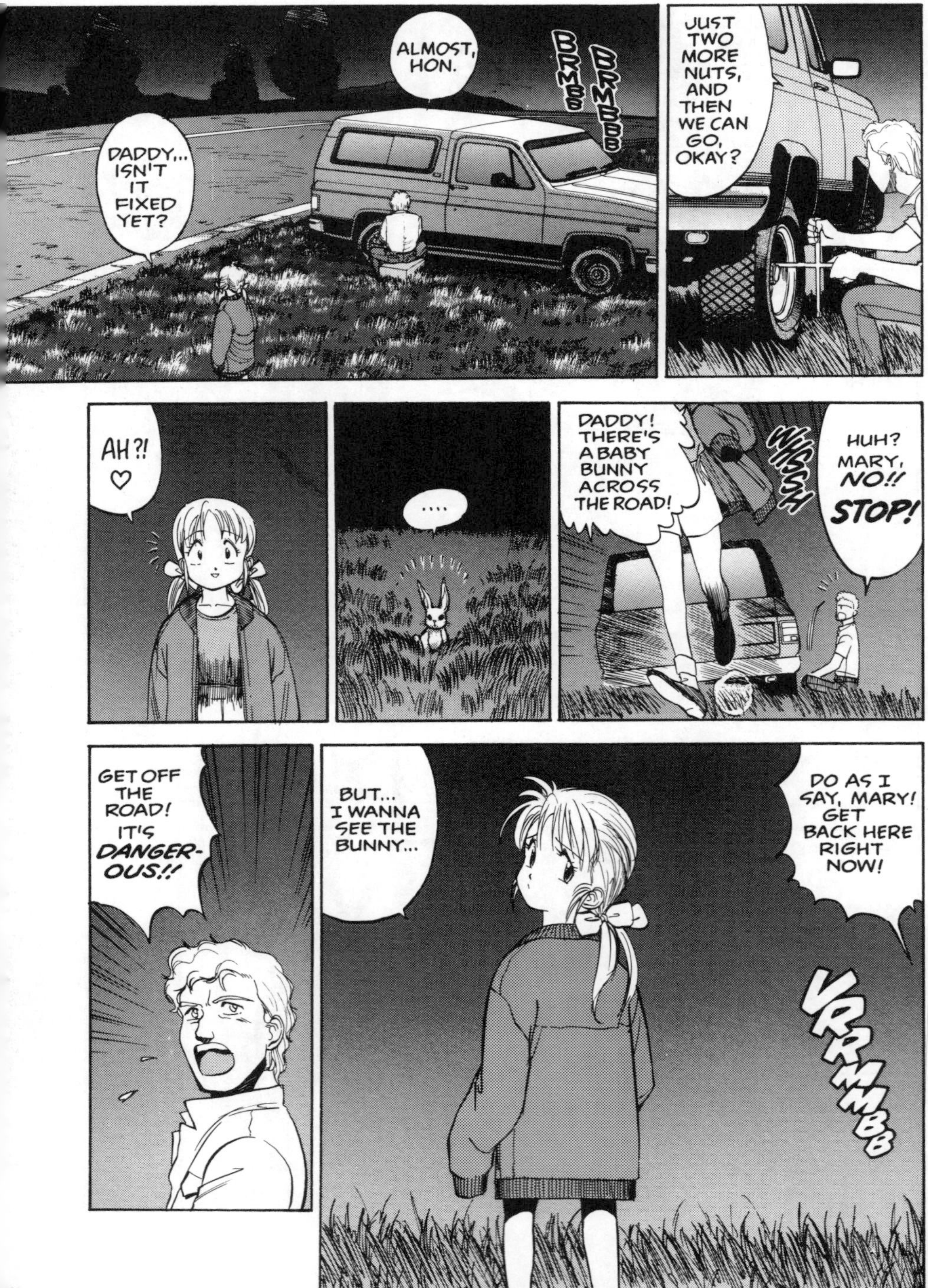
DADDY... ISN'T IT FIXED YET?
ALMOST, HON.
BRMBB BRMBBB
JUST TWO MORE NUTS, AND THEN WE CAN GO, OKAY?
AH?! ♡
....
DADDY! THERE'S A BABY BUNNY ACROSS THE ROAD!
WHSSH
HUH? MARY, NO!! STOP!
GET OFF THE ROAD! IT'S DANGEROUS!!
BUT... I WANNA SEE THE BUNNY...
DO AS I SAY, MARY! GET BACK HERE RIGHT NOW!
VRRMMBB

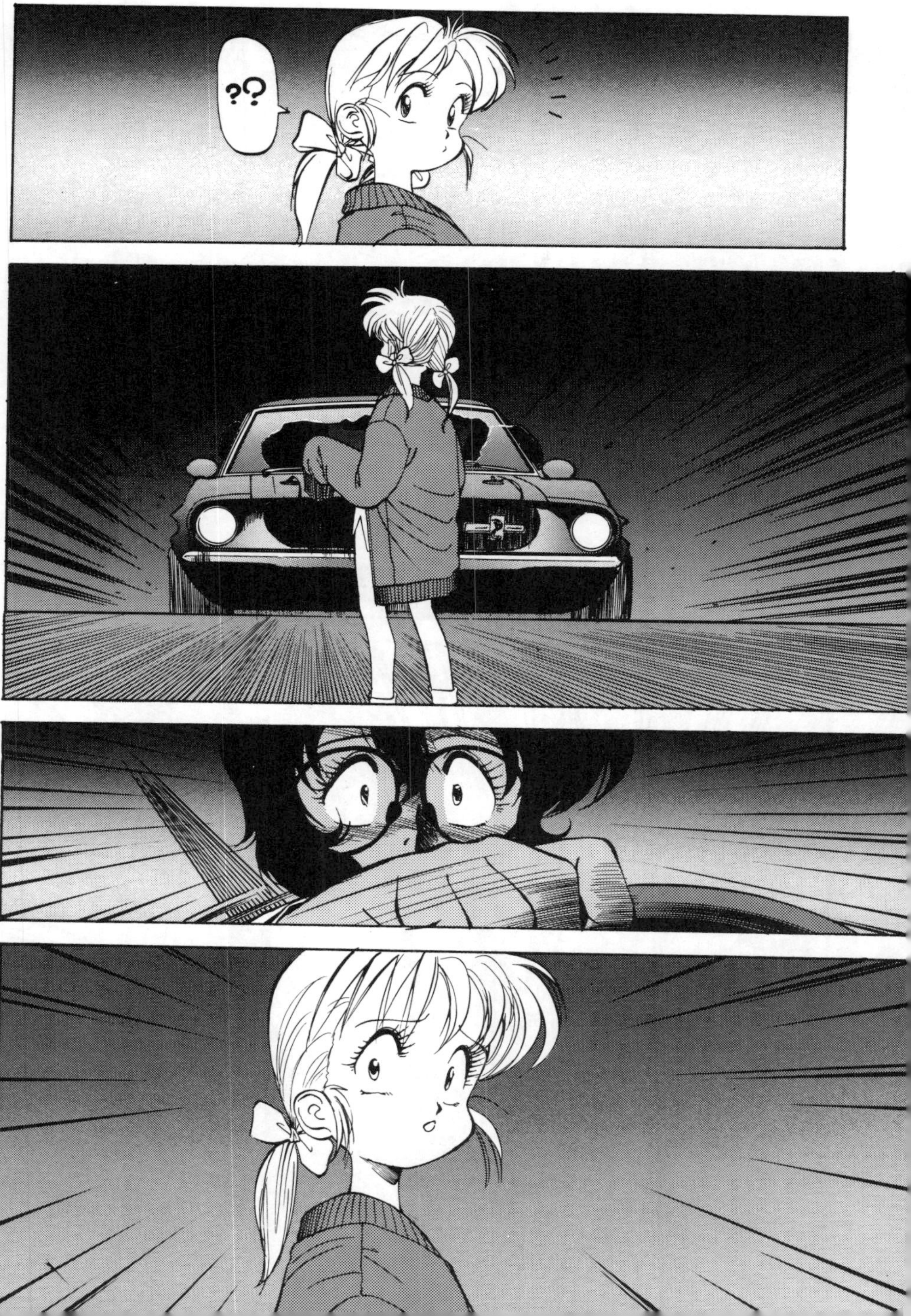
??

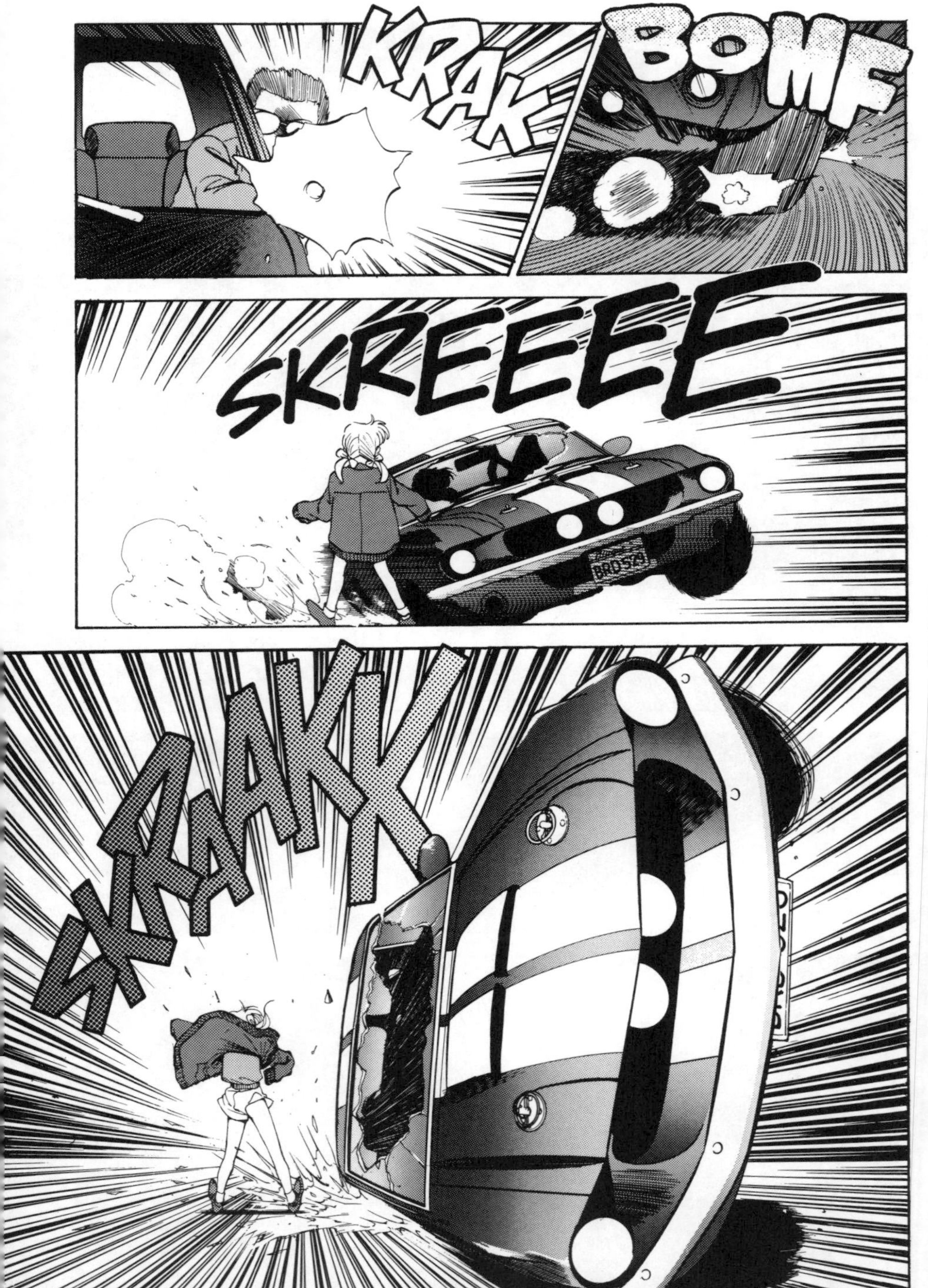
KRAK
BOMF
SKREEEE
BRD 529
SKAAAKK

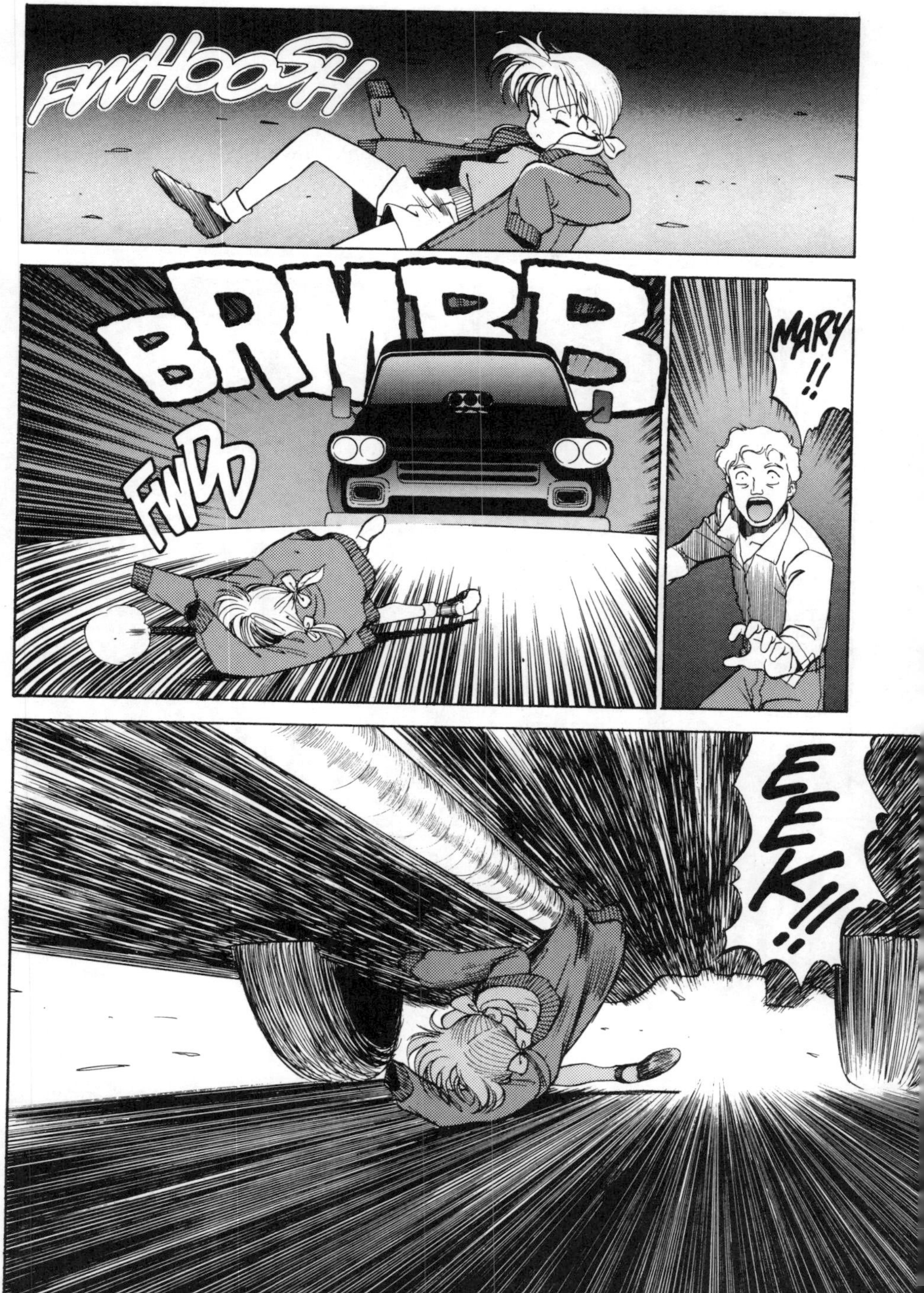
FWHOOSH
BRMBB
FWDD
MARY!!
EEEK!!

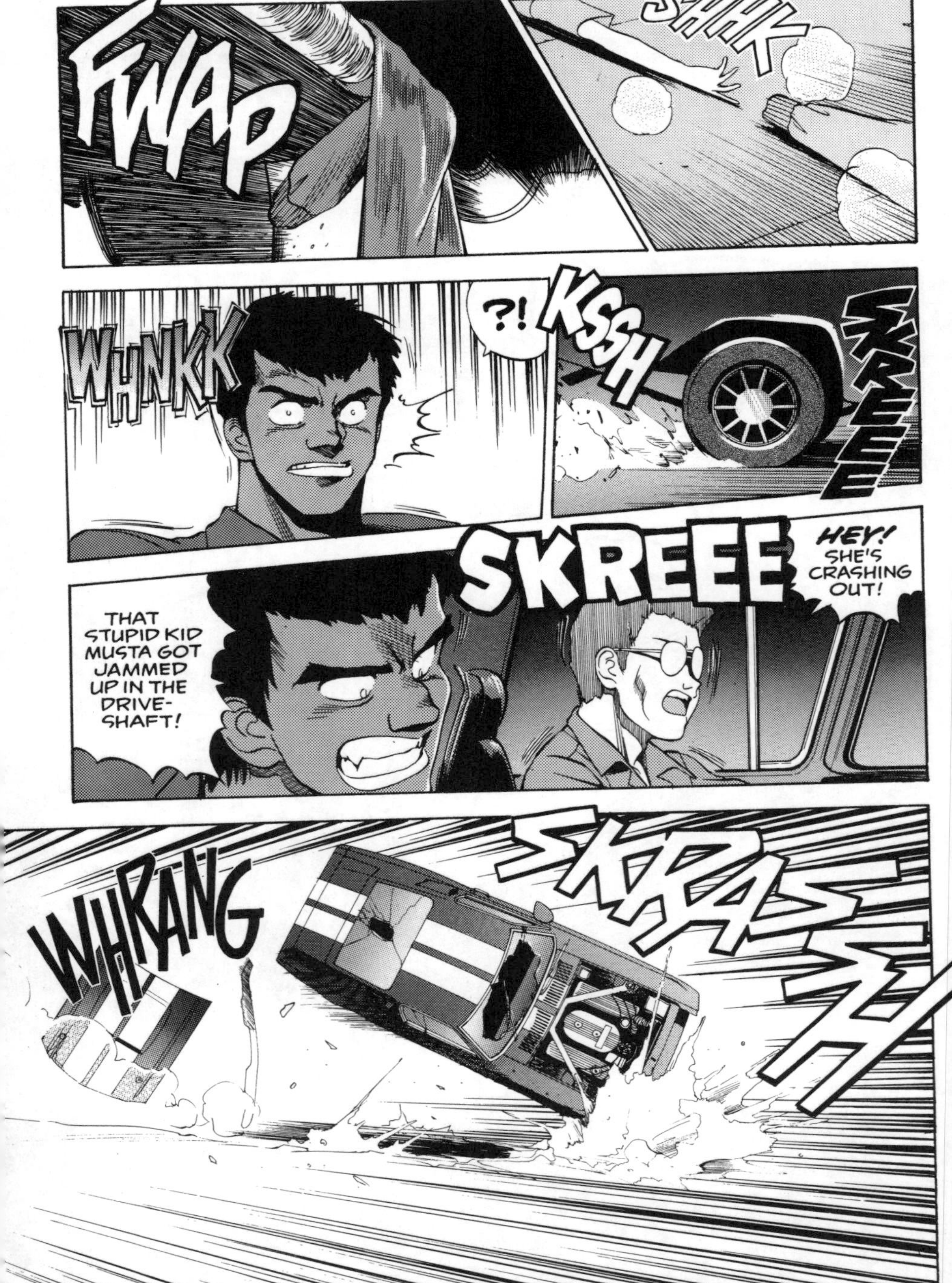
FWAP
SHHK
WHNKK
?!
KSSH
SKREEEE
THAT STUPID KID MUSTA GOT JAMMED UP IN THE DRIVE-SHAFT!
SKREEE
HEY! SHE'S CRASHING OUT!
WHRANG
SKRASSH

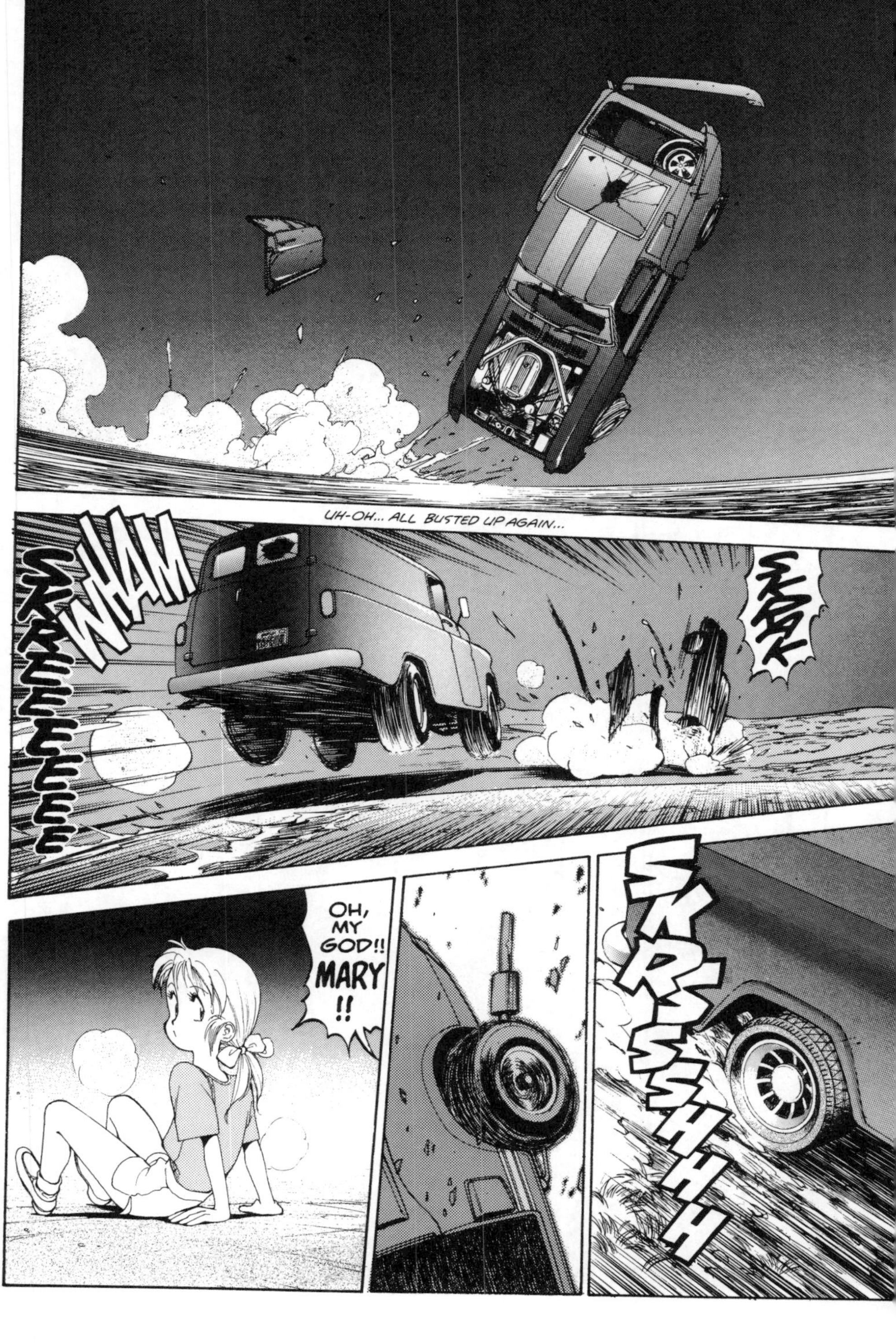
UH-OH... ALL BUSTED UP AGAIN...
WHAM
SKREEEEEEE
OH, MY GOD!! MARY !!
SKRSSHHHH

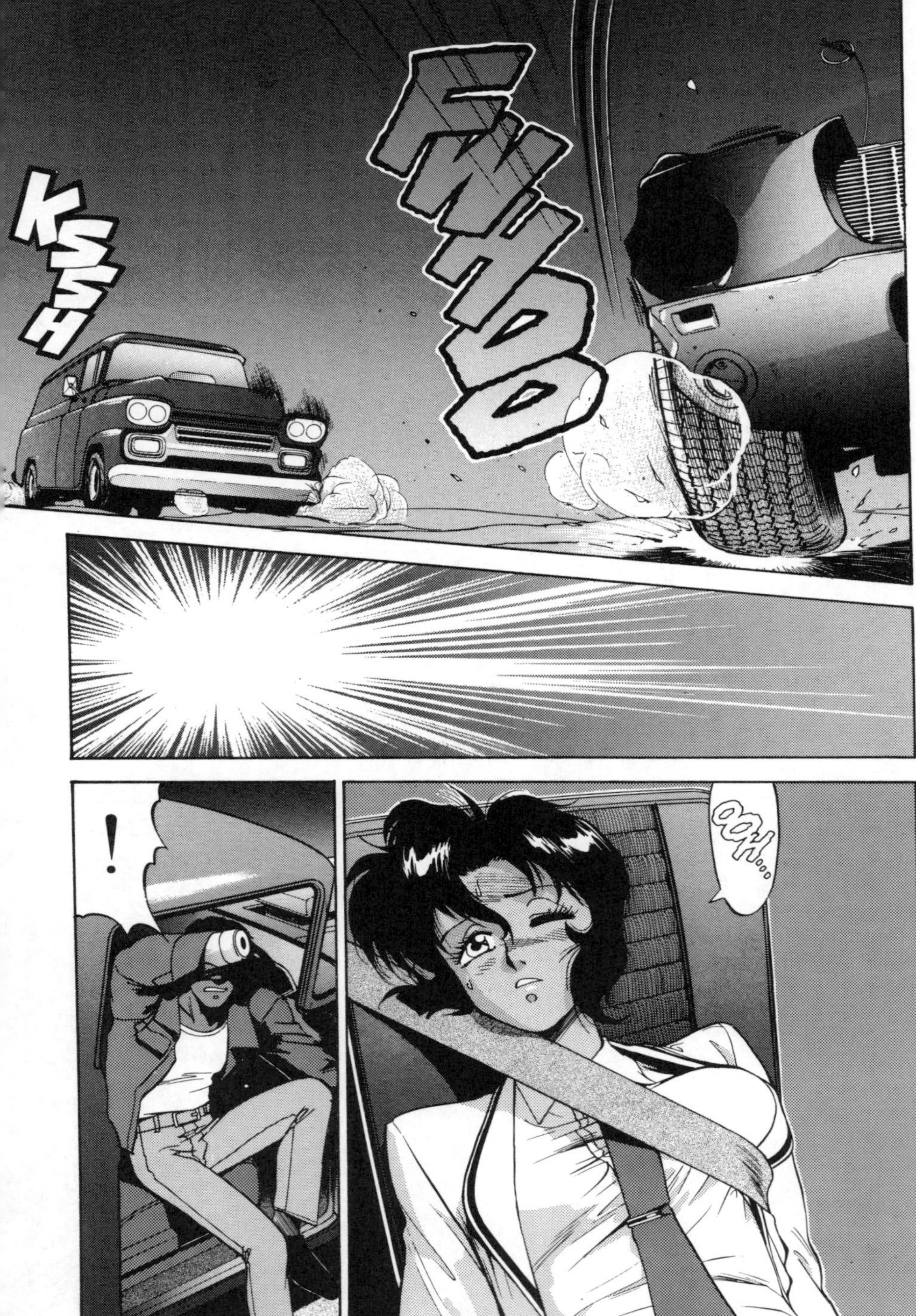
KSSSH
FWHOO
!
OOH...

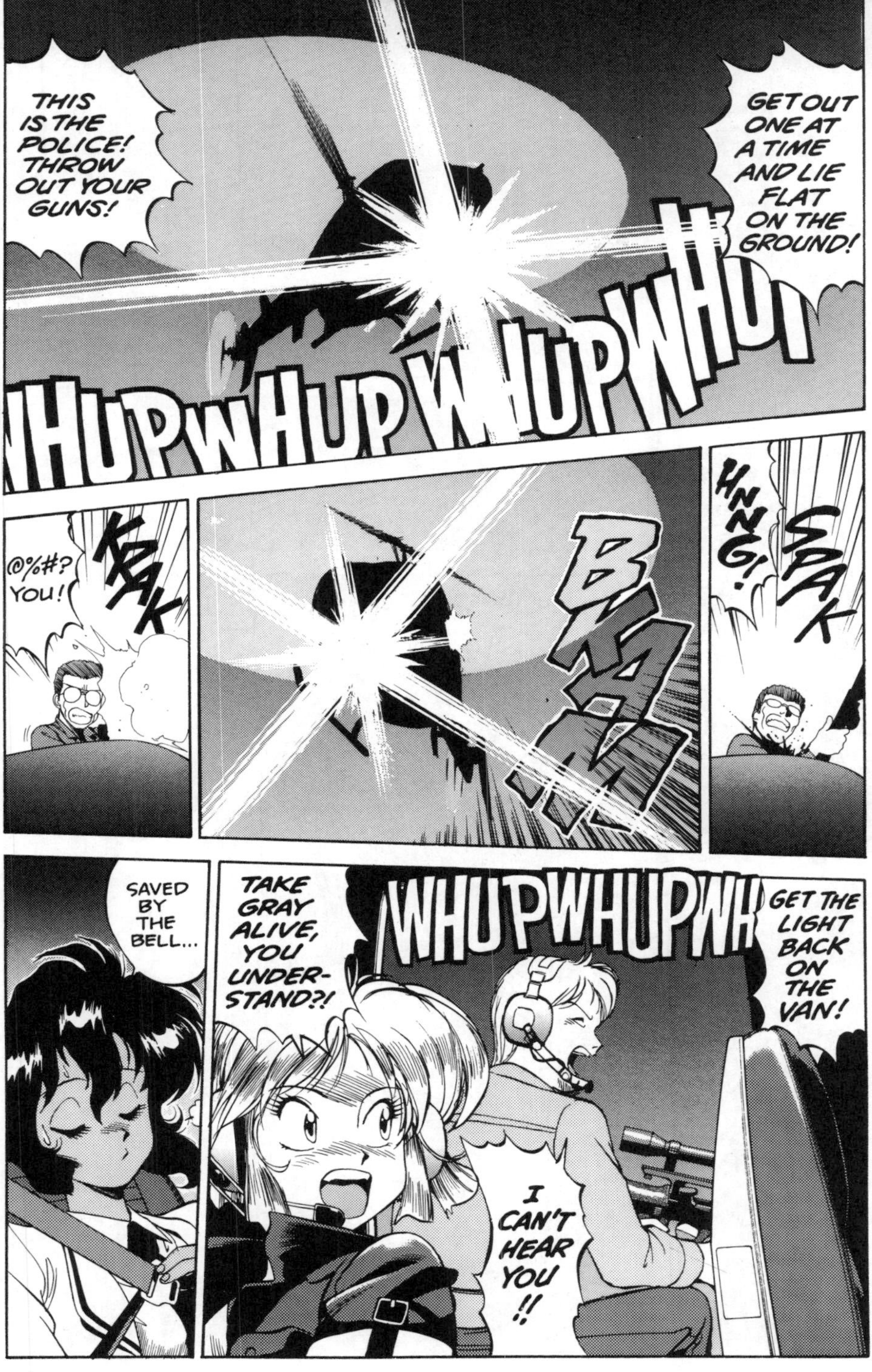
THIS IS THE POLICE! THROW OUT YOUR GUNS!
GET OUT ONE AT A TIME AND LIE FLAT ON THE GROUND!
WHUPWHUPWHUPWHUI
@%#? YOU!
KRAK
BLAM
HNNG!
SPAK
SAVED BY THE BELL...
TAKE GRAY ALIVE, YOU UNDER-STAND?!
WHUPWHUPWH
GET THE LIGHT BACK ON THE VAN!
I CAN'T HEAR YOU!!

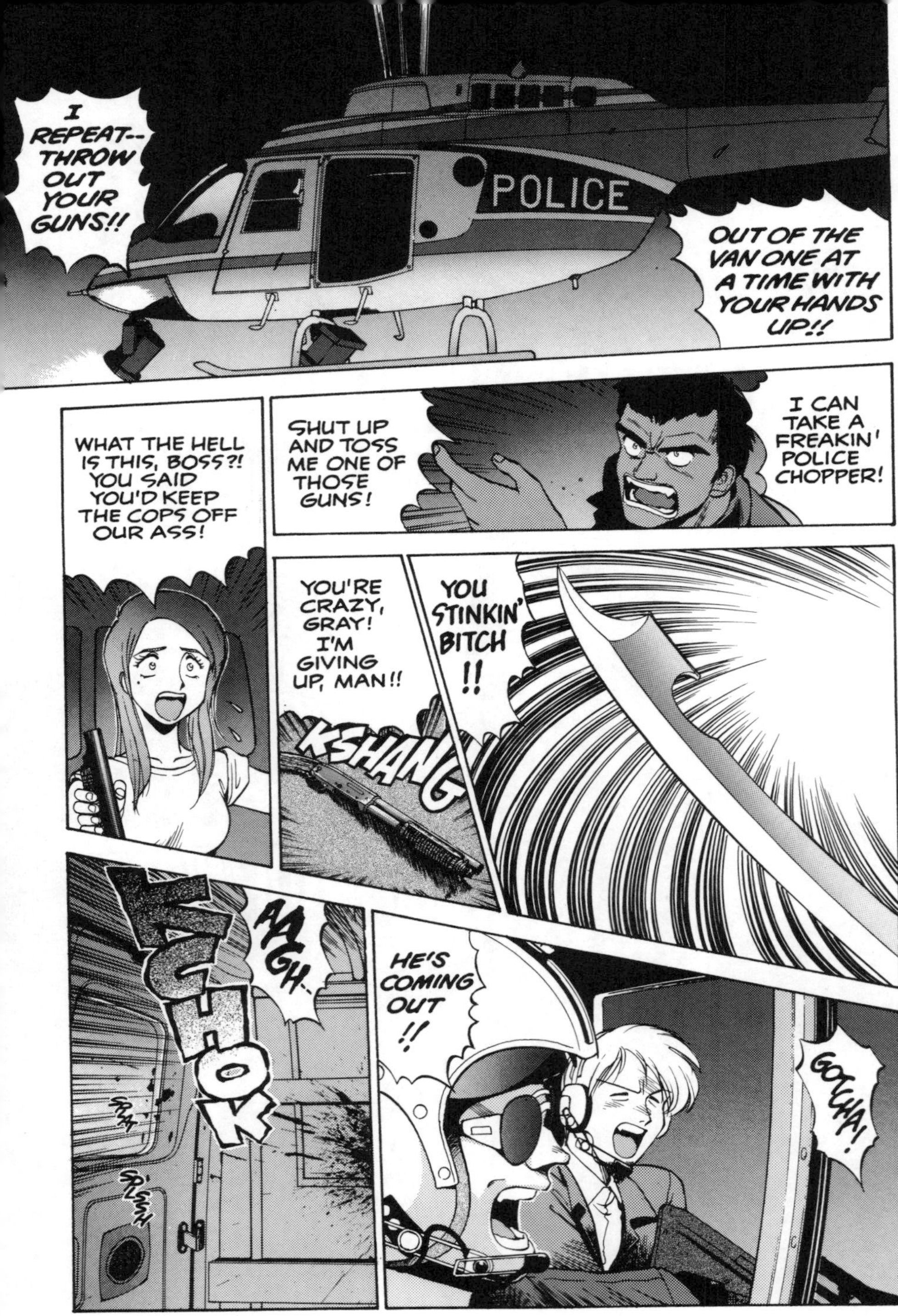
I REPEAT-- THROW OUT YOUR GUNS!!
OUT OF THE VAN ONE AT A TIME WITH YOUR HANDS UP!!
WHAT THE HELL IS THIS, BOSS?! YOU SAID YOU'D KEEP THE COPS OFF OUR ASS!
SHUT UP AND TOSS ME ONE OF THOSE GUNS!
I CAN TAKE A FREAKIN' POLICE CHOPPER!
YOU'RE CRAZY, GRAY! I'M GIVING UP, MAN!!
KSHANG
YOU STINKIN' BITCH !!
KCHOK
AAAGH..
HE'S COMING OUT !!
GOTCHA!

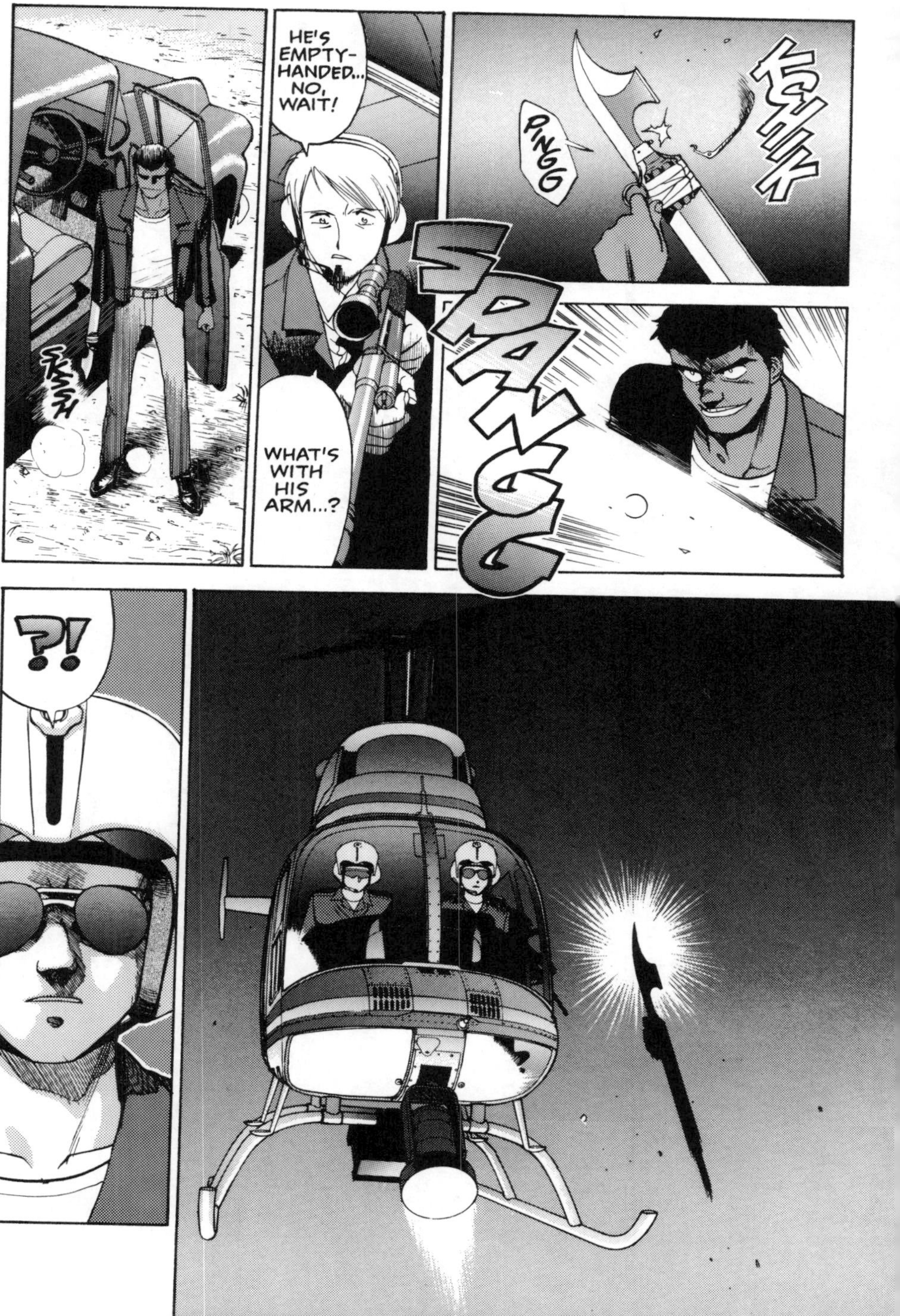
SKSSH
HE'S EMPTY-HANDED... NO, WAIT!
WHAT'S WITH HIS ARM...?
KCHIK
PINGG
SPANGG
?!

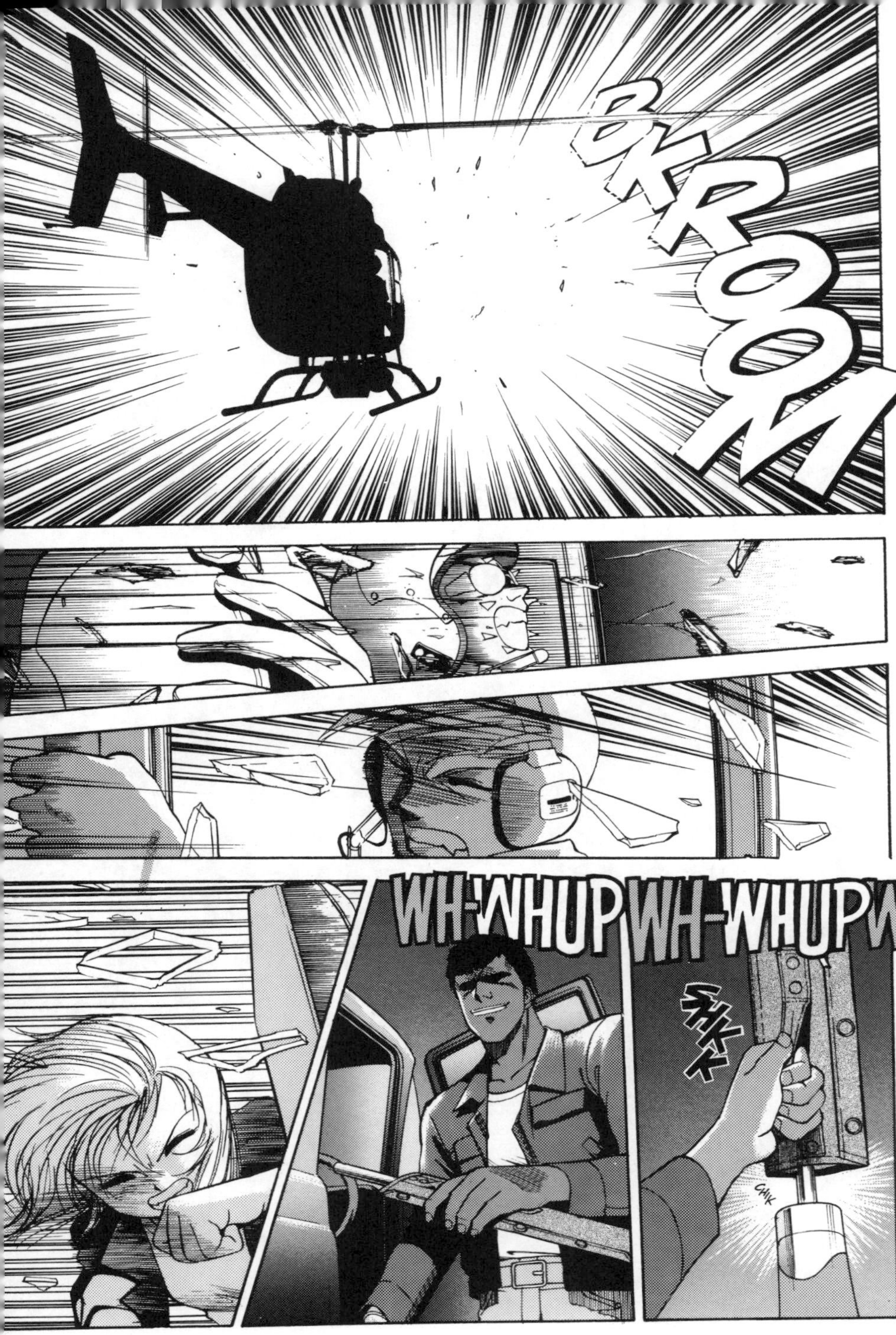
BKROOM
WH-WHUP WH-WHUPW
SHKK
CHIK

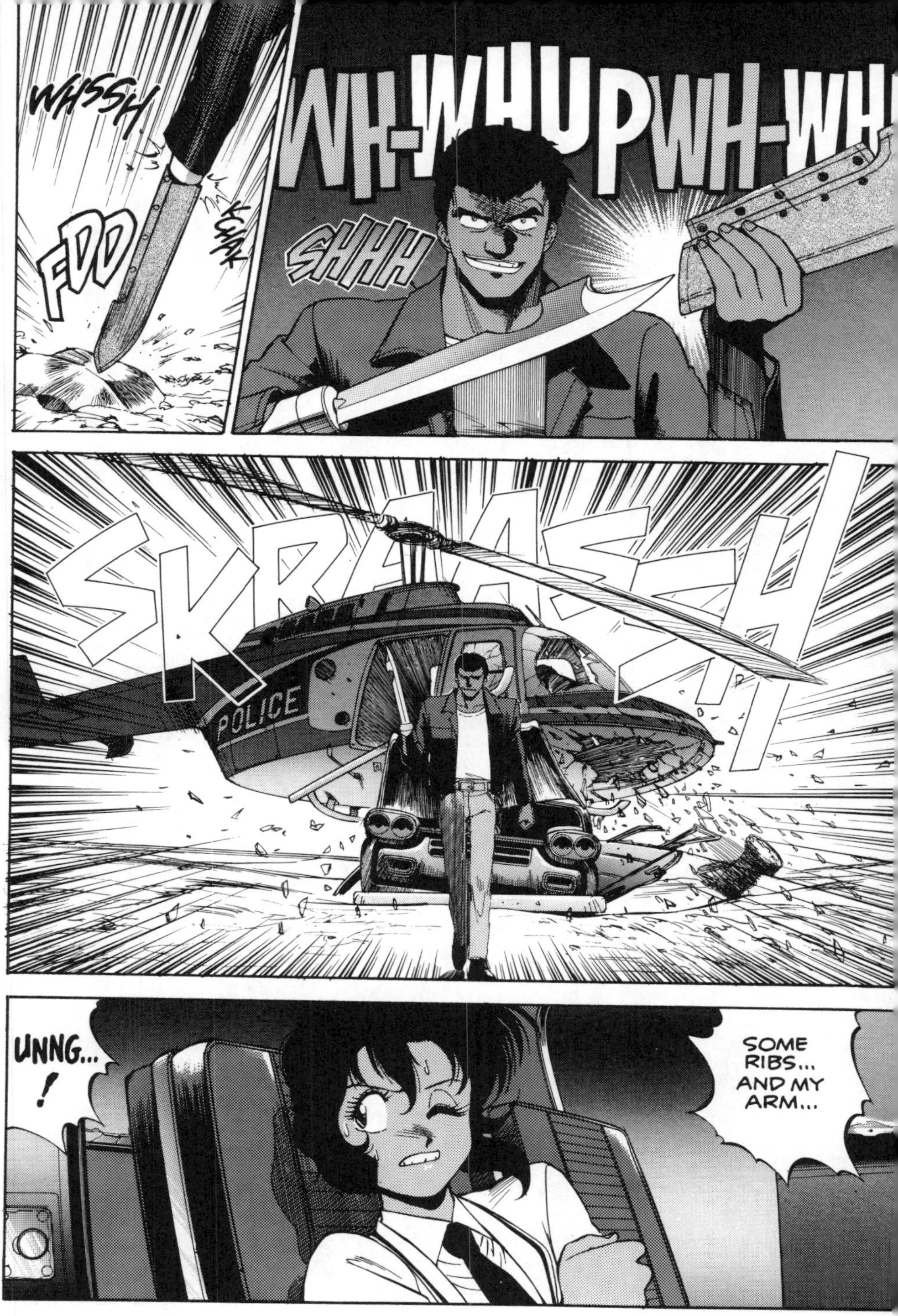
WHSSH
FDD
KCHAK
WH-WHUPWH-WH
SHHH
UNNG...
!
SOME RIBS... AND MY ARM...

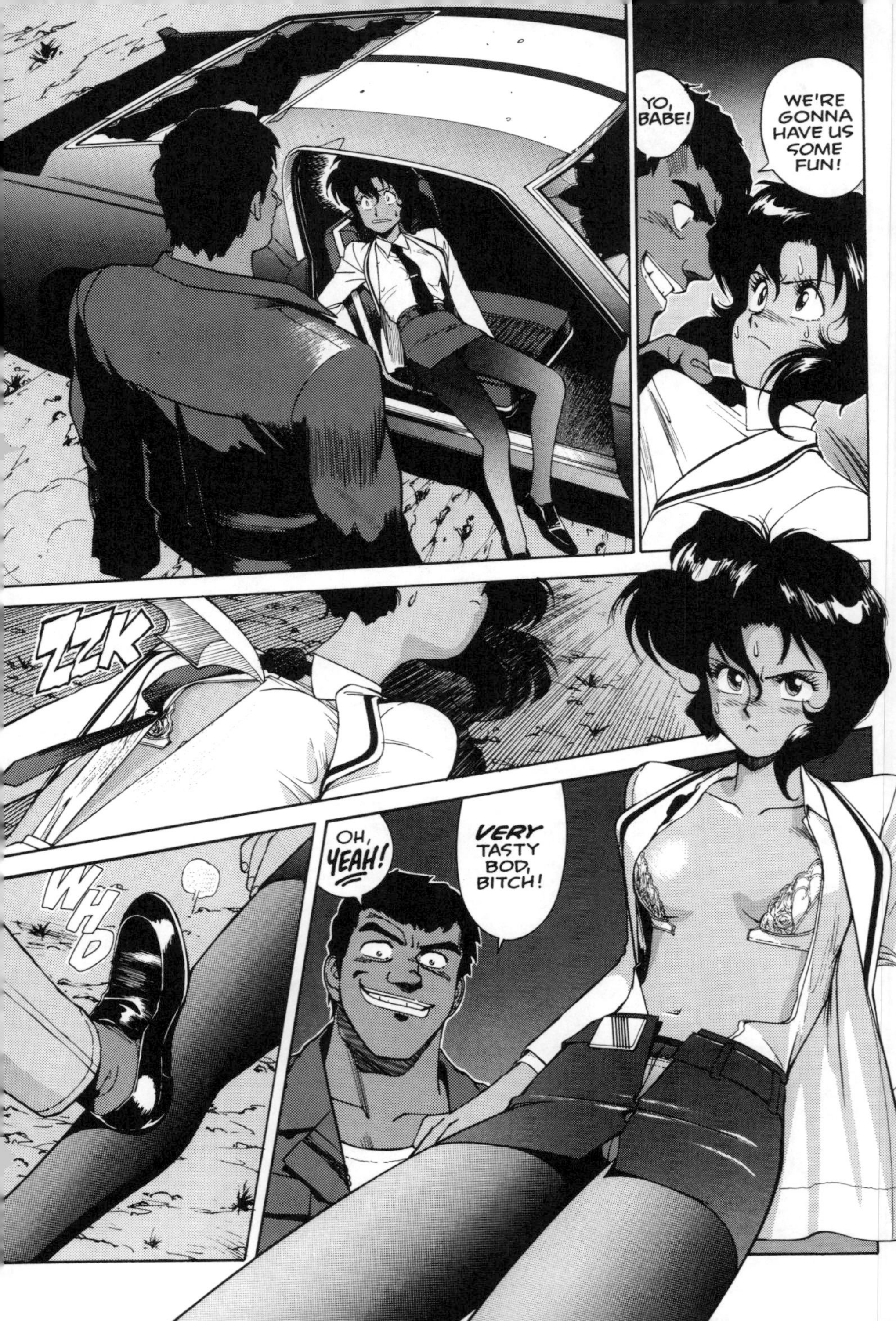
YO, BABE!
WE'RE GONNA HAVE US SOME FUN!
ZZK
WHD
OH, YEAH!
VERY TASTY BOD, BITCH!

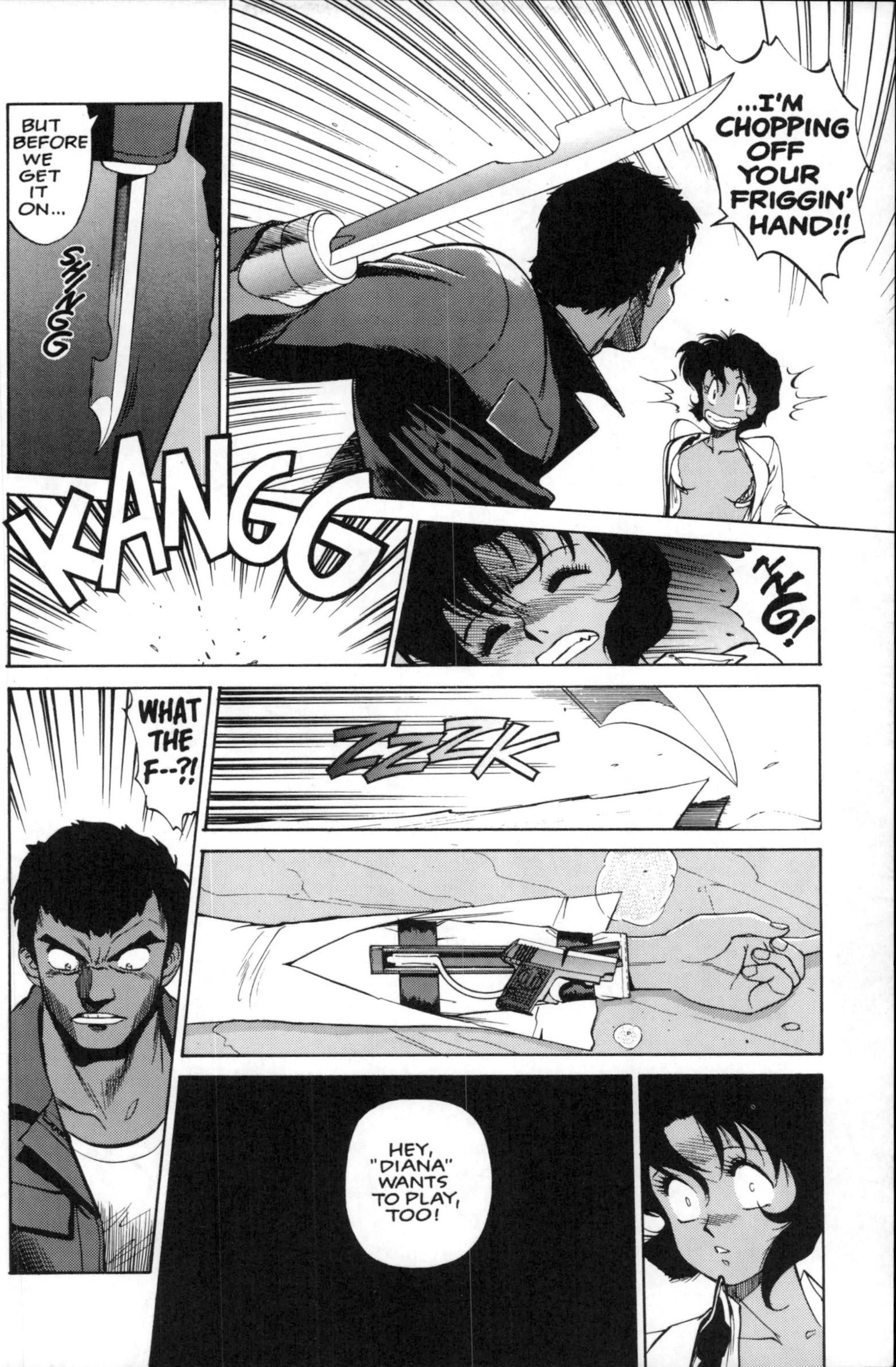
BUT BEFORE WE GET IT ON...
SHINGG
...I'M CHOPPING OFF YOUR FRIGGIN' HAND!!
KANGG
NNG!
WHAT THE F--?!
ZZZK
HEY, "DIANA" WANTS TO PLAY, TOO!

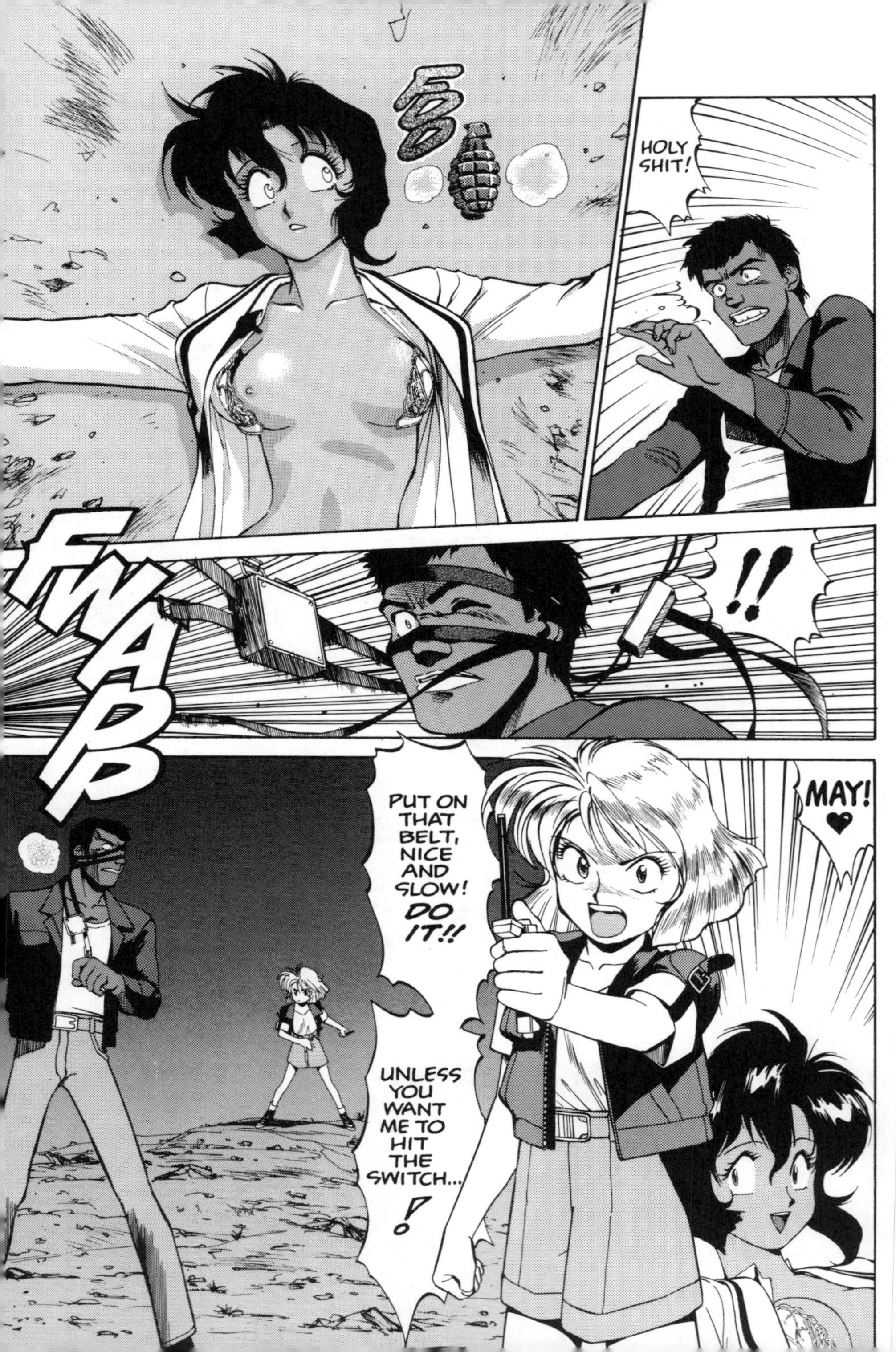
HOLY SHIT!
FWAPP
!!
PUT ON THAT BELT, NICE AND SLOW! DO IT!!
UNLESS YOU WANT ME TO HIT THE SWITCH...!
MAY! ❤

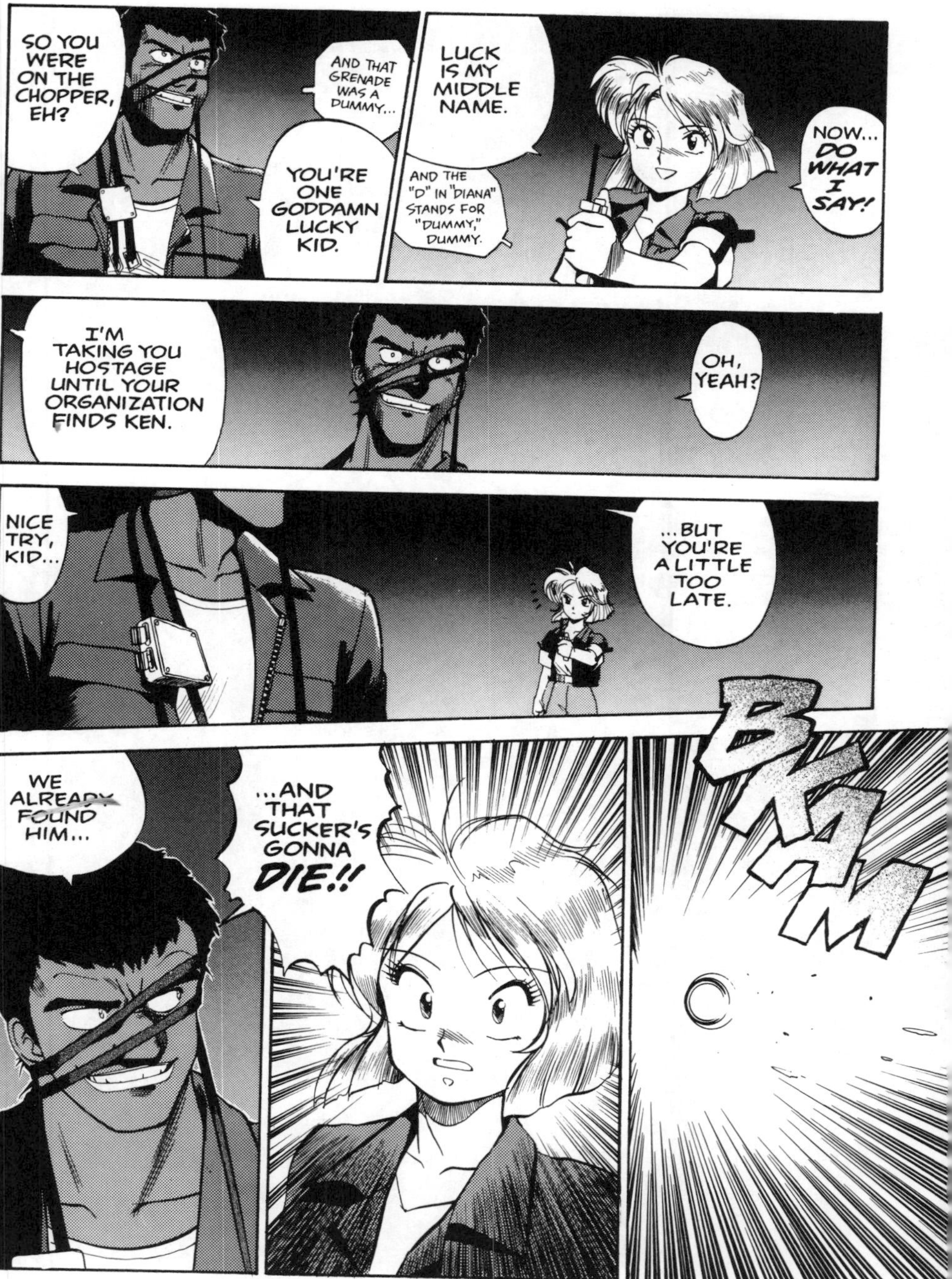
SO YOU WERE ON THE CHOPPER, EH?
AND THAT GRENADE WAS A DUMMY...
YOU'RE ONE GODDAMN LUCKY KID.
LUCK IS MY MIDDLE NAME.
AND THE "D" IN "DIANA" STANDS FOR "DUMMY," DUMMY.
NOW... DO WHAT I SAY!
I'M TAKING YOU HOSTAGE UNTIL YOUR ORGANIZATION FINDS KEN.
OH, YEAH?
NICE TRY, KID...
...BUT YOU'RE A LITTLE TOO LATE.
WE ALREADY FOUND HIM...
...AND THAT SUCKER'S GONNA DIE!!
BKAM

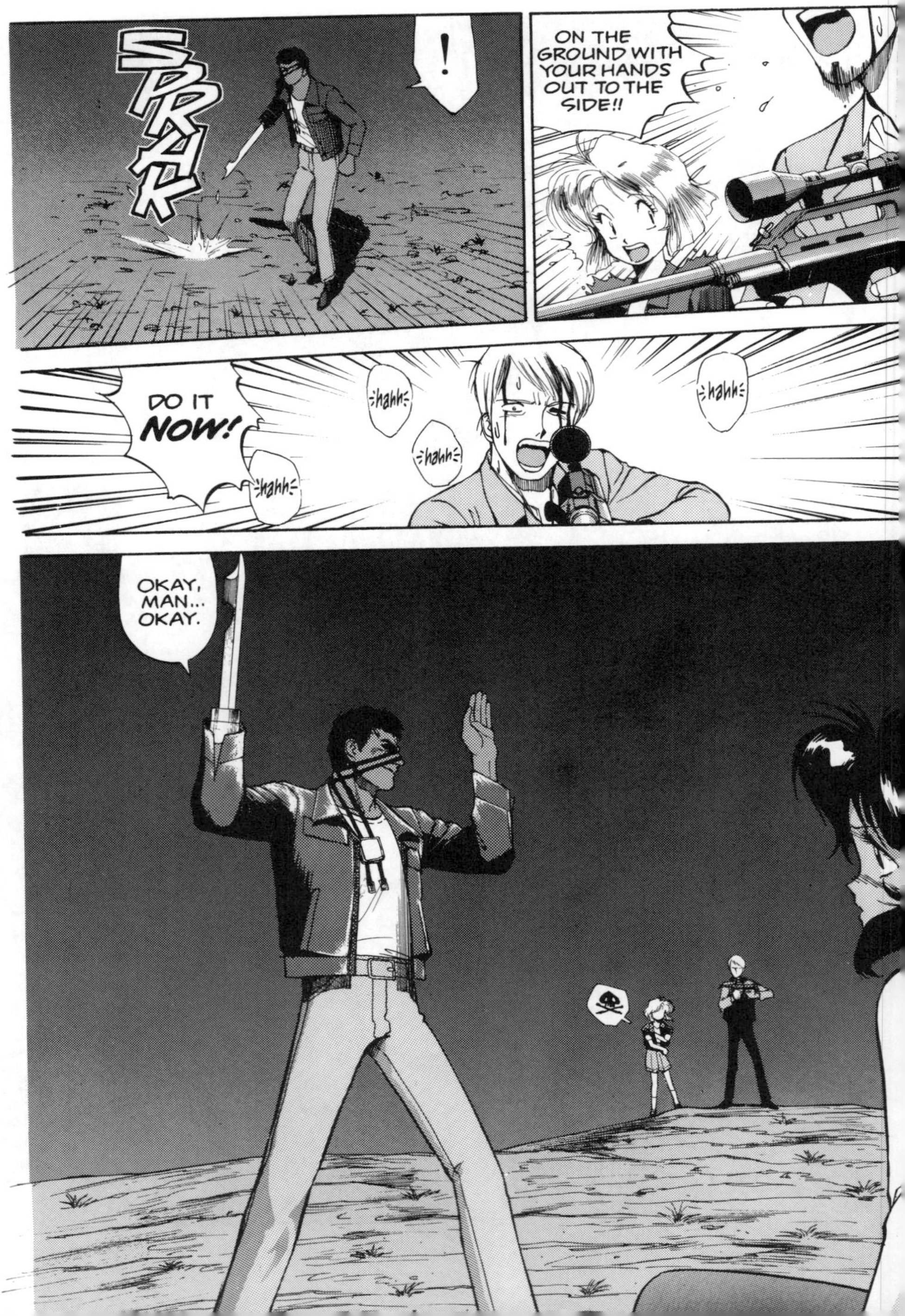
SPRAK
!
ON THE GROUND WITH YOUR HANDS OUT TO THE SIDE!!
DO IT NOW!
hahh
hahh
hahh
hahh
OKAY, MAN... OKAY.

KENICHI SONODA

cover art from Gunsmith Cats #7

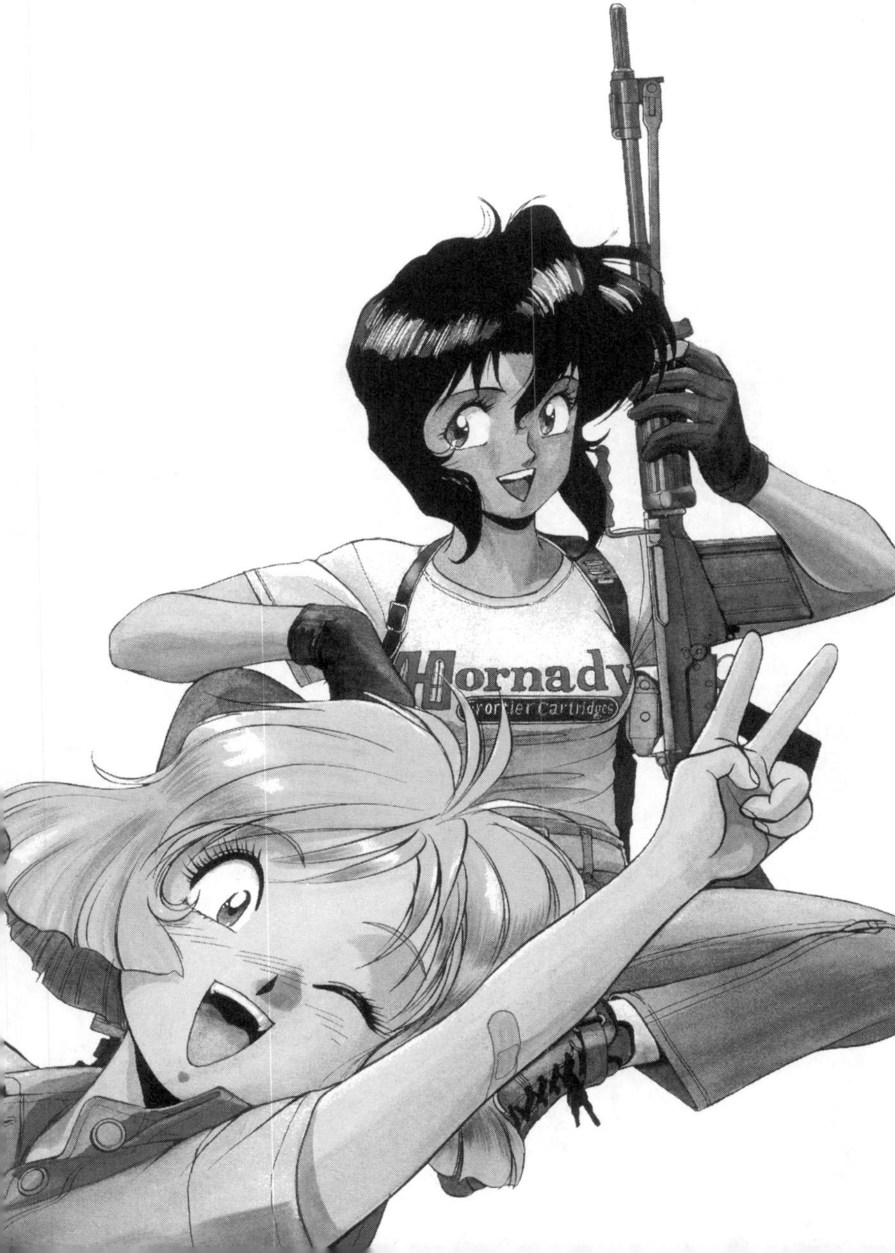
Hornady
Frontier Cartridges

KENICHI SONODA

***cover art from* Gunsmith Cats #9**

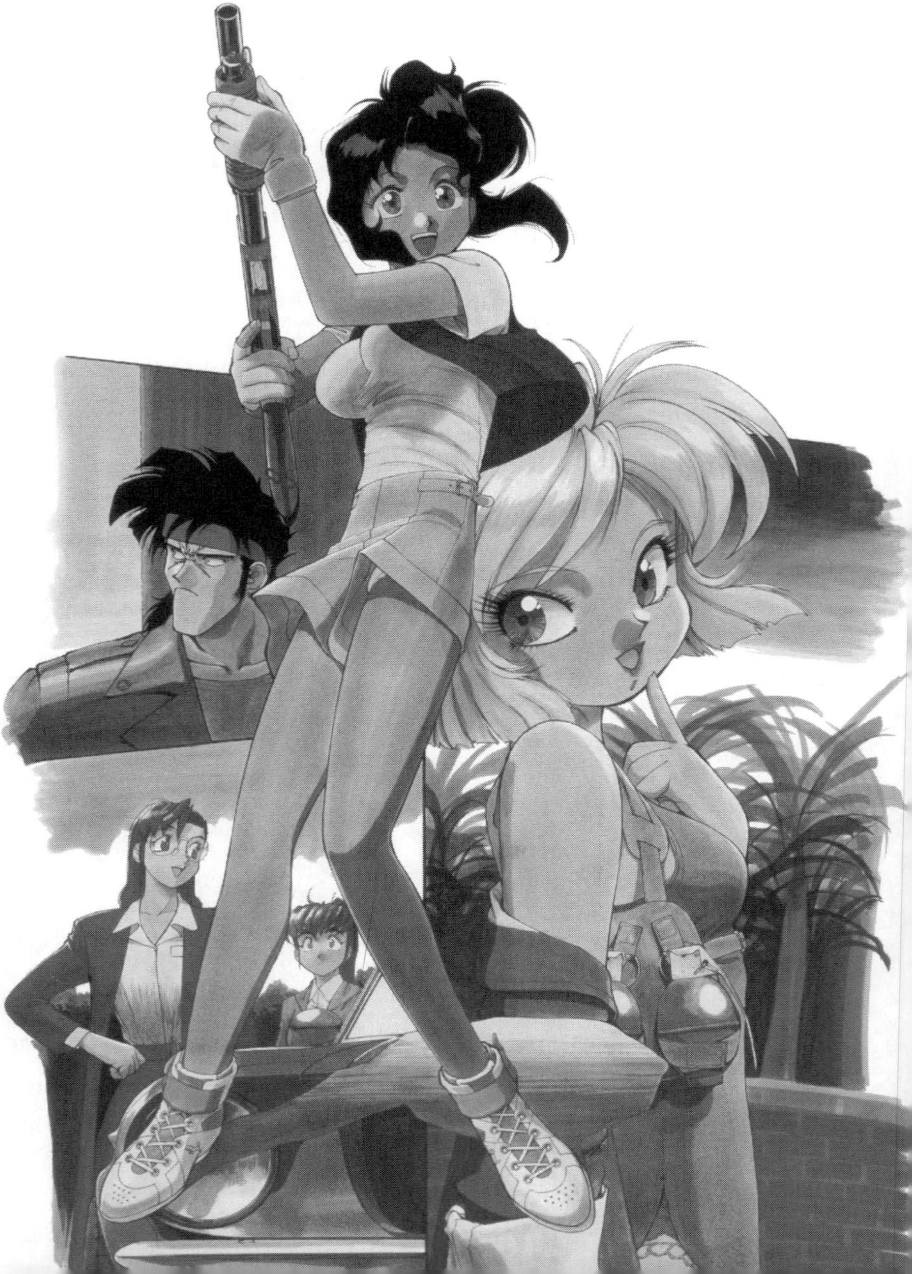

KENICHI SONODA

cover art from **Gunsmith Cats #10**

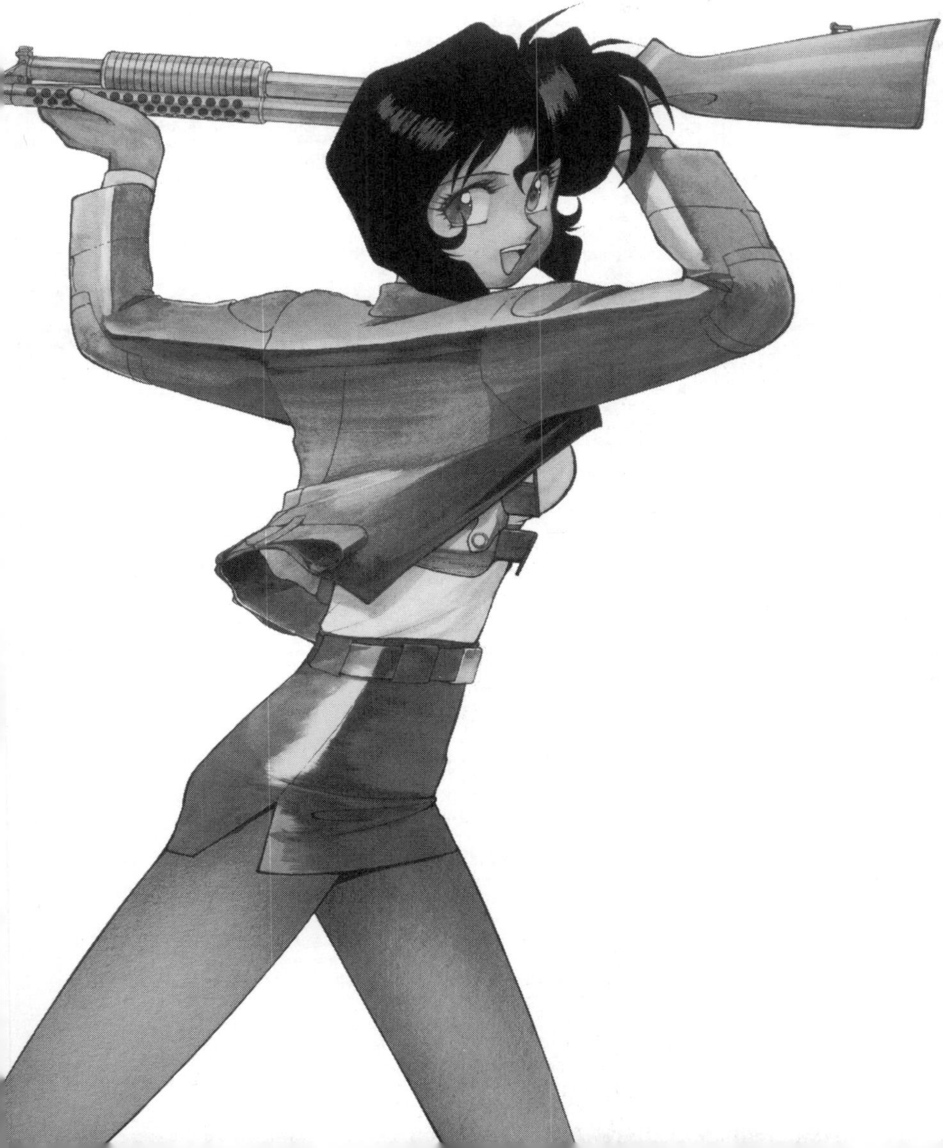

MANGA! MANGA! MANGA!
DARK HORSE HAS THE BEST IN MANGA COLLECTIONS!

AKIRA
Katsuhiro Otomo
BOOK 1
ISBN: 1-56971-498-3 $24.95
BOOK 2
ISBN: 1-56971-499-1 $24.95
BOOK 3
ISBN: 1-56971-525-4 $24.95
BOOK 4
ISBN: 1-56971-526-2 $27.95

APPLESEED
Masamune Shirow
BOOK ONE
ISBN: 1-56971-070-8 $16.95
BOOK TWO
ISBN: 1-56971-071-6 $16.95
BOOK THREE
ISBN: 1-56971-072-4 $17.95
BOOK FOUR
ISBN: 1-56971-074-0 $17.95

BLACK MAGIC
Masamune Shirow
ISBN: 1-56971-360-X $16.95

BLADE OF THE IMMORTAL
Hiroaki Samura
BLOOD OF A THOUSAND
ISBN: 1-56971-239-5 $14.95
CRY OF THE WORM
ISBN: 1-56971-300-6 $14.95
DREAMSONG
ISBN: 1-56971-357-X $14.95
ON SILENT WINGS
ISBN: 1-56971-412-6 $14.95
ON SILENT WINGS II
ISBN: 1-56971-444-4 $14.95
DARK SHADOWS
ISBN: 1-56971-469-X $14.95
HEART OF DARKNESS
ISBN: 1-56971-531-9 $16.95
THE GATHERING
ISBN: 1-56971-546-7 $15.95

BUBBLEGUM CRISIS
Adam Warren
GRAND MAL
color paperback
ISBN: 1-56971-120-8 $14.95

CARAVAN KIDD
Johji Manabe
VOLUME 2
ISBN: 1-56971-324-3 $19.95
VOLUME 3
ISBN: 1-56971-338-3 $19.95

THE DIRTY PAIR
Adam Warren • Toren Smith
BIOHAZARDS
ISBN: 1-56971-339-1 $12.95
DANGEROUS ACQUAINTANCES
ISBN: 1-56971-227-1 $12.95
A PLAGUE OF ANGELS
ISBN: 1-56971-029-5 $12.95
FATAL BUT NOT SERIOUS
color paperback
ISBN: 1-56971-172-0 $14.95

DOMINION
Masamune Shirow
ISBN: 1-56971-488-6 $16.95

DOMU
Katsuhiro Otomo
A CHILD'S DREAM
ISBN: 1-56971-611-0 $17.95

DRAKUUN
Johji Manabe
RISE OF THE DRAGON PRINCESS
ISBN: 1-56971-302-2 $12.95
THE REVENGE OF GUSTAV
ISBN: 1-56971-368-5 $14.95
SHADOW OF THE WARLOCK
ISBN: 1-46971-406-1 $14.95

GHOST IN THE SHELL
Masamune Shirow
color/B&W paperback
ISBN: 1-56971-081-3 $24.95

GODZILLA
Kazuhisa Iwata
ISBN: 1-56971-063-5 $17.95

GUNSMITH CATS
Kenichi Sonoda
BONNIE AND CLYDE
ISBN: 1-56971-215-8 $13.95
MISFIRE
ISBN: 1-56971-253-0 $14.95
THE RETURN OF GRAY
ISBN: 1-56971-299-9 $17.95
GOLDIE VS. MISTY
ISBN: 1-56971-371-5 $15.95
BAD TRIP
ISBN: 1-56971-442-8 $13.95
BEAN BANDIT
ISBN: 1-56971-453-3 $16.95
KIDNAPPED
ISBN: 1-56971-529-7 $16.95
MISTER V
ISBN: 1-56971-550-5 $18.95

INTRON DEPOT
Masamune Shirow
INTRON DEPOT 1
color paperback
ISBN: 1-56971-085-6 $39.95
INTRON DEPOT 2: BLADES
color paperback
ISBN: 1-56971-382-0 $39.95
INTRON DEPOT 2: BLADES CD-ROM
2 CDs with illustrated mousepad
ISBN: 1-56971-485-1 $79.95

OH MY GODDESS!
Kosuke Fujishima
1-555-GODDESS
ISBN: 1-56971-207-7 $13.95
LOVE POTION NO. 9
ISBN: 1-56971-252-2 $14.95
SYMPATHY FOR THE DEVIL
ISBN: 1-56971-329-4 $13.95
TERRIBLE MASTER URD
ISBN: 1-56971-369-3 $14.95
THE QUEEN OF VENGEANCE
ISBN: 1-56971-431-2 $13.95
MARA STRIKES BACK!
ISBN: 1-56971-449-5 $14.95
NINJA MASTER
ISBN: 1-56971-474-6 $13.95
MISS KEIICHI
ISBN: 1-56971-522-X $16.95
ADVENTURES OF THE MINI-GODDESSES
ISBN: 1-56971-421-5 $9.95
THE DEVIL IN MISS URD
ISBN: 1-56971-540-8 $14.95
THE FOURTH GODDESS
ISBN: 1-56971-551-3 $18.95

ORION
Masamune Shirow
ISBN: 1-56971-572-6 $19.95

OUTLANDERS
Johji Manabe
VOLUME 2
ISBN: 1-56971-162-3 $13.95
VOLUME 3
ISBN: 1-56971-163-1 $13.95
VOLUME 4
ISBN: 1-56971-069-4 $12.95
VOLUME 5
ISBN: 1-56971-275-1 $14.95
VOLUME 6
ISBN: 1-56971-423-1 $14.95
VOLUME 7
ISBN: 1-56971-424-X $14.95
VOLUME 8
ISBN: 1-56971-425-8 $14.95

SHADOW LADY
Masakazu Katsura
DANGEROUS LOVE
ISBN: 1-56971-408-8 $17.95
THE AWAKENING
ISBN: 1-56971-446-0 $15.95
SUDDEN DEATH
ISBN: 1-56971-477-0 $14.95

SHADOW STAR
Mohiro Kitoh
STARFLIGHT
ISBN: 1-56971-548-3 $15.95

SPIRIT OF WONDER
Kenji Tsuruta
ISBN: 1-56971-288-3 $12.95

STAR WARS MANGA
A NEW HOPE
George Lucas • Hisao Tamaki
VOLUME 1
ISBN: 1-56971-362-6 $9.95
VOLUME 2
ISBN: 1-56971-363-4 $9.95
VOLUME 3
ISBN: 1-56971-364-2 $9.95
VOLUME 4
ISBN: 1-56971-365-0 $9.95
THE EMPIRE STRIKES BACK
George Lucas • Toshiki Kudo
VOLUME 1
ISBN: 1-56971-390-1 $9.95
VOLUME 2
ISBN: 1-56971-391-X $9.95
VOLUME 3
ISBN: 1-56971-392-8 $9.95
VOLUME 4
ISBN: 1-56971-393-6 $9.95
RETURN OF THE JEDI
George Lucas • Shin-ichi Hirom
VOLUME 1
ISBN: 1-56971-394-4 $9.95
VOLUME 2
ISBN: 1-56971-395-2 $9.95
VOLUME 3
B&W paperback
ISBN: 1-56971-396-0 $9.95
VOLUME 4
ISBN: 1-56971-397-9 $9.95
EPISODE 1— THE PHANTOM MENACE
George Lucas • Kia Asamiya
VOLUME 1
ISBN: 1-56971-483-5 $9.95
VOLUME 2
ISBN: 1-56971-484-3 $9.95

3x3 EYES
Yuzo Takada
HOUSE OF DEMONS
ISBN: 1-56971-059-7 $12.95
CURSE OF THE GESU
ISBN: 1-56971-175-5 $12.95

WHAT'S MICHAEL?
Makoto Kobayashi
OFF THE DEEP END
ISBN: 1-56971-249-2 $5.95
MICHAEL'S MAMBO
ISBN: 1-56971-250-6 $5.95

YOU'RE UNDER ARREST!
Kosuke Fujishima
THE WILD ONES
ISBN: 1-56971-319-7 $12.95
LIGHTS AND SIREN!
ISBN: 1-56971-432-0 $10.95

*All titles are black-and-white paperback unless otherwise noted

Available from your local comics shop or bookstore!

To find a comics shop in your area, call 1-888-266-4226
For more information or to order direct:
•On the web: www.darkhorse.com •E-mail: mailorder@darkhorse.com
•Phone: 1-800-862-0052 or (503) 652-9701 Mon.-Sat. 9 A.M. to 5 P.M. Pacific Time
*Prices and availability subject to change without notice